Medical Malpractice

Medical Malpractice

Law, Tactics, and Ethics

Frank M. McClellan

Temple University Press

PHILADELPHIA

Temple University Press, Philadelphia 19122
Copyright © 1994 by Temple University. All rights reserved
Published 1994
Printed in the United States of America

The paper used in this publication meets the minimum requirements
of American National Standard for Information Sciences—Permanence
of Paper for Printed Library Materials, ANSI Z39.48-1984 ⊛

Library of Congress Cataloging-in-Publication Data

McClellan, Frank M.
    Medical malpractice : law, tactics, and ethics / Frank M. McClellan.
      p.   cm.
    Includes bibliographical references and index.
    ISBN 1-56639-065-6 (alk. paper). — ISBN 1-56639-066-4 (alk. paper)
    1. Physicians—Malpractice—United States.   I. Title.
KF2905.3.M37   1993
346.7303'32—dc20
[347.306332]   92-36045

THIS BOOK IS *dedicated to Ruby Brooks, Harrikah Stanton, and Allen Eaton, Esq., of Washington, D.C. Ruby is the mother of Harrikah, a beautiful young woman who in December 1971, at the age of nine months, suffered a catastrophic medical injury. Twenty years ago, Ruby placed her faith in two young lawyers—Allen T. Eaton and me—to pursue justice for her family. Allen had the wisdom and the courage to explore uncharted medical and legal territory in pursuit of a just result. (See* Stanton v. Astra Pharmaceutical Products, Inc., *718 F.2d 553 [3d Cir. 1983], discussed in Chapters 11 and 12 of this book.) I have benefited immensely from his friendship, criticism, and encouragement.*

Contents

Preface

Since the early 1970s, legislatures and courts have struggled to reform the law governing medical malpractice claims. Many of the proposed reforms seek to promote economic efficiency through some specific cost-containment or damage-limitation mechanism. Other proposals seek to deter the filing of "frivolous" claims. Much of the debate assumes—incorrectly, in my view— that the task of evaluating a medical malpractice case is simple, allowing quick and easy assessments of the merit of a particular case. In addition, most of the proposals give no attention to the law's role in protecting the dignity of the participants. Economic considerations command the reformers' exclusive attention.

This book seeks to achieve two primary goals. The first is to illustrate the multitude of considerations that influence the initiation and resolution of a medical malpractice case. In my view assessing the merits of a medical malpractice case entails a dynamic process of intelligence gathering that produces varying evaluations at different stages. Indeed, the process is so complex and challenging that efforts to judge the reasonableness of an attorney's conduct are more aptly focused on the process used to evaluate the case than on the conclusion the attorney reached as to the merit of a claim or defense.

The book's second goal is to highlight human dignity as an issue in medical malpractice law in particular and tort law in general. Concern over money serves as an important motivation for patients to sue and for health care providers (and their insurers) to defend lawsuits. Acknowledging this monetary concern, however, should not keep us from recognizing the significant role that the patient's or doctor's sense of worth and dignity plays in medical malpractice litigation. In a society where the number of people who are old or poor is likely to increase in the next two decades, human dignity will often surface as the dominant consideration in medical malpractice litigation. Reform proposals that ignore this issue are not likely to succeed in the long run.

This book explores both the philosophical and the practical underpinnings of medical malpractice litigation through the eyes of a litigator and law professor. Wearing different hats over the past twenty years, I have engaged in intelligence gathering in the camps of plaintiffs' and defendants' lawyers, in courtrooms, and in classrooms full of law students and medical students. My aim is to produce a book that challenges and informs a mixed audience, including law students, practicing attorneys, physicians, and allied health care professionals. I am particularly hopeful that the book will appeal to teachers and students of health law and related academic disciplines in law schools and medical schools. To make the book adaptable as a textbook, I have included in twelve chapters and in an Appendix problems that raise thorny issues of law, economics, or ethics. In addition, a list of Suggested Readings in Case Law presents leading cases that I believe law students should read to gain an appreciation of the specific conflicts that have shaped the law of medical malpractice as we know it today.

In order to avoid confusion, the plaintiff is always female, her attorney is male, the defendant is male, and his attorney is female throughout the book, except in Problems and in discussions of cases.

Acknowledgments

I express my appreciation to my former students at Temple Law School who made significant contributions to this book through classroom discussions and individual research projects. I would especially like to thank the following students: Emily Zitser Zuzelo and Stephanie Montgomery, who painstakingly researched and offered critical assessments of tort reform statutes; Vanessa Haley, who made substantial contributions to Chapter 9; and Loralee Choman, who provided outstanding assistance on Chapter 10. My long-term friend and law partner, Allen T. Eaton, Esq., not only planted the seed for this book but also offered many insights into substantive issues as well as the practical problems of lawyering. In particular, Allen made significant contributions to the discussion in Chapter 1 about interviewing the plaintiff. My associates and friends David Smorodin and Pat Williams contributed their ideas and drafting skills to Chapter 1 and Chapter 12. Brian E. Appel read earlier drafts of various chapters and offered many helpful suggestions. My editor, Doris B. Braendel, cheerfully prodded me along and challenged me to write in a form that would make the book understandable to nonlawyers. Any success that I achieved in that regard is due to her editing. Final production of the manuscript required a level of computer knowledge, word processing skills, discipline, and patience that I lacked. Cassie Stankunas and Shyam Nair came to my rescue on the computer. Jacquelin Latty provided diligent and reliable research and citation checking. Thanks also go to my production and copy editors, Joan Vidal and Jane Barry. Finally, my wife and friend, Professor Phoebe A. Haddon, consistently provided me with insightful criticism of the substance, organization, and style of the book. Equally important, she encouraged me to stick with it until it was done.

Part I

Legal, Medical, and Ethical Standards

Chapter 1

Threshold Considerations:
When Doctors and Patients Collide

Litigating a medical malpractice case is one of the most challenging tasks a trial lawyer can undertake. On the one hand, the injured patient's mental, physical, and financial well-being often depend on the outcome of the litigation. On the other hand, the physician naturally perceives the lawsuit as a threat to his reputation and a challenge to his knowledge, training, and skill; allegations of professional negligence strike at the core of his sense of self-worth. For both parties, large sums of money are at stake. Usually, the factual and legal issues are complex and the litigation expenses enormous (see Chapter 2 for a discussion of costs). Years may pass before the cumbersome legal proceedings unwind sufficiently to permit a true assessment of the claim, and the outcome may reflect a reasoned evaluation of the evidence and applicable law, or gut feelings of empathy or hostility toward one of the trial participants, or both.

The plaintiff's attorney carries a tremendous burden. The client is usually unable to finance the litigation or help her lawyer identify and clarify medical issues. Recovering the costs of the litigation and being paid for services rendered depend on winning the case. Winning the case most often depends on the willingness of one doctor to testify against another (see Chapter 11 for a discussion of the expert witness requirement). Finally, even with the help of an expert witness who is willing to testify in court, the plaintiff's attorney confronts the arduous tasks of educating a jury or judge on complex medical issues and persuading them to condemn the conduct of a person who enjoys the highest level of respect accorded any professional (see Chapter 13 for a discussion of jury considerations).[1] Defense counsel will attempt to reinforce the jury's feelings that medicine is so complex that a person who has earned the title "doctor" should not be condemned by hindsight. After all, counsel will argue, the defendant physician made a valiant effort to aid the plaintiff under difficult and complex circumstances and should not be held to an unrealistic standard of perfection. Moreover, the truth is that sometimes bad results follow good medical treatment, although no one can really say why. Medicine is both a science and an art, requiring the professional and his patient to accept a high degree of uncertainty about the human body and the ability of science to understand, predict, and control results.

Nevertheless, the job of defense counsel is not a cakewalk. Her client is often arrogant and defensive. The defendant physician is subjected to piercing cross-examination in an environment that is unfamiliar and potentially hostile. In this environment the doctor's ego, competence, and knowledge are challenged and scrutinized in a manner to which he is unaccustomed. Physicians live and work in a social structure that encourages them to act as if they are in control and indeed demands that they do so. The legal system, on the other hand, turns the defendant into a passive participant who must rely on others to play the dominant roles in resolving the dispute.

Plaintiff's counsel and the judge will certainly let the physician know that in this arena he is not running things. At the same time, the plaintiff may be an appealing person and her injuries may be catastrophic. Moreover, the jurors know from their personal experiences and from news reports that many mistakes made by health care providers are avoidable.

Given the high stakes, cost, and complexity of medical malpractice litigation, attorneys must pay careful attention to all the factors that influence decision making when evaluating or preparing a medical malpractice case. A systematic and comprehensive approach to intelligence gathering, evaluation, and preparation is essential. The client interview, medical research, selection and preparation of experts, and selection of jurors should not be approached haphazardly or necessarily in the same manner as in an ordinary personal injury case.

To set the stage for this complex world, let us look at four problems that reflect some fundamental legal, medical, and ethical issues confronting the medical malpractice attorney. Although some of the problems echo real cases, these illustrations are meant not to set the reader guessing how a particular court resolved a particular conflict, but rather to evoke thoughts about the values at stake in medical malpractice cases.

■ **Problem One:** *Inadequate Anesthesia*

Mrs. Green suffers from osteoarthritis in the ankle, which resulted, at least in part, from the failure of her surgeon, Dr. Brown, to complete an operation performed to reduce a severe trimalleolar fracture of her right ankle.

Clarke v. Gibbons

Dr. Brown did not complete the operation because he was advised by the anesthesiologist, Dr. White, that the spinal anesthesia she had administered was wearing off. Based on past experience, Dr. White had anticipated that the operation would take two hours; so she had selected an anesthetic agent that would last two hours and twenty minutes. According to Dr. Brown's notes in his operative report, he had anticipated that the operation would take about three hours because of the patient's obesity and the severity of the fracture. When told that the anesthesia was wearing off, he terminated the procedure without consulting with Dr. White about whether she could safely administer additional anesthesia because he was upset that she had not used the appropriate anesthetic in the first place. The surgeon and anesthesiologist had not discussed the expected length of the operation before the surgery.

When Dr. Brown terminated the operation, he had completed all the reduction except for reduction of the posterior fragment of the tibia. He intended to complete the operation at another time, but Mrs. Green developed infected skin blisters that did not heal in time to permit a second operation.

In this situation is Mrs. Green justified in filing a lawsuit against Dr. Brown or Dr. White without the support of expert testimony? If she needs expert testimony, what opinions must the experts express to justify a medical malpractice claim? Should she name the hospital as a defendant?

If a lawsuit is filed, what defenses should the doctor and hospital offer? Should either defendant cross-claim against the other? What effect would a decision to cross-claim have on the resolution of the merits of the case or on the ultimate payment of any award?

In *Clark v. Gibbons*,[2] a patient's lawsuit against her doctors based on facts similar to those in this problem provoked three different views on whether the evidence was sufficient to support a jury finding of negligence, in the absence of expert testimony specifically stating that the physicians were negligent. Justice Peters expressed the majority view that the evidence as a whole supported a finding of negligence based on the doctrine of res ipsa loquitur (see Chapter 3). Justice Trobiner took the position that the negligence concept failed to provide appropriate criteria for making a decision on loss distribution on these facts; in his view the doctors should have been held responsible based on the concept of strict liability. Concurring and dissenting, Justice Traynor opined that while there was specific evidence that the surgeon was negligent, the premature termination of the operation by itself did not support invoking the doctrine of res ipsa loquitur.

■ **Problem Two:** *Neglect of the Elderly Patient*

Mr. Clark, eighty-five years of age, died after two months of hospitalization as a result of severe disabilities associated with a stroke. The family wants to sue the hospital because at the time of his death they discovered that both his legs were covered with decubitus ulcers. A nurse-consultant who reviewed the medical records is prepared to testify that the ulcers were caused by a failure on the part of the nursing staff to bathe Mr. Clark regularly and turn him as required by the nursing protocol for treating patients in this condition.

The family members have retained counsel to represent them. Counsel has advised the hospital's attorney that she intends to file suit, and the attorney has responded that the lawsuit would be frivolous. Hospital counsel first notes that Mr. Clark died from causes not associated with decubitus ulcers. The attorney further asserts that he has interviewed the nurses who cared for Mr. Clark and they will testify that, notwithstanding the absence of entries in the medical chart, their conduct in caring for Mr. Clark fully conformed to standard nursing protocol.

This problem raises important questions concerning the economics of medical care and malpractice litigation. Should the family's attorney file suit? How much is it likely to cost to try this case to verdict? If the jury returns a verdict in the plaintiff's favor, how much money is the jury likely to award? Chapter 5 discusses the impact of financial considerations on medical practices. Chapters 6–8 address the methods by which the law measures damages and the factors that influence the size of a personal injury award.

■ **Problem Three:** *The Intimidated Expert Witness*

Two weeks before the scheduled start of the trial of a malpractice case against a dentist, the plaintiff's dental expert decides not to testify because his professional liability insurance carrier has threatened to cancel his policy if he does. It turns out, to the surprise of plaintiff's counsel and his expert, that the expert has the same insurance carrier as does the defendant dentist. Moreover, the only restriction in the policy on the insurance company's right to cancel the policy is a requirement that the company give thirty days' notice and refund the unearned premium.

What should plaintiff's counsel do? Should an insurance company be precluded from canceling the policy of an insured who engages in conduct that may make the company lose money? Would it be against public policy for malpractice insurers to include an express provision in a malpractice policy prohibiting an insured from testifying against any other professional who is insured by the company?

In *L'Orange v. The Medical Protective Company*,[3] which presents similar issues, the court observed:

> A member of the medical profession could hardly be expected to appear in court and testify for a plaintiff in any litigation if the penalty might be the cancellation of his own malpractice insurance. It manifestly is contrary to public policy to permit an insurance company to use policy cancellation as punishment against a doctor or dentist who appears as a witness to protect the rights of a plaintiff who has been wronged by another member of the profession. If the insurance industry can use the cancellation procedure to keep members of the medical profession from testifying as witnesses, malpractice litigation can be stifled.[4]

On the other hand, in *McDonnell v. Commission on Medical Discipline*,[5] where a physician-defendant attempted to intimidate two residents who were experts for the plaintiff, the court held that he could not be disciplined for "immoral conduct" because the Maryland Code limits the definition of unprofessional conduct to acts done by a physician "in his practice as a physician." The court thought that the defendant-physician's efforts to intimidate the opposing experts were not acts related to his practice as a physician.

In the subsequent trial of the *McDonnell* medical malpractice case, *Meyer v. McDonnell*,[6] another Maryland court held that the physician's conduct in attempting to intimidate the experts is admissible as tending to show his consciousness of the weakness of his case and a belief that his defense would not prevail without the aid of these improper and unfair tactics. This, in conjunction with the other evidence in the case, may lead to the further inference that the appellee considers his case to be weak because he is, in fact, guilty of the negligence that the appellant asserts he committed.[7] Later in this chapter I will offer some suggestions about how to keep this type of problem from occurring.

■ **Problem Four:** *The Altered Record*

Dr. Jenson is a defendant in a medical malpractice case in which the plaintiff alleges that he performed an unnecessary hysterectomy on her. The laboratory reports support the doctor's diagnosis of a malignancy that warranted the surgery. A nurse has advised Dr. Jenson's attorney to examine the medical records carefully, however, because she has reason to believe that Dr. Jenson has altered them or caused them to be altered. She also states that it is not the first time Dr. Jenson has done something like this.

What should Dr. Jenson's attorney do? If she determines that the nurse's observations are accurate, should she advise plaintiff's counsel, the court, or the hospital at which the surgery took place?

Rule 3.3 of the American Bar Association *Model Rules of Professional Conduct* (see the Appendix) provides: "(a) A lawyer shall not knowingly: (1) make a false statement of material fact or law to a tribunal; . . . (4) offer evidence that the lawyer knows to be false. If a lawyer has offered material evidence and comes to know of its falsity, the lawyer shall take reasonable remedial measures."

The challenge to the attorney in this situation is how to represent her client effectively if credible evidence suggests that he has engaged in dishonest and unethical conduct. Counsel cannot continue to represent the client without taking some remedial measures if the court is likely to be misled concerning material matters. It is clearly much easier to be a pure advocate in an adversarial system than it is to reconcile advocacy with ethics.

This book contains many problems designed to prompt reflection on how to reconcile advocacy with ethics.[8] Readers should consider not only particular medical malpractice issues but also the system of justice as a whole. Among the fundamental issues explored here are the roles that ought to be played by physicians, attorneys, courts, juries, legislators, and other members of the community who may be asked to participate in resolving individual disputes. In addition to examining the appropriate allocation of decision-making authority, the discussion tries to cast light on the criteria that should guide the ultimate decision to compensate the patient or require her to bear her losses on her own. Among the questions that underlie the discussion are the following:

1. What are the pivotal ethical, social, and economic considerations?
2. Which of these considerations, if any, should dominate the legal decision-making process?
3. Should a judge, jury, legislature, administrative agency, arbitrator, or mediator resolve any given dispute?
4. Should the health care provider be discouraged from engaging in similar conduct in the future?

Seeking the answers to these questions will lead us into some of the thorniest thickets in modern American jurisprudence.

Ethical and policy issues are not, however, the only important threshold considerations that command an attorney's attention at the outset of her evaluation of a potential medical malpractice case. Equally important are some practical considerations that determine whether the litigation is likely to be a challenging and rewarding experience or a harrowing and thankless ordeal. Primary among these factors are the personality and needs of the parties to the litigation. The initial stage, when attorney meets client, offers a unique opportunity not only to evaluate the potential merit of the case, but also to determine what it is going to be like to live with this client for a substantial period of time and how this client is likely to help or hurt his own case. In addition, the first meeting allows the attorney to assess the potential of conflicts or other ethical dilemmas arising during the course of the litigation. For these reasons, I regard the initial client interview as a critical stage in the evaluation of a potential medical malpractice claim or defense.

Fundamental Concerns about Clients

Whether a case is tried to a jury or a judge, the status and personalities of the parties to the lawsuit have an impact on the decision maker. The lifestyle, character, and values of the parties affect their credibility as witnesses and influence the amount of empathy they inspire. In other words, a medical malpractice case, like other civil lawsuits, is not just about facts and law bearing directly on the dispute; it is ultimately about people and their lives before and after the accident. Independent of the attorney's assessment of the merit of a client's claim or defense, the settlement, dismissal, or basic trial strategies may be heavily influenced by the client's psychological, emotional, or financial needs, or by her basic personality or character. Understanding and assessing the strengths and weaknesses of the parties is an important part of the attorney's job, and the initial interview of the client provides an ideal opportunity to focus on the client as a person. Spending the two or more hours necessary to conduct a comprehensive and sensitive client interview makes a substantial contribution to an evaluation of the case.

Whether the attorney represents the patient or the health care provider, the goals of the initial interview include gathering factual information, formulating legal issues, and assessing the client as a person and a potential witness. Though the need to assess the client exists in all types of litigation, it is especially important in medical malpractice cases because of the unique status of health care providers and the mystique associated with doctors. The initial interview presents an opportunity not only to assess the potential merit of the claim or defense, but also to evaluate the personal appeal of the patient or the doctor.

During the initial interview, counsel should project how the client will appear to the court and to the jury when the case goes to trial, perhaps several years later. Counsel should assess whether the client will take constructive suggestions with respect to dress, appearance, and speech. From the perspective of plaintiff's counsel, some cases should be rejected despite their merit if counsel feels he will be unable to sell this particular client to a jury. Accepting a plaintiff's medical malpractice case represents an exceptional commitment for an attorney, since he must usually work on a contingent fee basis, financing the costs of the litigation himself at the risk of never recouping these costs or earning a fee if he does not win. In these days of expensive expert witness fees, ranging from two to three thousand dollars a day or more, a bad decision can have dire or in the case of small law firms, perhaps even catastrophic consequences.

On the defense side it is tempting to delay a determination that the health care provider is likely to lose a case because defense counsel is paid on an hourly basis and thus an early settlement reduces the fee she will earn. Some health care providers, however, may be served best by developing an early settlement strategy if a judge or jury is likely to disbelieve or dislike them. A medical malpractice case may take a substantial toll on a doctor's emotional well-being and financial resources. Although it is important that a defensible case receive a vigorous defense, it is equally important to control and minimize financial and emotional costs if the case is likely to be a loser.

The remainder of this chapter highlights issues and techniques relevant to the initial client interview of the plaintiff and the defendant. Although the discussion aims primarily at the practicing attorney, others may find it useful in thinking about the impact that effective lawyering techniques or a litigant's personality and character may have on the outcome of a case.

Conducting the Initial Client Interview

A senior person should conduct the initial client interview. Relying on a paralegal or secretary for this task may be practical in simple accident and domestic cases, but in medical malpractice cases a lawyer who understands medicine, anatomy and physiology, and people should be in charge. If possible, an assistant should also be present to take notes and gather impressions about the case and the client.

The primary client should be interviewed alone unless there is good reason for including another adult, such as a spouse. In the privacy of a one-on-one interview the potential client will tell counsel about important matters that she may not reveal in front of another person. If the initial interview is conducted in the presence of family, counsel should conduct a private interview with the primary client at a later time.

Before the interview begins, counsel should assure the client that sensitive questions about personal matters will be asked only to assess the case properly. It is helpful to assure the client that there is little she can tell counsel that he has not heard before and that what a client tells her attorney is confidential and will not be repeated outside the room unless absolutely necessary and allowed by the Code of Professional Responsibility. Moreover, particularly sensitive matters need not be recorded. Indeed, sensitive data in counsel's possession should be placed in a safety deposit box or some other secure location that will preserve the client's right to privacy.

Identifying and Avoiding the Troublesome Plaintiff

A client may be troublesome because of expectations, demands, or personal needs that neither counsel nor the legal system will ever be able to meet. In the initial client interview, counsel should try to identify the troublesome plaintiff early, because once a medical malpractice case is accepted, it is difficult to withdraw without hurting the client. Bonding and dependency occur quickly, as does the expenditure of resources. An early discussion of the attorney's normal frequency of communicating with the client may enhance an understanding of the new relationship being formed and identify the client who has personal needs that counsel cannot meet. The potential client should be advised as to the limitations of counsel's availability for consultation. A good policy is to inform the client that she will be called at critical times in her case but will not be informed about routine questions and decisions that have little effect on the outcome of the litigation. Although it may sound insensitive, as a practical matter this approach is critical to counsel's ability to devote the requisite full-time efforts in effective representation of multiple clients.

It is helpful to tell a client during the initial interview that failure to be available for routine conferences at the client's wishes is due not to lack of interest, caring, or compassion but simply to the fact that counsel has a heavy case load and must allocate time judiciously to competing tasks. The client should be assured, however, that her case will receive attention on a timely basis.

In short, counsel should try to make it clear from the beginning that he will not be available to the client to converse about her personal life or about the process or progress of the case unless there is some good reason for it. Those clients who are unable or unwilling to be represented on this basis should be rejected and referred to attorneys who have more time available for interaction with clients or who have an approach or philosophy of practice that will satisfy the particular client.

This approach for establishing an understanding of limited lawyer-client communication should not be misunderstood to suggest that the lawyer will not allow the client to participate in important decisions that may affect the outcome of the case. Informed consent is as important in the context of lawyering as it is in the context of medical care. But just as it would be inefficient and detrimental to a patient to be consulted about every technical decision made after she has given an informed consent to the procedure, the same is true in the litigation process. On the other hand, material matters such as whether to make a demand or accept a settlement offer or whether to retain co-counsel clearly require client consultation and consent.

Sometimes a desirable client becomes a troublesome client because the interviewing lawyer creates unreasonable expectations or fails to temper them on the part of the client. I recommend adopting the following office rule: Never offer clients or referring lawyers an estimate of the expected value of the case. Unrealistic expectations based on a lawyer's representation of value cause serious harm to clients.

Rather than creating an expectation of a specific amount of money that will be recovered, during the initial stages of evaluating a medical malpractice case counsel should assure the client that the attorneys will put forth their best efforts to secure an adequate recovery and that if the case goes to litigation, the court or jury will set the amount. As far as settlement is concerned, the attorney should make it clear that the final decision will be made by the client. Counsel should advise the client what he believes is or is not an adequate and fair recovery; the client should also be advised, however, that no one can guarantee the outcome of the litigation, and thus, the client must make the final decision.

At the completion of the initial client interview the lawyers and paralegal or other assistants should compare notes and prepare a memorandum. If counsel decides to investigate the case, the memorandum should describe the information, such as medical records, other interviews, or further investigation, required. Should counsel reject the case, he should prepare a memo containing the reasons why. A prompt rejection letter should follow.

Sometimes a plaintiff will present a case that appears to represent a colorable claim of malpractice. In those cases attorneys are tempted to make a snap judgment: "Yes, we will take this case. They shouldn't be allowed to get away with that." The urge to make such decisions based on emotion should be resisted. Instead, counsel should afford himself the advantage of observing the client further and reviewing the evidence critically before undertaking the responsibility of litigating the case.

If it becomes apparent during the interview that counsel will be unable to take the case, the client should be told the decision and the reason why. This should be followed up with a letter. If the case is accepted for investigation, or is one of those rare cases that are accepted immediately for prosecution, the client should be informed about the decision and about the fee and expense arrangements. Many laypeople are not familiar with the specifics of a contingent fee arrangement, and explanations will be required after the client has read the agreement. Medical authorizations and a retainer agreement should be signed at that time.

Checklist for Interviewing a Plaintiff

The following checklist may prove useful in the initial client interview.

1. Assess the client's dress and physical appearance. See if she makes eye contact. Check for mannerisms, voice, and enunciation. Make a determination as to whether the person is telling you the truth. Is the story credible? Does there appear to be an undisclosed prior relationship with the opposing party? Is there a hatred of doctors or a distrust of medical personnel? Has the potential client suffered a wide variety of ailments?

2. Determine if other attorneys have examined the case. If so, their reputation is significant. If the case has been reviewed by attorneys known to you to be sloppy or incompetent, the review merits little weight. On the other hand, if the case has been reviewed by a respected practitioner, an extra measure of vigilance is warranted. Moreover, counsel may gain insight into the needs and personality of the client by determining whether she has consulted numerous attorneys and, if so, the reason for her going from lawyer to lawyer.

3. Evaluate the significant other persons who will have influence on the plaintiff during the course of the litigation. This is particularly important with respect to a spouse in the case of plaintiffs, and co-workers in the case of health care providers. A client who is constantly badgered and questioned during the course of litigation by a significant other is likely to pose a serious problem to her attorney. Significant other persons can include parents, children, other relatives or friends, or other attorneys in the family who may try to run the suit. All these factors are part of evaluating a case.

4. Determine the jurisdiction and venue where suit may be brought. A case may be good in one jurisdiction and worthless in another. For example, a case based on a botched sterilization giving rise to an unwanted pregnancy has little chance of success in a community dominated by persons who have strong religious beliefs opposing birth control. The dominant values of the court and jury should be considered at the outset of the case, rather than after it is over.

5. Determine the exact period of the statute of limitations involved. Several factors may cause the attorney to be brought into a case very late. First, the plaintiff may have hesitated to bring suit against her doctor. Second, manifestation of the injuries may have been delayed. And third, some have altered the statute of limitations as a part of tort reform. Plaintiff's counsel who discover that the case is close to being barred by a statute of limitations should advise the client in writing and complete the review expeditiously. If necessary, action should be taken to toll the statute of limitations pending final evaluation.

6. Personal history

   The client's personal history in medical malpractice cases is as important for the lawyer as it is for a doctor. Failure to take the history or omitting a part of it can mean numerous calls to the client, creating the appearance of incompetence. If the information is taken at the time the file is given to the lawyer, it will be readily available to aid in both the evaluation of the case and its eventual prosecution. In the initial client interview plaintiff's counsel should elicit the following information:

a. Name
b. Address
c. Phone numbers
d. Occupation
e. Place of work
f. Length of employment
g. Present earnings
h. Prior employment history
i. Brief earnings history
j. Name and occupation of spouse
k. Prior spouses
l. Dates of marriages
m. Dates of divorces
n. Prior involvement in lawsuits
o. Complete medical history beginning with childhood injuries, etc. Although not all cases require a complete history, it is still a good idea to get one to determine factors that could have assisted in causing the injuries.
p. Names of prior physicians and hospitals rendering treatment
q. All adverse information contained in an old medical record which could affect the case. The prior history should mention childhood illness, blood type, genetic factors. This is especially true in birth-injury cases and those involving predisposing factors.
r. Drug and alcohol use
s. Cigarette use
t. Arrest record, if any
u. Names and ages of children

Details of the suspected malpractice should include:

a. Who committed the alleged negligent actions
b. When each alleged act was committed
c. Where each alleged act was committed
d. What constituted each negligent act

At this point in the interview counsel may be able to determine whether any colorable claims of medical malpractice exist. If a bad result has occurred but no malpractice, the potential client should be advised that not all bad results are the product of negligence and that not every mistake rises to the level of malpractice. If there is negligence but it clearly did not cause the patient's harm, explain to the client the causation requirement in the law. This is a good point to stop the interview.

7. If counsel decides to continue the interview because the matter appears worth investigating, many additional details are needed, particularly concerning all hospitals where the patient was treated for the illness under question. The interviewer should elicit the following information:
   a. Names and addresses, if possible, of all treating doctors
   b. Names of all treating nurses
   c. Names of all other personnel on the ward whom the client remembers
   d. Names of all nurses, aides, and other medical personnel who may know the details of the injury
   e. Names of insurers and others who paid medical bills
   f. Names of witnesses, other patients, or persons who may have been present when the alleged malpractice occurred
   g. Rumors circulated by medical personnel concerning any discipline or prior reprimands of treating personnel
   h. Names of any medical personnel who suggested that the patient see a lawyer
8. Information concerning economic loss
   a. Nature of the injury, etc.
      (1) Document scars
      (2) Use videotape when necessary
      (3) In the case of a person who may die, make a special effort to videotape the interview with the person to preserve her testimony as best you can
   b. Determine who is entitled to compensation
      (1) Spouse
      (2) Children
      (3) Survivors
      (4) Estate. Has an executor/executrix been appointed?
   c. Detailed earnings history
      (1) Income tax returns, W-2 forms, etc.
      (2) Names of supervisors
      (3) Schools attended or special training received
      (4) Awards, promotions, safety record
      (5) Attendance
      (6) Information regarding future of job, job security
   d. Household expenses
   e. Services rendered to spouse, children, other eligible survivors
   f. Hobbies
   g. Services relevant to religious institutions
   h. Civic affairs
   i. Future care requirements
      (1) Wheelchairs
      (2) Prosthesis
      (3) Therapy
      (4) Home nursing care

(5) Future corrective surgery
(6) Nursing homes
(7) Evaluations and whom they were performed by

Interviewing the Health Care Provider

The circumstances under which defense counsel obtain clients in medical malpractice cases provide little opportunity to avoid the troublesome client. Most defense counsel are hired by the defendant's professional liability insurance carrier, who pays both the expenses of the litigation and counsel's hourly fee. Rejecting the client involves consideration of the impact on counsel's relationship with the insurance company as well as the particular client. Nevertheless, it behooves defense counsel to identify the troublesome client as early as possible. A doctor or nurse may be troublesome because of personality, character, professional knowledge and skills or lack thereof. Some sense of the potential problems may be gleaned from the referring insurance manager and from the initial interview.

Many of the observations and suggestions made in the discussion of the plaintiff's interview also apply to the health care provider's interview. This section concentrates on considerations unique to the health care provider. Clearly, the focus of the initial interview will be on the defendant's version of what occurred that caused the bad result at issue. Ostensibly a discussion of the facts of the case, a sensitive interview will also disclose much about the health care provider's personality, character, health, and professional skills and knowledge.

In most cases the two most credible sources of the medical facts of the case are the principal health care provider and the medical records. It is useful to learn at the initial interview how much the doctor or nurse recalls about the case independent of the medical records. If he recalls important matters that are not included in the records, counsel should get explanations concerning the defendant's normal practice of recording medical information and why important matters now remembered are not a part of the record.

The medical record should be reviewed by counsel in as much detail as possible before the initial substantive interview (see Chapter 9). This allows fruitful exploration of the plaintiff's theories and potential defenses while the defendant is reviewing the facts of the case. In addition, a detailed review of the medical record permits counsel and client to develop a rapport and, it is hoped, induces client confidence in counsel. The process of identifying important fact witnesses, medical authorities, and possible experts should begin at the initial interview.

Much of the initial interview should aim at disclosing the identity of the defendant as a person and as a professional. Since he will have received a copy of the complaint containing allegations about his acts of negligence and lack of professional skills and knowledge, how he responds to these allegations to his attorney provides an excellent opportunity to assess how he will appear at trial. If the matter goes to trial, the defendant, like most health care providers, will initially benefit from the respect and esteem that a majority of the public bestows on doctors and other health care professionals. Counsel should recognize, however, that her defense will be shattered if the defendant on trial is arrogant and unlikable or has betrayed the public trust. His social and economic background, family relationships, friendships, hobbies, community activities, and religious practices may be discovered by the jurors and affect their beliefs about the defendant as well as their judgment as to what really happened in this case. A person who is hardworking, thoughtful, sensitive, and concerned about the well-being of others is certainly easier to defend than an overbearing professional who cares only about his own power, prestige, and financial status.

Health care providers are human. They enjoy states of good mental and physical health; they also suffer from illness. Drugs and alcohol sometimes creep into their lives and the lives of those they care about. The stress of the practice may be exceptionally high at times and take a toll on both their personal lives and their professional performance (see Problem Two in Chapter 2). A mandatory part of the interview should involve a careful review of the defendant's past and present health. This may provide clues to past problems as well as to current techniques of handling the client.

Defense counsel must be just as concerned as plaintiff's attorney with the personality and character of the litigants. During the early stages of her investigation defense counsel should assure herself that she represents a health care provider who is both honest and competent. A medical malpractice case that turns on factual disputes concerning whether the doctor or nurse employed the knowledge and skill required under the circumstances presents a different challenge from a case that rests on a contention that the health care provider lacks the ability required to practice. The claim that the doctor or nurse has altered the medical records or engaged in some other deceitful conduct may be the worst type of case to defend. Allegations of professional dishonesty may shock a jury and induce a large damage award driven by anger. Allegations of incompetence may arouse empathy with the unfortunate victim who trusted the professional. Both types of cases raise difficult issues of trial strategy as well as ethical issues for defense counsel.

Assuming that the health care professional is in good health and honest, his credibility may turn on the jurors' perception of his general professional competency. This does not mean that competent people do not on occasion make mistakes, as plaintiff's counsel is sure to remind the jury. It does mean, however, that a defendant who presents himself as a knowledgeable, skilled, honest, and trustworthy professional enhances his chance of being believed both as to what happened in this case and as to the required standard of care.

If counsel familiarizes herself with the medical record and the medical issues in the case before the initial interview, she can conduct a preliminary evaluation of whether the defendant has kept abreast of the state of medical knowledge. In addition, she can make appropriate inquiries about the skill and training necessary to provide the care that was rendered to the plaintiff.

To accomplish the goals of the initial interview, counsel should insist that the meeting occur in an environment where the client will give his undivided attention to the matter with minimum interruption. Counsel's office offers this advantage in addition to providing the opportunity to evaluate how the defendant responds to an unfamiliar environment, since he will have to function in such an environment throughout most of the litigation.

Checklist for Interviewing the Physician

A general guideline is to ask all the questions that a competent plaintiff's attorney will likely ask either through interrogatories or at a deposition. This process will reveal matters that may need to be protected from discovery as well as some that may hurt the defense. The interview should elicit the following information:

> Personal information
> Education
> Training
> License to practice
> Board eligibility or certification
> Hospital staff privileges
> Publications
> Professional associations
> Continuing education programs
> Textbooks and periodicals customarily relied on in field
> Names of all health care providers who treated plaintiff
> Names of witnesses to care rendered to plaintiff
> Differences of view among plaintiff's health care providers or others as to propriety of care rendered to plaintiff
> Prior disciplinary proceedings
> Prior criminal proceedings
> Prior civil lawsuits

The defendant should be given the following instructions:

> Do not alter medical records.
> Do not contact opposing experts.
> Do not discuss the case with anyone, especially the plaintiff or her family.

Conclusion

In this chapter I have tried to show the need for both a philosophical and a practical understanding of the various factors that influence the prosecution and defense of a medical malpractice case. The threshold considerations include the standard of care required of health care professionals and institutions. Other basic issues, which have roots in ethics, economics, psychology, sociology, and politics, should also be addressed as threshold matters, rather than ignored or set aside for later consideration. Chapter 2 raises these issues.

Chapter 2

The Lawyer's Duty of Care

The attorney's primary responsibility in a medical malpractice case is to learn enough medicine to assess whether the conduct of the treating doctors and nurses caused the plaintiff's injuries and, if so, whether these health care providers were negligent. Counsel for each side must depend on experts to help sort through the mass of technical information related to the care that the plaintiff received. Often the experts disagree, placing the burden on the attorneys to judge which expert is most credible. Moreover, expert opinions are frequently premised on the attorney's ability to prove certain facts. As counsel obtains more information through formal or informal investigations and research, the opinions of the experts may change. A basic problem for the medical malpractice attorney is deciding when he has gathered sufficient information to evaluate the merits of the case fairly. In making this determination, counsel usually must operate within the constraints of a financial budget. Unlimited resources are rarely made available to either side to the litigation.

Physicians complain that lawyers file too many frivolous medical malpractice suits. Although studies of medical malpractice cases do not support the physicians' view that this problem is widespread,[1] it is undoubtedly true that plaintiffs' attorneys accept and prosecute through some stage of the litigation process claims that ultimately prove devoid of merit. Assessing the significance of the frivolous claim problem, however, requires taking into account the reality that a lawyer rarely has all the facts he needs to assess the merits of a case accurately when it is first presented to him. Only after he has spent substantial effort and time reviewing the medical records, interviewing fact witnesses, obtaining an expert witness's opinion, and conducting medical research will the merits of a case appear. Consequently, it is not unusual for a case that initially seems meritorious to turn out to be a clear loser.

Intensive pretrial investigation and research is critical to evaluating a medical malpractice case. An attorney's initial goal should be to gather all the information that an expert witness will need in order to formulate an opinion about whether malpractice has occurred. Unfortunately, it is not always possible to obtain all that information before the suit is filed. Medical records do not tell the full story even when they are relatively complete and legible— which is often not the case. Fact witnesses such as residents and nurses frequently move away, and even after they are located, they may be reluctant to discuss the case for fear of repercussions or out of loyalty to a colleague. Those witnesses who will discuss the case may be understandably biased.

Despite the obstacles, counsel on both sides have an obligation to get as complete a picture as possible before deciding whether a potential medical malpractice case has merit. Methods and techniques for developing that picture are discussed throughout this book. The remainder of this chapter considers the standard to be employed in evaluating whether the claim or defense has merit.

■ **Problem One:** *Tongue Paralysis*

After a tonsillectomy Mrs. Smith suffered paralysis of her tongue. She sought representation to sue Dr. Sand, who performed the tonsillectomy. At her first meeting with the attorney, Mr. Carl, Mrs. Smith and her husband stated that Dr. Sand told them that the cause of the tongue paralysis was probably too much pressure exerted by the clamp used during the course of the operation. After this initial conference Mr. Carl conferred with the physician who was currently treating Mrs. Smith for the paralysis; this doctor informed Mr. Carl that although she had never seen or heard of paralysis resulting from a tonsillectomy, she felt that it must have been caused by something that had occurred during the operation and that pressure on the tongue was a possible explanation. Mr. Carl then obtained a report from a neurologist who had evaluated the plaintiff; the report stated that the paralysis reflected a complete interruption of the twelfth nerve. Mr. Carl interpreted that report to be consistent with his theory that the interruption had been caused by excessive pressure exerted on Mrs. Smith's tongue by the clamp. After he obtained and studied the plaintiff's complete medical records and found no other explanation for the paralysis, Mr. Carl filed suit against Dr. Sand. The jury took only twenty minutes before returning a verdict in favor of the doctor. Is this a frivolous lawsuit?

The facts set forth in this problem are taken from <u>*Rorrer v. Cooke*</u>. [2] After losing her medical malpractice case, Mrs. Rorrer sued the lawyer, Mr. Cooke, who had represented her for legal malpractice, alleging, among other things, that he had been negligent in his failure to obtain adequate expert consultations from physicians qualified to evaluate her medical malpractice claim. In support of her legal malpractice claim, she retained another attorney to testify as an expert witness concerning the legal malpractice. This lawyer submitted an affidavit to the court, stating in part, "In my opinion, it is very important in the preparation and trial of a medical malpractice case to have at least one medical witness who enthusiastically and convincingly will support the plaintiff's attorney's medical theory of negligence."[3] The affidavit goes on to state that the lawyer had been negligent in his failure to obtain the advice of a specialist not associated with the plaintiff's care, noting the availability of medical consulting agencies that could have reviewed the claim objectively. It further stated that Mr. Cooke had weakened his chances of getting an objective and full assessment of the merits of the medical case by locking himself into a medical theory that medical experts did not support.

The appellate court in *Rorrer* ruled that the expert witness's affidavit was insufficient to support Mrs. Rorrer's claim of legal malpractice. Its insufficiency lies in the expert attorney's failure to describe the legal standard of care required of Mrs. Rorrer's attorney in terms of the standards of the legal profession. In the view of the appellate court Mrs. Rorrer's expert had said no more than that he would have handled the case differently. According to the court, that was not enough to prove that the way in which Mrs. Rorrer's attorney carried out the case constituted negligence.

Legal malpractice claims are governed by the same general standards as medical malpractice claims. The first standard is that the lawyer must possess that degree of skill and knowledge ordinarily possessed by members of the profession rendering the service for which he is employed.[4] In *Rorrer*, the defendant's possession of that skill and knowledge was not challenged.

The second standard is that the lawyer must employ that skill and knowledge in rendering the particular service. The issue in *Rorrer* was whether the defendant had employed that skill in evaluating, preparing, and presenting the case. The plaintiff's claim that Mr. Cooke had failed to use the requisite skill was based on the assertion that an essential ingredient of a plaintiff's medical malpractice case is an expert who will "enthusiastically" support the plaintiff's claim that a particular act of medical negligence has occurred. There was no question that the defendant attorney did not present an expert who enthusiastically supported his theory that the plaintiff's tongue paralysis resulted from pressure exerted by the clamp during the tonsillectomy. The pivotal question was whether it was negligent to proceed to trial without making a greater effort to obtain such testimony. The appellate court does not address this issue. In its view the opinion of the expert witness did not adequately allege that the support of an enthusiastic expert was essential for meeting the standard of care required of a lawyer handling a medical malpractice case. Rather, according to the court, the affidavit simply represented the individual opinion of the lawyer who wrote it.[5] In other words, to support a claim of malpractice, the plaintiff's expert must define the standard that the defendant failed to meet in terms of what a competent professional would have done in similar circumstances; it is not enough simply to say what the particular expert would have done in similar circumstances.

It is certainly ideal to have an enthusiastic medical expert who will express an opinion that the medical defendant deviated from the required standard of care and that such deviation was the cause of the plaintiff's injuries. Moreover, there probably are cases where the nature of the medical negligence and the cause of the plaintiff's injuries are clear enough that it would be negligent to evaluate, initiate, or present the case without an enthusiastic expert. Unfortunately, the ideal is often not achievable. Experienced medical malpractice attorneys know that most physicians hesitate to testify unequivocally unless the act of malpractice is blatant and the cause of the plaintiff's injuries is clear. Physicians are much more forgiving of mistakes in judgment or deviations from desirable medical practices than are plaintiffs' lawyers and injured consumers, in part because they recognize the complexity of medicine and in part because they are reluctant to condemn a colleague.

Furthermore, legal language blocks communication between lawyer and doctor. The term *cause* when used in law connotes that "more probably than not" X produced Y. Experts are expected to testify that "to a reasonable medical certainty" X produced Y. But what does that mean? Does it mean the same level of certainty that a physician would require in diagnosing a patient's condition and prescribing a therapy? The answer is probably yes, but the courts do not expressly define the legal standard for causation by using language that physicians understand.[6] An attorney must usually work hard to get his witness to grasp the legal meaning of *causation*. But the effort is worth it. Only then will the expert gain the confidence to express opinions on causation to a reasonable medical certainty.

The bottom line is that an attorney must exercise reasonable care and diligence both in identifying appropriate expert witnesses and in communicating with them. Once these tasks are performed, the attorney will learn whether the case can be effectively evaluated in its present posture or whether material information must still be acquired.

In addition to diligently investigating the factual and medical basis of the claim, the attorney who undertakes to represent a client in a medical malpractice case has numerous other specific obligations. They include supervising associate counsel, communicating with the parties, communicating with witnesses, conducting discovery, giving timely notice to governmental entities that are potential defendants, and filing claims with medical review panels. Each of these specific duties has served as the basis of a legal malpractice claim.[7]

Like their professional counterparts in the medical community who are the primary subjects of this book, attorneys who venture into the field of medical malpractice litigation must maneuver around potentially devastating traps. The duty to possess and employ the degree of skill and knowledge possessed and employed by a professional acting in the same or similar circumstances exists every time a professional provides a service. Consequently, even the most highly skilled and conscientious doctor or lawyer may commit malpractice at some point in his or her career.

With respect to the issue of attorney malpractice in *Rorrer*, one must draw the line between ideal professional conduct and unacceptable professional conduct. Though the failure of plaintiff's counsel to obtain an enthusiastic expert may not constitute a deviation from the required standard of care for attorneys in every medical malpractice case, attorneys for both the plaintiff and the defendant should always strive to obtain such testimony. Since the plaintiff bears the burden of proof, plaintiff's counsel proceeds to trial in great jeopardy if he does not have a credible expert. Though it is possible to get a case to a jury in the absence of persuasive expert testimony, the chances of obtaining a favorable verdict are substantially reduced. Accordingly, from the moment that a lawyer begins evaluating a medical malpractice case, he should think about what kind of expert he needs and how to get her.

The chances of getting such an expert are significantly influenced by the amount of preparation the lawyer puts into gathering facts and understanding the medical issues. The ability to read, understand, and summarize medical records and conduct medical research is critical. The expert's impression of the case and her willingness to be involved in it will be influenced by the first communication she has with the lawyer. For this reason, the lawyer should view the expert as a partner in the potential litigation with reciprocal obligations for assessing the merits of the claim. To be a partner in evaluating the case's medical aspects merely requires that the attorney learn some medicine, and that is not as difficult as it sounds. Spending some time in medical libraries and talking to health care professionals about particular medical issues will accomplish wonders.

But just as it is a serious error to rely totally on the expert to evaluate the medical aspects of the case, it is a mistake to try to dictate the medical theory of the case to the expert. The cardinal principle that should govern a lawyer's conduct in evaluating and preparing to try a medical malpractice case is that he must retain the "best" expert available to assess the case and testify at trial if the case is meritorious. The art of applying this principle so that he knows who the "best" expert is and how her expertise can be maximized is the ultimate challenge. Since identifying and communicating with medical experts will have the greatest influence of any factor on the evaluation of a medical malpractice case, we return to a discussion of the "best expert" in Chapter 11.

■ **Problem Two:** *The Impaired Doctor*

Dr. Axelrod is alleged to have caused a plaintiff to suffer severe injuries by negligently performing an operation while intoxicated. Carlton Community Hospital is also named as a defendant based on allegations that the hospital's medical staff had been aware of Dr. Axelrod's drinking for several years but had ignored the problem. Ms. Douglas represents Dr. Axelrod; Mr. Gold represents the hospital.

After initiating the lawsuit, plaintiff submitted to the hospital a request that documents be produced, including all committee reports and investigative reports concerning complaints filed by patients and staff members against Dr. Axelrod relating in any manner to the performance of his professional duties over the past five years. The request also sought the doctor's personnel file, including disciplinary and impaired-physician reports. In addition, during the course of Dr. Axelrod's deposition, plaintiff's counsel asks the doctor the following questions: Have you ever been enrolled in a rehabilitation program for alcoholics? Have staff privileges ever been limited at any hospital on the grounds that your consumption of alcohol interfered with the performance of your duties as a staff physician? Have you ever been investigated by any professional licensing body or any hospital based on charges that you were intoxicated while performing your professional duties? Have you ever been convicted of operating a motor vehicle while under the influence of alcohol? Have you ever been ejected from a social affair sponsored by a professional association on the basis that you were intoxicated? Isn't it true that you keep alcohol in your office in the hospital where you performed the surgery on this plaintiff? Was the hospital aware that you kept alcohol in your office on hospital premises? Did you consume any alcohol during the eight-hour period preceding the operation you performed on the plaintiff? Have you ever performed surgery while intoxicated? Have you ever performed surgery when you had consumed alcohol within two hours of the start of the surgery?

Should Ms. Douglas permit the doctor to answer the questions? If she instructs the doctor not to answer, is the court likely to require answers at a later time and/or impose sanctions on the doctor and/or Ms. Douglas? As a member of the bar, if Ms. Douglas believes Dr. Axelrod does in fact have a serious alcohol problem, does she have a professional responsibility to take some action to prevent him from causing harm to future patients?

What position should Mr. Gold take concerning the request for production of documents? What position should he take on the questions posed during the deposition? What position should Ms. Douglas take on the request for documents?

Some of the issues set forth in this problem were taken from *Bay Medical Center v. Sapp*.[8] That court ruled that the committee reports requested by the plaintiff were protected from discovery by the state peer-review statute and the state's public policy in favor of the confidentiality of such records. To gain access to the records, plaintiff would have to show exceptional necessity or extraordinary circumstances.

Determining the extent to which a plaintiff may discover details about a physician's past bad acts may turn on specific provisions in a peer-review statute. Generally, such statutes immunize from discovery evidence presented to a peer-review panel, but the statutes do not prevent the plaintiff from obtaining statements from witnesses based on knowledge acquired outside the peer-review process or documents generated independently of that process. Consequently, the plaintiff may be permitted to obtain the testimony of other health professionals who observed the defendant practicing medicine while impaired, either by way of their recollections or by way of letters or memos written to persons other than the peer-review committee.[9]

In addition to concerns about the effect of evidence of a physician's impairment on the outcome of the particular case, ethical defense counsel must consider what steps to take to protect her client and the public if there is persuasive evidence that her client suffers from a serious impairment. One commentator offered the following observations regarding the extent of the problem of impaired physicians:

> No one knows exactly how many physicians are practicing despite alcoholism, drug addiction, or psychiatric disorders; estimates range from 5 to 12 percent of the 485,000 licensed physicians in the United States. The American Medical Association (AMA) estimates that there are 10,000 alcoholic physicians and that 7 to 8 percent of doctors are now or will become alcoholics. While the alcoholism rate among physicians is comparable to that in the general population, the drug addiction rate is thirty to a hundred times higher. Some physicians are addicted to both alcohol and narcotics. Some psychiatric problems experienced by physicians are related to their addictions; depression is also common. Suicide is more fre-

quent among physicians than the general population, and for women physicians the rate is three times higher than in the general female population. These statistics probably understate the problem because until recently it was largely ignored or concealed.[10]

Most states today have some type of "impaired physician" program. The typical program takes a remedial rather than a punitive approach. Thus, if the physician acknowledges the problem and enrolls in a treatment program, punitive sanctions are withheld.[11]

An attorney has both an ethical and a legal duty to seek help for the impaired health care worker.[12] Moreover, if the impaired professional has privileges at a hospital, counsel for the hospital is obliged to take some steps to protect the hospital's patients from future negligent acts by that professional, lest the hospital be held legally responsible in the future for failing to avoid a foreseeable risk to its patients.[13] Whether or not such ethical issues arise, the fundamental obligation of defense counsel when she first agrees to represent a health care provider is to gain his trust so that honest communication can take place. The relationship of trust may prove critical to counsel's ability to help the impaired physician. It may also prove pivotal to counsel's efforts to defend the health care provider effectively.

Moreover, if an evaluation of the merits of the case leads counsel to conclude that the case ought to be settled, an acceptable resolution of the claim will require both trust and good communication. The failure of defense counsel to advise the client of the intent to settle a case in accordance with the insurer's directions has spawned some reported opinions affirming the potential merit of the legal malpractice claims on the basis of defense counsel's conflict of interest. In *Rogers v. Robson, Masters, Ryan, Brumund & Belom*,[14] for example, the insurer authorized defense counsel to settle without the doctor's consent, but the court nevertheless held that a conflict arose when the doctor advised his attorney of opposition to any settlement. The court took this view despite the provision in the insurance contract that gave the insurer the authority to settle without obtaining the consent of the doctor. In *Arana v. Koerner*,[15] the court held that the doctor should have been advised of a conflict of interest and allowed to obtain alternative counsel when he disagreed with the decision to settle.

Counsel on both sides should give serious attention to potential conflicts of interest early in the representation and err on the side of telling the client more than he may want to know about counsel's ethical concerns. Plaintiff's counsel has the persistent problem of reconciling his economic interest with the client's in light of the contingent fee and cost advancement custom. At all cost, the plaintiff's lawyer must be able to defend his advice and strategy as promoting the best interest of his client. The same is true of defense counsel, who will make less money on a particular case if it is resolved quickly, since she is paid an hourly fee. Rationalization of decisions will undoubtedly occur, but constantly raising the standard of "best interest of my client" serves a constructive role in the decision-making process. In addition, it is not unusual to represent more than one plaintiff or defendant (backed by an insurance company) with different perspectives, expectations, and demands regarding the outcome of the litigation. If the interests are not reconcilable, the attorney must insist on the retention of separate counsel (or an independent guardian, in cases involving an incompetent) to ensure that the interests of all parties are vigilantly protected.

Chapter 3

The Common Law of Medical Malpractice

At first blush, the law applicable to medical malpractice claims seems nothing more than the basic legal rules and precepts applicable to every member of the community. Further examination of the rules as applied to health care professionals, however, reveals some significant variations that can make the difference between winning and losing a medical malpractice case. These cases rely on the legal theories that a doctor was negligent or failed to obtain an informed consent. A theory that a doctor or hospital should be held strictly liable for a bad result, regardless of whether negligence occurred, has been invoked but is almost always rejected. To prevail in her medical malpractice claim, in addition to proving negligence or a lack of consent, a plaintiff must also prove that the conduct of the health care professional caused her harm. This chapter reviews the basic common law rules governing medical malpractice claims. It starts by painting the picture with a broad brush and then goes on to focus on some of the important but subtle details that require attention if the picture is to be fully appreciated. The discussion in Chapters 4 and 5 builds on the pivotal facts and issues of the seminal cases presented here.

■ **Problem:** *The Heart Attack Victim*

Mr. Prince, fifty-five years of age, consulted Dr. Jackson, a specialist in internal medicine, complaining of shortness of breath and discomfort in his chest. Dr. Jackson examined Mr. Prince and performed some tests, but he did not administer a perfusion lung scan, which would have revealed that the patient suffered from pulmonary embolic disease. Dr. Jackson advised Mr. Prince that the tests were inconclusive and scheduled another appointment for four weeks later. The next week Mr. Prince was unable to get out of bed. Since his wife could not reach Dr. Jackson by telephone, she called for an ambulance. Mr. Prince was taken to the Mercy Hospital Emergency Room, where he was examined by Dr. Rocket, who ordered an electrocardiogram, X rays, and other tests. After reviewing the test results, Dr. Rocket diagnosed Prince as suffering from pneumonitis and released him from the hospital. Mr. Prince returned home, where he died two days later. An autopsy revealed that a pulmonary embolism was the cause of death.

Mrs. Prince has filed suit in behalf of herself and her husband's estate against Dr. Jackson, Dr. Rocket, and Mercy Hospital. She has an internal medicine specialist who has expressed the opinion that Dr. Jackson was negligent in failing to perform a perfusion lung scan and that Dr. Rocket was negligent in misreading the electrocardiogram, which revealed gross abnormalities warranting Mr. Prince's immediate hospitalization. Dr. Rocket has responded that she advised Mr. Prince to see Dr. Jackson the next day, since Mr. Prince had told her that he was under Dr. Jackson's care. She also has produced hospital regulations stating that while emergency room physicians may recommend admission, they do not have the authority to admit patients to the hospital; rather, all patients must be admitted by an attending physician. The hospital documents further show that Dr. Rocket was an employee not of the hospital but of Emergency Services, Inc., a private corporation that contracted with the hospital to provide emergency room services.

In addition to denying liability to the plaintiffs, Mercy Hospital has filed a cross-claim against Dr. Rocket, Emergency Services, Inc., and Dr. Jackson seeking indemnification from each of them for any money that the hospital may have to pay to the plaintiffs.

The following, discussions illuminate the claims, defenses, and cross-claims raised by this problem. For a case presenting a similar fact pattern, see *Mehlman v. Powell.* [1]

Negligence

A patient cannot hold a professional responsible for her injury based solely on proof that the professional did or failed to do something that caused the injury. Nor is it sufficient for the patient to prove that the doctor made a mistake in judgment that caused her injury.[2] Although some commentators and judges have suggested that strict liability may have a place in medical malpractice law, no jurisdiction holds a health care professional strictly liable. Thus a bad result alone is not a sufficient basis for commencing a malpractice

action. Rather, the predominant principle governing the common law is that
a patient bears the risk of injury associated with medical treatment, except
where the risk ensues because the doctor or nurse was negligent. Proof of
negligence requires evidence that the defendant's health care provider failed
to conform to the conduct required of a reasonable person acting in the same
or similar circumstances.

A threshold problem for the plaintiff's lawyer is to identify the person
to whom the defendant is to be compared so that the court will appreciate
the level of skill and knowledge the defendant should have possessed when
he rendered care to the plaintiff. The modern trend is to apply a national
standard of care to doctors, especially those practicing in a medical specialty,[3]
but there are other standards as well. Some jurisdictions continue to apply a
"same community" standard.[4] Others apply a "same or similar" community
standard.[5] Finally, some permit case-by-case consideration of the medical resources available to the health care professional as a factor in assessing the
skill and care requirements.[6]

While the standard adhered to by other, similarly situated professionals
serves as the general guideline for determining whether a particular defendant was negligent, there are two important qualifications. First, the level of
knowledge and skill that the professional is required to possess and employ is
evaluated in light of the advanced state of medical knowledge. In other words,
if a community of professionals continues to employ outdated practices, the
courts reserve the authority to declare the entire group negligent. Second, a
professional who has more knowledge or skill than the average is required to
use that skill and knowledge and will not be shielded by what others do if
the evidence shows that he knew the others were exposing the plaintiff to an
unreasonable risk.[7]

To prove the skill and knowledge required under the circumstances demands the testimony of an expert witness.[8] To qualify as an expert, a witness
must have sufficient education, training, and experience to assist the court
and jury in determining the knowledge and skill that is required of a professional and the customary behavior engaged in by a prudent professional in
diagnosing and treating a condition like the plaintiff's (see Chapter 10). If the
jurisdiction has not followed the trend of eliminating locality considerations,
the expert must be familiar with the knowledge and skill possessed and employed by professionals in the locality where the plaintiff was treated. If the
treatment rendered falls within a particular branch of medical specialty, the
expert need not be certified in that particular specialty but must have sufficient education and experience to testify to the skill and care required of a
person rendering care in the specialty.[9]

Incollingo v. Ewing[10] illustrates the scope and limitations of the general rule that a physician is to be judged in accordance with the customary knowledge and skill possessed and employed by physicians acting in the same or similar circumstances. The plaintiffs in *Incollingo* charged that two physicians and a drug company negligently caused the death of a child. The child's family doctor had prescribed Chloromycetin, an antibiotic drug, to treat a minor throat infection. A second doctor renewed the prescription in response to the mother's telephone request. The drug caused the girl to suffer aplastic anemia, which in turn caused her death.

The manufacturer's package insert, which accompanied the drug, warned that the drug should not be prescribed for minor infections and that it should not be prescribed for prolonged use unless blood studies were first performed. The negligence charge against the child's physician, who first prescribed the antibiotic, rested on his failure to perform blood studies before prescribing the drug. In addition, the plaintiffs contended that a drug known to have such serious side effects should not have been prescribed to a child who had only a minor infection. The plaintiffs made the same allegations of negligence against the second physician. In addition, he was charged with negligence in failing to examine the child before prescribing the drug.

Relying on evidence that the salespeople of the drug company encouraged doctors to prescribe the drug for minor infections and that in their conversations with doctors the salespeople minimized the importance of the warnings in the drug's package insert, the plaintiffs charged the drug company with negligence in overpromoting the drug. The jury found all three defendants negligent.

On appeal the first doctor contended that he could not be found negligent because he properly prescribed the drug to treat an infection and did not renew the prescription because he was aware of the danger that prolonged use could cause aplastic anemia. The Pennsylvania Supreme Court held that he could be found negligent, notwithstanding evidence that his conduct conformed to that of a majority of physicians in the Philadelphia community, because his own testimony demonstrated that he had more knowledge and a better appreciation of the drug's risk than other physicians who may have engaged in similar conduct.[11] In addition, the evidence showed that the child had only a minor infection when the doctor first prescribed the drug rather than the kind of serious infection that would have justified its use.[12]

The second physician contended that he could not be found negligent because uncontroverted evidence established that 75 percent of the physicians in the community would have prescribed the drug for a minor infection notwithstanding the warning in the package insert. The community custom was argued to be reasonable in light of the alleged overpromotion of the drug, which diluted its warning.

In rejecting these arguments, the Pennsylvania Supreme Court emphasized that while custom is evidence of due care, it is not always controlling.[13] The court took the view that the alleged custom in this case could be found by the jury to be unreasonable in light of the drug's known risks, noted in the package insert. Moreover, the court emphasized that a physician may not allow himself to be duped by a drug company's salespeople and thereby insulate himself from liability on the basis of custom. Rather, he has a responsibility to exercise his best judgment to render proper care and to engage in reasonable conduct notwithstanding the existence of a custom to the contrary.[14]

Incollingo illustrates the ambivalence of courts toward the effect of custom in a medical malpractice case. On the one hand, if a plaintiff attempts to get a case to the jury without expert testimony as to custom, the case is likely to be dismissed on the basis that proof of professional negligence requires proof of custom and deviation from that custom. On the other hand, if the court is provided with evidence as to custom, it may still allow a finding of negligence, notwithstanding conformity to custom, on the ground that the circumstances of the case make it unreasonable to follow the custom. On the basis of expert testimony, the court may find that the custom is unreasonable in itself or in light of the current state of medical knowledge.

Informed Consent

Since the seminal case of *Canterbury v. Spence,*[15] the doctrine of informed consent has demanded serious consideration in connection with medical malpractice litigation. *Canterbury* involved a claim by a nineteen-year-old male against a surgeon who performed a laminectomy on him. Before performing the surgery, the physician, Dr. Spence, had performed a myelogram in an effort to determine the source of Mr. Canterbury's chronic back pain. The myelogram indicated that the patient had a filling defect in his spinal column which required surgery to relieve his pain. The physician had contacted the patient's mother by telephone before the operation and, in response to her inquiry regarding the seriousness of the operation, had advised her that it was no more serious than any other operation. After the operation the patient at first did well; but after falling from his bed, he experienced loss of feeling in his lower extremities. He sued the surgeon, alleging, among other things, that the doctor was negligent in failing to advise him that a laminectomy could lead to paralysis, even if the surgeon did everything right.

At trial Dr. Spence testified that there was a 1 percent risk of paralysis associated with a laminectomy even in the absence of negligence. The trial court dismissed the patient's informed consent claim, and the appellate court reversed. In explaining its reasons for reversing the decision, the court developed standards for the doctrine of informed consent which soon gained adherents nationwide.[16]

Building on the established principle that every adult of sound mind has a right to determine what is to be done with his or her body, the court declared that a physician who performed an operation without advising the patient of all the material risks, benefits, and alternatives to the procedure subjected himself to liability based on a negligence cause of action.[17] The materiality of the information that required disclosure was to be determined on the basis of the information that a reasonable person in the patient's position would deem important in deciding whether to undergo the procedure.[18] If material information was not disclosed, the physician would be liable if the lack of disclosure was the cause of harm. Nondisclosure would in turn be deemed the cause of the harm if the jury concluded that a reasonable person in the patient's position would have elected to forgo the procedure if the information were disclosed.[19]

The critical weapon that *Canterbury* provided to plaintiffs was the ability to present a medical malpractice claim to a jury without the support of expert testimony that the doctor had violated a professional standard of care. The *Canterbury* court expressly held that experts were required only to educate the jury about the risks inherent in the procedure. The jury could then decide whether the undisclosed risks were material.[20] Most jurisdictions have embraced the basic doctrine of informed consent announced in *Canterbury*, although a substantial number of courts have held that the risks required to be disclosed are only those that doctors customarily disclose in similar circumstances.[21]

Despite the proclivity of physicians to withhold information from patients,[22] plaintiffs' counsel face a formidable hurdle in assessing the viability of an informed consent claim: proving that a reasonable patient would have declined the procedure if the risks had been disclosed. If the physician has skillfully employed an appropriate procedure, the plaintiff will have a hard time persuading a jury that a reasonable person in his position would have elected to forgo the procedure if he had been adequately informed. In addition to the difficulty of proving causation in terms of what a reasonable patient would have done, informed consent cases present the usual problem of proving the actual physical cause of the plaintiff's injury. It should be sobering to those who view the informed consent doctrine as a mighty sword that Mr. Canterbury lost his case on retrial because the jury believed the testimony of the defendant doctor and his expert witnesses that the patient's paralysis and other injuries were caused not by the laminectomy but by a preexisting ailment.[23]

The courts' adoption of the informed consent doctrine has probably had more impact on physicians' perception of the law than on the actual practice of medicine. As Jay Katz has observed in a perceptive and comprehensive assessment of the informed consent doctrine, physicians overreacted to the court's embrace of the doctrine by creating exaggerated and erroneous descriptions of its scope and meaning.[24] This response may be due in large part to the fact that the doctrine was first applied to surgeons, the class of physicians probably most resistant to the notion that choosing an appropriate therapy for a sick patient is properly viewed as a joint venture between doctor and patient.[25]

Res Ipsa Loquitur

The doctrine of res ipsa loquitur (roughly translated as "the thing speaks for itself") provides that the circumstances of an accident may by themselves furnish a reasonable basis for a jury to infer negligence on the part of a defendant. Three conditions must exist to justify the use of the doctrine:[26] (1) the accident must be one that ordinarily does not occur in the absence of negligence; (2) the injuries must be caused by an instrumentality or agency under the exclusive control of the defendant; and (3) the plaintiff must not have produced or contributed to the accident by some voluntary conduct on her part. If these three conditions are met, the common law of torts allows the jury to draw an inference that the plaintiff was injured because of some negligent behavior on the part of the defendant, even though the plaintiff may not be able to prove the specifics of that negligent behavior.

In a typical medical malpractice case the plaintiff will not be able to meet the first condition, because most medical procedures pose an inherent risk of an untoward result.[27] Accordingly, expert testimony that the result produced in the plaintiff's case was due to negligent conduct is usually required. Exceptional cases warranting the application of the doctrine usually involve leaving some foreign object in the patient during the course of an operation.[28]

Ybarra v. Spangard[29] was an unusual case where the doctrine was successfully invoked even though no foreign object was involved. In *Ybarra*, the plaintiff awoke the morning after his appendectomy with a sharp pain about halfway between his neck and the point of his right shoulder. He had never experienced this condition before, and the doctors and nurses who attended him could not explain it. The trial court's entry of a nonsuit in favor of all the doctors and nurses who were sued was reversed by the Supreme Court of California, which held that "where a plaintiff receives unusual injuries while unconscious and in the course of medical treatment, all those defendants who had any control of his body or the instrumentalities which might have caused the injuries may properly be called upon to meet the inference of negligence by giving an explanation of their conduct."[30] On remand the case was tried without a jury and resulted in a judgment in favor of the plaintiff against all the defendants. This judgment was subsequently affirmed by the California Court of Appeal.[31]

The applicability of the doctrine of res ipsa loquitur has been considered in many jurisdictions with varying results, depending on the factual setting.[32] In the light of this doctrine, it is also interesting to review Problem One in Chapter 1, involving the premature termination of surgery because the anesthesia wore off, where the majority ruled that the circumstances warranted invoking the doctrine of res ipsa loquitur.

Negligence as a Matter of Law

Rarely does a court rule that a physician was negligent as a matter of law. Usually, the court defers to expert medical testimony regarding custom and allows the jury to determine whether negligence existed in light of conflicting expert testimony. *Helling v. Carey*[33] represents the exceptional case where the court concludes that it is better situated than the medical experts and the jury to resolve the negligence issue. In *Helling*, the plaintiff suffered severe impairment of her vision from glaucoma. She had been under the care of ophthalmologists for nine years, and during this time, despite numerous complaints about problems with her vision, the defendants never performed an eye-pressure test to determine whether glaucoma was present.

In the negligence action brought against the physicians, uncontroverted evidence was introduced that it was a customary practice of ophthalmologists not to perform a glaucoma test on patients under the age of forty because the incidence of glaucoma in that age group was only one in twenty-five. All the experts testified that the defendants had followed the accepted practice of not giving the glaucoma test to the plaintiff.

On appeal the court held that despite customary practice the defendants were negligent as a matter of law. The court explained: "Under the facts of this case reasonable prudence required the timely giving of the pressure test to this plaintiff. The precaution of giving this test to detect the incidence of glaucoma to patients under 40 years of age is so imperative that irrespective of its disregard by the standards of the ophthalmology profession, it is the duty of the courts to say what is required to protect patients under 40 from the damaging results of glaucoma."

The radical nature of the court's holding in *Helling* may be appreciated by comparing it to the approach taken by the Pennsylvania Supreme Court in *Incollingo v. Ewing*,[34] discussed earlier, where the court declined to accept testimony of medical custom as controlling on the ground that there are some circumstances in which a reasonable person would not follow the custom. But the court did not find the defendant physicians negligent as a matter of law. Rather, it held that the question of negligence was properly one for the jury. In contrast, the court in *Helling* found it unnecessary to remand the case for consideration by the jury, reasoning that under the circumstances in the case no reasonable person could reach any conclusion other than that the defendants were negligent despite their adherence to custom.

Although in some cases the court directs a verdict for the plaintiff on the grounds that expert testimony establishes negligence as a matter of law, *Helling* represents one of the few cases where the court finds negligence as a matter of law notwithstanding expert testimony to the contrary.[35] It did so by relying on the famous statement by Justice Holmes in *Texas & Pac. Ry. v. Behymer:* "What usually is done may be evidence of what ought to be done, but what ought to be done is fixed by a standard of reasonable prudence, whether it usually is complied with or not."[36] In the absence of compelling expert testimony that a medical custom is unreasonable in light of the advanced state of medical knowledge, a court is unlikely to find a physician negligent as a matter of law if the physician has conformed to customary medical practices.

If we reconsider Problem One in Chapter 1, it is interesting to speculate whether the court in that situation should declare that the surgeon and anesthesiologist were negligent as a matter of law for not discussing the expected length of the operation before commencing the surgery. Alternatively, should the surgeon be declared negligent as a matter of law for terminating the surgery without asking the anesthesiologist whether the anesthetic could be safely extended long enough to allow completion of the surgery?

Breach of Contract

As we saw above, a physician does not ordinarily guarantee a particular result merely by undertaking to render professional care to a patient. In the rare case where a physician has made an express promise that a particular result will or will not follow the medical care, he may be held liable for breach of contract if an untoward result occurs.[37] Skepticism about patients' claims that physicians have made such express promises has, however, led some courts to hold that the plaintiff must prove not only that the physician made an express warranty, which the plaintiff relied on, but also that the plaintiff gave separate payment for the warranty.[38] In addition, some jurisdictions dislike holding a health care provider liable on the basis of contract and have enacted statutes requiring that such warranties must be in writing.[39]

In jurisdictions where the breach of contract theory is recognized, the following expressions have been deemed sufficient to support the cause of action: a statement that a sterilization procedure will prevent pregnancy;[40] a statement by a physician that he would cure internal lesion polyps in the bladder within two days;[41] a physician's promise to care for the plaintiff during pregnancy and delivery when he failed to attend the birth and the child was stillborn;[42] and a statement by a physician that he would not perform a radical mastectomy.[43]

On the other hand, the following statements have been deemed insufficient to support a breach of contract claim: a statement that the chance of pregnancy after a tubal ligation is one in a million;[44] an assertion that the hernia operation will be "simple and without problem";[45] and an assurance that the care rendered will be careful, skillful, and prudent.[46]

Wrongful Birth

A fertile and controversial area of medical malpractice litigation involves claims that the negligence of a health care provider has resulted in the birth of an unwanted child. When such a claim is made by a parent, it is termed a *wrongful birth claim.*[47] When the claim is made by a child, it is termed a *wrongful life claim.*[48]

Until the late 1960s, courts refused to recognize such claims, either by the child or by the parent, on the grounds that it would be bad public policy to categorize a child's coming into existence as an injury.[49] Probably because of the change in public policy announced in the U.S. Supreme Court's abortion decisions, courts began to take a new look at these tort claims.

With California a notable exception,[50] most courts have continued to reject the claim of a child that she should be awarded damages because her birth was produced by negligent medical care. In such cases the child is not contending that the health care provider caused her to be born with a physical or mental handicap. Rather, the claim made is that if proper care had been rendered, the child would not have been born at all. Courts have been reluctant to recognize such claims partly because of their concern with the difficulty in measuring damages to the child.

On the other hand, most recent cases recognize that parents have a valid cause of action for wrongful birth.[51] This is especially true when the child is born with disabilities; when the child is born healthy, there is more disagreement.[52] But even where there is agreement that a cause of action for the parents should be allowed, there is disagreement as to the appropriate elements of damage. Parents have sought recovery for emotional distress, medical expenses required to raise an impaired child, and the cost of rearing a child born healthy but not wanted. To date, little uniformity exists in the law as to the propriety of these specific claims.[53]

Hospital Corporate Liability

Until the 1960s many hospitals enjoyed legal immunity from medical malpractice claims based on the notion that they were charitable institutions and as such should not be burdened with responsibility for any unfortunate results that occurred in the course of providing their charitable services. Today, in most jurisdictions, the doctrine of charitable immunity no longer shields a hospital from medical malpractice claims.[54] The courts have acknowledged that the public relies on the modern hospital for quality medical treatment,[55] and consequently it expects the hospital to provide competent physicians, competent allied health personnel, and adequate equipment. As a result of this shifting attitude, courts have examined the organizational structure of a hospital to determine if it may be held liable for improper care rendered by its medical staff.[56] The concept of hospital corporate negligence is the result of this judicial scrutiny.

Corporate negligence is defined as "the failure of those entrusted with the task of providing accommodations and facilities necessary to carry out the charitable purposes of the corporation to follow, in a given situation, the established standard of conduct to which the corporation should conform."[57] The responsibility of ensuring that the corporation provides adequate accommodations and facilities falls on the governing body of the hospital, as distinguished from those charged with rendering medical treatment. Corporate negligence differs from the doctrine of respondeat superior because it imposes on the hospital a nondelegable duty owed directly to the patient without regard to the details of the doctor-hospital relationship.

In 1952, in response to the concern for improving patient care, standardizing surgical procedures, and improving hospital record keeping, the American College of Physicians, the American Hospital Association, and the American Medical Association formed the Joint Commission on Accreditation of Hospitals (JCAH), a widely recognized, nonprofit organization that inspects and accredits hospitals in compliance with its standards.[58] Although the accreditation process is strictly voluntary and lacks any legal or governmental status, accreditation by the JCAH identifies a hospital as complying with standards established by national professional organizations.[59]

The landmark case holding a hospital liable on the ground that it breached an independent corporate duty owed to the patient is *Darling v. Charleston Community Memorial Hospital*,[60] in which the plaintiff claimed that his right leg had to be amputated because the hospital emergency-room physician applied a cast to his leg in an improper manner and the nurses did not test for circulation as required by the standard of care. He further alleged that the nurses did not heed the obvious signs that the circulation in his leg was impaired. The hospital defended against the claim of corporate liability on the basis that it could not be held independently liable to the plaintiff because as a hospital it was not permitted to practice medicine and the duty it owed to the patient was limited to the use of reasonable care in selecting medical doctors.

Focusing on the relationship between the hospital and its patients, the court concluded that the evidence would support a finding of negligence against the hospital. When a serious impairment of the circulation in the plaintiff's leg manifested itself, "it became the nurses' duty to inform the attending physician, and if he failed to act, to advise the hospital authorities so that appropriate action might be taken."[61] In addition, the court held that the hospital could be found negligent for failing to review the emergency physician's work or failing to require a consultation in light of the dangerous conditions that should have been obvious to the hospital nurses.[62]

The *Darling* decision was significant not only because it ruled that a hospital is obliged to provide and care for patients entrusted to it but also because it set new evidentiary requirements for proving the standard of professional negligence. Instead of providing expert witnesses, the plaintiff introduced as evidence JCAH standards, the Illinois Department of Public Health Regulations, and Medical Staff Bylaws of Charleston Community Medical Hospital. In the court's view this evidence "performed much the same function as did evidence of custom. [It] aided the jury in deciding what was feasible and what the defendant knew or should have known."[63] The use of this type of evidence to establish the standard of care has the potential to enable a plaintiff to establish a prima facie case even in the absence of expert testimony.[64] One commentator has identified the following items that may be admissible as evidence of the standard of care: hospital records, hospital bylaws, departmental rules and regulations, risk management records, nursing manuals, standing orders, state licensing requirements, medical staff review committee records, JCAH manuals, federal statutes and regulations, and department protocol.[65]

The theory of corporate liability has greatly expanded over the years as a result of the *Darling* decision.[66] Courts have recognized the following areas of direct corporate liability.[67] First is the hospital's responsibility for supplying and maintaining equipment and facilities. Hospitals have been held responsible for defective, improper, or inadequate equipment or facilities in a number of cases. For example, in *American Bank and Trust Co. v. Community Hospital of Los Gatos Saratoga, Inc.*,[68] the hospital was found liable for a patient's burns caused by overheated shower water. In *Bellaire General Hospital, Inc. v.*

Campbell,[69] the hospital was liable for injuries caused by inadequate oxygen supply equipment in the hospital room. And in *Grubb v. Albert Einstein Medical Center,*[70] the hospital was held responsible for a patient's paralysis caused by a defective electric drill used in surgery.

The hospital also has a duty to its patients to select its staff physicians carefully and periodically review their credentials. While the duty to make the initial investigation and recommendations regarding an applicant's qualifications for staff privileges may be delegated to a medical staff committee, the ultimate authority to grant or deny staff privileges remains with the hospital administrator. In *Johnson v. Misericordia Community Hospital,*[71] the court relied on hospital bylaws and state statutes to charge the hospital with constructive knowledge of a doctor's negligence.[72]

An area of increasing concern is the hospital's duty to supervise physicians. The leading case in point is *Purcell v. Zimbelman,*[73] in which a hospital was held liable for permitting a physician to operate even though he had been successfully sued before for the same surgical procedure. Other interesting cases addressing the corporate negligence issue include *Bost v. Riley*[74] (physician failed to keep daily progress notes in direct violation of hospital rules); *Utter v. United Hospital Center Inc.*[75] (hospital was found liable for nurses who failed to comply with hospital regulations requiring reporting of suspected improper treatment by physician); *Brook v. St. John's Hickey Memorial Hospital*[76] (failure of radiologist employed by hospital to recognize and report injection into unusual site did not render hospital liable); *Ziegler v. Superior Court of County of Pima*[77] (negligent supervision in implantation of pacemaker); and *Poor Sisters of St. Frances Seraph of Perpetual Adoration, Inc. v. Catron*[78] (failure of nurses and inhalation therapists to report endotracheal tube left in patient longer than customary period).

A natural outgrowth of the basic corporate liability theory is that a hospital has a duty to formulate medical rules or policies. The landmark case is *Airshields, Inc. v. Spears,*[79] where a premature newborn child was placed in an incubator that continually administered a prescribed amount of oxygen. The infant later developed retrolental fibroplasia, which resulted in total blindness. The court held that the hospital was liable for constructive knowledge that the amount of oxygen administered was too great and would likely result in blindness. In *Bilonoha v. Zubritzky,*[80] the court held that a jury must be instructed that a hospital can be held negligent for not devising adequate rules and regulations governing the procedures followed by its operating room personnel. And in *Scott v. Brookdale Hospital Center,*[81] the court found the hospital liable for failure to require a consultation after examination by an intern and that such omission from its rules constituted a departure from accepted standards of medical practice.

In addition to liability for failure to formulate operating rules and procedures, the hospital may face liability for negligence in enforcing medical rules or policies. For example, in *Pederson v. Damochel*,[82] the hospital was held liable because the plaintiff was administered anesthesia without a medical doctor present, in violation of a hospital rule. In *Polischeck v. United States*,[83] a patient was discharged from the emergency room before being examined or having his chart reviewed by a licensed physician, and this resulted in corporate liability of the hospital. Finally, *Fjerstad v. Krusten*[84] involved a finding of hospital liability for a patient's negligent treatment by an intern who failed to obtain consultation with an on-call physician before the patient was released from the emergency room.

In contrast to the preceding cases, which reflect hospitals' increased liability, some jurisdictions have placed statutory limitations on recovery against a hospital, imposed caps on recovery,[85] or allowed recovery only to the extent of the existing liability.[86] Others have limited recovery to paying patients.[87]

The corporate liability theory does not exclude the alternative theory of vicarious liability (see below). But if the evidence establishes that the individual who committed the negligent act was acting as an independent contractor—meaning that he was not subject to the hospital's direction and control as to the manner of providing the service—the hospital will be liable to the plaintiff not on the basis of vicarious liability, but only on the basis of corporate liability. The corporate liability theory, in conjunction with an increasingly competitive health care delivery market, has prompted many hospitals to rethink and challenge the traditional allocation of exclusive power to physicians on questions of appropriate medical care (see Chapter 5 for the implications of the corporate liability theory to health maintenance organizations and other health insurance companies).

Vicarious Liability

A hospital and a physician may be held liable for the negligent conduct of staff physicians and nurses based on vicarious liability, meaning that in some circumstances the law holds one person responsible for the conduct of another.

In tort law, vicarious liability of the hospital and/or the physician turns on the pivotal question of who has the right to control the work that is being done and the manner in which it is done.[88] When a physician is held liable on this basis of control, the liability is sometimes rationalized on the grounds that the physician is the captain of the ship.[89]

In addition, a hospital may be held liable under the ostensible agency doctrine for the negligent conduct of a physician who was in fact an independent contractor. Such liability is premised on two factors: the patient's reasonable belief that the physician was a hospital employee and the hospital's "holding out" the physician as its employee.[90] The ostensible agency doctrine reflects the modern view that a patient frequently enters a hospital expecting a wide range of hospital services rather than merely the personal care of a particular physician. The courts have thus deemed it unfair to limit the hospital's liability for negligent medical care on the basis of the technical legal relationship of the hospital and the treating physician unless the evidence compels the conclusion that the patient knew or should have known that the treating physician was not a hospital employee.[91]

Causation

Frequently, the most difficult burden the plaintiff has in a case against a health care provider is proving that a breach of the standard of care in fact caused the plaintiff's injuries. The causal connection must generally be established by expert testimony stating to a reasonable medical certainty that the injury was the result of the health care provider's negligence.[92] This presents a serious problem, because in many cases a plaintiff's injuries can stem from multiple potential causes, including the illness for which she was being treated, and experts may therefore be reluctant to express an opinion at the level of certainty required by the law.

An important case that acknowledged the conflict between legal standards of certainty and the limited ability of science to meet those standards was _Hamil v. Bashline_,[93] in which an emergency room physician failed to employ a cardiac monitor to evaluate a patient who came into the hospital complaining of chest pain, because the machine in the emergency room was not working. The patient was allowed to leave the emergency room and later died as a result of a cardiac arrest.

In the trial of the negligence action the expert witness, a pathologist, testified that the patient would have had a 75 percent chance of surviving if the emergency room physician had complied with the required standard of care.[94] The trial court found the testimony insufficient to allow the jury to find a causal connection because the expert did not state to a reasonable medical certainty that the medical negligence in fact caused the death.

Invoking the Restatement (2d) of Torts,[95] the Pennsylvania Supreme Court reversed, holding that the testimony was sufficient to allow the issue of causation to go to the jury. The court noted that the Restatement provides for a relaxed standard of proof of causation in a case against a person who has failed to render services that he had a duty to render to a plaintiff.[96] In such a case, the court held, it is not necessary that the plaintiff introduce evidence of a medical expert to a reasonable medical certainty that the negligence caused the harm. Rather, the expert need only testify that the negligence increased the risk of harm to the plaintiff that in fact came about. Once the expert testifies to this effect, it is then a question for the jury to decide whether the negligence was a substantial factor in producing the plaintiff's harm.[97] In reaching this conclusion, the court relied on a line of cases that adopted the view that it is unfair to impose the normal standard of proof of causation in a case where the defendant's failure to act both increases the risk of harm to the plaintiff and diminishes the plaintiff's ability to prove what would have occurred had the defendant acted.[98]

The *Hamil* approach has been approved in some jurisdictions[99] and rejected in others.[100] In addition, some courts have adopted a variation of *Hamil* by allowing recovery for the "loss of chance" caused by the defendant's medical negligence.[101] Plaintiff may recover under the "loss of chance" doctrine if the judge or jury concludes that the defendant's negligence was a substantial factor in reducing the patient's chances for a better result.[102] If such a determination is made, recovery is allowed based on the percentage of chance lost.[103]

Chapter 4

Discovering and Proving the Standard of Care in a World of Specialization

─────

Few physicians today devote their careers to the general practice of medicine. Indeed, if *general practice* means a practice in which a physician sees and treats patients without regard to their age or chief complaint, general practice by a single physician probably occurs only in remote rural areas where the population lacks access to specialists. Certainly, emergency room physicians, family physicians, and pediatricians see patients with a wide variety of ailments, but each makes claim to specialized knowledge and training beyond the minimum required to obtain a medical license.

Recognizing the extent of medical specialization, most attorneys who depose doctors in medical malpractice cases carefully explore each doctor's education and training in a specialty. With great solemnity the witness is asked whether he is eligible for board certification or already certified. The doctor's answers are noted and presumably filed away for later use in evaluating and trying the case. But does this ritual serve any meaningful purpose? Under the law prevailing in most jurisdictions today, it does not. At most, a doctor's eligibility for or certification by a specialty board is useful to an attorney only in building or diminishing the doctor's credibility in the eyes of the jury. As for qualification as an expert, the specialty training of a physician may make it easier for him to qualify, but it is by no means essential. As for the applicable standard of care, the court adopts the standards of a particular specialty only where the treating doctor has represented to his patient, expressly or by implication, that he possesses the qualifications of a particular specialist and adheres to the standards of the specialty.

The court's unwillingness to treat board certification or eligibility as a pivotal consideration in a medical malpractice case is peculiar in light of the large numbers of specialists and society's acknowledgment of the increasing complexity of medicine. Since World War II most licensed physicians have pursued enough graduate training to make a claim to some specialized medical knowledge. Significantly, however, such claims are not certified by any professional body or governmental agency. Indeed, the law does not require a licensed physician to obtain any type of license or certification to practice a specialty.

The lack of legal or professional regulation of medical specialization in the United States has resulted from society's struggle to accommodate clashing values: democracy, equality, and professionalism. An understanding of this historical collision is essential to appreciating the tentative and ambiguous way in which the law has addressed the issue of the impact of medical specialization on the legally mandated standard of care. The historical forces are considered below.

This chapter explores the discovery and proof of the required standard of care in light of physicians' proclivity toward specialization. This inquiry is particularly important because the legal doctrine applicable to the standard of care states that the physician must possess and employ that degree of skill and knowledge ordinarily possessed and employed by the ordinary physician acting in the same or similar circumstances. But who is the "ordinary physician"? If generalists, specialists, and subspecialists treat the same patients for the same conditions, but their knowledge and skills vary widely, what level of skill governs—the advanced skill and knowledge of the specialist or the minimal knowledge and skill of the generalist?

Two legal rules offer guidance. One provides that if a physician holds himself out as a specialist, he is governed by the standards applicable to the specialty.[1] The problem with this rule is that courts have not deemed that providing a service ordinarily provided by specialist in itself constitutes "holding oneself out" as a specialist. Rather, "holding out" has usually been found to occur only where the physician makes an express representation to the patient that he is a specialist. The bottom line is that if community custom allows both specialists and generalists to provide the care in question, the practitioner needs to meet only the criteria of a physician with skills and training similar to his own.

The other legal rule provides that a physician has a duty to seek consultation or refer a patient[2] to a specialist if he knows or ought to know that the care required is beyond his skill and knowledge. The relevant inquiry here concerns the circumstances in which the physician ought to have known that he was "over his head."

One way to clarify the issues is to identify the minimum standards for medical knowledge and skill and then to identify the factors and circumstances that will support a patient's claim to the right to expect a higher standard. This in turn requires comparing the approaches of the generalist and the specialist to clinical decision making. To facilitate the inquiry, consider the following problem.

■ **Problem:** *Obstetrician Treats Cardiovascular Problem*

Dr. Gordon, a specialist in obstetrics and gynecology, treated Ms. Schultz during her pregnancy. Dr. Gordon was aware that Ms. Schultz had a history of cardiovascular disorders. During a routine examination the doctor determined that Ms. Schultz was suffering from elevated blood pressure, which she diagnosed as pregnancy-induced hypertension. Dr. Gordon instructed Ms. Schultz to get her bed rest. After bed rest Ms. Schultz's blood pressure returned to normal. A month later, however, during another examination, Dr. Gordon found that the patient's blood pressure was once again elevated. She also noted swelling of Ms. Schultz's extremities. She admitted Ms. Schultz to the hospital, and that evening Ms. Schultz went into labor and delivered prematurely. The baby was healthy, but five days later Ms. Schultz died of a rupture of a dissecting aortic aneurysm of the ascending aorta.

What is Dr. Gordon's liability? Since Ms. Schultz's death was due to a cardiovascular disorder, may Dr. Gordon be found negligent for failing to consult with or refer Ms. Schultz to a cardiologist? Should she be held to the standard of care required of a specialist in cardiology?

Minimum Standards of Skill and Knowledge

The minimum standards governing medical care rendered by physicians depend on the identity of the evaluator. The state, the general medical community, the medical specialist, the hospital, and last but not least the patient all have expectations about the level and kind of care that a patient should receive.

The minimum standards for obtaining a license to practice medicine are established on a state-by-state basis. Today the standards adopted by the states are quite similar. The applicant must obtain a degree from an accredited medical school, pass a national medical examination administered by a voluntary board, and complete one year of postgraduate training in a residency. Graduates of foreign medical schools may obtain a special license to practice in residency programs for a limited period of time.

Until the twentieth century the education obtained by physicians varied widely. Many physicians gained their education and training through apprenticeships. Often doctors did not even possess a high school diploma or college degree. Moreover, there was little uniformity in education, even among those who attended medical schools. Many of the schools were proprietary schools, and no governmental agency or professional accrediting association prescribed standards to govern the admission or graduation of students. Understandably, then, at the end of the nineteenth century the knowledge and skills of persons who held themselves out as doctors were highly variable.

In the early twentieth century a report prepared by Abraham Flexner disclosed the vast disparity in the education and training of physicians. The Flexner Report proposed uniform standards for medical school curricula and admission. These proposals, adopted nationwide by the medical profession, led to the development of uniform standards for medical education and training, among them the current stipulation that the medical school curriculum must include specific science courses. Because many of the schools lacked the resources to meet the new standards, one of the major effects of the reforms was a reduction in the number of medical schools and graduates.[3]

Today the typical medical school curriculum is fairly standardized. During the first two years the medical student studies the basic sciences: biology, biochemistry, physiology, pharmacology, anatomy, and so on. During the last two years the focus shifts to the development of clinical skills, through exposure to physicians treating patients in teaching hospitals. Occasionally, a course on medicine and law, ethics, or economics is offered.

At a minimum, then, a physician must possess some knowledge about such fundamental subjects as anatomy, physiology, pharmacology, biochemistry, internal medicine, and infectious diseases. In addition, she must possess some basic clinical decision-making knowledge and skills. For example, she is expected to know what information to seek when taking a history from a patient or someone communicating in the patient's behalf. She should know that certain symptoms presented by a patient warrant performing specific diagnostic tests or providing specific advice or treatment. She should be able to perform certain tests and provide specific treatment in a skillful manner. Moreover, she should be able to interpret particular test results accurately and to make appropriate assessment of the treatment or additional testing indicated in light of the results.

A helpful book for understanding a doctor's approach to clinical decision making is Robert H. Fletcher, Suzanne W. Fletcher, and Edward H. Wagner, *Clinical Epidemiology*.[4] The authors begin by posing the following problem:

> A 52-year-old man is admitted to the hospital because of abdominal pain and weight loss. He was well until 8 weeks prior to admission when he noticed the gradual onset of epigastric pain radiating to the back. Over the next several weeks this pain increased in intensity and became constant. In retrospect, he has had a

poor appetite and has lost about 15 pounds in the past few months. He consulted his physician and a diagnostic evaluation, including a complete history, physical examination, a complete blood count, and serum chemistries disclosed no specific cause for his symptoms.[5]

The authors describe the challenge this patient poses to the physician:

[T]he physician must differentiate between carcinoma of the pancreas and peptic ulcer disease, among other possible causes for this patient's complaints. If an upper gastrointestinal series is performed and it is reported to be "normal," the doctor must have some idea of how frequently a "false negative" result can occur in the presence of these diseases, and must decide if further testing is warranted. If a subsequent abdominal computerized tomography scan shows a pancreatic mass and a diagnosis of pancreatic cancer is made, the patient will probably want to know the prognosis of pancreatic cancer—how long such patients live and how well they fare. Finally the physician must decide which kinds of treatment—surgery, chemotherapy, or simple palliative care—offer the most help to the patient.[6]

The authors observe that in seeking solutions to such problems, physicians usually rely on their own experiences, the experiences of colleagues, and the medical literature. In view of these considerations, this chapter addresses several questions: How much skill and knowledge does the law require the treating physician to have in light of the highly specialized world of medical practice? When should the treating physician recognize that the patient is entitled to the skill and knowledge of a more highly trained physician, so that consultation or referral is in order? Which medical specialist is the appropriate person to serve as an expert in providing answers to the questions of standard of care and causation raised in the medical malpractice case at hand?

The patient described by the authors of *Clinical Epidemiology* may have been evaluated and treated by a general practitioner, an internist, an infectious disease specialist, a surgeon, or a gastroenterologist. In addition, in evaluating the test results, the treating physician may have elected to consult with one of these specialists, a radiologist, or no one. Presumably, each type of specialist has different knowledge and skill in light of his professional training and practice experience. Whose knowledge and skill should we use to compare with the knowledge and skill of the treating physician? The answers are unclear. In effect, courts and legislatures have avoided resolving the fundamental question of the legal significance of medical specialization.

Legal Review of Medical Decision Making

The search for a standard boils down to a search for what a competently trained physician should have known and done in light of a patient's particular symptoms. A bad result by itself does not mean that a physician is legally responsible. Nor does a mere mistake in judgment make him liable. The plaintiff must prove that bad result would not have occurred and the error in judgment would not have been made if the physician had employed the skill and knowledge required under the circumstances.

When attorneys are asked to evaluate a case because a bad result has occurred, they rely on the same sources physicians use to assess the appropriate standard of care to which the patient is entitled, namely, the experiences of trained physicians and the medical literature. Attorneys ask expert witnesses to evaluate the care rendered to a patient by addressing the following issues: Did the treating physician make the correct diagnosis? If so, was it made in a timely manner? If an incorrect or untimely diagnosis was made, was the mistake the result of a failure to perform examinations or tests or properly to evaluate the test results in accordance with standard medical practices? Was the proper treatment rendered or prescribed in light of the diagnosis that was made or should have been made? Was the treatment rendered in a timely manner? Was the treatment rendered in a technically correct manner? If not, was the error an inherent risk of the procedure? Was there appropriate monitoring of the patient? Was the patient given adequate directions and warnings? Was the follow-up care appropriate? Finally, and of critical importance, were any of the mistakes the cause of the bad result?

Some of the fundamental problems posed by medical specialization in terms of medical and legal standards for patient care are presented in *McDaniel v. Merck, Sharp & Dohme.*[7] The material facts are as follows. On February 25, 1982, Carol M. Lee, twenty-six years old, visited the Western Pennsylvania Hospital emergency room, complaining of a sore throat. The physician in charge diagnosed her as having an infection, streptococcal pharyngitis; he prescribed an antibiotic, erythromycin, and discharged her. When her condition worsened, she returned to West Penn's emergency room on February 28, 1982. The events that unfolded thereafter are succinctly presented in the opinion of the Pennsylvania Superior Court.

> Decedent was diagnosed by . . . Dr. Kavic [a surgical resident at West Penn] as having acute appendicitis. Decedent was admitted for surgery and put under the supervision of the hospital's surgery staff. The attending physician on that date was Dr. Dunmire. Blood studies were ordered, and the first dose of the antibiotic Mefoxin was prescribed by Dr. Kim, and administered. . . .
>
> By noon, decedent was anemic. Following an appendectomy performed by Dr. Dunmire on the evening of February 28, Mefoxin was again administered. Because the supervising physician is generally assigned to the surgery staff for only a thirty-day period, Dr. Goodworth assumed supervision of the case the next day, replacing Dr. Dunmire.
>
> Post-operatively, the decedent developed a wound infection and manifested

an elevated temperature. Mefoxin was continuously administered from February 28 until decedent's death on April 4, 1982, except for a three-day period
while Dr. Kavic was on vacation. Decedent underwent three subsequent operations to treat her infection. Nevertheless, her fever continued and she developed a
severe case of hemolytic anemia with bone marrow depression, which ultimately
precipitated her death.[8]

The product liability and medical malpractice action that followed raised
two central questions: what had caused the decedent's fever, hemolytic anemia, and bone marrow depression, and whether the drug company, the hospital, the attending surgeon, and the surgical resident were legally responsible
for her death based on theories of negligence against the health care providers
and the sale of a defective product by the drug manufacturer. Using experts'
review of the medical records and deposition testimony of the treating physicians, the plaintiff asserted that the decedent's fever, hemolytic anemia, and
bone marrow depression were caused by the administration of Mefoxin. The
plaintiff's principal theories of negligence were that the surgeons were negligent for continuing the administration of the antibiotic beyond seven days
when they had not by that time identified the source of the infection and
for not obtaining a consultation from an infectious disease specialist when it
became clear after ten days that they had neither discovered the cause of the
infection nor established an efficient treatment plan.

After the case was remanded for retrial, the plaintiff reached a settlement
agreement with the drug company. The case was then tried to a jury against
the surgeons and the hospital. The jury found negligence on the part of the
attending surgeon but held that the negligence was not a substantial factor in
causing the decedent's death. Accordingly, a verdict was rendered against the
plaintiff.

From a public policy perspective, the method by which the case was resolved highlights many of the difficulties that medical specialization poses for
the medical community and the courts. The trial court and the appellate court
took radically different approaches to the issue of the qualifications of expert
witnesses who have different specialties. The trial court took the view that
a physician serving as an expert in a case involving complex medical issues
should be limited to expressing opinions about subjects that fall exclusively
within his highest specialty. Thus, the court ruled that an infectious disease
specialist should not be allowed to express an opinion as to the cause of the
plaintiff's blood disorder; a hematologist should not be allowed to express an
opinion as to whether a fever is induced by drugs rather than by an infection;
and a physician who specializes in internal medicine and clinical decision
making should not be allowed to express any opinions as to the standard of

care for managing a patient who experiences complications after undergoing an appendectomy. The trial court's rationale was that the complexity of the medical questions presented in the case allowed each specialist to have sufficient expertise to provide helpful insights only on narrow issues falling within his particular specialty. Accordingly, the hematologist could talk about blood and nothing else. The infectious disease specialist could talk about infection and nothing else. The internal medicine specialist had expertise, in the court's view, about none of the relevant issues and could not even express opinions as to whether the circumstances required the physicians handling the postsurgical care to call in consultants in the various specialties. According to the trial court, this issue should be appropriately addressed only by a surgeon. The court did allow, however, that a hematologist could testify to the need for a hematologic consultation and an infectious disease specialist could testify to the need for an infectious disease consultation.

The appellate court disagreed. According to that court, each of these expert-physicians proffered by the plaintiff had a "reasonable pretension" to specialized knowledge regarding the standard of care applicable to managing a patient in a teaching hospital who after undergoing an appendectomy experienced fever and anemia.[9] Each was also viewed as competent to testify as to when a hematologist or infectious disease specialist should have been consulted.[10] Moreover, the hematologist and infectious disease specialist were each competent to testify as to the cause of the plaintiff's infection, anemia, and death.[11]

The multiple issues arising out of the role of the expert in medical malpractice litigation are fully explored in Chapter 10. Here we examine the impact of specialization on the delivery of medical care and the appropriate legal response to medical specialization in terms of the legal standard of care and the qualifications of medical experts.

The view adopted by the trial court in *McDaniel* ignored several important considerations. First is the process by which a physician becomes a specialist and the inferences that are fairly drawn from that process regarding the skill and knowledge that the specialist gains and retains. Second is the history of specialization and the peculiar impact that this history has on the significance of the certification of specialty process. Third is the culture of specialization and its impact on the ability of the legal system to evaluate a medical malpractice claim fairly. Fourth is the impact of adopting a standard for qualifying an expert witness in terms of specialization and limiting her testimony accordingly.

Before I address these considerations in detail, it is helpful to review two other recent cases that focus on the standard of care owed to a patient in light of specialization. In *Denton v. U.S. and Cushing Memorial Hospital*,[12] a Kansas trial court sitting in a nonjury trial accorded great weight to the testimony of a board-certified cardiologist that the heart condition of the forty-three-year-old decedent, who had died of a myocardial infarction four days after being admitted to the hospital, was so serious that it was negligent for the defendant-doctor, who was an internist but not a cardiologist, to continue to treat the patient without obtaining a consultation with a cardiologist. In finding that the internist was negligent, the court explained:

> Mr. Denton's status, following his severe myocardial infarction, was precarious. His condition demanded the most careful scrutiny of both fluid balances and dosages of administered medicines. The separate aspects of Mr. Denton's heart difficulties, congestive failure, hypotension, etc., were such that the inappropriate use of one medicine would counteract the beneficial effects of another. Dr. Hill confronted a most difficult and complex set of circumstances regarding the treatment of Mr. Denton.[13]

In contrast, in *Lane v. Skyline Family Medical Center*,[14] the Minnesota Court of Appeals found that a trial court correctly refused to instruct the jury that the defendant, a specialist in family practice, could be found negligent for failing to consult a specialist in obstetrics and gynecology, in diagnosing and treating the plaintiff, who presented an abnormal pregnancy with twins. In support of her theory the plaintiff presented the testimony of a specialist in obstetrics, gynecology, and maternal-fetal medicine: "He testified that the family doctor is well qualified to take care of many problems and those that he's qualified to take care of, he must take care of those patients with the same standards as the specialist [*sic*]."[15] He went on to explain: "What I am saying is that they must be able to recognize an abnormal pregnancy and get consultation or help when the pregnancy deviates from normal, beyond their capabilities."[16]

Based on this testimony, elicited through cross-examination, and the expert's testimony on direct examination that the standard of care for mothers expecting twins is the same for family practitioners as for specialists, the court concluded:

> [P]laintiffs did not present the foundational evidence entitling it to an instruction under Larsen. No testimony introduced at trial tends to support the conclusion that an expert would have been better qualified to treat a woman with Sally Lane's symptoms. Plaintiff's own expert witness, Dr. Bendel, testified that only one standard of care exists in Minnesota for the treatment of mothers with twin pregnancies.
>
> . . . Even if a duty to refer existed and Dr. Hiza breached that duty, plaintiffs still need to establish the final element under Larsen: that Hiza's care did not meet a specialist's standards. Since the same standard of care applies for family practi-

tioners as specialists, according to Dr. Bendle, breach of the duty to refer in this case would not change the standard of care.[17]

The approaches taken by the courts in *McDaniel*, *Denton*, and *Lane* provide some sense of the confusion that courts experience when confronted with questions about what medical problems various physicians are truly qualified to treat. The courts have acknowledged that specialty training helps qualify a physician as an expert on particular medical questions, but the effect of the acknowledgment has been only to allow the specialist to express an opinion as to the required standard of care that the judge or jury as factfinder may accept or reject. Significantly, a rejection of the specialist's opinion as to the standard of care need not rest on its conflict with the testimony of another board-certified specialist; so long as another licensed physician expresses a different opinion, the factfinder may accept her opinion as stating the appropriate standard of care even though she makes no claim to having completed the education and training required to become board eligible or board certified.

To understand the law's cavalier approach to this issue first requires an appreciation of the medical profession's cavalier approach to the issue. This in turn requires an excursion into the history of the development of medical specialty boards.

The History of Medical Specialization

In an enlightening book on the history of the medical profession in America, *American Medicine and the Public Interest*,[18] Rosemary Stevens discusses the history of medical specialization. Stevens argues persuasively that the present system of allowing medical specialty boards to set the criteria for recognizing the qualifications of doctors claiming specialized knowledge and skills is explained by two concerns that have dominated the thinking of the medical profession in the United States since the beginning. The first is that democratic values of equality—rather than hierarchical values of status, prevalent in England—should govern the manner in which medicine is practiced. The second is that the practice of medicine should remain as free as possible from government regulation. The second concern has led the American Medical Association (AMA) not only to wage a historic fight against national medical insurance (a fight that continues today), but also, in conjunction with the belief about democratic values, to defeat efforts requiring that physicians claiming a specialty obtain a license evidencing their skill and competency in that specialty.[19]

The result of these concerns was a series of compromises. As specialties emerged, specialty boards also emerged, controlled by the medical community and serving a quasi-public function similar to licensing boards. The public, however, has almost no input or control over these boards.[20] To Stevens's thesis we might add the observation that since the specialty boards have always declared that it is not their function to determine whether a physician possesses minimum competence to practice the specialty (see discussion below), the courts and legislatures have remained passive in their responses to claims that the standards of a specialty should govern the performance of medical services that fall within the specialty.

Surgeons were the first group of physicians to gain formal recognition in the United States as medical specialists.[21] Until the early twentieth century, general practitioners had performed surgery as a regular part of their medical practices. In 1913, however, the American College of Surgeons was founded and proceeded to establish standards for the qualified surgeon.[22] Two events between 1880 and 1920 prompted recognition of surgery as a specialty. One was the founding of most of the hospitals now in existence; the other was the development of the surgical technique of opening the abdomen.[23] The establishment of hospitals produced a split in the medical profession between those physicians who performed surgery and those who did not, with the former spending much of their professional time in a hospital. The opening of the abdomen, together with the introduction of anesthetics and the discovery of antisepsis, led to the piecemeal development of surgical subspecialties such as gynecology; urology; ear, nose, and throat; and neurosurgery.[24]

The sum effects of these developments were the disappearance of generalism in surgery and the rise of concern about the safety of surgery performed by the general practitioner. A search for a system of controls began. In Britain the medical system excluded the general practitioner from performing surgery and mandated that general practitioners refer patients to surgeons. American notions of egalitarianism produced stiff resistance to adopting the British system. Instead, most hospitals maintained open staff policies, giving access to surgical facilities to all staff. For a while, individual practitioners developed a referral system of surgeons for a "fee split," but the American Medical Association code of ethics of 1912 condemned this system.[25]

For our purposes, two features of the recognition of the American College of Surgeons as a specialty organization stand out. First, by establishing standards for recognizing a qualified surgeon, this group set a precedent for allowing a voluntary professional group, rather than the government, to define professional qualifications. Second, in 1917, when the American College of Surgeons held its first conference on hospital standardization, it became much more than a guild or specialist society; it gained the power to evaluate and grade hospitals and surgeons, a power that would allow it to play a dominant role in the medical profession, alongside the AMA.[26]

The internists were the next specialists to separate themselves from general practitioners. Whereas surgeons had used surgical techniques and the hospital as a base of practice to set themselves apart, from 1913 to 1915 internists began to distinguish themselves from general practitioners by focusing on the physiological and chemical bases of disease rather than on the generalists' more folksy approach to disease and cure. In imitation of their surgical colleagues, internists formed the American College of Physicians in 1915. Unlike the American College of Surgeons, however, this organization decided not to require an examination for admission, thus acting more like a specialist society than a quasi-licensing agency.[27]

Perhaps because it did not acquire quasi-licensing authority, the internists' organization did not gain the allegiance of other medical groups that embraced a scientific focus on disease. Psychiatrists, pathologists, neurologists, and pediatricians had already formed separate specialist societies that continued to maintain separate identities. Each group of specialists grew up around technical approaches to treating some particular medical problem. Much of the battle for recognition was aimed at improving the specialist's ability to compete by gaining enhanced prestige and controlling access to the practice.[28]

It is significant that the specialty societies did not attempt to control practice by license or legal regulation. Control was based on voluntary professional recognition. As a result, the specialty societies set standards through boards that established educational and training criteria for board recognition. Such recognition was obtained through the combined efforts of the specialty societies, the American Medical Association, and the American College of Surgeons.[29]

Determining which specialty boards warranted recognition proved to be influenced more by the politics of the medical profession than by scientific considerations. Tied up in the struggle were the demands of general practitioners that recognition of specialties not lead to any lessening of the authority, power, and respect accorded the general practitioner. Also involved were the competitive goals and allegiances that various specialists developed. The function of the board was to establish the standards of fitness to practice the specialty and to conduct the examinations for qualification. The founding of the first ophthalmologist board in 1916,[30] for example, resulted from a battle with optometrists for a monopoly over the right to provide eye care. The new board allowed the ophthalmologists to determine that an eye doctor must take systematic courses and demonstrate proficiency to be admitted to the specialist society. On the other hand, by the time anesthesiologists established a specialty board in 1937,[31] surgeons were accustomed to using nurse anesthetists in their practice; consequently, anesthesiologists were unable to gain a monopoly to provide anesthesia in surgical suites.[32]

During World War II the federal government recognized the significance of board certification by assigning different ranks in the army to the medical specialist and the general practitioner: general practitioners became first lieutenants; certified specialists became captains. After the war a 1946 statute provided that no one was to be rated a medical specialist unless board certified. Specialists earned the basic rate of pay of the generalists plus 25 percent. This recognition conferred new importance on board certification.

Stevens observes:

> With the recognition of specialty board certification by the armed services and by certain public medical programs, a cycle of professional development was complete. There had been one cycle of development from emerging specialization to demands for formal recognition of medical specialties; this cycle had extended from the early part of this century to the early 1930s, culminating in suggestions for specialist licensure. The period immediately following World War II marked the end of a second cycle, from the establishment of the specialty boards as a system in the 1930s to their formal acceptance, however limited in scope, by the public. But at the same time a third cycle was beginning with the movement toward some eventual and further rationalization of specialist services, which would be linked both with the specification and supervision of graduate education and training for all medical practitioners with publicly and professionally articulated manpower needs.[33]

Medical Specialization Today

Today there are twenty-four specialty boards that set the criteria for eligibility for certification in the specialty.[34] The American Board of Medical Specialties (ABMS) includes the following member specialty boards: allergy and immunology, anesthesiology, colon and rectal surgery, dermatology, emergency medicine, family practice, medical genetics; internal medicine; neurological surgery; nuclear medicine, obstetrics and gynecology, ophthalmology, orthopedic surgery, otolaryngology, pathology, pediatrics, physical medicine and rehabilitation, plastic surgery, preventive medicine, psychiatry and neurology, radiology, surgery, thoracic surgery, and urology.[35] In addition, there are now seventy subspecialties recognized by the ABMS.[36]

Obtaining formal recognition of one's special skill and knowledge usually requires a residency of three to six years. When the residency is successfully completed, the physician is declared "board eligible," meaning that she is eligible to take the oral and written examinations for certification. Some physicians who achieve board-eligible status never become board certified, either because they cannot pass the certification tests or because circumstances divert them from taking and passing the required tests.

A person who is neither board certified nor board eligible for a particular medical specialty may provide the medical services performed by board-eligible and certified specialists without violating any law. All that is required to practice medicine is passing a national examination administered by a voluntary board and meeting the qualifications for licensure within the particular state in which the physician intends to practice. The state requirement for licensure most commonly includes graduation from an accredited medical school and one year of postgraduate training. So long as a licensed physician does not misrepresent his qualifications to the public, the common law relies on market forces and hospital boards to control the areas of medicine within which physicians practice.

The American Board of Internal Medicine's 1990 statement of policies and procedure reflects the typical schizophrenia of the specialty boards. It declares that the purpose of the board is "to improve the quality of medical care by developing standards to ensure that the certified internist possesses the knowledge, skills, and attitudes essential to the provision of excellent care. Certification is recognition by peers of a superior level of ability." The statement then emphasizes: "Certification by the Board is not a requirement to practice internal medicine, and the Board does not intend either to interfere with or to restrict the professional activity of a licensed physician because the physician is not certified."

The American Board of Thoracic Surgery offers an even more explicit statement as to the limited significance of board certification:

> Board certification in a medical specialty is evidence that a physician's qualifications for specialty practice are recognized by his peers. It is not intended to define the requirements for membership on hospital staffs, to gain special recognition or privileges for its Diplomates, to define the scope of specialty practice, or to state who may or may not engage in the practice of the specialty. Specialty certification of a physician does not relieve a hospital governing board from responsibility in determining the hospital privileges of such specialist.

In view of all these disclaimers as to the significance of certification, one outside the profession is prompted to ask, "Why bother?" The answer of the American Board of Thoracic Surgery is, "The primary purpose of the Board, and its most essential function, is the protection of the public through the establishment and maintenance of standards in the specialty of thoracic surgery."

In medical malpractice litigation the question of the significance of board eligibility or certification often arises in connection with either establishing the standard of care or evaluating someone's qualifications as an expert. The reality of medical practice is that physicians practicing in the same or similar communities may possess widely varying skills and knowledge. In light of this reality, the standard of care required of physicians practicing in a world of specialized medicine often eludes easy definition if the attempt to establish the standard focuses on testimony as to what the "ordinary" physician does in particular circumstances. It appears, then, that board certification or eligibility has little effect on legal requirements or definitions of the medical standard of care to which a patient is entitled.

But does specialization influence the outcome of medical malpractice cases through mechanisms other than legal doctrine? The answer is probably yes. The way specialists see the world has an impact on the evaluation and litigation process from beginning to end.

The Subculture of Medical Specialists

In a book entitled *The Culture of Professionalism*,[37] Burton Bledstein examines the desire of large numbers of Americans to be regarded as professionals. This desire reflects a view that being seen as a professional enhances a person's prestige and wealth. This attitude is now solidly established in the United States and must be reckoned with if we are fully to appreciate the factors that influence individuals involved in medical malpractice cases. Attitudes about professional status affect the way patients, jurors, judges, and health care providers respond to medical malpractice claims and the evidence produced to prove or refute those claims.

To appreciate its impact, one needs first to acknowledge that professionals are held in high regard and paid well as a group because society presumes that the education, training, and work experience of members of the group have produced a shared method of evaluating and solving problems. At the same time, the group sees itself as sharing certain unique characteristics that set its members apart from the larger society. To be sure, members of the profession do not shed other important characteristics—such as race, ethnic background, gender, religion, and economic background—that affect the way they see the world or are seen. Nevertheless, the commonality of professional attitudes, beliefs, and values competes for a place in the individual's culture.

Doctors are first a part of a professional culture in America. They are next a special professional group that devotes itself to promoting and protecting health. Finally, in today's world of specialization, doctors become a part of a subculture of medical specialists. In other words, there are significant differences in how various medical specialists see the world and go about the business of solving problems.

Surgeons stand out as a prominent subgroup. In a splendid book describing modern surgeons from the perspective of an anthropologist, Joan Cassell offers many insights about surgeons and a useful approach to assessing the culture of other medical specialists.[38] Cassell distinguishes three features of the surgeons' culture: the art, craft, and science of surgery; the temperament of surgeons; and the fellowship of surgeons. Attorneys sometimes mistakenly focus solely on the art, craft, and science and neglect temperament and fellowship, matters that may have a tremendous impact on the outcome of a medical malpractice case.

With respect to the art, craft, and science of surgery, Cassell observes that the public and many surgeons regard the practice of surgery as the production of miracles, which she defines as follows:

> A miracle is *rapid*. A cure that takes months may be remarkable and gratitude-inducing, but it is not miraculous. . . .
>
> A miracle is *spectacular*. Consisting of a reversal or transformation, it propels the beneficiary from a disvalued to a valued state: sickness to health, death to life, water to wine.
>
> It is *definitive*. The beneficiary was sick, is well; disease was excised; the patient is cured. The surgical miracle is irreversible; the patient's body will never be the same.
>
> A miracle is *attributable*. Everyone knows who was responsible.
>
> It is *performed by someone with extraordinary powers*. Specialized knowledge and training, access to marvelous substances, or a relation to mystical or supernatural forces can be cited to explain these powers.
>
> A miracle is *unpredictable and mysterious*. Although it may be involved with rationality, in some ways it transcends rational, known, natural forces; it inspires hope, fear, and wonder.[39]

Cassell observes that both surgeons and patients are affected by this perception of the surgeon's art. Typically, the good surgeon is held in awe and becomes accustomed to being viewed as a special person. Cassell notes, however, that a surgeon may be technically good, particularly in terms of having good hands and the ability to cut well, but may not be a "good" person in the sense of caring about patients and interacting well with them. Nevertheless, it is the well-rounded surgeon whom most people have in mind when they invoke superlatives: "The 'complete' hero is admired and loved by patients and their families and is honored and emulated by younger colleagues, who observe the effects of caring and learn the significance of healing from his interactions with patients. The complete hero is the Exemplary Surgeon; technical and moral excellence are joined. He is a good *surgeon*, and he is a *good* surgeon."[40]

With respect to the surgeon's temperament, Cassell observes that a surgeon is a person who thrives on being the center of attention.

Operations, like miracles, are *attributable*. . . . Bad results are visible, blamable—and blamed. . . . Good results are equally visible and attributable. . . . Surgeons may be blamed more than other specialists for bad results, but then, they are admired, praised—even adored—for good ones. A surgeon requires immediate, rapid, and positive feedback; the intellectual interest of the problem, in and of itself, is rarely enough. We might speculate that the kind of person who becomes a doctor is someone who likes to be admired, while the kind of person who becomes a surgeon is someone who *needs* to be admired. Performing a "miracle" may be as essential to the self-image of the surgeon as to the well-being of the patient.[41]

Unfortunately, the same characteristics and temperament that produce miracles may also produce disasters. Cassell presents a thoughtful discussion of four categories of "Deadly Surgical Sins": "vices of excess; generative sins; defects, or character flaws; and deficiencies."[42] In essence, Cassell argues that we need to understand that substandard care by surgeons may be the result of various factors, including temperament, skills, or character, and we must identify the cause in order to adopt an appropriate response.

Moreover, in responding to misconduct on the part of surgeons (or any professional, for that matter), we must be aware of the group's "fellowship." Cassell contends: "Every hospital seems to have an almost invariant cast of surgical characters: the Prima Donna, the Old-Time Surgeon, the Sleazy Surgeon, the Buffoon, the Compassionate Young Surgeon, the Exemplary Surgeon."[43] This cast of characters forms a network within the hospital whose members take fellowship with and judge one another. Since some are also on the staffs of other hospitals, individuals may participate in more than one network. In addition, there are nationwide networks based on the institutions where surgeons trained or currently work, and networks of academicians, chiefs of surgery, and so on. Finally, and of great importance to medical malpractice litigation, the local fellowship rests within a larger fellowship of doctors:

> Surgeons work closely with radiologists, who x-ray and scan their patients and help interpret the results, and with pathologists, who analyze tissue specimens sent from the operating room. They share patients with "medical doctors," who are frequently responsible for the decision to send the patient to a particular surgeon, rather than a competitor. Certain specialists "feed" patients to certain surgeons; their goodwill is essential to a surgeon in private practice.[44]

A basic appreciation of the specialists' art and craft, temperament, and fellowship is essential to anyone involved in medical malpractice litigation. This understanding provides clues to discovering and providing the general standard of care as well as to ascertaining what actually occurred in a particular case. The legal community will benefit greatly from further studies of surgeons and other medical specialists.

Conclusion

Medical specialization has a minimal impact on the content of legal standards. Except for egregious cases—for example, where a general surgeon decides to perform a heart transplant—specialization has little influence in defining the standard of care or applying that standard in the courts. Since legislatures have refused to attach any importance to a physician's being board eligible or board certified, the law is likely to remain in this state as long as the medical profession itself attributes so little significance to the specialist's education and training. On the other hand, the culture of specialization has a tremendous impact on the effective assessment and proving of the merits of a case. Before accepting or rejecting an assessment of the merit of a claim or defense offered by a defendant or an expert, counsel for both the plaintiff and the defendant should gather some basic information about the nature and culture of the specialty. Is it a closely knit, egocentric group or a broad-based altruistic one? Are its members self-oriented or patient-oriented? What is the group's position within the profession in terms of power and wealth? Is the group particularly sensitive or vulnerable to medical malpractice claims or professional insurance issues? Is there currently a dominating political agenda? Asking these and similar questions may produce some exceptionally helpful insights into how best to evaluate and prosecute or defend the medical malpractice case.

Chapter 5

Economics, Ethics, and the Standard of Care: Emerging Issues

—

Before the 1970s the medical care decision-making process reflected few value conflicts. Physicians dominated the process. The doctor's profit motive usually remained below the surface. Making the patient well stood foremost in everyone's mind as the dominant value. Accepted medical practice guided medical decisions and answered most ethical questions. Physicians and family members expected patients to comply with the doctor's advice without challenging it or seeking second opinions. No one would have thought of suggesting that a patient might be denied an appropriate diagnostic procedure or treatment because it cost too much.

Today's medical decision-making model reflects a much more complex and dynamic picture. The cost of medical service sometimes overrides physicians' medical and ethical judgments. Many individuals participate in the decision-making process, in addition to the doctor. Often the patient plays an active role in deciding the course of the therapy. In addition, nurses, hospital administrators, and insurance-company physicians frequently seek to alter or veto the decisions reached by the treating physician and patient.

■ **Problem One:** *Insurer Refuses to Pay*

Mr. Woodson was admitted to City Hospital while suffering from major depression, drug dependency, and anorexia. His treating physician determined that he needed three to four weeks of in-patient care at the hospital. Ten days later, through its agents, his insurance company announced that it would not pay for any further hospital care. Mr. Woodson was an employee of a federal government agency and received health insurance coverage from his employer under a contract governed by the Federal Employees Health Benefits Act.[1] Since neither Mr. Woodson nor any of his family members were able to pay for further in-patient hospital care, he was discharged. Two weeks later he committed suicide.

If a negligence claim is filed against the treating physician, City Hospital, and/or the insurance company, should the trial court grant a motion to dismiss? In considering the issues raised by this problem, it is interesting to consult *Wilson v. Blue Cross of Southern California.*[2]

■ **Problem Two:** *Decision to Forgo a Test or Referral*

Over the course of a year Dr. Frugal, an ophthalmologist, evaluated Mr. Fields, forty years of age, for eye problems. After performing a number of tests on Mr. Fields, Dr. Frugal concluded that Mr. Fields suffered from low-pressure glaucoma, a rare disease that causes a loss in peripheral vision due to excess pressure on the lens in the eyes. Mr. Fields was enrolled in a health maintenance organization (HMO) plan that required him to get approval for any consultations or referrals from his primary physician, who had referred him to Dr. Frugal. She prescribed eye drops, the customary treatment for glaucoma.

Unfortunately, Fields did not have glaucoma; he had a slow-growing tumor that was causing him to go blind. Concerned about his continuing loss of vision over the coming year, on his own initiative and at his own expense Mr. Fields consulted an ophthalmologist who also specialized in neurology. After he underwent a computerized tomography (CT) scan, the tumor was detected and surgery was performed.

It is undisputed that a substantial portion of the vision that Mr. Fields lost could have been saved if a CT scan had been ordered and evaluated by an ophthalmologist with specialized training in neurology. It is also undisputed that Dr. Frugal considered ordering a CT scan or making a referral but decided not to because of cost considerations. Given the financial incentives built into the HMO reimbursement plan, however, Dr. Frugal undoubtedly did just what most ophthalmologists would have done in light of the patient's symptoms, the risks, and the cost of the CT scan and the referral. On the other hand, Mr. Fields has an expert who will testify that 95 percent of the physicians treating a patient with Mr. Fields's symptoms and history would have immediately ordered a CT scan or made a referral if the patient had a non-HMO plan such as Blue Cross and Blue Shield or Medicare.

Does Fields have a meritorious claim against his primary care doctor, Dr. Frugal, or the HMO insurer? In this connection it is worth looking at *Helling v. Carey*.[3]

The Winds of Change

In the traditional medical decision-making model a doctor employs her medical skill and knowledge to diagnose a patient's ailment and prescribe an appropriate medical treatment. She provides this service on a fee-for-service basis. This means that the patient or his insurer pays the doctor's fee and the hospital bill as service is rendered rather than on a prepaid or other insurance-reimbursement basis. Blue Shield (coverage for doctor's services) and Blue Cross (coverage for hospital services) dominated the health care insurance market. Blue Cross paid the doctor's fee based on the prevailing rate in the area, and Blue Cross paid the hospital fee based on the hospital's cost. Thus neither the patient nor the health care provider had an economic incentive to limit medical care or provide it at the lowest cost.

Before to the mid-1960s indigent patients received care from charitable hospitals, public clinics, and physicians who were willing to provide services for free or at reduced rates. With the passage of statutes in 1966 authorizing medical benefits for the elderly under Medicare and for the poor under Medicaid, federal and state governments entered the health care financing field on a large scale. Economist Paul J. Feldstein offers the following relevant factual background:

> Medicare is a federal program for financing the medical services of the aged; Medicaid is a federal-state financing program for the medically indigent. . . . In 1965, 8 percent of medical expenditures were privately financed. . . . By 1985, although the private sector had increased its total expenditures (from $28 billion in 1965 to $224 billion in 1985), this total represented a declining share of total personal medical expenditures, 6 percent. The federal rather than state government is paying an increasing share (3 percent) of personal medical expenditures. In 1965, the federal government spent $3.6 billion on personal medical services, while states spent $4.1 billion. By 1985, the federal government was spending $112.6 billion a year and states were spending $34.8 billion.[4]

During the late 1960s and throughout the 1970s the cost of medical care continued to increase at a rate significantly higher than the rate of inflation. The cost of health care insurance, which had become a significant part of employee benefit packages, rose at a rate that was alarming to businesses, unions, and government officials. All agreed that something had to be done to control medical costs.

With the enactment of Medicare and Medicaid, the aged and the poor had increased access to medical care. Hospitals were paid according to their costs and physicians received their usual and customary fees. Private medical insurance was also becoming more widespread during this period. The consequence was that provider prices began to increase more rapidly, as did expenditures on medical services. As both private insurance and government payments lessened the financial burden on the patient, there were few constraints remaining to hold down the use of services and prices charged by providers. The federal and state governments became alarmed as they saw their expenditures under Medicare and Medicaid exceed their budgets for these two programs. . . . Business and labor also became concerned with the rapid increase in employees' health insurance premiums.[5]

In an effort to control medical costs, government and private industry sought mechanisms that would make suppliers and consumers more sensitive to cost considerations. Most of the reforms focused on the supply side of medical services. The first approach that was adopted relied on regulatory rather than market mechanisms to control costs.

One regulatory mechanism, known as the certificate of need review (CON review) required hospitals to obtain approval from a regional agency before purchasing, constructing, or acquiring expensive health care equipment or facilities. To gain permission for such purchases, the hospital had to convince the local agency that there was a need in the community for this particular hospital to have this particular equipment or facility. If successful, the applicant received a certificate of need. The justification for CON review lay in the belief that, if left to their own devices, health care providers would purchase "excess" equipment and facilities. In this context, *excess* meant that supply would exceed consumer demand, in that potential patients, if informed, would be unwilling to pay the increased cost of the additional equipment or facilities when the same product was already available from another source. Through the CON review, the government hoped to discourage hospitals from purchasing expensive equipment such as CTs as a way of competing in the marketplace. Health care providers felt that they were in a better position than the government to determine what they needed to compete effectively, however. Moreover, the first health care provider to obtain new equipment or facilities had an incentive to use the CON review process to limit competition. The result of these conflicting perceptions and goals was that many health care providers fought to escape the limitations of the CON review process.

Utilization review represented another regulatory mechanism used by private and governmental health insurers. The insurer would review the medical care rendered to the insured while hospitalized to determine the propriety of the treatment and the length of the hospital stay. Although private insurers had conducted such retrospective reviews in the past, the increasing costs incurred in the 1970s prompted both private and public insurers to conduct more stringent and more frequent utilization reviews.

In addition, many insurers began conducting concurrent reviews during the 1980s. A concurrent review meant that rather than waiting until the end of the medical care to assess its propriety, physicians and nurses hired by insurers reviewed the proposed treatment while the treating physician was rendering it. Through concurrent reviews, insurers hoped to nip unnecessary care in the bud.

Experiencing only limited success with retrospective and concurrent reviews, the federal government followed the lead of some states and implemented a radical reimbursement scheme known as diagnostic review groups, or DRGs. Under this approach, techniques for diagnosing and treating common diseases and illnesses were categorized and average costs designated for each. The insurer would then pay the health care provider a set amount, regardless of the health care provider's actual cost incurred in providing the care.

The goal of DRGs was to make health care providers in general and hospitals in particular provide an optimum level of health care. According to classical economic thinking, "The optimal rate of output of medical care will be achieved when the price of that care (which is presumed to equal the costs of producing that care under a competitive system) is equal to the marginal benefit of that care."[6] The method of reimbursing hospital costs that existed before DRGs was thought to be inefficient because the patient had no incentive to seek less expensive hospital care because she did not directly pay the cost. In addition, since the hospital gained reimbursement on a cost basis, it had no incentive to restrain costs. The DRG reimbursement system sought to place the burden on the supplier of hospital services to reduce costs by limiting reimbursement to a fixed price. With a fixed price, profits could be increased or maintained only by reducing costs.

Reimbursing hospitals on a fixed-price basis addressed only part of the problem, however. Similar fixed-price reimbursement for physicians was necessary to place direct pressure on the principal health care decision maker to control costs. In addition, some mechanism was needed to make patients as the ultimate consumers more sensitive to the cost of medical care. Finally, reimbursement schemes alone would not do the job. Ultimately, according to traditional economic analysis, achieving an optimal level of health care services required some fundamental changes in the health care delivery system that would produce true competition.

The reasons for the emergence of market competition in health care were similar to other deregulated industries. Business and federal government each developed a concentrating interest in holding down the rise in their medical expenditures.

As a result of the 1981 recession and severe import competition, business moved toward self-insurance; their increased concern with health care costs stimulated insurance companies to introduce cost-saving innovations in their benefit packages. The federal government introduced DRGs as a means of controlling rapidly rising Medicare and Medicaid expenditures. Low cost substitutes to traditional providers developed, namely HMOs and outpatient surgery clinics. These new delivery systems decreased hospital and physician revenues. The excess capacity among physicians and hospitals and the change in business incentives and in government were important preconditions for market competition. . . . The judicial system assured market competition would occur when the Supreme Court upheld the applicability of antitrust to the health care industry.[7]

As Feldstein observes, the principal stimulant to competition in the health care field proved to be the emergence of HMOs and the application of antitrust principles to the health care field. Nourished by federal legislation passed in 1973 that required all employers of twenty-five or more persons to offer employees HMO coverage as an alternative to the fee-for-service reimbursement scheme adhered to by Blue Cross and other private insurers, HMOs assumed a substantial role in the health care decision-making process in the 1980s. The competitive activity of HMOs prompted the traditional health care insurers to reevaluate and revise many of their reimbursement policies and practices.

Though HMOs now symbolize competition in health care, they are but one form of response to fixed payments or capitation reimbursement schemes. Preferred provider organizations (PPOs) are a significant alternative form. Because PPOs offer medical care at reduced rates, the insured has an incentive to use these particular health care providers. Unlike the HMO user, the insured has the option to use other health care providers but must absorb some portion of the higher cost of the nonplan health care provider. In addition, HMO plans themselves take different forms. Some HMOs employ the doctors and own the hospitals that provide the care to the insured. Others enter into contracts with independent practice associations (IPAs) that provide care to HMO subscribers while also providing care to patients who are insured under other health plans.

The cost-containment efforts of the government and private insurers have caused physicians and hospitals to take a different approach to the business of medicine. At the same time, patients have found it necessary to respond to the new market forces in order to gain access to medical care at an affordable cost.

Market competition has changed the incentives facing the purchaser as well as the supplier of medical services by transferring financial risk. Purchasers, whether they are patients, employers, or insurance companies, have an economic incentive to search for those providers that can provide a given quality product at the lowest price. Purchasers also have an inventive to consider the trade-off between price and quality; increases in quality that are worth less than their increased cost are less likely to be purchased. Regardless of whether the supplier is for-profit or nonprofit, they have an incentive to minimize the cost of the product they are producing when they face a fixed price, either market or government determined.[8]

We are only beginning to appreciate and assess the fundamental changes produced by the new competition and financing arrangements. The next section explores tip of this iceberg.

The Cost of Cost Containment

To date, only a few reported cases depict health care decisions clearly made to save money at the risk of seriously jeopardizing the life or well-being of the patient. More will surely emerge in the near future. Such cases are likely to attract much public attention. The cases that pose an even greater threat to the standard of care in the medical community, however, will attract much less scrutiny because they lack the clarity of value choices and the drama of immediate catastrophic injury. Problem One above represents the first category. Problem Two represents the second category, that of everyday medical decisions that gradually lower the standard of care in order to cut costs. Each problem commands careful analysis.

In Problem One, a patient committed suicide after the hospital discharged him against his wishes and despite a professionally diagnosed need for hospital care to treat his mental illness. The reason for the discharge is clear. His insurance company refused to pay, and he had no other means of financing his care. Potential defendants in a lawsuit include his treating doctor, his insurance company, and the hospital. Complex legal and ethical questions flow from a consideration of the propriety of subjecting any of these parties to liability for the catastrophic result of a health care decision clearly driven by financial considerations. Before reaching conclusions on the legal responsibility, as distinguished from the ethical responsibility, we need more facts.

Whether the decedent's health insurance policy expressly included or excluded coverage for hospitalized treatment of mental illness is a pivotal factual issue. The facts clearly establish the treating physician's view that the decedent needed hospitalized care. The facts do not, however, tell us what coverage the decedent had purchased in his policy. For analytical purposes, then, let us assess the legal consequences based on three different factual assumptions. First, let us assume that the policy expressly covered hospitalization for thirty days for treatment of the precise type of mental illness from which the decedent suffered but that the potential defendants did not know of the clear provisions in the policy. Second, let us assume that the policy authorized hospitalization for treatment of mental illness, but that reasonable people could disagree concerning whether the coverage applied in this instance. Third, let us assume that the policy expressly excluded hospitalization but covered out-patient treatment.

If the policy contained provisions expressly covering hospitalization, Problem One would closely reflect the facts in *Wilson v. Blue Cross of Southern California.*[9] In *Wilson*, the decedent voluntarily admitted himself to a hospital in California for treatment for mental depression and drug addiction. His treating physician determined that he needed four weeks of hospitalized treatment. His health insurance policy, issued by Blue Cross of Alabama, included as a benefit thirty days of hospital treatment for a mental disorder. Blue Cross of California, acting through an agent, Western Medical, conducted a concurrent utilization review, however, and determined that the decedent's hospitalization was not medically justified. As reported by the court, the plaintiff alleged the following additional facts:

> Dr. Taff informed the decedent of Western Medical's decision "that the patient did not meet the admission criteria for his particular insurance policy and that his further stay was not justified or approved." The decedent was informed that he would "not be covered financially by his insurance company and that the liability [for hospital costs] would then be his." . . . The decedent cried while talking to an aunt about the determination that he was to be released from the hospital because the insurance company would not pay for the benefits. The decedent's aunt testified at her deposition that the family did not have enough money to pay for the cost of in-patient hospitalization. Dr. Taff told the aunt of the decedent "to come and get him." Dr. Taff told the decedent's mother and father that Western Medical "terminated his [the decedent's] stay" and the decedent's father was told that this was a "problem" that had occurred on other occasions.[10]

The trial court granted a summary judgment in favor of Western Medical and both insurance companies. The appellate court, however, reversed, ruling that, based on allegations, a jury could hold the defendants legally responsible for the decedent's death.

In their argument the defendants in *Wilson* relied on *Wickline v. State of California.*[11] In that case Ms. Wickline underwent surgery in which a part of an artery in her leg was removed and a synthetic artery inserted to replace it. On the same day, she underwent a second operation because a clot formed in the graft. Five days later she underwent a lumbar sympathectomy, a major operation in which a section of the chain of nerves that lies on each side of the spinal column is removed. With the last operation the physicians attempted to relieve spasms that she was experiencing in her leg. Four days after the lumbar sympathectomy her treating physicians concluded that it was medically necessary for her to remain in the hospital for an additional eight days. Since her medical care was paid for by the California Medical Assistance Program (Medi-Cal), however, they submitted a request for approval of the additional stay to the on-site duty nurse employed by Medi-Cal to conduct concurrent reviews of such requests. The on-site duty nurse passed the form on to a physician employed by Medi-Cal. The Medi-Cal physician reviewed the form and concluded that only four additional days in the hospital were justified.

At the end of the fourth day Ms. Wickline was discharged and her husband received instructions for home care: antibiotic powder for the groin incision, medication, warm water baths, and bed rest. After she arrived home, her leg became grayer and finally bluish. Nine days after discharge she was readmitted. Unfortunately, it was too late to save her leg, which was first amputated below the knee and then above the knee.

At trial of the lawsuit against Medi-Cal, her treating physician testified that in his opinion she would not have lost her leg had she remained in the hospital for four additional days of observation and treatment. In his view the Medi-Cal doctor concerned himself more with saving Medi-Cal money than with the patient's well-being. Moreover, in the view of the treating physician it was negligent for the Medi-Cal doctor to reach a conclusion regarding the medical necessity of the requested eight-day stay without examining the medical records, seeing the patient, and discussing her condition with her treating physician.

In contrast, Medi-Cal produced an expert who testified that the Medi-Cal consultant conformed to the required standard of care in making an assessment based on the Medi-Cal form. In his opinion the treating physicians had a duty to use the available Medi-Cal procedure for appeal to overturn the rejection of the hospital stay request, if they thought that the discharge posed a danger to the patient. On the facts of the case the court agreed that the treating physicians bore the responsibility for the discharge decision.

In relying on *Wickline*, the *Wilson* defendants made three arguments in support of their contention that California's tort law shielded them from liability on these facts. First, they contended that *Wickline* held that the sole liability for a discharge decision rests with the physician who makes the decision, even if it is based on an insurance company's refusal to pay benefits. Second, they argued that public policy considerations supporting concurrent review require the courts to immunize the reviewers from tort liability. Third, the defendants argued that the court should immunize reviewers from liability in cases where the treating physician fails to appeal the reviewer's denial of benefits.

In rejecting each of these arguments, the appellate court placed substantial weight on the facts that the insurance policy in question clearly provided for the benefits that the reviewer denied and, furthermore, that the policy at issue contained no provisions authorizing a concurrent review of a treating physician's determination of medical need.

Addressing the defendant's reliance on *Wickline*, the court noted that *Wickline* presented a special case of insurance coverage benefits and a review process governed by a state statute. Moreover, that state statute expressly provided that entitlement to benefits should be determined in accordance with the usual standards of medical practice in the community. In *Wickline*, the treating physician decided to accept the reviewer's determination that the postsurgical discharge of the patient should occur in four days rather than eight. The experts who testified in the case all agreed, however, that discharge in four days accorded with medical standards—even though the treating physician originally expressed the judgment that his patient's condition warranted additional hospitalization. Consequently, the statutory provisions combined with the expert opinions to justify a ruling as a matter of law that the insurance-benefit reviewers could not be held liable for bad results that

 followed the early discharge. The *Wickline* court's decision immunizing the reviewer was appropriate, according to the *Wilson* court, notwithstanding the testimony of the treating physician that in his view the patient's condition required more hospitalization and that a longer hospitalization in his opinion would have allowed the health care providers to treat the infection and avoid the necessity of amputating the plaintiff's leg.

 In the present case, however, the *Wilson* court reasoned that no public policy justified immunizing the insurer from liability. According to the court, the laudable goal of containing medical costs did not justify the reviewer's decision. Indeed, in this case, unlike *Wickline*, the evidence would allow a jury to conclude that the goal of cost containment had been allowed to corrupt medical judgment.

Wilson did not render an opinion on the potential liability of the treating physician or hospital. Neither did *Wickline*. The plaintiff in *Wickline* did not sue the health care providers. Through dicta (i.e., statements of law not required to decide the particular case), however, the *Wickline* court offered some suggestions as to the potential liability of the treating physician for allowing the discharge of a patient when the physician's judgment favors continued hospitalization. The *Wickline* court opined that the physician could not be absolved of responsibility to render appropriate professional care to her patient based on the decision of an insurer. Rather, the responsibility to render reasonable care to a patient may require the treating physician to appeal a decision that she believes fails to meet the standard of care. A curious aspect of *Wickline* was that the treating physician and all the experts who testified agreed that the treating physician's decision to discharge Mrs. Wickline in four days, rather than in eight days as he originally requested, conformed to the standard of care required. Clearly, if the plaintiff had sued the treating physician along with Medi-Cal, she could have obtained a more critical assessment of the conduct of the treating physician, who might have been held liable to her for not appealing the rejection of the requested eight-day hospital stay.

Wickline makes it plain that, if the treating physician appeals the original decision of the insurance company, and the insurer rejects the appeal, the treating physician should fully inform the patient that additional care is warranted. If he does, it is unlikely that a court would hold him responsible for a bad result where the only option that the insurer has left him is to provide medical care at no cost. Such a scenario requires the court to confront directly the responsibility of insurers for interfering with medical judgment, as occurred in *Wilson*.

Similar cautions apply to the hospital. The evolving doctrine of corporate responsibility provides a basis for a patient discharged for financial reasons to contend that a hospital has breached its duty. A patient may argue that a hospital has a duty to adopt procedures and safeguards to guide attending physicians, staff, and patients in appealing reimbursement decisions that dictate health care treatment below the standard of care. A hospital should reasonably foresee that disputes will arise among treating physicians and reviewers, necessitating an expeditious review of decisions denying approval for medical treatment that is medically necessary. Accordingly, a hospital should develop rules and procedures for determining when a denial of treatment by a third-party payor will dictate the treatment regimen. As in the case of the physician, however, no liability should follow a decision to deny or limit care in nonemergency situations after the attending physician or hospital staff has exercised reasonable care to reverse the insurer's decision.

Finally, if the patient's insurance policy expressly excludes coverage of a service such as mental health counseling, and the treating physician views the treatment as critical in order to avoid serious harm, the liability of the health care provider should turn on whether the situation rises to the level of an emergency. If it does not, from a legal perspective, the risk of nontreatment lies with the patient. If it does, the health care provider, under both the common law and a federal statute (COBRA), discussed below, must err on the side of treatment until such time as the threatening condition has stabilized.

Decisions to Order Tests, Make Referrals, or Acquire Equipment

Problem Two presents a different type of medical decision dictated by the patient's health care insurer. The doctor acknowledges that a fee-for-service reimbursement plan such as Blue Shield would prompt most physicians in the community to order the CT scan to rule out a tumor. Responsive to the goals of this patient's HMO plan, however, the physician has attempted to contain costs by not ordering a test that would rule out a serious risk but in all likelihood would reveal no significant positive findings. Should the insurer or health care provider enjoy immunity from tort liability for making such a decision on account of a cost-containment plan?

On the one hand, the unfortunate victim will contend that life and good health are too precious to be subordinated to the dictates of cost containment. On the other hand, the beneficiaries of reasonable cost containment include all persons in the insurance group, health care providers participating in the plan, and the insurance company investors, who will reap greater profits. The *Wickline* and *Wilson* decisions suggest that insurance reimbursement plans that corrupt medical judgment may subject the insurer and the health care provider to tort liability. The *Wilson* court specifically held that the public policy supporting cost-containment goals does not override the public policy entitling patients to reasonable medical care. The question, then, is whether cost containment and quality medical care are compatible goals. If not, legislatures or courts must declare which policy should govern.

The same issue arises when a hospital administrator decides for financial reasons not to purchase or make available equipment that a health care provider considers important to providing appropriate medical care. *Washington v. Washington Hospital Center*[12] provides an excellent fact pattern for considering this issue. In *Washington*, the chairman of the hospital's department of anesthesiology, by way of a written requisition, asked that the hospital purchase an end-tidal carbon dioxide monitor, which would allow the anesthesiologist to determine more quickly and accurately whether an anesthetized patient was receiving adequate oxygen. The hospital declined the request, even though the anesthesiologist had stated in the memorandum that the hospital would fail to meet the national standard of care if it did not provide the monitor in each of its operating rooms. One year later, while undergoing a minor surgical procedure, the plaintiff did not receive adequate oxygen and suffered permanent and profound brain damage. The anesthesiologist and nurse anesthetist, who anesthetized and intubated the plaintiff, settled the medical malpractice claim against them after the trial of the suit commenced. The hospital, however, refused to settle, choosing instead to argue to the court and the jury that the standard of care of a tertiary care hospital in the Washington, D.C., area did not require it to have this expensive equipment at the time the care was rendered. In addition, the hospital contended that the anesthetists were solely responsible for the bad result. The jury disagreed and rendered a verdict against the hospital for $4.6 million. The appellate court affirmed the verdict. In the court's view the testimony of the plaintiff's expert, statements in several medical journal articles, and the memorandum of the hospital's anesthesiology department chairman combined to provide sufficient basis for a jury to conclude that the standard of care required the use of the monitors. In effect, the jury and the court informed hospitals in unmistakable terms that a hospital will be held responsible for financing decisions that cause health care providers in the institution to provide substandard care.

Cost Containment and the Standard of Care

The desire to contain costs can tempt decision makers to choose strategies that clash with the goal of maintaining a high quality of health care. It seems likely that the goals are not inherently irreconcilable. The challenge is to employ strategies that allow decision makers to balance the goals properly. Given the variety of administrative and health care decision makers involved in the process, however, some form of tort liability seems to be an essential element of the reconciliation. Immunizing cost-containment plans and decisions from meaningful outside scrutiny would ensure that financial considerations would receive too much weight in the minds of insurers and health care providers. Potential tort liability, on the other hand, would compel decision makers to take into account not only the cost of the proposed care but also the cost to the patient and the community of denying the care. As Feldstein observes, the malpractice system serves both as competition and as a quality assurance mechanism: "Poor quality care is too costly to an organization if it results in an increase in lawsuits and in large awards to the aggrieved parties. The threat of malpractice suits should inhibit the provision of poor quality care."[13]

The conflict between cost containment and health promotion has prompted HMO insurers to argue that federal legislation authorizing the cost-containment plans exempts the insurers and participating health care providers from common law tort liability. Such arguments have evoked favorable responses from the courts when presented in connection with breach-of-contract actions where the insured claims a right to expanded coverage of benefits under an HMO policy. Where the decision to deny coverage has caused the insured to suffer serious personal injuries, thus giving rise to a tort claim, however, courts have rejected the immunity argument. In effect, under current law, judges and juries may assess the reasonableness of the cost-containment plans in light of the impact on the patient.

Standard-of-care assessments are made against the background of seminal cases such as *Wilkinson v. Vessey*[14] and *Helling v. Carey*,[15] both of which condemn the conduct of physicians who fail to use available medical technology to diagnose risks of serious disease or illness. In finding two radiologists negligent for, among other things, rendering radiation therapy to treat a suspected cancer in the plaintiff's chest cavity, the *Wilkinson* court noted that the physicians had started the therapy without first reviewing earlier X rays of the plaintiff's chest area and without obtaining a biopsy. The court observed that a physician may be held liable for exposing a patient to serious therapeutic risks without first using all available technology to confirm the diagnosis that prompts the undertaking of the high-risk therapy. The *Helling* court held that a pressure test to detect glaucoma was so simple and inexpensive that the patient's eye doctors were negligent as a matter of law for not performing the test when the plaintiff continued to lose her eyesight while under their care for a number of years. The negligence existed, according to the court, notwithstanding the undisputed evidence that ophthalmologists as a group considered the pressure test unnecessary for persons under forty years of age.

Viewed out of context, tort law presents a threat to sound decision making by doctors. Critics contend that decisions such as *Wilkinson* and *Helling* cause physicians to practice defensive medicine. They argue that, when combined with rapidly developing expensive technology, defensive medicine contributes substantially to rising health care costs, which the cost-containment plans are designed to address. On the other hand, health care financing plans, driven by a cost-containment goal, present an equally serious threat to sound health care decision making. Cutting costs in the face of serious illness that is treatable is not only cruel but "penny wise and pound foolish."

In truth, what the proponents of both systems desire is to influence professional health care providers to take both the patient's individual well-being and the cost of medical care into account. Such balanced decision making will require a fundamental restructuring of power and authority among the participants in the process so that the person with the final word is a trained health care professional who views himself as having the patient's welfare as his primary responsibility. In the past the treating physician played that role. Today, despite valid criticism of the treating physician's insensitivity to cost, the treating physician must continue to have significant power to influence the health care decision, serving as the patient's representative in negotiations with the health care financiers. In emergencies reasonable care mandates that doubts must be resolved in favor of treatment and against cost containment. In nonemergency situations it is important that a system exist that places ultimate decision-making authority in the hands of someone other than an employee-consultant of the insurer. At a minimum an independent hearing officer or panel must have authority to resolve conflicts, taking into account both cost and health considerations. The failure of a health care financier or insurer to have in place some system that allows for prompt and objective resolution of health care financing decisions that impinge on standard-of-care decisions should be viewed as negligence in itself.

Chapter 6

Tort Reform: Legislation, Courts, and State Constitutions

———

Since the early 1970s, insurance companies, medical organizations, and bar associations have battled over the need to reform the law governing medical malpractice claims and the process used to resolve such conflicts.[1] Today that battle continues in the midst of a larger struggle concerning fundamental reform of the health care system as a whole. Proposals for reform of the health care system include encouraging competition for managed care, creating a one-party payer system similar to the one used in Canada, rationing the type of care for which the government or insurer will pay, as in Oregon, and establishing a national health care plan, like the one used in Great Britain.[2] Whether the reform produces minor or major changes in the health care system, careful consideration must be given to the impact of the existing tort system on the goals of health care reform. Intelligently assessing the compatibility of the current tort system with a reformed health care system requires that we first understand the role that the tort system has played in producing desirable or undesirable effects within the existing health care system.

Health care providers, personal injury lawyers, and insurers approach this issue with strong convictions about what is wrong with the current system and what ought to be done about it. Often, the assumptions behind those convictions are wrong. It is commonly assumed, for example, that the tort system produces far more litigation than is justified by the medical negligence that occurs. Recent studies of the operation of the malpractice system reveal, on the contrary, a large gap between the number of meritorious medical malpractice claims that could be brought and those that are actually brought.[3] Indeed, one research group examined medical malpractice claims brought in New York and concluded: "[F]or every 8 potentially valid claims, only 1

77

claim was actually filed; of the claims filed, we estimated that no more than 1 in 2 would eventually result in money paid to the plaintiff."[4] Those studies, if accurate, suggest that the most popular legal reforms adopted in most states during the past twenty years have not only missed their mark; they have aimed at the wrong target.

Another assumption, often made by health care providers, among others, is that a consumer with a serious injury will probably be paid by an insurance company through a settlement because of fear that a jury's decision will be based on sympathy with the plaintiff rather than reason. Yet a recent study of 8,231 closed malpractice cases in New Jersey produced this conclusion: "In malpractice cases, physicians provide care that is usually defensible. The defensibility of the case and not the severity of patient injury predominantly influences whether any payment is made. Our findings suggest that unjustified payments are probably uncommon."[5]

As long as health care providers are human, instances of negligent medical care causing serious injuries to patients will occur. Accordingly, three categories of potential medical malpractice claims will continue to exist: (1) frivolous claims (those which no competent attorney or health care provider would regard as meritorious); (2) claims of egregious negligence (those which every competent attorney or health care provider would regard as meritorious); and (3) reasonably disputed claims (those in which competent attorneys and health care providers might reasonably disagree about the claim's merit). Reforms of the tort system in the past two decades have rested on the assumption that frivolous claims pose the greatest problem. Reasonably disputed claims have prompted procedural and process reforms, discussed in this chapter. Claims of clear and egregious departures from accepted medical standards have received minimal attention, other than occasional media coverage of large jury verdicts. The assumption is that such egregious cases are so rare that we need not spend a great deal of time worrying about them. In reality, careful evaluation of such claims would reveal a need to adopt strong deterrent measures to avoid a recurrence because of faulty practices or impaired health care providers.

By arguing that popular reforms have rested on faulty assumptions, I do not intend to suggest that the current tort system works well and should not be changed. Indeed, scholars are now beginning to offer proposals for reform that would reduce or eliminate the need to assess fault in every case in order to make a compensation decision.[6] Such proposals, I believe, warrant serious consideration.

The basic proposition on which the discussion and analysis in this chapter rest, however, is that we need to better understand the positive and negative effects of the tort system on the health care system if we are to fashion reforms that are rational, effective, and fair. Understanding the tort system as it applies to health care providers means more than simply conducting and reviewing empirical studies of the outcomes of various negligence claims and assessing the merit of the claims. It means we must gain a deeper insight into the culture of the medical malpractice litigation system. In other words, we must attempt to gain a better understanding of why patients, health care providers, lawyers, judges and insurers do what they do when medical care produces a bad result. Unless we pay attention to the beliefs and values of the participants in this process, we will not understand how they see the world, why they see it that way, and how they are likely to respond to changes in the tort law or health care systems. Understanding the culture of malpractice tort law, like understanding the culture of medicine, can help all the parties to a lawsuit appreciate the complexity of finding an approach to medical malpractice that is both fair and efficient.

I believe that we need to place less emphasis on institutional reform and more emphasis on individual reform. In my view, the fairest and most efficient way to reform the medical malpractice system is to change the culture by better educating the members of both professions as to the causes of bad results in the health care system and the appropriate role of the legal system in responding to compensation claims based on medical injuries. This education must be accompanied by a re-examination and clarification of the professional responsibilities of health care providers and attorneys, placing special emphasis on the duty to engage in ethical conduct. I believe that structural reform of the tort system holds far less potential for improving the quality of care of health care and reducing its cost than does improving the skills of professionals and demanding that all members of the profession engage in ethical conduct guided by the principle that the interest of the consumer comes first.

This chapter presents an overview of statutory trends in tort reform, a description of the constitutional challenges to the new legislation, and a critical assessment of the most popular tort reform measures and the assumptions underlying them. It concludes with a discussion of the central role of ethics in achieving the goals sought by tort reform.

Overview

Until the 1970s medical malpractice cases represented a small segment of tort litigation and evoked only sporadic outcries. In the 1970s, however, insurance companies grabbed the nation's attention by announcing that a dramatic increase in suits against health care providers made it imprudent for them to continue to write malpractice insurance.[7] According to the insurers, the tort law of the various states made it difficult if not impossible to predict future liability verdicts and thus to assess appropriate premiums that would allow a reasonable profit. The insurers insisted that staying in the medical malpractice insurance business made good business sense only if they could increase premiums by huge amounts. Many threatened to stop writing insurance for doctors and hospitals if the legal system was not reformed. Greedy lawyers and emotional juries attracted special blame. The media and a small number of incompetent doctors also received criticism.

The insurance companies' threats precipitated close examination of the legal system's handling of medical malpractice claims. Some reviewers attributed the crisis to the breakdown in the physician-patient relationship. They observed that specialization and other modern approaches to the delivery of health care depersonalized the doctor-patient relationship and encouraged lawsuits when a bad result followed medical treatment. In addition, the complexity of medical practice from both a scientific and an economic perspective raised expectations of a quality of care that many doctors could not meet. Consumer advocates complained that the medical profession failed to employ effective disciplinary measures to rid itself of incompetents.[8]

Many doctors took a different view. They agreed with the insurance companies that the crisis had been caused by unscrupulous attorneys motivated by contingent fee arrangements that gave them an opportunity to make large sums of money by bringing frivolous lawsuits.[9] The solution to the crisis lay in diminishing the incentive on the part of attorneys to bring the claims.

Lawyers in turn pointed to a closed shop of physicians who protected incompetent colleagues at the expense of the public. In addition, they charged that the insurance companies that had precipitated the crisis by threatening to abandon the health care system had an ulterior profit motive—namely, the need to increase their premiums in order to recoup the losses they had suffered by investing unwisely in the stock market during the seventies.[10]

Other commentators who had no direct economic stake in laying blame felt that the public shared responsibility for the crisis. A general mood of litigiousness prevailed among the American public during the 1970s.[11] They contended that the publicity given to million-dollar awards in personal injury cases had fueled a belief that a medical malpractice victim could easily become rich if she sued.[12]

In short, the refusal of insurance carriers to issue malpractice policies alarmed the medical profession,[13] which in turn demanded that state legislatures come to its aid.[14] In an effort to respond to this crisis, many states pushed through various forms of emergency remedial legislation, much of which did not withstand subsequent constitutional challenges.[15]

After the initial wave of tort reform legislation in the 1970s, the issue left the public eye for a decade. Then, in the 1980s, insurance companies and health care providers again asserted that a medical malpractice crisis had developed, threatening the ability of the medical community to deliver quality health care. Once more state legislatures responded to the cry with a barrage of emergency medical malpractice reforms.

The new reforms represented a myriad of approaches.[16] They did, however, share a few goals: to expedite meritorious claims and weed out frivolous suits, to provide the public with qualified and competent health care providers while curtailing the practice of those not competent to practice medicine, to reduce damage awards in medical malpractice actions, and to ensure the availability of medical malpractice insurance.

Reforms aimed at weeding out frivolous claims included setting up pretrial screening panels; requiring a certificate of merit, and/or an affidavit of an expert who can attest to its merit, before filing a suit; permitting a cause of action for baseless and vexatious claims; establishing special qualifications for expert witnesses; and shortening the statute of limitations. Reforms directed at reducing the incidence of substandard medical treatment included requiring a risk management unit in every health care facility; reporting all malpractice claims to the insurance commissioner and to a disciplinary board for health care providers; and establishing disciplinary committees to expedite the curtailment of incompetent physicians' privileges.

Reforms intended to reduce the size of damage awards included setting limitations on recovery of malpractice damages, and specifically, caps on non-economic damages; permitting periodic payment of future damages; abrogating the collateral source rule (under which a plaintiff is permitted to recover in full from the defendant even though the plaintiff also receives compensation from other sources, such as her own insurance or worker's compensation); limiting attorneys' contingency fees; and eliminating punitive damages.

Finally, to ensure the availability of insurance, many states created patient compensation funds.[17] Others established joint underwriting associations[18] to ensure the availability of health care insurance to health care providers and hospitals. Hawaii, Idaho, and Minnesota made these associations temporary, with specific time limitations,[19] while Missouri postponed their implementation until the insurance commissioner declared a malpractice crisis.[20] To protect the funds from quick exhaustion, many states set a maximum amount recoverable by one claimant or for all claimants under one policy. Other states set minimum amounts of insurance that a health care provider or hospital must carry in order to practice within the state. Statutes in Indiana, Louisiana, Puerto Rico, South Carolina, and Wisconsin provided for an excess liability fund,[21] which is available to the prevailing plaintiff if the award exceeds the maximum insurance available through the defendant's insurance policy. In Hawaii, Illinois, Indiana, and Kentucky patient compensation funds also may provide that they will not pay any amount of punitive damages.[22]

Medical risk prevention programs in health care facilities and hospitals represent a final category of reforms that attempt to achieve several of the goals at once. These programs entail closer monitoring of the medical staff, mandatory insurance reporting requirements, and the institution of a hospital risk management program. As of 1992, only Florida, Indiana, and Kansas had enacted risk management programs.[23]

The medical malpractice reform statutes of the 1970s and 1980s prompted a plethora of constitutional challenges. The challengers argued most frequently that the reforms violated the health care consumer's rights to due process, equal protection, and a jury trial. Many of the challenges in the 1970s succeeded, apparently because judges believed that the legislatures were reacting to crisis lobbying rather than thinking through the issues. Most of the challenges in the 1980s failed because courts deferred to legislative declarations that the medical malpractice litigation process needed to be reformed in order to avert a crisis of availability of insurance or runaway jury verdicts.

Constitutional Challenges

Most federal law challenges to state reform legislation have invoked the equal protection and due process clauses of the Fourteenth Amendment of the United States Constitution. The equal protection clause prohibits a state from denying "to any person within its jurisdiction the equal protection of the laws."[24] The due process clause provides that a state may not deprive any person of "life, liberty and property without due process of law."[25]

The U.S. Supreme Court has analyzed equal protection claims traditionally under two standards of review: strict scrutiny and minimum rationality.[26] The strict scrutiny standard directs the court to uphold the statute only if doing so is necessary to achieve a compelling governmental interest.[27] The Court has reserved a strict scrutiny standard to certain suspect classes, including classification based on race,[28] national origin,[29] alienage,[30] or religion,[31] or where a statute has a material impact on a fundamental right or interest.[32] The minimum rationality standard applies to statutes that are not based on suspect classifications and do not impair a fundamental right.[33] The test to be used for the mere rationality approach is whether the classification conceivably bears a rational relationship to an end of government that is not prohibited by the Constitution.[34]

A third level of review that has recently been introduced is commonly referred to as *middle-level scrutiny*.[35] In a few situations courts have appeared to engage in scrutiny that is more probing than the mere rationality test but less rigid than the strict scrutiny standard. Middle-level scrutiny has principally been limited to classification based on gender,[36] alienage,[37] and illegitimacy.[38] The test is usually stated as follows: The means chosen by the legislature must serve important governmental objectives and must be substantially related to achieving those objectives.[39]

Some plaintiffs in medical malpractice actions have requested use of a strict scrutiny approach, arguing that the state statute discriminates against victims of medical malpractice and that plaintiffs have a fundamental right to recover damages in a medical malpractice suit as they would in any personal injury tort claim.[40] In such a suit a Montana Supreme Court held unconstitutional a statute that abolished noneconomic damages against the state, county, or municipality and that also put a cap of $300,000 on economic damages for each claimant.[41] The court found that the right to bring a civil action for personal injuries was fundamental.[42] Similarly, states that have constitutional provisions that explicitly prohibit placing limits on personal injury awards would subject a damage limitation statute to a strict scrutiny review because the statute would infringe on a fundamental constitutional right.[43]

Middle-level scrutiny has been used, for example, by the New Hampshire Supreme Court in *Carson v. Mauer*[44] in ruling that a statute of limitations was unconstitutional. The *Carson* court stated, "[W]e conclude that the rights involved herein are sufficiently important to require that the restriction imposed on those rights be subjected to a more rigorous judicial scrutiny than allowed under the rational basis test."[45] Other states have also applied a substantial relationship test indicative of middle-level scrutiny.[46]

The following courts have employed the rational review analysis in determining constitutional issues: Arkansas, California, Florida, Iowa, Louisiana, Nebraska, New Jersey, New Mexico, New York, and Wisconsin. Under a rational basis standard, the majority of legislation has withstood constitutional challenges.[47] The courts have held that a legitimate purpose is being served by remedial medical malpractice legislation aimed at ensuring an adequate health care system. A 1983 Rhode Island decision,[48] however, concluded that the legislation furthered no legitimate purpose, reasoning that no medical malpractice crisis existed.[49]

The due process clause of the Fourteenth Amendment precludes deprivation of life, liberty, and property without due process of law.[50] The standard of review is similar to either the strict scrutiny standard or the rational basis test employed under an equal protection analysis. To pass muster under the strict scrutiny review test, the objective must be compelling.[51]

Plaintiffs in medical malpractice actions have challenged statutes on procedural due process grounds,[52] on the right of access to the courts,[53] and on the right of access to trial by jury,[54] as well as on the grounds of separation of powers.[55] These theories have not fared well, however, because the majority of courts view the right to recover money damages as an economic or social benefit rather than as a fundamental right (such as the right to vote, to marry, and to travel).[56] In addition, in most cases a plaintiff is not denied total access to the courts because a majority of the statutes allow a plaintiff ultimately to litigate her case on the merits. The right of access to the courts is blocked only until the plaintiff has successfully navigated the pretrial hurdles set up by the new legislation, such as a pretrial screening panel.

Some Popular Tort Reform Measures

Pretrial Screening Panels

Most states have enacted some form of pretrial mediation or screening[57] for the express purpose of weeding out frivolous claims and encouraging the early settlement of meritorious claims.[58] Pretrial screening panels vary from state to state.[59] Some are mandatory and some may be waived with the approval of both parties. Generally, a panel is composed of an attorney and/or a judge, a doctor or health care provider, and a layperson. The procedures and evidentiary rules are informal and relaxed. In some states recommendations made by the panel may be admissible as evidence in a later trial.[60] Panel members may be called to testify at a subsequent trial in some states, while other states forbid this.[61] Most jurisdictions that allow the panels' findings of fact or recommendations on the amount of damages as evidence require instructions that the panels' findings are not binding and should be given weight as the jury may deem appropriate.[62]

The controversy over the mediation panels focuses on the constitutional claims of separation of powers, equal protection, due process, and the right to trial by jury. Plaintiffs have complained that the panels cause unnecessary delays in the final disposition of the case and that this slowdown runs counter to the intended goal of expediting claims.[63]

An interesting assault on pretrial screening panels is found in *Bernier v. Burris*,[64] in which the panels were attacked on due process and equal protection grounds. In declining to follow the middle-scrutiny standard used by New Hampshire[65] and North Dakota,[66] the Supreme Court of Illinois explained, "We do not believe that the provisions in question implicate a suspect or quasi-suspect classification and accordingly the appropriate standard for determining the plaintiff's equal protection challenges under the Illinois and Federal Constitutions is whether the legislation bears a rational relationship to a legitimate governmental interest."[67] Despite the legislators' addition of numerous procedural safeguards to protect the pretrial screening from constitutional challenge, the court found the panels constitutionally unacceptable.

To avoid the claim that the procedure entailed an unlawful delegation of judicial power, for example, the new legislation had made the judicial member of the panel the sole authority over legal issues. The court in *Bernier* explained its view of why the arrangement did not work:

> Under these provisions, the role of the judicial member of the panel must take one of two forms. Either he serves on the panel in his judicial authority to make factual determinations, or he is denied his judicial authority and has no greater authority than the two other panel members. In essence, the panel procedures at issue here do not adequately distinguish between the judicial members; the fact finding functions are still blended as they were in *Wright*. . . .[68]

To withstand a separation of powers argument the statute must meet a two-pronged test. The first is whether an act improperly vests judicial functions in nonjudicial members; the second is whether the act makes the panel decision final and binding on the parties.[69] The new legislation attempted to separate the duties of a nonjudicial member from that of a judge by providing that the panel could apply the law only as determined by the judge and a new trial could be granted after the proceedings. No one was bound by the decisions of the hearing unless agreed on in writing by both parties. The Illinois Supreme Court rejected even this much delegation of judicial power to nonjudges.

In contrast to *Bernier*, most courts have upheld pretrial screening panels against constitutional challenges.[70] In many states that have found the panels constitutional, however, the procedures often produce a tremendous backlog of cases, resulting in losses of time and money.[71] Pretrial screening panels need to be refined to prevent such a backlog, and the Illinois legislation offers a good example of how such panels could be established, despite the drubbing it suffered in *Bernier*.

Limitations on Amount of Recovery

The simplest way to reduce skyrocketing malpractice awards—though at tremendous cost to potential medical malpractice victims—is to place ceilings on the amount recoverable by a plaintiff. Some states have resorted to placing maximum dollar limits on the amount recoverable, others have eliminated awards of punitive damages, and some have abrogated the collateral source rule.

Measures that directly curb damages have evoked criticism. They are vulnerable to constitutional attacks on the grounds of due process and equal protection. Florida, Texas, Idaho, New Hampshire, North Dakota, Ohio, and Illinois have all declared ceilings on recoveries unconstitutional.[72] Courts in California, Louisiana, Indiana, Nebraska, and Wisconsin have upheld constitutional challenges to caps on awards.[73] The California Supreme Court found the $250,000 cap on noneconomic damages to be constitutional. The U.S. Supreme Court dismissed that appeal, thereby leaving decisions on the constitutionality of such limitations to the individual states.[74]

As with the ceilings on recovery, the abrogation of the collateral source rule has met with some controversy. Courts in Kansas, New Hampshire, North Dakota, and Ohio have found violations of due process and equal protection.[75] In Arizona, California, Florida, Iowa, and Illinois, courts have upheld abolition of the rule under a rational basis review, reasoning that eliminating certain overlapping recoveries bears a rational relationship to government's legitimate interest in reducing the costs of malpractice actions.[76]

A few jurisdictions have eliminated punitive damages from medical malpractices cases, primarily reasoning that adequate deterrence of egregious conduct may be achieved by other means.[77] Since punitive damages are usually awarded in addition to compensatory damages in order to punish the wrongdoer, if there are other mechanisms by which the wrongdoer may be punished, the need for punitive damages may be diminished. In 1986 the Illinois Supreme Court declared constitutional a statute that prohibited awards of punitive damages.[78] The court held that the prohibition did not offend equal protection. The statute was found to be rationally related to the legitimate governmental interest of avoiding excess liability.[79]

Periodic Payment of Future Damages

Some states have enacted provisions for periodic payment of future damages.[80] Periodic payment provides that the damage award be disbursed periodically rather than in a lump sum. Many states provide for election of periodic payment by a party and also may require the defendant to post adequate security. Various courts have upheld these periodic payment provisions against constitutional challenges.[81] New Hampshire is the only state to declare such provisions unconstitutional, with the court declaring that this provision deprived severely injured persons of equal protection of the law.[82] The court reasoned that there was no justification for treating a severely injured person who is a victim of medical malpractice differently from a person severely injured in any other non-work-related accident.[83]

Attorneys' Fees

Another measure that states have taken to reduce malpractice awards is the reduction of fees recoverable by attorneys. Many states have enacted legislation regulating and controlling the contingent fees that an attorney may charge in representing parties in a medical malpractice suit.[84] However unpopular such laws may be with the plaintiffs' attorneys, they have withstood constitutional challenges.[85] New Hampshire struck down its legislature's entire medical malpractice statute,[86] but it is the only state to declare a contingent fee scale unconstitutional. The prevailing view has been that such statutes do not violate due process or equal protection challenges under a rational basis review.

Reactions to a Perceived Medical Malpractice Crisis

As we have seen, during the 1970s the threat by insurance companies to stop writing professional liability insurance policies for physicians precipitated panic in the medical community, which in turn provoked state legislatures throughout the country to pass statutes protecting the medical community from various common law rules governing medical malpractice claims. The legislative reforms had three principal thrusts. The first shortened the time period within which claims must be brought. Accordingly, insurers replaced their "occurrence" policies with "claims made" policies, which limited coverage to claims made during the policy period and consequently made it easier for insurers to make a fair projection of claims that might have to be paid at the expiration of the period. Under an occurrence policy, an insurer risked facing a claim being made for substantial sums after the policy period expired, so long as the claim was based on conduct by the insured that occurred while the policy was in effect and the statute of limitations did not bar the claim.

The second thrust allowed health care providers to create captive insurance companies supported by some form of catastrophic injury fund ("cat fund"). The cat fund effectively spread the risk of large verdicts to all health care providers, who in turn could pass the costs to the health care consumer.

The third thrust established arbitration or screening panels as a prerequisite to the court action. It was hoped that these panels would allow a fast assessment of the merit of claims.

The reforms of the seventies were followed by a period of calm. In the late 1980s, however, insurance issues once again prompted panic. This time it was the cost of insurance rather than its availability that claimed the attention of reformers. Proponents of tort reform cited the high cost of medical malpractice insurance to support their contention that the tort system could not properly handle medical negligence claims. They contended that the system adversely affected the availability of medical services needed by the public and discouraged the practice of medicine in accordance with sound medical standards. Based on the premise that too many medical malpractice claims were being filled and that the size of the awards made in these cases was often too large, the trend of legislative reform in the 1980s was to place caps on damage awards and adopt a presuit requirement that plaintiff's lawyers assure the court that there was merit to the claim before any action could be filed.

Judging from the avalanche of responsive legislation, an overwhelming consensus has developed that the medical malpractice crisis is real. Neverthe-less, in light of the scant empirical evidence, the seriousness of such a crisis still warrants examination. The courts in Rhode Island, for example, have questioned its existence[87] and, in its absence, have declared their medical malpractice provisions unconstitutional. At present they are the only courts to invalidate these reform statutes on the basis that there is insufficient evi-dence of a crisis. But the issue of whether courts and legislatures are reacting rationally to clear and objective evidence or are yielding to the scare tactics of the powerful insurance lobby remains.

In *Medical Malpractice on Trial*, which reviews empirical studies of medical malpractice,[88] Paul C. Weiler summarizes the medical community's criticisms of the legal system's treatment of medical malpractice claims:

> [T]ort costs have soared because patient attorneys seeking hefty contingent fees are filing far too many spurious allegations of medical negligence, and because unsophisticated juries, moved by the plight of often seriously disabled plaintiffs, too often give in to the temptation to use the doctor's insurer to award huge dam-age sums as redress for the patient's needs, irrespective of whether there is any tangible evidence of fault on the part of the doctor.[89]

Weiler contends, however, that this indictment of the tort system is based largely on myth rather than fact: "[I]t is wrong to charge the tort system with inflating the true incidence of medical negligence. In fact the contrary is true: there is a large gap between the number of tort events taking place inside hospitals and the number that eventually filter into the court system."[90]

In support of his position Weiler cites several extensive studies. Each used essentially the same methodology: a careful review of the medical records of hospitalized patients (who make up the vast majority of patients with any kind of significant injury). The first study, done in California in the mid-1970s, examined the records of roughly twenty thousand patients. It was discov-ered that 1 in 22 of these patients suffered a disabling iatrogenic (treatment-generated) injury from hospitalization; of these injuries, 1 in 6 was caused by careless treatment as judged by the reviewing doctors. When these injury estimates were compared with another data set of closed malpractice claims reported to the National Association of Insurance Commissioners, rough cal-culations indicated that only 1 tort claim was actually filed for 10 such events, and only 1 in 25 was actually paid.

The California study was replicated in New York state in the late 1980s:

> . . . Our results showed a somewhat lower rate of patient injuries than in Califor-nia (roughly 1 in 27 hospitalizations) but a much higher proportion of injuries due to negligence (slightly more than 1 in 4) and a bottom line estimate that 1 negligent

adverse event (1 "tort") occurred for every 100 patients hospitalized. Extrapolating our New York population estimates to the nation as a whole implies that every year there are more than 150,000 fatalities and 30,000 serious disabilities precipitated by medical treatment in this country [91]

In the light of these conflicting claims, it may be helpful to consider the following problem.

■ **Problem:** *Typical Reform Statute*

A prominent legislator has proposed the following statute:

Whereas the tort system has adversely impacted on the accessibility and quality of medical services available to the public, the following statute is hereby enacted to promote the health and welfare of our citizens:

No tort claim may be filed against any health care provider seeking compensation for injuries arising out of medical care provided to the claimant unless the claimant has first obtained an expert opinion from a qualified expert that the health care provider named as a defendant deviated from the standard of care required of him and that such deviation was the cause in fact of the injuries for which the claimant seeks compensation. In addition, the claimant's attorney must certify his good-faith belief that the claim is meritorious. To qualify as an expert, a person must have practiced within the same field of medicine in this same or a similar community as the defendant for three years before and three years following the time that the alleged negligent medical care was rendered. If a claimant or her attorney files a claim in violation of the requirements of this act, the claimant or her attorney, in the discretion of the court, shall be liable for all losses sustained by the health care provider who was improperly sued, including attorney's fees and costs incurred in defending the action, as well as economic losses sustained by the health care provider.

No claim may be filed in court unless it has been considered by an arbitration panel composed of one health care provider, one attorney, and one member of the public who is neither an attorney nor a health care provider. Either party may appeal de novo from the findings of the arbitration panel, but the findings of the panel shall be admissible evidence in the court action.

If the claimant prevails on her liability claim, no award may be made for pain and suffering and other noneconomic losses in an amount in excess of $100,000; and the total award may not exceed $500,000 per person or $1,000,000 in the aggregate for each occurrence.

Attorneys may represent claimants on a contingent fee basis, but any contingent fee in excess of 25 percent of the claimant's gross recovery shall be deemed void as violative of public policy.

The statute of limitations for medical malpractice claims is one year. No action shall be brought more than two years after the cause of action arose; provided, however, that if the claimant can prove with clear and convincing evidence that the claim was not brought in a timely manner because the health care provider against whom the suit is brought fraudulently concealed the existence of the cause of action, the action may be brought within one year of the date that the victim or her representative discovered, or should have discovered, the fraudulent concealment.

If we assume that the basic goals of tort law are corrective justice, deterrence of negligent conduct, and administrative efficiency in resolving tort claims, what arguments may be made to support this statute? To oppose it? What justifies limiting the statute to medical malpractice claims? Is the scheme embodied in the statute fair? Should the statute withstand constitutional challenge? Does it make a difference whether this is a state statute or a federal statute?

The statute set forth in this problem reflects a conglomeration of the most popular tort reforms adopted in a piecemeal fashion by various states during the past two decades. Putting all these reforms into one statute allows some important observations that apply generally to the trend of medical malpractice tort reform statutes.

First, the injured patient must certify the merit of her claim, but the health care provider need not certify a good-faith belief in his defense. The criteria for qualifying as an expert witness significantly narrow the range of competent persons who will be willing to testify against their colleagues in a professional negligence case. Such a narrowing will have a negligible effect on the health care provider as a defendant because he will experience little difficulty in obtaining the services of a colleague in the same community to defend his conduct. Caps are placed on potential damage awards, but no corresponding floors are established to ensure that a plaintiff who proves her case receives adequate compensation. The plaintiff's attorneys' fees are limited, while the defendant remains free to spend as much as he or his insurer sees fit to defend the case. One may reasonably predict that this measure provides health care providers with a substantial litigation advantage to add to their existing advantage in access to expertise and money. The arbitration panel screening process exacerbates the defendant's resource advantage by requiring that the plaintiff try her case twice, if she wishes to have a jury resolve the issue of fact. Finally, the statute of limitations is revised to provide the health care provider with additional protection against stale claims, but no protection is given to minors or incompetents who depend on the judgment of others to protect their rights; nor is any protection offered to the unfortunate victim of malpractice who through no fault of her own discovers after two years that someone left a foreign object in her body or injured her in another way that took time to manifest itself.

This review is intended to suggest that, in the interests of assuaging the very real fears of the medical and insurance communities, legislatures have overreacted. The result has been a series of one-sided reforms based on insufficient evidence of the crisis that they are supposed to address. At the least, lawmakers should pause and gather more complete factual information before adopting particular reforms. Ultimately, the question of fairness and justice will revisit the legislature by way of issues raised in the media or the courts. Consequently, both courts and legislators will benefit from a critical analysis of the rationale and justifications for these popular tort reforms.

As Weiler points out, the reforms that have been instituted by state legislatures since the early 1970s rest on perceptions not supported by empirical data. The reforms clearly promote the value preferences of the reformers to reduce the number of malpractice claims and lower the awards in those where the patient prevails. The reforms do not, however, address the need to deter substandard medical practice. Indeed, the reforms, standing alone, undermine the goal of identifying and deterring conduct engaged in by health care providers that exposes patients to undue and unreasonable risks of harm.

The Need for Rational Tort Reform

If corrective justice and deterrence remain goals of the litigation process, then empirical studies, case studies, and critical analysis of alternative dispute resolution and compensation systems must be undertaken. The insights gained from such studies should enable lawmakers to develop tort reform that is fair and more efficient than the one-sided, piecemeal reforms that have carried the day during the past two decades.

One's view of the tort system—as a major contributor to the medical malpractice problem or as an important solution to the problem—depends on one's perspective. Individuals not only see the world of medical practice and legal processes differently, but their personal experiences also produce strongly held views fanned by powerful emotions. Insurers, doctors, nurses, hospital administrators, plaintiffs' lawyers, and defendants' lawyers have vested interests in maintaining or changing the tort system. Each group seeks to enact its view as the law of the land through the use of political and economic muscle as well as intellectual persuasion. Lawmakers—legislators and judges—seeking to promote the public interest must demand more of the proponents and opponents of tort reform than bald assertions and political pressure.

The extensive studies of medical records of hospitalized patients in the 1970s and 1980s provided surprising answers to the question of whether there were too many medical malpractice claims filed in a tort system that allows compensation based only on proof of negligence. The answer was that many more negligent acts occur in medical practice than ever give rise to lawsuits. Rather than continuing a debate marked by much heat and little light, we need answers to the following factual questions: Does the existing tort system cause health care providers to take safety measures they would not otherwise take? If so, is this good or bad? To what extent do juries or judges award damages that are excessive or inadequate? Do arbitration panels do a better job than juries or judges in assessing fault and awarding damages? Does the contingent fee system promote or retard effective evaluation and representation of injured consumers? Are plaintiffs' attorneys overcompensated or undercompensated by contingent fee arrangements that range from one-third to one-half of the gross recovery? What effect would a limitation of attorney's fees for defendants have on the litigation process? What effect would an award of attorneys' fees to the prevailing party have on meaningful access to the judicial system by patients or health care providers? What effect do caps on noneconomic losses or total awards have on the goal of fair and adequate compensation to victims of medical negligence? Is the tort system a major contributor to inadequate access to medical care on the part of any segment of the community? Is peer review, when undertaken in good faith, an effective deterrent to bad medical practice?

Answers to these questions are so critical to rational policy making that lawmakers should insist that proponents and opponents of tort reform come forward with relevant data. The need for a moratorium on the enactment of piecemeal reforms based on inadequate information is further demonstrated by a review of seminal cases decided under the common law system and judicial responses to the reform of medical malpractice law in the seventies and eighties. Chapters 1–5 describe and analyze many of the cases that developed standards of liability applied today in medical malpractice cases. Chapters 7–8 explore leading cases on damage awards. What gets lost in these chapters, however, and in the tort reform debate generally, is the concrete impact of the existing system or proposed alternative systems on individual human beings who deliver or receive care that produces devastating injuries. Attorneys who represent health care providers or injured patients or their family members appreciate the profound impact that bad results of the health care system have on all the participants.

In an age dominated by impersonal medical care, patients and their families demand honest evaluations of the causes of bad results. That is not to say that personal liability is necessary. Rather, patients require a satisfactory explanation as to why and how tragic results occur. The process of demanding, exploring, and receiving a credible explanation not only allows the affected parties to understand what has happened, but also serves in many instances as a key to the painful process of adjusting to the reality of the present situation. The same is true for many health care providers.

When legislators consider radically altering the common law system to protect health care providers from liability or to make them strictly liable, the following considerations are worth pondering. First, what impact will tort reform have on the educational and law-reform functions currently served by the common law system? Some important cases have raised this concern to national prominence. The court's ruling in *Canterbury v. Spence*,[92] for example, that a patient's right to determine what happens to her body entitles her to participate in the medical decision as to what therapy will be rendered, provoked a healthy and enlightening debate over the duty of doctors to obtain an informed consent from their patients. *Darling v. Charleston Community Memorial Hospital*[93] prompted fundamental rethinking about the responsibility of a hospital for patient care. *Wickline v. State of California*[94] opened a discussion regarding the relative responsibilities of HMOs and other insurers for the quality of care rendered to their insured. Will such cases be eliminated by proposed tort reforms that seek to deter the filing of purportedly frivolous and unjustified lawsuits?

Second, do one-sided reform statutes serve the public interest? We are all potential beneficiaries and victims of the health care system. There are good doctors and bad doctors, miraculous procedures and tragic procedures. The case of Dr. John G. Nork, a California surgeon who, according to lawsuits, victimized hundreds of people through negligently performed back surgery,[95] should cause us to critically assess the impact of shielding health care providers from the tort system without first putting in place an effective system that allows the public to scrutinize the conduct of health care providers.[96]

The need for serious reflection by legislators on these questions is underlined by an appreciation of the role played by courts in reviewing tort reform legislation. The federal courts have taken a hands-off approach to tort reform. The state courts, with notable exceptions, have done the same, almost completely deferring to the legislatures in their legislative tort reform activities in the 1980s.[97]

No person has a vested interest that precludes a state from changing a particular rule of the common law governing tort liability. So declared the U.S. Supreme Court in *New York Central Ry. Co. v. White*,[98] when it rebuffed an employer's argument that a worker's compensation statute deprived employers of due process of law. The employer argued that the statute was unconstitutional because it subjected an employer to liability for a worker's injuries without requiring proof that the employer was negligent. In rejecting the argument, the Supreme Court reasoned that there was a rational basis for the legislature to conclude that the no-fault system embodied in the new statute promoted the public welfare by providing workers with a more certain and efficient method of recovering for injuries sustained on the job, thus placing more of the inherent risks of the workplace on the employer.

The Court observed that the statute gave and took away rights from both sides. The employee lost the right to sue for full recovery of the damages allowed by the common law. In exchange for no-fault recovery, the employee could no longer recover for pain and suffering and could recover for only a portion of his economic losses. The employer lost the ability to assert defenses based on the employee's negligence, assumption of risk, or negligent conduct of a fellow employee. At the same time, the employer gained protection from huge damage awards.

A few years before, on the other hand, a New York state court in *Ives v. South Buffalo Ry. Co.* [99] had found an earlier version of the worker's compensation statute violative of the due process clause of the state constitution. The New York court believed that holding the employer liable without proof of fault took property from the employer without due process of law. The court concluded that the no-fault scheme could not be justified on the basis of the state's power to promote the health, safety, and welfare of the community because there was no rational connection between promotion of such interests and the selected no-fault scheme. Today, of course, the New York court's decision seems peculiar; we are accustomed to paying workers for on-the-job injuries based on state worker's compensation statutes and to holding manufacturers strictly liable not only for their workers' injuries but for injuries suffered by consumers due to defects in products.

Interestingly, legal historians tell us that it was not until the mid-nineteenth century that American courts required proof of fault before a plaintiff could recover for a personal injury caused by the conduct of another. Before that time a person was held responsible for injuries that he caused even if he was not negligent. Within a half-century, however, American courts became so accustomed to viewing tort law from a fault perspective that a no-fault scheme appeared not only radical but unconstitutional. The New York court that decided *Ives v. South Buffalo Ry. Co.* in 1911 and the state legislature that passed the first worker's compensation statute obviously held fundamentally different values. The legislature valued highly a worker's health and well-being; the court valued highly an employer's right to maintain the wealth he had acquired through legitimate capitalistic enterprise. The views of the court carried the day, temporarily, because it interpreted the state constitution as embodying its own value preferences. Subsequently, the New York state constitution was amended to allow for a no-fault worker's compensation statute, and the U.S. Supreme Court did not find that the U.S. Constitution protected an employer's wealth from such a compensation scheme.

Today we are witnessing a similar struggle over values among the state courts and legislatures with respect to medical malpractice litigation. Most state courts, however, now give great deference to the power of the legislature to create new schemes for handling tort compensation. Using a rational basis standard, most courts have upheld pretrial screening panels, limitations on plaintiff's attorney fees, caps on awards, and shortened statutes of limitations to promote community health, safety, and welfare. Nevertheless, there are notable exceptions to this trend, usually based on the reading of specific provisions of a particular state's constitution. For example, courts have held that pretrial screening procedures violate a constitutional requirement of separation of powers, that delays in processing claims through the arbitration process violate a claimant's right to a day in court, that selecting only medical malpractice claims for tort reform violates the equal protection clause, and that caps on awards violate the right to a jury trial. As we have seen, most medical malpractice tort reform to date has been one-sided, giving health care providers protection from tort claims without addressing the problem of malpractice itself and without considering the problems that plaintiffs confront in prosecuting meritorious claims. Florida stands as a significant exception to this trend. While conforming to the tendency of revising tort law to protect physicians from perceived injustices, Florida addressed the problem of malpractice itself by requiring health care providers and institutions to set up risk management programs that will ferret out doctors and nurses who are shown to engage in repeated acts of substandard medical care.

The goal of identifying repeat offenders has also been pursued by the federal government through provisions in the Health Care Quality Improvement Act of 1986.[100] That statute establishes a national data bank in which health care providers must file reports of malpractice claims that have resulted in payment to the claimant or discipline to the health care provider. The main goal of the statute is to prevent doctors and nurses from fleeing the jurisdiction in which they were disciplined and starting anew in another jurisdiction without disclosing their past problems. It is hoped that legislators will continue to consider measures that may protect the public from unnecessary exposure to health care providers who demonstrate that they fail to possess or employ the degree of knowledge or skill required of them.

In addition, legislators need to consider the needless barriers that exist to a patient's presenting a meritorious claim, including the difficulty of finding experts willing to testify as to the required standard of care, delays in the litigation process, and the tremendous cost of prosecuting a meritorious claim to final judgment. One relatively simple reform that could be implemented is to allow experts to testify to the standard of care required to diagnose or treat certain conditions without being required to express an opinion that the defendant physician or nurse deviated from the standard. Plaintiff can prove deviation from the standard without having the expert express such an opinion. The value of the modification would be that the expert would be able to perform her more customary role of analyzing and describing medical standards rather than condemning the conduct of a colleague in a direct, pointed, and antagonistic manner.

I am not attempting here to outline a statute for tort reform to benefit patients. Rather, the point is that tort reform should aim at revising the system to promote the public interest. And surely, the public interest includes protecting the rights of patients who have suffered injury at the hands of health care professionals. Such patients are at a decided disadvantage under the present system.

The Role of Ethics

Neither health care reform nor tort reform can achieve its goals if the members of the respective professions do not adhere to high ethical standards, placing the interest of patient and client above the economic gain to be derived by the professional. Because they possess specialized skill and knowledge and perform most of their work outside the public eye, health care providers and lawyers have a unique ability to engage in unethical conduct that cannot be detected. They also possess a level of knowledge, power, and wealth that allows them to manipulate whatever system is created so that it serves their ends. The same may be said of ethical drug manufacturers. Changing the system without gaining the commitment of such key decision-makers to the fundamental goals of the system is an inept approach to reform. The more one reflects on the social and economic roles of health care providers and lawyers, the more apparent this becomes.

From a social and economic perspective, health care providers (especially doctors) and lawyers have more in common than they care to admit. Socially, each is the object of the public's love and hatred. They are loved because, when they perform their jobs well, they bestow tremendous benefits on consumers. They are hated because catastrophic consequences sometimes flow from their services, and it is difficult for the public to assess blame. Again, drug manufacturers fit the bill. The hallmark of the consumer's relationship with health care providers, lawyers, and drug companies is the consumer's dependency. While informed consent plays an important role, it can never obviate the need for a deep level of trust. Thus, when bad results follow the professional's service, it should not be surprising that frustration often sets in. When the disappointed consumer decides to evaluate the professional's conduct of the professional, he quickly learns that he must rely on another member of the professional's club to provide the assessment. This often increases the consumer's frustration and breeds cynicism and distrust of the legal system.

Economic considerations add fuel to the fire. In the eyes of most of the public, health care providers and lawyers make a lot of money. For this they are admired by some and despised by others. The public finds it difficult to judge whether the professional makes too much money in general or has charged too much for a particular service. The impersonality of many relationships nourishes skepticism and distrust.

For their part, health care providers and lawyers are often shocked when they obtain a license to "practice a profession" and discover that, in addition, they must "run a business." Many health care providers and lawyers lack the training, skills, and temperament to do so. In one sense, practicing law or medicine presents the professional with a unique opportunity to make money in that, unlike most business people, doctors and lawyers are well situated to persuade the potential consumer not only that she needs to buy the service offered, but also how much of that service is good for her. For example, the more patients who can be persuaded that they need to have cataracts removed, the more money the eye doctor can make. Similarly, persuading more clients that they have good negligence claims or defenses generates more litigation and more money for medical malpractice attorneys.

Without a strong sense of professional ethics, the goal of running a successful business could easily dominate the goal of practicing a profession in accordance with high ethical standards. Moreover, as economic competition intensifies, it becomes more difficult to allow ethics to constrain the business instinct. Witness the problems currently faced by health care providers who must respond to the cost-containment policies of third party payers (see Chapter 5). The situation is probably even more frustrating to health care providers and lawyers who choose—as most do today—to practice as employees rather than as entrepreneurs. As an employee, the professional must balance a desire to make a good salary, the employer's desire to make a profit, and the consumer's right to competent and ethical professional services—a significant challenge.

Facing the reality that profit-making opportunities frequently clash with ethical obligations compels an exploration of how well the professions are preparing their members to resolve these clashes and how effective ethical

standards will be in enabling professionals to serve the consumer in a reformed health care or tort system. In connection with the reform of the
medical malpractice system, we must consider how attorneys for plaintiffs
and defendants get medical malpractice business; assess the merits of claims
and defenses before and after filing suit; decide when to continue the
fight and when to quit; go about resolving claims without initiating litigation or without going to verdict. Can the approaches to these tasks be improved to better serve consumers and adhere to higher ethical standards?
These and many other ethical questions important to the tort reform debate
need to be explored in depth. In an effort to contribute to that exploration,
I have included in the Appendix a series of problems raising ethical issues
relevant to medical malpractice litigation. I believe that examination of ethical issues may prove to be of tremendous value to all who are genuinely
committed to tort reform in the public interest.

Part II

*Assessing and
Proving Damages*

Chapter 7

Assessing and Proving Compensatory Damages

■

Predicting the potential damage award in a medical malpractice case is a hazardous business. Indeed, much of the process is subjective. The goal of this chapter is to identify the multitude of considerations that influence the presentation of the case on damages and the ultimate verdict.

Counsel for each party in a medical malpractice case should evaluate the potential damage award from at least two different perspectives: first, what award will the law permit in light of the evidence? And second, what award is likely to be made in light of the law, the evidence, and the dominant psychological and emotional factors bearing on the case? The following problem illustrates the importance of asking both questions.

■ **Problem:** *Valuing a "Personal Injury"*

Joe Jenks is paralyzed from the waist down as a result of negligently performed surgery on his back. At the time of the surgery he was thirty years of age and employed as a forklift operator for Wheeling Manufacturing Co. He graduated from high school at age eighteen, spent two years in the army (receiving an honorable discharge), and immediately after discharge went to work for Wheeling. Before the surgery he was in good health, except for chronic back pain that plagued him for six months after he fell while playing basketball. He earned $30,000 as a forklift operator in the year before the accident. In addition, that same year he earned $20,000 moonlighting as a security guard on evenings and weekends. He has never been married and lives alone.

He was a below-average student in high school, graduating at the bottom of his class. He was, however, a well-liked and ambitious young man who had a strong aptitude for mechanics. His paralysis is permanent.

Jenks has filed suit against his orthopedic surgeon, alleging that the surgery was negligently performed and that he was not adequately informed of the risks of the surgery. If a jury decides the case in favor of Jenks, what is the likely award? How much is the case worth if it is settled without a lawsuit? How much is the case worth if it is settled after commencement of a lawsuit but before substantial discovery? How much is the case worth if it is settled on the day of trial when the parties are ready to pick a jury?

What additional information would you want before placing a value on the case?

Basic Considerations in Assessing Damages

For plaintiff's counsel, assessing and preparing for proof of damages begins with the initial interview with the client. The cost of evaluating and litigating medical malpractice cases compels plaintiffs' attorneys to reject some meritorious cases because the money that could be recovered does not justify the cost of the suit or the risk of losing. Assessing the merits of any case usually costs at least $2,000 (as of 1991), and most cases will require an expenditure of $5,000 to $10,000 before counsel can be sure that the case is meritorious. If the case goes to trial, costs may exceed $50,000, and expenditures of $75,000 or more are not extraordinary.

Since most personal injury victims cannot afford to pay an attorney's hourly fees, legal representation is almost always provided on a contingent fee basis. This means that the plaintiff's attorney will be paid only if he wins the case at trial or settles it. Consequently, it is critical from a business standpoint that he evaluate not only the likelihood of winning the case but also the probable size of the verdict or settlement.

The elements of damage recoverable in most medical malpractice cases are the same as those recoverable in any personal injury action. The plaintiff may recover for past and future medical expenses, diminution in earning capacity, pain and suffering, emotional distress, and, in appropriate cases, punitive damages (see Chapter 9). In reality, however, the medical features of the case may substantially influence the size of a verdict. Even if jury members believe that the physician or nurse made a mistake, his professional aura may convince them that he should not be stigmatized for it, and they may return a small verdict or a defense verdict.[1] On the other hand, if they believe that the physician has betrayed the trust the patient and the public have placed in him, their sympathy for the patient may lead them to render a large award.

If the defendant is a hospital or a drug company, the common wisdom is that the jury is likely to be more sympathetic to the plaintiff because the defendant is an institution rather than an individual. They may feel that an institutional defendant places more weight on financial costs than on human costs. Indeed, a narrow cost-benefit analysis may lead a defendant to believe that it can draw on its resources of lawyers and experts to overwhelm the individual plaintiff. It is important that defendant's counsel avoid any hint of complacency or arrogance. If jury members sense that the defense is trivializing (as opposed to minimizing) the injuries, their sympathies will almost certainly swing to the plaintiff.

In short, it is a mistake to assume that the value of the medical malpractice case correlates with the proof the plaintiff can muster as to such economic losses as medical expenses and lost wages. In any case that involves the projection of future losses over a period of many years, expert testimony will vary widely as to the dollar amount needed to compensate even these concrete losses. Intangible losses like pain and suffering are necessarily subjective, and the compensation that a jury may deem appropriate will depend on empathy. The pain and suffering of an attractive plaintiff is undoubtedly worth more in the courtroom than the pain and suffering of a mean or obnoxious person. Moreover, a life may be valued by a jury in pure economic terms or in emotional or philosophical terms, depending on the nature of the case and the profile of the plaintiff or her family. For example, a report in the *National Law Journal* in September 1992 was entitled, "Juries Place Less Value on Homemakers."[2] The report stated: "The conventional wisdom is that 'about the top for your typical housewife is $450,000.'. . . It is a ceiling plaintiffs' lawyers don't dispute, although they prefer to emphasize the exceptions."[3]

Similarly, the size of a punitive damage award will depend on whether the jury believes that the defendant deserves to experience serious discomfort. A sympathetic defendant is less likely to be penalized than one who seems arrogant or incompetent. Large verdicts follow proof of large economic losses only in cases where the juries are willing to believe the evidence. It is foolhardy to evaluate a medical malpractice case without taking this reality into account.

The jury's perspective is not the only pivotal factor. The trial judge also plays a crucial role. Proof of intangible injuries such as pain and suffering, mental distress, or loss of ability to enjoy life requires the trial judge to make many rulings as to the admissibility of different types of evidence and the permissibility of various arguments. For example, a trial court's ruling on the admissibility of a film showing a typical day in the plaintiff's life (discussed later in this chapter) will be reversed only if there is proof of a manifest abuse of discretion. In addition, the extent to which plaintiff's counsel may assist the jury in arriving at a monetary figure to compensate the plaintiff for intangible losses will be determined both by the attitude of the court in exercising discretion on evidentiary questions and arguments and by the jurisdiction's legal rules governing arguments suggesting specific sums for pain and suffering or sums based on units of time such as a minute, an hour, or a day.

Moreover, since the early 1970s state legislatures have enacted reform statutes that have changed some of the basic legal rules governing the measurement of damages (see Chapter 6). Consequently, damage assessments may vary significantly from state to state. The jurisdiction's approach to the following issues has a substantial effect on the potential size of the damage award:

Is there a statutory ceiling on awards for losses in earning capacity, medical expenses, or pain and suffering?

What approach does the jurisdiction take to the impact of inflation on future losses?

Has the collateral source rule been changed?

What arguments are permissible on the measurement of pain and suffering, and what is the proper jury instruction?

In a death case does the jurisdiction allow for awards to compensate for both pecuniary and nonpecuniary losses?

Are punitive damages permissible? If so, what proof is required regarding the conduct, and how are the damages measured?

From a psychological perspective, the most influential consideration in the jury's assessment of damages may be the credibility of the evidence of plaintiff's present injuries and the probable effect that these injuries will have on him in the future. Important aspects affecting credibility include whether the plaintiff's damage experts are believable and whether plaintiff's counsel can make effective use of demonstrative evidence such as day-in-the-life films. A threshold consideration is whether the jury is likely to be receptive to or skeptical of the plaintiff's damage claim. The answer is influenced by the makeup of the jury, the evidence, and the attitude of the court, all of which are in turn affected by the social-economic values prevalent in the community in which the case is being tried.

The Goals of Damage Awards

The principal goal of a damage award in a negligence case is to return the victim to the economic position she enjoyed before the tort. Courts recognize that there are some losses that can be measured precisely in terms of money, some that permit a rough estimate, and some that are not susceptible to measurement at all. When losses are difficult to measure, a policy judgment must be made as to whether to allow *any* award for the loss in light of the difficulty of assessing it in monetary terms.

Tort law has offered different answers to claims for compensation of losses that are difficult to measure. The inconsistencies can sometimes be reconciled by looking at whether the injury is serious and the causal connection between the tortious conduct and the injury clear; in such cases the courts try to provide a theoretical tool for the jury members to use as they apply their common sense to the task of determining a monetary award. Doubts about either the seriousness of the injury or the causal connection usually prompt the court to reject the claim. This trend in the law governing damage awards in tort cases is probably explained by the secondary goal of tort damage awards: deterrence. If the plaintiff's injuries were caused by negligence, the court is motivated to allow for compensation not only to make the plaintiff whole but also to deter others from repeating such tortious conduct. If the injury is not serious or the causal connection doubtful, courts usually decline to spend their own or the jury's time on wrestling with thorny issues of compensation measurement.

Each medical malpractice case should be evaluated with these general goals and trends in mind. The specific rules governing the measurement and award of damages should always be critically assessed in light of these goals, because few courts or juries will be willing to apply the specific damage rules mechanically if it seems to serve no purpose in the case at hand.

Legally Cognizable Losses

In most jurisdictions the law allows specific elements of damage. These damages can be itemized as follows:

Physical Injuries
   Past loss of earning capacity
   Future loss of earning capacity
   Medical care expenses
        Physicians
        Hospitals
        Physical therapists
        Nursing care
        Supportive equipment
        Pharmaceuticals
   Physical pain and suffering
   Mental pain and suffering
   Disfigurement
   Loss of ability to enjoy life
   Curtailment of life expectancy

Mental Distress
   Past loss of earning capacity
   Future loss of earning capacity

Medical care expenses
    Psychologists or psychiatrists
    Hospitals
    Pharmaceuticals
Harm to relationships
Loss of ability to enjoy life
Fear of future injury

Loss of Consortium
Spouse's loss of affection and sexual relationship
Children's or sibling's loss of affection

Death Cases
Decedent's losses
    Future earning capacity (less personal and family maintenance expenses)
    Funeral expenses
    Medical expenses
    Pain and suffering
Family members' losses
    Financial contributions of decedent to family
    Services   •
    Society
    Sorrow (available in a few jurisdictions)

Wrongful Birth (parents' damages)
Birth expenses
Medical care expenses
Education expenses
Mental distress
Diminution of earning capacity

Wrongful Life (child's damages)
Education expenses
Medical care expenses
Mental distress
Pain and suffering

A preliminary assessment of the potential for a large verdict can usually be reached by looking at whether the plaintiff has credible evidence of a substantial loss in one of these categories, a loss that the jurisdiction acknowledges to be legally cognizable. To do this, however, an early determination must be made as to which jurisdiction's law is likely to govern the assessment of damages. Comparing the plaintiff's profile before and after the injury in light of the specific elements of legally cognizable losses will produce a rough sketch of the potential damage verdict. This sketch can then be refined by taking into account, among other things, the profile of the judge assigned to the case and the profile of the potential jury, in addition to the considerations discussed in the rest of this chapter.

Serious Physical Injuries

In a personal injury case a serious physical injury is one that severely diminishes a person's ability to engage in an activity for a substantial period of time, adversely affects her physical appearance, or substantially impairs her emotional health. Such an injury is usually accompanied by credible evidence of mental or physical pain and suffering. A plaintiff's lawyer who undertakes a medical malpractice case on the hope that he can trick a jury into thinking an injury is serious when it is not is flirting with economic and professional disaster.

The challenge is to measure the injury in monetary terms. Some components of the injury are easy to measure; others prove close to impossible. Measuring medical expenses already incurred, for example, is simply a matter of assembling the evidence of expenses and proving the reasonableness of the costs and the propriety of the care. Assessing future medical expenses is more difficult. First, the contingencies surrounding future care are likely to provoke differences of professional opinion both about whether a particular kind of treatment will be required and about how much it will cost. The law does not require proof to a reasonable medical certainty that each item of future medical care will be incurred. Rather, a plaintiff is entitled to compensation for all future medical expenses that she will probably incur.[4] Most serious injuries, for example, eventually force the caretaker to choose between institutional care or home nursing care. Home care is usually much more expensive than institutional care, but family members who are responsible for victims often prefer it, provided it is affordable. Jurors ordinarily understand this choice, and both sides are well advised to assess the credibility of their positions before deciding whether to argue that either home care or institutional care is appropriate for the injured plaintiff.

The same credibility question must be considered when claiming loss of income. The law measures this loss in terms of diminution in earning capacity.[5] A person need not have been actually earning wages at the time that the injury occurred in order to recover for diminution in earning capacity. Children, students, unemployed workers, and homemakers have a capacity to earn substantial income in the future even if they have elected or been forced to forgo earning wages at a given point in time.[6] The determinative question is how much money the individual would have been capable of earning on the market, in light of her education, experience, training, intelligence, and personality.

Again, counsel must carefully assess the credibility of this damage claim from a juror's perspective. The profile of the plaintiff as she existed before the injury is particularly important. Plaintiff's counsel should avoid presenting exaggerated claims of earning capacity that offend the jurors' common sense. And if the claims are exaggerated, defense counsel should not pass up the opportunity to point it out to the jury. The plaintiff's case will lose a great deal of its credibility if the plaintiff's counsel attempts to create a person who never existed. Similarly, defense counsel should avoid a nitpicking cross-examination of the plaintiff or her expert on the loss-of-income claim if her injuries are serious and the evidence of her future earning capacity is reasonable. Otherwise, defense counsel risks angering the jurors and inducing them to give the plaintiff more benefit of the doubt than they might otherwise be inclined to do.

The jurors' attitude toward the damage evidence is perhaps more important in a medical malpractice case than in the average personal injury case because the sums being talked about are likely to astound the jury, at least initially. Most people are neither educated nor experienced in assessing the costs of long-term medical care, nor are they aware of how much money the average worker earns over her lifetime. A personal injury lump-sum verdict demands long-term thinking and detailed analysis, possibly including such complex economic and financial issues as the likely rate of inflation and the reduction of money to present value. A juror can reject the challenge of dealing with such abstractions because he believes that the plaintiff or her claim lacks credibility, or he can become engaged in a painstaking, detailed assessment of the claim and its monetary value.

If the jurors' attitude toward evidence of economic losses is critical, their feelings about intangible damages such as pain and suffering, loss of ability to engage in activities, mental suffering, loss of consortium, and loss of ability to enjoy life are determinative. Jurors will either believe that these injuries are real and warrant monetary compensation or they will not. Plaintiff's counsel and witnesses must help the jurors empathize with the plaintiff and measure the plaintiff's noneconomic losses in monetary terms. Two common techniques for proving and measuring noneconomic losses are the "day in the life" film and the per diem argument on pain and suffering. As discussed below, plaintiff's counsel should make full use of these techniques, while defense counsel should attempt to limit their use on the basis of undue prejudice.

In addition, defense counsel must gingerly, and in most cases gently, bring to the jurors' attention unattractive features of the plaintiff that might otherwise be missed. At the same time, defense counsel should attempt to present a picture of the defendant doctor or nurse as a caring human being who works hard for a living and has family and friends who will be affected by the outcome of this litigation. Since the plaintiff or her family will be primarily in the spotlight, however, we turn to approaches to painting their portrait.

Portrait of the Plaintiff

Since a courtroom atmosphere is unique and often stilted, considerable thought must be given to how to present a meaningful portrait of the plaintiff, both in person and through her own words and the words of family members, friends, and associates. The portratal of the plaintiff as she was before the accident may be based on a variety of evidence, much of which is tangible and objective. Counsel should conduct a detailed and comprehensive investigation of the plaintiff's education, employment history, civic affiliations, hobbies, and recreational activities. Important information concerning the plaintiff's education includes degrees obtained, standardized test scores, academic awards, service awards, athletics, artistic activities, and social organizations to which she belonged. Investigation of her employment history should include her earnings history and performance reviews as well as other more personal accounts of work experience if possible. Research concerning the plaintiff's civic and social activities, recreation, and hobbies should elicit the picture that plaintiff's peers and acquaintances had of her.

The purpose of this exploration is to present to the jurors a picture of a real human being with whom they can identify. It is through this identification that the jury can come to appreciate the impact that the accident has had on the plaintiff's life. The other goal is to lay the foundation for experts to offer testimony regarding the economic losses suffered by the plaintiff as a result of the accident. Since the goal of tort law is to place the plaintiff in the position that she would have been in but for the accident, this information is critical to making an assessment of this position. Making a credible projection of what might have been is indispensable for a large personal injury verdict that is based on a goal of compensation rather than punishment.

The importance to the plaintiff's attorney of the initial client interview was emphasized and discussed in depth in Chapter 1. During this interview counsel should envision how his client is likely to appear at trial. Plaintiff's attorney must be familiar enough with his client's personal background and characteristics to make an intelligent judgment as to how to present her to the jury in light of the specific claims of damage involved in the case.

If the plaintiff is living and able to attend the trial, her appearance and behavior are crucial. The personal characteristics initially perceived by the judge and jury are age, gender, race, and general physical appearance. Counsel should carefully evaluate the relevance of these factors under a legal measurement of damages and then assess the jurors' sense of them in light of the instructions the jury will receive from the court. In addition, at the initial personal interview plaintiff's counsel should have gained valuable information about the type of presentation the plaintiff is capable of making in an unfamiliar environment where she is under stress. By the date of the trial considerable time should have been invested in improving her ability to communicate with a judge and jury. If the jury has been carefully selected and sensitized through voir dire (questions of jurors prior to their selection to serve on the case), the opening statements, and the court's instructions, the personal characteristics that will have the greatest impact on the size of the verdict will not be those that are discoverable by a visual examination of the plaintiff. Rather, they will be subjective impressions based on her interactions with other people in various environments. Characteristics such as intelligence, discipline, honesty, reliability, assertiveness, patience, tenacity, and generosity must be identified and portrayed before the jury if the personal injury verdict is to reflect the full extent of the damage caused by the negligent act. It is the responsibility of plaintiff's attorney to illustrate these characteristics for the jury.

Obviously, the effectiveness of the case presentation depends a great deal on whether counsel really knows the plaintiff. For this reason, it is important to spend some time with the plaintiff not only in counsel's office, but also in the plaintiff's home, at her job, and at a public place such as a restaurant. To portray the plaintiff effectively requires a knack for detail and a capacity to see the world through the eyes of another. The attorney can appreciate the facts about the plaintiff's life and communicate them more realistically and vividly the closer he gets to the experience.

The "Day in the Life" Film

A motion picture depicting a typical day in the plaintiff's life can be one of the most powerful forms of demonstrative evidence presented at trial. Sympathy engendered by the plaintiff's injuries is likely to fade during a long trial or after spirited jury deliberations. A plaintiff who is asking a jury to award millions of dollars for years of expected medical and nursing care and pain and suffering needs some way of making the jury appreciate the impact that the injuries and required care will have on her life. Charts and blackboard diagrams listing elements of damages are helpful only if the jury is willing to be guided by the information they contain. If the goal of the charts is to assist the jury in assessing losses, then the figures on the chart must be realistic. A significant part of the credibility of the figures depends on the persuasiveness of the plaintiff's medical and economic experts. Equally important, however, is the demonstrative evidence that allows the jury or judge to touch, feel, and experience the injuries—if only for a few moments.

To increase the probability that the film will effectively portray the plaintiff's injuries in a manner that both evokes sympathy and meets legal standards of admissibility, plaintiff's counsel should arrange for a nonlawyer as well as an attorney to attend the shooting and editing of the film. At both stages—shooting and editing—counsel should put himself in the position of the judge and ask himself whether he would admit each portion of the film if he had to rule on its admissibility. The nonlawyer should respond purely to the effectiveness of the film in educating her about the impact that the injuries have had on the plaintiff's life and in helping her empathize with the plaintiff.

In addition, because so much rides on the admissibility of the film and because it is likely to cost a minimum of five thousand dollars to make, it is important to have a skilled professional shoot the film. If a reliable and well-referenced local company is not available, it may be possible to contract with a producer or camera operator from a local television news crew to do the job on a free-lance basis or at least to suggest someone who is qualified.

Recognizing the impact that a motion picture—commonly referred to as a "day-in-the-life" film—may have on the factfinder's assessment of damages, defense counsel should ordinarily fight vigorously to prevent the admission of the film into evidence. Any objection that the film is not relevant, however, will usually be overruled by the court. Clearly, a film depicting the impact that the injury has had on the plaintiff's daily life is relevant to any damage question. On the other hand, an objection that the probative value of the film is outweighed by its prejudicial effects calls for more careful consideration by the court.

The first question the court must consider is whether the film is an accurate and objective depiction of the plaintiff's condition as it relates to her damage claim. If the answer is yes, the court must assess the probative value versus the prejudicial effects of the evidence based on the particulars in the film and the overall evidence available in the case. Obviously, resolving this question requires an exercise of discretion, and the trial court's decision cannot be reversed unless the circumstances indicate an abuse of discretion.

Both the judicial exercise of discretion and the impact of such films as evidence are well illustrated by *Roberts v. Stevens Clinic Hospital*,[7] a West Virginia case involving a wrongful death claim against a physician and hospital for allegedly performing a biopsy on a child without the parents' consent. The jury returned a verdict against both the physician and the hospital, awarding damages of $10 million. On appeal, defendants alleged, among other things, that the trial court had erred in admitting a twenty-minute, professionally prepared film that combined home-movie video recordings of the child taken by a neighbor with a series of still, colored photographs of the child as well as the mother's voice singing and talking to the child. Affirming the trial court's admission of the videotape, the appellate court stated:

> The purpose of the videotape was to demonstrate that Michael was a healthy, intelligent, enthusiastic, and well-loved child. So as a preliminary matter, the videotape was relevant. *W. Va. R. Evid. 401, 402.* In our review of the tape, we find no artistic highlighting that emphasizes some scenes or photographs more than others, and we find no merit in the defendant's assertions that because the mother's voice went on several seconds after the screen turned black, an unduly sentimental atmosphere was evoked that would have prejudiced the jury.[8]

In contrast, the court in *Bolstridge v. Central Maine Power Co.*[9] excluded the plaintiff's day-in-the-life videotape on the basis that it might distract the jury and unfairly prejudice the defendant. The court reasoned that open court testimony could demonstrate the relevant matters the plaintiff sought to prove through the film.

The cases discussing the admissibility of day-in-the-life films[10] demonstrate the importance of the trial court's attitude and philosophy to the evaluation of medical malpractice cases. The admissibility of the evidence that plaintiff must rely on to prove substantial intangible losses is almost totally dependent on the discretion of the trial court. Consequently, the size of the potential verdict is influenced significantly by the philosophy and temperament of the court.

Pain and Suffering

In many medical malpractice cases pain and suffering constitute one of the most substantial injuries that the plaintiff incurs. Since there is no market for the sale and purchase of pain and suffering, no source other than the legal process exists for determining whether the awards made for pain and suffering are reasonable or unreasonable. Since the loss is intangible and subjective, the debate as to whether tort law should continue to allow for pain and suffering compensation continues in the legislatures and in academia. Meanwhile, courts struggle to articulate proper guidelines for evidence and arguments for assessing an award. One of the most difficult aspects of evaluating the likely damage verdict in a medical malpractice case remains predicting what the court or jury is likely to award for pain and suffering.

In settlement evaluations lawyers and claims adjusters customarily put a monetary value on pain and suffering by multiplying the special damages—

medical expenses and diminution in earning capacity—by some figure ranging from 3 to 5. The product of the multiplication serves as a reference point for discussing the potential award. While acknowledging this custom, one court found the practice of assessing pain and suffering by some multiple of the special damages inexplicable—except possibly as the remnant of a belief adopted in some ancient societies that the numbers 3 and 5 have a mystical significance—and held that it should be confined to settlement discussions and not extended to the assessment of damages at trial.[11]

Another method commonly used to assess pain and suffering is to look at past verdicts in the same jurisdiction for similar injuries sustained under similar circumstances. Although helpful in drawing the contours of the potential verdict range, this approach is not likely to provide a basis for accurately predicting the pain and suffering verdict. Invariably, these past cases seem to present (or fail to present) some influential factors that distinguish them from the one being evaluated. Each human being, jury, and set of facts is in some way materially different.

Since pain and suffering awards are so difficult to predict, effective representation of the parties requires a focus on the evidence and trial techniques that may be used to influence the award. The techniques include the approach to the voir dire, jury selection, the opening statement, the presentation of evidence, and the closing argument. Because voir dire, jury selection, and the opening statement are addressed in detail in many trial books, the remainder of this section focuses on the closing argument as it relates to pain and suffering.

Most published trial court and appellate court opinions addressing the pain and suffering award begin by acknowledging that there is no specific yardstick against which to measure the permissible range of this award. Courts do, however, take positions on what counsel can say about the award. In the case of permissible coverage in closing arguments, there are three different approaches. Some jurisdictions hold that counsel may not suggest any specific sum of money as being appropriate—either in total or per diem.[12] Other jurisdictions allow counsel to suggest a sum for a total pain and suffering award but not a per diem sum.[13] Finally, some jurisdictions permit counsel to express a view as to an appropriate award for pain and suffering on a per diem or time-unit basis *and* in total.[14]

Another issue that concerns the courts is whether the plaintiff should be able to make the so-called golden rule argument to the jury. This argument asks the jury to make an award for the plaintiff's pain and suffering that the jurors would consider fair if they were in the plaintiff's shoes. Most of the reported cases addressing this issue prohibit the making of the golden rule argument. In *Henker v. Prebylowski*, [15] an intermediate appellate court in New Jersey considered and rejected the following argument made by plaintiff's counsel:

> Remember the wisdom tooth, a little canker sore in your mouth. You can't get rid of it. You may take Tylenol. Or take a fractured tooth, finger, a cut, a burn. What is the pain worth for one hour? You've gone to doctors and dentists. An anesthesiologist, you know how much he charges just to limit or prevent pain during the course of an operation. You know how much a dentist charges to give a shot of Novocain so you don't feel pain for ten, fifteen minutes. How much is that pain worth for one hour? When you get that hour, think about the thousands of hours that Ken Henker has suffered pain just the last three years. [16]

In reversing the judgment in favor of the plaintiff (the trial court attempted to save the verdict by ordering a remittitur, or reduction, from $250,000 to $45,000 for the husband and from $45,000 to $33,000 for the wife), the court reasoned first that the argument abused the permissible time-unit argument; under the rule adopted in New Jersey, counsel may argue that the award should be measured on a time-unit basis but may not suggest a specific sum of money. The principal reason for disapproving the argument, however, was what the court saw as an effort to invoke the golden rule argument. In the court's view,

> [T]here are suggestions that the members of the jury consider the few extra dollars they would be willing to spend to avoid the pain of a tooth extraction and to think what it means to suffer on a daily basis. This is a subtle appeal to the "golden rule," i.e., that the members of the jury consider what one day of pain and suffering or, conversely its avoidance, would be worth to them. [17]

The problem that both the per diem and golden rule arguments present to courts and to counsel is that if plaintiff's counsel is not permitted to make some argument to the jury on the pain and suffering claim, the jury is presented with no effective advocacy or reasoning as to how to render a monetary verdict that takes this component of the plaintiff's damages into account. On the other hand, if the court allows plaintiff's counsel to make either argument, the jury may respond with pure emotion and embrace the suggested standard as simply the best measure available. If the arguments are allowed, defense counsel must alert the jury to the danger inherent in a mechanical acceptance of either of these guides to measuring immeasurable losses; at the same time, she must exercise care that she does not inflame the jury. Sometimes the most effective response to the per diem argument is an appeal to the jurors' common sense regarding the lack of rationality of the monetary measure the plaintiff proposes. In a similar vein, an effective response to the day-in-the-life film is to acknowledge the seriousness of the plaintiff's injuries while urging the jury to fulfill its pledge to be fair to both sides by carefully weighing all the evidence offered by both parties on liability and damages and to follow the court's instructions in reaching a verdict.

The charge that the courts typically make to the jury on this issue—that the jury is to use its common sense, experience, and sense of fairness in assessing the injury based on the evidence presented—is of little assistance. Such an instruction is tantamount to the court's throwing up its hands and telling the jurors (who usually have little, if any, experience in the administration of justice), "When you reach this part of your damages assessment, do the best you can because neither the law nor counsel can offer you any guidance." Perhaps it is dissatisfaction with leaving the jury in this predicament that has persuaded many jurisdictions to approve the per diem or specific-sum argument in some form.[18] New Jersey once claimed the most influential court decision disapproving the per diem argument, but this jurisdiction now allows that argument on the basis of a rule of civil procedure.[19]

One of the most thorough and thoughtful discussions of the pros and cons of the per diem argument is presented in a California Supreme Court decision, *Beagle v. Vasold*,[20] where the majority approved that argument. In reaching its conclusion, the court seemed most influenced by its concern that prohibiting the argument kept plaintiff's counsel from being able to advocate effectively on an issue of damages that is often the most contested one in the trial. The court observed:

> Under some circumstances, the concept of pain and suffering may become more meaningful when it is measured in short periods of time than over a span of many years, perhaps into infinity. The "worth" of pain and suffering may become more meaningful when it is measured in short periods of time than over a span of many years, perhaps into infinity. The "worth" of pain over a period of decades is often more difficult to grasp as a concept of reality than is the same experience limited to a day, a week or a month. It is this very consideration which underlies much of the controversy over the issue before us. The fact that the "per diem"ARGUMENT provides a more explicit comprehension and humanization of the plaintiff's predicament to lay jurors makes this approach an effective tool in the hands of his attorney. This alone is not, however, a sufficient reason to condemn it.[21]

In contrast, Chief Justice Traynor took the view that a per diem argument was so arbitrary and prejudicial that it should never be allowed:

> It is one thing to urge that in view of all of the evidence of pain and suffering including its total duration, some specific sum or range of sums is reasonable. It is

quite another to urge the jury to use a formula such as a mill or penny per second, or penny or nickel or dime per minute, or $10 or $20 or $100 per day. None of these formulas appears unreasonable on its face, for there is no basis in human experience for testing their reasonableness. For a year of pain and suffering, however, they yield damages ranging from $3,650 to $315,360, sums that in light of all of the evidence in particular cases might appear to be grossly inadequate or grossly excessive. It is therefore unrealistic to seek an appropriate award for pain and suffering by the use of any so-called per diem formula. Only after counsel has determined how much damages for pain and suffering he is going to ask for can he select a per diem ratio to support his request. He could arrive at any amount he wished by adjusting either the period of time to be taken as a measure or the amount surmised for the pain and suffering for that period.[22]

Although to my knowledge there are no reliable empirical studies that attempt to measure the impact of the per diem argument on the size of a personal injury award, it seems clear that judges and experienced trial counsel believe that the arguments made by counsel to the jury with respect to the method of assessing damages for pain and suffering have a substantial impact on the verdicts rendered. Since medical malpractice cases are so complex and costly to try to verdict, counsel for both parties should give careful attention to the specific arguments that the jurisdiction allows counsel to make to the jury on the pain and suffering issue. Clearly, ignoring this important issue in evaluating the potential size of the verdict does a disservice to the client.

Loss of Ability to Enjoy Life

A severely injured plaintiff not only endures physical pain and suffering but also experiences severe limitations on her ability to engage in activities that she finds personally satisfying—taking long walks, coaching a kids' baseball team, singing in the church choir, and a whole range of activities that make each individual's life unique and enjoyable. Compensation for physical pain and suffering alone leaves a substantial injury uncompensated. For this reason, several courts have explicitly recognized the loss of ability to enjoy life or engage in one's customary activities as an element of damage separate from physical pain and suffering.[23] Other jurisdictions acknowledge that this aspect of a plaintiff's injuries warrants compensation but allow for compensation only as a part of physical pain and suffering or mental distress.[24] From a plaintiff's perspective, it is better to treat this injury as a separate item because it will presumably prompt the court or the jury to award a larger verdict if the damages are itemized and then added together to produce a lump-sum verdict.

A good example of the conceptual and evidentiary problems posed by a claim for loss of ability to enjoy life appears in a Maryland case, *McAlister v. Carl*,[25] where the court denied this aspect of the plaintiff's claim on the ground that it was too speculative. The plaintiff, who suffered physical injuries in an automobile accident, was advised by her physician not to pursue a career in teaching physical education, as she had planned before the accident. While the court acknowledged that a showing of an inability to engage in familiar physical activities was a legitimate damage claim in a personal injury action, in the court's view the evidence in the case before it did not establish any substantial loss of enjoyment that plaintiff would suffer as a result of having to choose another career. The court placed heavy reliance on the fact that the plaintiff was just graduating from college and had neither begun working in the physical education field nor secured a definite job offer in that field. The result in this case is consistent with the result reached in many of the older cases that deny a separate recovery for loss of ability to enjoy life but base the result on different reasoning—namely, that such a recovery is likely to duplicate the recovery awarded under the general category of pain and suffering.

Curtailment of Life Expectancy

Many injuries pose the possibility of premature death as the result of an increased risk of infection or other physical danger. The probability that one's life will be shorter because of someone else's negligence is an injury that the law of damages has tried to address in recent years. The principal argument advanced against allowing compensation for a decreased life expectancy is like the one denying recovery for loss of ability to enjoy life: that it would allow double compensation because the plaintiff would also recover for this injury as a part of the award for her diminution in earning capacity or for pain and suffering. Plaintiff's counsel needs to emphasize that, while this risk exists, it also seems clear that a shortened life expectancy has an adverse impact on an individual independent of its effect on her income-earning capacity and her pain and suffering. Though it is possible to take this injury into account in connection with emotional harm, there is a great risk from the plaintiff's point of view that it will be overlooked by the factfinder if it does not receive special emphasis.

Downie v. United States Line Co.[26] recognized curtailment of life expectancy as an independent injury provided that it was based on measurable components of injury such as the ability to swim, bowl, or dance. The view that curtailment of life expectancy deserves treatment as an injury separate from diminution of one's earning capacity or pain and suffering has apparently met approval in several English cases,[27] and the courts in the United States seem inclined to head in the same direction.[28]

Disfigurement

In addition to subjecting the plaintiff to physical pain and suffering, many accidents subject her to temporary or permanent physical disfigurement. One method of compensating the plaintiff for such an injury is to assess the cost of surgery or other medical care required to treat or repair the disfigurement. This alone, however, may be inadequate compensation. If medical treatment such as plastic surgery is feasible and effective, the cost of such treatment is certainly warranted. In many cases, however, cosmetic repair will be either risky or ineffective. In addition, the principal harm to a plaintiff who has been disfigured may be psychological or emotional.

A recent decision in Rhode Island, *Arlan v. Cervini*,[29] which overruled a line of precedent to the contrary, is representative of jurisdictions that now recognize the psychological component of the disfigurement injury and allow for compensation for this injury. The court held in *Arlan* that "mental suffering, which may include nervousness, grief, anxiety, worry, shock, humiliation, embarrassment, or indignity, arising from consciousness of a facial or bodily scar, is a compensable element of damages."[30] A year later the Rhode Island court affirmed its confidence in the correctness of this approach by holding that the new rule should be applied to cases on appeal because it would "promote justice and would not . . . have any significant adverse impact upon judicial administration since the purpose of the new rule would be only to allow full compensation for an already existing and demonstrable physical injury."[31]

Mental Distress and Fear

In most medical malpractice cases the plaintiff is entitled to recover for any mental distress caused by the tort as a secondary consequence of the physical injury. In such cases the mental distress recovery is often called *parasitic*, in that it feeds on the physical injury recovery. Since the development of the tort of negligent infliction of emotional distress, however, courts have had to confront the issue of the extent to which mental distress alone is a compensable element of damage.[32] Typically, the question arises when a close family member watches a loved one undergo physical suffering as a result of an act of medical negligence. Or rather, since medical malpractice is not usually self-evident, it is more realistic to say that the family member witnesses the suffering and later learns that the suffering could have been avoided if the health care professional had rendered proper care.

Four general criteria are employed by courts to recognize the tort of negligent infliction of emotional distress: (1) the existence of death or serious physical injury caused by negligence; (2) a close family relationship between plaintiff and the accident victim; (3) observation of the injury at the scene of the accident; and (4) severe emotional distress experienced by the family member.[33]

Several New Jersey cases illustrate the difficulty courts are having in reaching a satisfactory approach to the issue of whether a bystander should be able to recover for the mental distress caused as a result of witnessing harm suffered by a family member.[34] In *Lindemuth v. Alperin*,[35] the court rejected an effort of parents to recover for emotional harm they suffered in watching their child die as a result of a physician's failure to diagnose and treat an intestinal blockage. In rejecting the emotional distress claim, the court reasoned that failure to treat and diagnose an intestinal blockage was not an event that could be the subject of a layperson's sensory perception.[36]

In two subsequent cases the court reached a different conclusion. The first involved a claim of misdiagnosis of a ten-month-old child's intracerebral hemorrhage caused by his fall down some stairs. The superior court held that the parents' allegation that they were forced to witness the deterioration and death of their child as a result of misdiagnosis provided adequate support for a claim of negligent infliction of emotional distress.[37] The court distinguished the earlier decision as follows:

> In *Lindemuth* the parents learned of the accident after its occurrence, thus negating the observance of the alleged negligence that gave rise to those results. By contrast, in the present case defendants verbally communicated to plaintiffs the diagnosis before and while the parents were forced to witness the deterioration of their son's condition. This communication by telephone together with the observation of their child's condition fulfills the "observation" requirement for plaintiffs' prima facie case to recover for negligent infliction of emotional distress.[38]

In a similar vein the New Jersey court held that the requirement that the family member observe the death or injury at the scene was satisfied when a mother saw the postoperative introduction of hyperalimentation fluid into a catheter that had been improperly positioned in her six-year-old daughter's right internal jugular vein during surgery and then watched the child during the next two hours, which concluded with fatal cardiac tamponade.[39]

The problem presented by these cases is obviously a difficult one. On the one hand, it is clear that the emotional trauma experienced by family members is severe and devastating. On the other hand, courts want to draw the line somewhere on the physician's liability for an act of medical malpractice. The issue takes on particular importance in a death case because most jurisdictions do not allow family members to recover for the emotional distress and sorrow suffered as a result of the premature death of a loved one (see discussion below). In other cases the damage award has potential only if emotional harm is recognized because it is the principal injury sustained. A good example is *Molien v. Kaiser Foundation Hospitals*, [40] where the court held that a husband could recover for the emotional distress he suffered as a result of his wife's doctor's misdiagnosis that she had a venereal disease and advice that the husband should be examined. The ability to make an independent claim for such emotional distress significantly increases the verdict potential in such a case. In light of the potential impact of this type of damage claim in medical malpractice cases, counsel for both sides should carefully analyze the law in the jurisdiction to assess the potential and contours of a claim of negligent infliction of emotional distress.

Death Cases

How much is a life worth? The question provokes responses ranging from emotional diatribes to yawns, depending on the values of the responder, the importance of the answer to the interrogator, and the details provided to the responder as to the circumstances that led to the death and the character and personality of the decedent and her dependents. Posing the question at a cocktail party as an abstract proposition is likely to produce a shrug or a courteous philosophical discussion. Posing the same question when a decision has to be made about what methods to employ to save a sick child's life will provoke shouts, tears, and even physical violence. Posing the question to a jury will probably evoke both emotional and philosophical responses.

The issue of how or whether this question is posed to the jury is of the utmost importance. If the question is to be raised in some form, determinations as to the evidence that can be considered, the arguments that may be made by counsel, and the instructions that will be given to the jury about how to measure the loss are pivotal. In the early common law of torts in the United States all these knotty issues were avoided, because the law took the position that a tort died with the victim and thus no cause of action could be brought if the potential plaintiff died before a verdict was rendered.[41] It was thus much cheaper to kill a person than to maim him.

All states today have statutes providing a remedy for tortious conduct that has caused a death.[42] The statutes vary widely, however, as to who benefits from the action and the method of measuring damages.[43] Moreover, it remains true in most instances that the tortfeasor who kills her victim will pay less in damages than the tortfeasor who severely injures the victim but does not kill him.

Is a $10,000 or a $10 million verdict outrageous in a medical malpractice case? Some argue that the answer depends on the identity of the victim. Others contend that the answer should turn on the identity of the defendant and the nature of his conduct. Some focus on the needs of the victim's family. Others question whether any of these considerations can justify a multimillion dollar award in a death case. Where we stand on this issue depends on our background, our values, and the facts available to us. Do we agree that all human life is priceless? Do we feel that one person's life is worth more than another's? Should the law measure all lives the same, or should it measure them differently? Should the law measure lives in monetary terms at all? Our feelings about these issues may vary depending on whether the victim was an astronaut, a convict serving a life sentence, an eighty-five-year-old retired steelworker, or a two-year-old child with severe leukemia; on whether the defendant is a thousand-bed private hospital, a nursing home, a small-town family doctor, a heart-transplant specialist, or a drug company; on whether the death was caused by a biopsy performed without the patient's informed consent, a complicated heart transplant operation, the administration of a drug that had not been properly tested before being sold for clinical use, or the administration of a drug to which the patient had an allergy that was clearly marked on her chart. Should any of these considerations bear on the size of the damage award? These and many other provocative questions have been addressed by the various state legislatures that have enacted wrongful death and survival statutes.[44]

In one case of malpractice, brought against a hospital and a physician for the death of a child that was caused by the performance of a biopsy to which the parents did not consent, the jury rendered a verdict in favor of the decedent and his parents for $10 million.[45] During closing arguments and after suggesting that the proper award for the wrongful death of a racehorse worth $10 million would be $10 million, plaintiff's counsel questioned whether the child's life was worth less than a horse's. He observed that if someone had offered the parents an envelope containing a million dollars' worth of winning lottery tickets in exchange for the child's life, the parents would have declined the offer. He went on to note the billions of dollars the United States spends to make sure that the astronauts are brought home safely.[46] The doctor and the hospital were both found negligent.

In posttrial motions and on appeal the defendants argued, among other things, that the verdict should be set aside because plaintiff's counsel had made impermissible arguments to the jury and that, in any event, the verdict was excessive. The appellate court agreed that some of the arguments made by counsel improperly prompted the jury to place a value on the decedent's life, a valuation effort that West Virginia law does not permit. For this reason, the court ordered a subtraction of $7 million, reducing the collectible verdict to $3 million.[47]

Compensation schemes under the wrongful death and survival statutes may seek one of the following ends: preserving the probable economic value of the decedent's estate, protecting the economic or pecuniary interests of designated classes of family members of the decedent, and protecting the pecuniary and *emotional* interests of designated classes of family members of the decedent. The first form of statute is known as a *survival statute* because it focuses on the decedent and attempts to provide her with a tort remedy similar to the remedy she would have had if she had survived to pursue it. The second form is known as a *wrongful death statute* because it provides a remedy to the decedent's family members who suffer pecuniary losses as a result of the decedent's wrongful death. Lord Campbell's Act is the source of the form of wrongful death statutes that focus on the financial losses of the decedents' dependents.[48] The third form is of more recent vintage and represents a distinct minority approach to measuring losses in death cases. It is noteworthy because it allows the jury to compensate family members for both pecuniary losses and the intangible losses that are often the most severe in wrongful death situations: sorrow and mental anguish.[49]

The difference in approaches among the statutes may be best appreciated if we itemize the losses sustained by the decedent, the decedent's estate, and decedent's family members and then identify the elements considered under a typical survival statute, those recoverable under a typical wrongful death statute, and these cognizable under a statute such as that adopted in West Virginia, where family members may recover both pecuniary and nonpecuniary losses.[50]

The losses sustained by the decedent depend, to some extent, on whether she is instantly killed. If death is not instantaneous, the decedent is likely to incur medical expenses, experience pain and suffering, and suffer losses in earning power between the time of the accident and the time of death. In all death cases the decedent suffers an earning capacity loss of the difference between her earning capacity and her cost of personal maintenance. The decedent's estate loses the savings and other pecuniary accumulations the decedent was likely to make over her lifetime. Her family members lose the financial contributions she would probably have made to them over her lifetime. In addition, the decedent's untimely death is likely to inflict severe emotional distress on her family.

None of these injuries was compensated in death cases under the common law because a cause of action for tortious conduct dies with the victim. Lord

Campbell's Act, the first effort to correct this injustice, had the limited goal of providing compensation to close family members who were financially dependent on the decedent. It and its progeny provide compensation in death cases for *pecuniary* losses suffered by the decedent's spouse, children, parents, or siblings. The actual beneficiaries vary under the statutes.[51] The obvious injustice of this type of wrongful death statute is that it ignores the tremendous emotional harm and other nonpecuniary injuries suffered by the family. If none of the designated family members survives the decedent, this type of statute provides no remedy at all because it does not preserve any remedies for the decedent's estate per se.

In contrast, a survival statute focuses exclusively on the decedent's estate. It preserves the decedent's personal injury action for the benefit of the estate. If the decedent survived the accident for a period of time, medical expenses and pain and suffering are compensable. Decedent's loss of income from the date of the injury until the date of death is also recoverable. From the time of the decedent's death through the end of her work-life expectancy as it existed before the injury, a survival statute typically allows a recovery of gross earning capacity minus the cost of personal maintenance.

Some jurisdictions today have both a wrongful death and a survival statute or one statute that protects the interests of the decedent's estate and the designated beneficiaries.[52] If both statutes exist, the survival action usually allows recovery for the decedent's medical expenses, pain and suffering, past loss of income, and loss of future income minus personal maintenance and contributions to family members. If both survival and wrongful death actions may be brought, counsel must carefully analyze the damage claims to ensure that no permissible element of damage is missed and that no element of damage is claimed twice.[53]

The West Virginia death statute involved in *Stevens Clinic*,[54] discussed above, represents the current trend in legislation in this area. It provides:

> The verdict of the jury shall include, but may not be limited to, damages for the following: (A) Sorrow, mental anguish, and solace which may include society, companionship, comfort, guidance, kindly offices and advice of the decedent; (B) compensation for reasonably expected loss of (i) income of the decedent, and (ii) services, protection, care and assistance provided by the decedent; (C) expenses for the care, treatment and hospitalization of the decedent incident to the injury resulting in death; and (D) reasonable funeral expenses.[55]

In the absence of explicit allowance of recovery for sorrow and mental anguish, the jury is straitjacketed in trying to assess damages in any death case where the victim is neither the principal breadwinner nor a homemaker. In such cases juries have typically attempted to make some small award to the plaintiff, and the courts have struggled to rationalize the verdict in economic terms.[56] The radical aspect of the West Virginia statute lies in its allowance of recovery for "sorrow, mental anguish, and solace." Historically, this type of harm has been excluded from most statutes that provide tort remedies in death cases. The allowance for recovery for these very real but intangible injuries significantly increases the value of death cases because it vests in the jury much more discretion regarding the appropriate monetary award for the loss of life. Thus the allowance offers a fair and rational approach to achieving adequate compensation in death cases.

Delay Damages

Because the defendant and his insurer derive income from holding onto the potential settlement sum for as long as possible, it is often worth their while to delay the settlement of a medical malpractice case until the parties are on the courthouse steps. One court, however, recently expressly cited this practice as a factor that should be considered in reviewing whether a verdict is excessive. That court declared: "Without the occasional jury award that is at least ten times greater than what the parties would have settled for immediately after the tragedy, there would be no incentive on the part of clients to temper the file building, anti-settlement proclivities of their lawyers by urging quick payment of just claims."[57] More commonly, jurisdictions attempt to discourage defendants from engaging in this practice by adding interest of some sort to the ultimate award so that the economic incentive for delay is diminished.[58]

Such situations are fairly straightforward. The difficulties courts and legislatures are confronting in this regard involve developing appropriate standards for assessing delay damages in situations where the plaintiff rather than the defendant is the cause of the delayed settlement. The plaintiff's counsel may be slow in conducting discovery that demonstrates the strength of a case, and the merits of the case may not be readily apparent to the defendant at the time the action is filed. The plaintiff's monetary demand may be unreasonable. Alternatively, the demand may be reasonable, but a multiple-party situation may cause the parties to disagree about what proportion of the damages each party should pay. Such possibilities for delay in settlement lead jurisdictions to continue to struggle to develop standards of delay damage that will prompt all parties to the litigation to compromise and settle cases.[59]

Although the standards that will ultimately govern the award of delay damages in medical malpractice cases are not yet settled, counsel for all parties should begin to consider the possible impact of an award of delay damages early in the litigation. Both sides stand to lose a great deal of money in potential large-verdict cases, and the eventual decision of the court or jury as to the propriety of delay damages may be made on the basis of conduct that occurs long before the trial ever takes place.

Projections for the Future

In a medical malpractice case with the potential for a significant verdict, a major portion of the damage claim is likely to be based on injuries the plaintiff may continue to suffer after the verdict has been rendered.[60] Absent the passage of a statute, the jury will be required to render a lump-sum verdict based on its best judgment as to what harm the plaintiff is likely to incur for many years to come. Whether the focus is on diminution in earning capacity, medical expenses, or pain and suffering, projecting losses over a period of years into the future is a formidable task. The expert testimony will likely be in sharp conflict, and the data on which the experts base their opinions will be far from conclusive in support of the projection being made. No portion of the damage case demands greater attention from counsel than the standards and evidence relevant to the projection of future losses.

As we have seen, presenting a realistic portrait of the plaintiff to the jury requires a detailed and comprehensive investigation. One reason this portrait is so important is that it will make or break the credibility of the projections that plaintiff's counsel is asking the jury to accept for purposes of reaching a monetary verdict. The earlier discussion of the plaintiff's portrait identified some personal characteristics that may influence the jury in reaching a verdict. We now consider the approach the law takes concerning these characteristics.

The threshold question is whether the law allows the witnesses, counsel, or jury to acknowledge these characteristics explicitly in assessing damages. In other words, since the objective in making the damage award is to place the plaintiff in the position she would have been in but for the accident, the only characteristics that should be considered in projecting the plaintiff's future are those that truly affected her potential at the time the accident occurred.

The most sensitive personal characteristics are race and gender. Since a person's race or gender per se does not affect the intensity or duration of the pain he or she suffers as a result of an injury, it seems obvious that these characteristics should not be considered in connection with a pain and suffering award. Whether they should be considered in assessing future losses in earning capacity depends on whether one assumes that historical evidence of earnings and work-life expectancies for minorities and women serves as the best evidence of what the future would have been for a particular individual had she not suffered an injury. Here it is helpful to look at the specific factual determinations the law requires a jury to make in awarding a lump sum for future losses.

The two critical facts that a jury must determine in projecting either loss of income or medical expenses are the amount of money that will be lost in each year and the number of years that the plaintiff will continue to incur the loss. These determinations must be calculated on a different basis for income losses, medical expenses, and pain and suffering because the appropriate time period for assessing these losses is likely to differ. The key concepts involved are life expectancy and work-life expectancy. Life expectancy governs claims of future medical expenses and pain and suffering. Work-life expectancy governs asessments of losses in earning capacity. The outside limit of the term for which a person can make a claim for medical expenses or pain and suffering is that person's life expectancy as it exists after the accident and as of the time of trial. The plaintiff's life expectancy may be longer or shorter than her work-life expectancy, which is determined by the plaintiff's condition before the accident. If the injury has not shortened the plaintiff's life expectancy, her position, despite her injury, does not differ from that of most people, who expect to live beyond their years of active work, provided their health and lifestyle permit.

On the other hand, a severe injury often shortens a person's life expectancy. Thus, for example, a five-year-old who has suffered brain damage as a result of medical malpractice may have had a seventy-year life expectancy before the accident. The neurological insult, however, may have subjected the child to an increased risk of infections and other hazards, reducing his actual life expectancy to twenty years. Consequently, the medical expense and pain and suffering claims must be limited to the twenty-year life expectancy. His loss-of-income claim, however, applies to his work-life expectancy as it existed before the tort, a period probably more in the neighborhood of forty-five years.

Publications of the U.S. Department of Labor containing statistics on both work-life expectancy and life expectancy are recognized as authoritative by economists and actuaries, and when authenticated and relied on by expert witnesses in the trial, they are admissible as evidence. The same is true for publications of the insurance industry. It is important to remember, however, that these statistics reflect averages, and their use to project the life expectancy and work-life expectancy of any individual is problematic, since that individual may or may not fit the average mold. For this reason, evidence of the plaintiff's personal characteristics—such as her health, lifestyle, and environment—is admissible and may be relied on by the jury to reach a conclusion different from the one suggested by the statistics.

It is in this regard that defense counsel may contend that race and gender should affect damage assessments. Courts have traditionally ruled that race and gender are relevant to projections of life expectancy because scientific studies have shown these characteristics to be correlated with long or short life spans. The same rationale has been used to justify the consideration of gender in projecting work-life expectancy, although this assumption is subject to serious challenge today in light of changing social patterns.

The U.S. Department of Labor also publishes statistics on the earnings of workers, which are tabulated by race and gender and are relied on by expert economists and employment specialists. Courts have traditionally allowed the use of such statistics, but compelling arguments exist for dispensing with this practice. The primary argument is that these statistics are remnants of a period of time when discrimination based on gender and race was perpetrated under color of state law.

Since such discrimination is now prohibited by state and federal law as against public policy, using them to project an individual's future earning capacity is irrational. Although the issue has not yet reached the appellate courts for resolution, it is likely that this argument will eventually prove persuasive and that the amount of earnings projected for individual plaintiffs will have to be made on a race- and gender-neutral basis.

Gender and race aside, the personal characteristics that the law acknowledges to be most important in projecting a person's future earning capacity are age, health, intelligence, education, work history, and personality. Together these characteristics provide a reasonable basis for projecting what the individual is capable of earning in a particular economy.

An excellent demonstration of how rationally to project an individual's lost earning capacity appears in *Feldman v. Allegheny Airlines*,[61] which should be mandatory reading for the personal injury lawyer. *Feldman* involved a wrongful death claim brought under Connecticut law in behalf of a twenty-five-year-old woman who died in an airplane crash, leaving a surviving spouse but no children. The defendant acknowledged to liability, and the damage claims were tried to the court. In resolving the damage issues, the district judge authored an extraordinarily illuminating opinion regarding the assessment of damages in death actions in particular and in personal injury actions in general.

At the time of her death the decedent was in the process of relocating from New Haven, Connecticut, to Washington, D.C., because her husband had just graduated from law school and had secured a job in Washington. A graduate of the University of Pennsylvania, the decedent had several years of experience in work relating to governmental functions and processes. She was in the process of deciding whether to attend law school—she had been accepted at George Washington University Law School—or secure a new job in the Washington, D.C., area concentrating on governmental relations. To assess the economic losses caused by her death, the court first had to develop a profile of her relevant characteristics and then project her earning potential over her lifetime in light of those characteristics.

After noting the positive performance ratings the decedent had earned in her previous employment and recounting the testimony her employers and associates offered regarding her personality, the court concluded:

> While predictions as to the precise course her future career would have taken may not be made with certainty, the Court has not the slightest doubt that the qualities of intelligence, aggressiveness, enthusiasm, and tenacity which she demonstrated in her working life would have carried her far, especially in view of the fact that she was pursuing a career in and about the federal government at the very time when the equalization of career opportunities for women was emerging as a major federal policy.[62]

The court adopted the conservative assumption that the decedent would have opted to take a job in government rather than attend law school. The court then projected her diminution in earning capacity based on a career in government. In order to have some basis of comparison tailored to the decedent rather than to some average college graduate, the court relied on testimony regarding the career patterns of two individuals, one man and one woman, with similar educational backgrounds, who chose careers in different areas of government relations. On the basis of this evidence, the court selected a GS salary scale that it believed would have applied to the decedent had she elected to pursue a job with the federal government in the District of Columbia.[63]

To project diminution in earning capacity of an individual, two, and possibly three, basic pieces of information are required. First is how much the person could earn during each period (week, month, year) of the future in which a loss is being projected. Second is how long that person could be expected to work so that earnings can be for the entire term. Third, depending on the approach the jurisdiction takes to inflation, is what discount rate should be used to reduce a projected loss to present value or what rate of inflation should be taken into account in projecting a future loss. *Feldman* offers an illuminating analysis of each of these considerations.

As for the amount that the decedent could have earned in each year in the future, the *Feldman* court relied on government tables setting forth the GS salary scale and projected periodic promotions and raises for the decedent. The court took the decedent's gender into account by assuming that she would have left the employment market for a period of eight years to have two children and to stay home with them. This assumption, however, was not based solely on the general statistics regarding women's historical work patterns. Rather, it was supported by testimony from her husband as to plans he and his wife had discussed regarding their future.[64]

Significantly, during the eight years that the court assumed that the decedent would have elected to be a homemaker rather than a government employee, it did not deny her a recovery for loss in earning capacity. Noting that the item of damage for which she is being compensated is diminution in earning capacity and not lost earnings per se, the court simply held her salary constant for those years and computed her loss in each of those years based on the annual salary she would have had on the date that she elected to stay home. This analysis reasoned that the decedent would not lose her earning capacity during those years; rather, a decision to stay at home would simply be her way of expressing a preference for another activity that was worth more to her than the salary at that point in time.[65]

As for the term for which she could be expected to have an earning capacity, the court relied on stipulations entered into by the parties and the assumptions made by each party's expert. Based on the stipulations and testimony, the court projected a working life expectancy for the decedent of forty years as of the time of her death.[66]

The next question was whether to reduce the compensation for future losses because of the fact that the personal injury judgment would result in an immediate lump-sum collection of an income that would have been collected only periodically, at specified dates in the future, had the decedent lived. It is generally recognized that the immediate possession of a dollar is worth more than the right to collect that same dollar in the future. For example, a decedent who is earning $10,000 annually at the time of her death and has a ten-year work-life expectancy can be projected as losing a total of $100,000 if we simply multiply $10,000 by ten years. If we award the decedent's estate $100,000 in a lump-sum today, however, the estate can invest the $100,000 and earn interest. If the estate earned interest at a rate of 10 percent (for ease in computation), it could withdraw $10,000 each year to match the expected annual earnings loss and still end up with the $100,000 principal at the end of the ten-year term.

In the past this kind of reasoning prompted courts to require that an award for future losses in personal injury cases be reduced to present value, usually at an arbitrarily set interest rate such as 6 percent. The assumption underlying the reduction was that the lump-sum award would allow the plaintiff to make a safe investment and therefore the amount awarded for each projected period of a future loss should be one that, when invested at that safe rate of interest, would grow to the amount of the projected future loss when it was needed.

For an appreciation of the cumulative impact of a reduction to present value even under a conservative assumption of a discount rate of 1.5 percent, we may refer again to *Feldman*. The computation of damages for loss of earning capacity made by that court reflects the fact that, if no reduction is made, the award for diminution of earning capacity (net after a subtraction for taxes) would be $662,874. In contrast, the award after making a reduction to present value using the modest discount rate of 1.5 percent was $499,953. In other words, a 1.5 percent discount rate over a forty-year period cost the plaintiff $162,921.[67]

In response, plaintiffs generally argue that the reduction-to-present-value requirement is unfair because it ignores the reality that inflation will eat away at any money awarded for a future loss. eir example, a teacher who received a lump-sum award for a total diminution in earning capacity in 1950 based on a projection of each year's future loss in earnings from 1950 through 1990, reduced to present value, would have been significantly undercompensated because teacher salaries increased greatly during that period. Thus, if one projected in 1950 that a teacher needed an amount necessary to grow to $5,000 (when invested at 6 percent per annum, compounded) for the year 1990, and did not take into account that teacher's salaries were likely to be substantially higher in 1990, at least in part to address inflation, the award would be seriously deficient. Using an extremely conservative assumption that teachers would gain raises of 5 percent per year based on merit, one could expect the teacher to earn $15,000 a year, even if the raise was limited to $250 a year, based on a simple interest rate rather than a compound one. Add another $250 a year for inflation, and the teacher would be earning $25,000 a year, again assuming a constant 5 percent inflation rate with no compounding.

In the past, courts refused to listen to the inflation argument, reasoning that it was speculative and confusing. The last fifteen years have, however, prompted a different judicial attitude, and many jurisdictions take inflation into account through some means. *Feldman* represents one approach, using a small discount rate to reflect the difference between interest paid on an investment, less the inflation. The Pennsylvania decision *Kaczykowski v. Boulabasz* represents another.[68] In *Kaczykowski*, the court held that no reduction to present value was required because it is fair to assume that any interest earned on a lump-sum award for future losses would equal inflation. Both warrant careful reading.

The court in *Feldman* decided to take inflation into account by factoring it into the interest rate that the court assumed the plaintiff could earn on the lump-sum award. The court reasoned that a certain portion of interest paid on money invested is real return on the investment, while a certain portion simply represents inflation—the decline in the purchasing value of the dollar. The task was to determine what portion of interest paid on a safe investment represented a true gain to the investor. The court settled on 1.5 percent, based on a review of interest paid on a variety of treasury bills over a period of 23 years. The court simply compared the interest rate in each of those years with the inflation rate and determined the real rate of return in each of those years. The court then determined the average rate of real return on investment during those years, which it calculated at 1.5 percent, and assumed that this same rate would be returned in the future.[69]

The Pennsylvania Supreme Court in *Kaczykowski* considered the *Feldman* approach but rejected it in favor of what is called the "total offset" approach.[70] This approach assumes that whatever interest is earned on the money invested over a period of time will be equal to inflation, and the two will thus totally offset each other. Thus there is no need to reduce a lump-sum award to present value.

A third method used by some courts to account for inflation is the evidentiary approach. Under this approach, the court considers expert testimony concerning the likely effect of inflation as another piece of evidence for the jury to consider and resolve. Each side must thus present evidence and argument to the jury on this issue.[71]

The total offset approach is obviously the easiest approach to administer in a courtroom because it allows the court and the jury to avoid the issue entirely. But it is probably less defensible in economic terms than is the reduced discount rate approach adopted in *Feldman*. It is possible, however, to defend the total offset approach on broader economic grounds, on the assumption that interest paid to the plaintiff will equal the combination of inflation and increases in productivity in the economy in a given year. On this assumption, supported by some economists, a court can justify ignoring issues of inflation and present value if, when projecting future losses, it does not increase an expected future loss on the assumption that the loss will be higher in a given year because wages will increase by that time due to increases in productivity.

The last argument can be best explained if we explore two common considerations often relied on by economists and actuaries when they are projecting future wage losses: productivity increases and merit increases. Economic studies have found that since World War II, workers in the United States have gained wage increases that average about 2.5 percent above the average rate of inflation during that period. The explanation for this inflation-adjusted average wage increase is the distribution of increased profits based on increases in productivity in the workforce. According to this economic theory, the introduction of a technological advance such as a word processor allows an employer to earn greater profits with the same input of labor because of increased productivity, a portion of which will be passed on to the worker. The average increase based on this phenomenon is said to be 2.5 percent.

If workers do enjoy the benefits of increased wages due to increased productivity, a projection of diminution in earning capacity should take into account the probability of such increases occurring and compensate a plaintiff for such a loss. This can be done by increasing the projected future losses by the average annual rate of the expected productivity-induced wage increase, or by subtracting the productivity-increase percentage from the interest rate that one assumes a lump-sum award for loss of income could produce. The last approach, together with a subtraction of the expected rate of inflation from the discount rate, may justify the total offset method in economic terms.

Wage increases based on general productivity increases in a particular industry or in the general economy should be distinguished from wage increases that are projected for an individual based on merit. The latter type of increase is subjective and is necessarily based on proof of personal characteristics and factors affecting the particular individual's attractiveness in the marketplace. To the extent that the evidence provides a reasonable basis for projecting a merit increase, such evidence should be admissible for the trier of fact to consider.

Another factor that counsel should weigh is the consideration, if any, that the jurisdiction requires the court or jury to give to income taxes. In a personal injury case the Internal Revenue Code provides that an award for personal injuries is not taxable. Interest earned on a lump-sum award is taxable. Thus, the question arises as to whether the trier of fact should consider federal income taxes at all in making the award. Defendants believe the award for diminution in earning capacity should be reduced to reflect the fact that wage payments would ordinarily be taxed if they were not a part of a personal injury award. Plaintiffs contend that it would be unfair to reduce the lump-sum award based on income tax concerns without increasing the award to take into account future taxation of the interest on the lump-sum award. Obviously, these arguments can be confusing to a jury. Consequently, some courts now advise the jury that the personal injury award will not be subject to federal income taxation and thus the jury should neither increase nor decrease the award based on concerns about income taxes.[72] A recent U.S. Supreme Court decision construing a claim for personal injuries under the Federal Employers' Liability Act held, however, that income taxes were relevant and that the jury should be instructed that an award is not subject to federal income tax.[73] Most courts, however, still take the position that income taxes should not be considered in making an award for impairment of earning capacity.[74]

In contrast, in wrongful death or survival cases a different approach is required in some jurisdictions. In death cases some jurisdictions—such as Connecticut in *Feldman*—provide for a recovery of gross income minus projected federal income taxes for the particular year. Other jurisdictions, such as Pennsylvania, allow the jury to make an award based on projections of losses of gross income for particular years, with no consideration of projected income taxes that would have been paid had the decedent lived.

Determining a Settlement Value

Having surveyed the field of damages, I would like to reexamine the problem set forth at the beginning of this chapter to illustrate an approach to deriving a settlement figure. Recall that Joe Jenks was injured at age thirty. At the time of the injury he was earning $30,000 a year. He now suffers a permanent disability. Defense counsel will, however, challenge his contention that he is unable to engage in any gainful employment. In addition, defense counsel will dispute the plaintiff's projected work-life expectancy and future medical needs.

In assessing the settlement value of the case, it is useful to list the dominant factors that may influence the verdict and assign a grade to each factor. First, counsel should identify the elements of damage that the plaintiff is likely to get before the jury and total the figures that he may put on the blackboard. This total should include an amount representing pain and suffering. If the jurisdiction does not permit a per diem argument for pain and suffering, counsel should derive a figure for the potential pain and suffering award by multiplying the special damages by a factor of from 0.25 to 5, depending on the nature of the injury and the strength of the evidence. As for example, suppose that the plaintiff has suffered a serious physical injury that requires substantial medical care and has left her with a severe permanent disability that limits or eliminates her earning capacity. Counsel might come up with the following figures:

Past diminution in earning capacity	$ 30,000
Future diminution in earning capacity	900,000
Past medical expenses	120,000
Future medical expenses	650,000
Pain and suffering and other intangibles	1,700,000
High verdict potential	$3,400,000

The figure used for pain and suffering equals the special damages. As such it is relatively conservative in terms of multiples customarily used by attorneys and adjusters in settlement negotiations.

Next counsel must assess the potential impact of the factors that influence damage awards on this potential high verdict. In our example counsel will assign a percentage value to each of the considerations and arrive at an average percentage that he will use to multiply the high potential verdict. If a particular factor supports the high potential verdict, he will assign a high percentage, and if it is detrimental to the verdict, he will assign a low percentage.

Strength of liability evidence	75%
Attitude of judge	50%
Attractiveness of plaintiff	100%
Attractiveness of defendant	50%
Strength of damage experts	75%
Attitude of jury in jurisdiction	10%
Total	360%
Average percentage	60%

In this example the probable award would come to 60 percent of $3,400,000, or $2,040,000. The probable award was derived by multiplying the average percentage attributed to the factors that influence verdicts by the high verdict potential. The same formula may be used to project the probable low verdict if there is a serious dispute as to such special damage items as income loss or future medical expenses.

Obviously, this kind of computation is not a scientific exercise, and it lacks an empirical basis to support its use. In addition, the illustration does not address the important considerations of inflation and reduction-to-present-value approaches that may be required in the jurisdiction. The goal of the illustration is simply to emphasize the various factors that may influence the ultimate damage award. One purpose of engaging in the exercise is to alert counsel to aspects of the case that need strengthening, if possible, or, if not, that must be acknowledged as irremediably weak. By focusing on these and other relevant factors, counsel can conduct a realistic evaluation of the settlement value of the case and prepare an effective case on damages in the event that the case cannot be settled.

The art of proficient lawyering requires analyzing and balancing a multitude of objective and subjective considerations in order to make strategic judgments as to which matters warrant further development and which must be strengthened or abandoned for effective presentation at trial. Many of these judgments will involve assessing the plaintiff's profile and projecting the impact that the alleged malpractice will have on her life.

Checklist of Damage Issues

Preparing the portion of the damage case that addresses future losses is one of the most intellectually challenging aspects of a medical malpractice case. A grasp of matters such as present values and projected inflation rates is essential if counsel is to address the damage issues effectively through direct or cross-examination. The following checklist of items should be fully discussed with each party's expert and understood by counsel before trial:

1. Plaintiff's life expectancy before the accident
     Gather plaintiff's medical records.
     Consult plaintiff's physicians.
     Explore plaintiff's lifestyle with family and friends
         (smoking, drinking, drugs, exercise, work habits, etc.).
     Secure life-expectancy tables from U.S. Department of Health and Human
         Services
         Department of Labor and life insurance companies.
     Retain appropriate expert (economist or actuary, physician).
2. Plaintiff's life expectancy after the accident
     Secure expert report and assess.
     Plaintiff's work-life expectancy before the accident.
     Review information in 1 above.
     Obtain reports from U.S. Department of Labor.
3. Plaintiff's work-life expectancy after the accident
     Retain appropriate experts and obtain expert reports.
     Interview fact witnesses (family, friends, employer, co-workers).
4. Plaintiff's earning capacity before the accident
     Interview fact witnesses.
     Obtain education records.
     Obtain employment records.
     Review learned treatises and government publications.
     Retain expert and obtain expert report.
5. Plaintiff's earning capacity after the accident
     Retain appropriate expert (rehabilitation medicine specialist, physical
         therapist, occupational therapist, economist).
     Review learned treatises and government publications.
6. Plaintiff's future medical expenses
     Retain appropriate experts and obtain expert reports.
7. Plaintiff's pain and suffering—physical and mental
     Interview fact witnesses.
     Retain appropriate expert witnesses.
     Obtain pictures.
     Retain expert to make day-in-the-life film if appropriate.

Chapter 8

Punitive Damages: Goals and Standards

Punitive damage claims provoke emotional responses from litigants, lawyers, and the courts. Hurt and anger often fuel a plaintiff's quest for punitive damages. On the other hand, a punitive damage claim impugns the motives and threatens the reputation of the defendant. And because a punitive damage award must usually be paid from the personal assets of the defendant and not by his insurance company, he will fear losing the material things for which he has worked hard.

Many judges dislike punitive damage claims. Judicial hostility is sometimes cloaked in semantics, in a description of the egregious conduct that must be shown to justify such an award. Other courts may take the first opportunity available to dismiss the claim as lacking evidentiary support. Courts seem particularly resistant to a punitive damage claim made against a health care professional. Perhaps because of their experience in providing professional services, many judges believe that personal injuries caused by professional negligence should not expose the professional to a loss of personal assets, and it takes substantial proof of egregious wrongdoing to persuade a court otherwise. The trial judge supervising tort claims against health care professionals is called on to screen out frivolous claims and insulate professionals who have merely made mistakes from the risk of such a severe sanction. To do so, judges consider the goals of the award and the stringent standards that a plaintiff's case must meet.

The goals of a punitive damage award are to punish the tortfeasor for having engaged in egregious conduct and to deter her and others from engaging in such conduct in the future. In light of these goals, a punitive damage award may not be made on the basis of ordinary negligence or even gross negligence. As one court has observed: "The question in medical malpractice cases, as in tort actions generally, is whether there has been sufficiently aggravated conduct contrary to the plaintiff's interests, involving bad motive or reckless indifference, to justify the special sanction of punitive damages. That sanction serves the dual function of penalizing past conduct constituting an aggravated violation of another's interests, and of deterring such behavior in the future."[1]

Nevertheless, articulation of the goals and standards for the invocation of punitive damages offers scant guidance to the practitioner. The precedent presents too many inconsistent and irreconcilable results.

Medical malpractice cases present particularly difficult challenges to courts with respect to punitive damages. Judicial responses reflect the ambivalent feelings that most of us have toward health care professionals. On the one hand, we admire them and trust them to help heal us and our loved ones. We assume that they adhere to the Hippocratic Oath and believe that instances of negligent harm are rare, representing mistakes that any professional could make when faced with a demanding patient population and rapidly changing technology. On the other hand, we have all heard of shocking accounts of tragic results that occurred when health care professionals failed to provide minimally acceptable health care. Such stories shake our image of the professional's infallibility and provoke a desire to punish. A punitive damage claim requires the court and jury to decide whether the health care provided the plaintiff falls so far below the expected level that it warrants not only economic compensation to the victim but also a monetary sting prompted by outrage. Clearly, those instances occur. When they do, courts and juries are angered at the professionals' breach of trust and reflect it in their judgments and verdicts.

The plaintiff's lawyer who includes a punitive damage claim in his complaint is thus usually choosing to sail in uncertain waters. Although courts agree on the standards and goals of this remedy, they disagree on the application of the standard in particular circumstances. What one judge finds offensive, another may characterize as ordinary negligence. If the claim is omitted from the original complaint and plaintiff seeks to add it after discovery, the trial court will weigh the considerations governing amendments and exercise its discretion to preclude the amendment. Injecting a punitive damage claim into a case may provoke the court's ire if done too early in the proceeding, on the basis that plaintiff lacks concrete proof of the outrageous conduct. Injecting the claim late may elicit a denial from the court on the ground that the claim should have been made earlier to give the defendant a fair chance to disprove it. Whether and when to include a punitive damage claim in a medical malpractice case is thus an exceptionally important strategic decision.

If a punitive damage claim is included in the complaint, the defendant should file an objection to the claim and seek to have it dismissed. If the count remains in the complaint, not only will the defendant's personal assets be placed in jeopardy, but conflict may arise between the defendant's interests and his insurer's. The defendant may in fact need to retain an additional attorney to deal with issues involving insurance coverage (see the discussion below).

■ **Problem:** *Physician Paternalism or Greed*

Dr. Clark performed a radical mastectomy on Ms. Doyle to remove a malignant tumor. After the surgery Ms. Doyle learned that in light of the size and location of the tumor, most surgeons would have offered her a choice of either more limited surgery or radiation treatment. Dr. Clark acknowledges that others would have offered those choices but states that he did not because he believes generally that radical surgery is the best treatment plan for such tumors. Based on information received from nurses and other patients treated by Dr. Clark, Ms. Doyle suspects that Dr. Clark's approach is motivated as much by money as by his medical opinion. Does she have a valid medical malpractice claim against Dr. Clark? If so, should the jury be allowed to consider a punitive damage award?

A 1987 New Jersey case, *Edwards v. Our Lady of Lourdes Hospital*,[2] demonstrates the difficulty of predicting the outcome of a punitive damage claim and the importance of a court's attitude in assessing that outcome. *Edwards* involved a litany of negligence claims against a hospital, physicians, and nurses for care rendered to a premature infant (twenty-seven weeks, two and a half pounds). Plaintiffs contended that inadequate medical care caused the infant to suffer brain damage and necessitated the amputation of one leg at the hip.

At birth the child had no heartbeat and had to be resuscitated, which was done successfully. Thereafter, numerous events occurred that contributed to the child's injuries. The respirator in the newborn intensive care unit (NICU) malfunctioned, and there was no back-up source of oxygen. The infant's heartbeat slowed drastically, and the absence of oxygen significantly delayed his resuscitation. After he was reconnected to the respirator, he was not properly restrained, which allowed him to dislodge the endotracheal tube on at least six occasions, depriving him of oxygen.

There also were problems with circulation in the infant's lower extremities. At first an intravenous line was inserted to improve circulation. When he had trouble maintaining the line, however, the director of the NICU allowed a neonatal fellow on duty to write an order for a cutdown to allow insertion of a line into the child's vein. The cutdown was performed by a surgical resident, who mistakenly inserted the catheter into an artery instead of a vein. The surgical resident ignored repeated warnings from the nurse on duty that there was a problem with the catheter. As a result of the improper insertion of the catheter, the infant's leg had to be amputated.

The plaintiffs sued the hospital, the respiratory therapy department of the hospital, the nurse who did not report the surgical resident's refusal to inspect the catheter, and several other physicians, nurses, supervisors, and administrators of the hospital. Both compensatory and punitive damages were sought against all the defendants.

A jury found the surgical resident, the respiratory therapy department, and the nurse negligent, assessing their comparative responsibility as 90.2 percent, 5.1 percent, and 4.7 percent, respectively. None of the other defendants was found negligent. The jury awarded the infant and his mother $1,267,530 in compensatory damages. The jury also awarded punitive damages against the hospital in the amount of $225,000.

On appeal the New Jersey Superior Court set aside the punitive damage award. In explaining why the award against the hospital could not stand, the court directly expressed its contempt for the plaintiffs' claim and the way it was presented. The court noted that the punitive damage claim came into the case by leave of court to file a fourth amended complaint. The fourth amended complaint sought punitive damages from the surgical resident who had ignored the nurse's warnings. The plaintiffs also sought punitive damages from the hospital. In the court's words: "Plaintiffs alleged that the hospital failed to supply adequate staffing for clinical supervision of the 11–7 nursing shift, that the hospital had knowledge that the staffing was inadequate and not qualified, and that the hospital therefore engaged in wanton misconduct in reckless disregard of Eugene's rights."[3]

At the end of the plaintiffs' case, in response to the defendant's motion to dismiss the punitive damage claim, the plaintiffs stated that punitive damages were sought against the hospital only and did not argue that the surgical resident's conduct should be considered. Rather, the plaintiffs rested their claim of right to punitive damages on the contention that the hospital's failure to provide oxygen on a twenty-four-hour basis constituted gross negligence. The jury apparently agreed and awarded punitive damages.

The appellate court believed that the plaintiffs did not present sufficient facts to support a punitive damage award against the hospital. On appeal the plaintiffs sought to broaden the factual basis of the punitive damage claim by citing the hospital's failure to monitor the endotracheal tube and the infant's blood levels as well as its duty to provide a trained staff. In rejecting the plaintiffs' efforts, the court stated:

> [W]e are convinced that plaintiffs are relying on the same evidence to establish negligence and the elements for punitive damages. Conduct decidedly more culpable than ordinary negligence was required. . . . Plaintiffs did not prove that the hospital through its Respiratory Therapy Department, or Nurse Farlow for that matter, committed a deliberate act or omission with knowledge of a high degree of probability of harm and reckless indifference to consequences.[4]

The *Edwards* decision presents a sharp contrast to *Medvecz v. Choi*,[5] a federal court decision applying Pennsylvania law to a punitive damage claim in a medical malpractice case. The plaintiff in *Medvecz* underwent an elective renal arteriography to determine whether she suffered from any tumors in her right kidney. The X-ray procedure required the injection of a radio-opaque dye into her blood vessels. The dye was transferred into her spinal cord, causing paralysis from the waist down. Plaintiff sued the surgeon, the anesthesiologist, and the manufacturer of the dye. The drug company and surgeon settled with the plaintiff before trial, but the anesthesiologist joined both as well as the hospital as third-party defendants in the plaintiff's case against him.

The plaintiff's theory of liability against the anesthesiologist was that he had not properly monitored her blood pressure during the course of the procedure. She also contended that the anesthesiologist was negligent for allowing the administration of neosynephrine to raise her blood pressure, since this drug constricts blood vessels, causing the dye to be squeezed into her spinal cord. Although the jury found both the surgeon and the anesthesiologist negligent, the trial court did not allow it to consider the punitive damage claim.

The Third Circuit reversed, ruling that the plaintiff's proof could support a punitive damage award under Pennsylvania law. In Pennsylvania, Section 908 of the *Restatement of Torts* governs punitive damage claims. Comment (b) to Section 908 states: "Punitive damages are awarded only for outrageous conduct, that is, for acts done with a bad motive or with a reckless indifference to the interests of others." According to the Third Circuit, the difficult problem in assessing a punitive damage claim in the medical malpractice context is to define "reckless indifference."

Case law had approved the view that reckless indifference occurs "where there is great danger to others from the course of conduct in question, and, second, where the actor may be assumed to know or to have reason to know of the magnitude of the risk involved in the conduct at issue."[6] In the case before it, the Third Circuit concluded, evidence that the anesthesiologist had left the operating room without waiting for a replacement allowed the jury to reason that he had abandoned his patient. In the court's view abandonment of a patient by a doctor in circumstances where the doctor knew of the significant risk to his patient would meet the definition of reckless indifference.

If the reckless indifference standard is applied to the facts of *Edwards*,[7] discussed above, the New Jersey Superior Court would seem to be correct in finding that the proof did not justify holding that the hospital as a corporate entity had engaged in conduct reflecting a reckless indifference to the patient. The plaintiffs' claim against the surgical resident who refused to acknowledge the nurse's warnings that he had inserted the catheter into the child's artery as opposed to his vein, however, would present a sound punitive damage claim. Ignoring a warning of serious risk of harm to one's patient would certainly qualify as reckless indifference.

A frequent source of punitive damage claims is unauthorized surgery. As the court stated in *Pratt v. Davis*,[8] deliberately to perform unauthorized surgery reflects an intentional disregard of the rights of others. Punitive damages are thus appropriate.

Intentional misrepresentations also support punitive damage claims. Using the reckless indifference standard, courts have allowed punitive damages for statements reflecting less than intentional misrepresentation. Thus, in *Los Alamos Medical Center Inc. v. Coe*,[9] the physician reassured the patient that she need not be concerned about becoming addicted to the morphine he was prescribing for her. In the court's view the patient's inquiry put the doctor on notice of the danger. His reassurance that there was no risk of addiction in these circumstances was sufficient evidence of reckless indifference to the safety of others to justify a punitive damage award.

Inattentiveness in the face of obvious evidence of a great risk of physical harm may also justify submitting a punitive damage claim to a jury. In *Hoffman v. Memorial Osteopathic Hospital*,[10] the appellate court held that the trial court should have submitted a punitive damage claim to the jury where the evidence showed that an individual, subsequently diagnosed as suffering from Guillain-Barré syndrome, which causes neurological paralysis, was left sitting on the floor of the emergency room for one and a half to two hours, although unable to move, after the physician in charge could not find anything wrong with him and thus insisted that he leave. Similarly, in *Rennewanz v. Dean*,[11] a physician who compelled a patient who suffered a rectal hemorrhage while in his office to lie down on a couch unattended for forty-eight hours was found to present the requisite reckless indifference or gross negligence to warrant an award of punitive damages.

In some cases physicians have been found to be so lacking in skill and competence to undertake a certain procedure as to justify a punitive damage award. In *Mandeville v. Courtright*, [12] an unlicensed dentist who worked for a dental corporation that did not have a charter to carry on business in the state broke a patient's jaw by extracting a piece of the jawbone on the erroneous assumption that it was a root. The court held that performing the procedure while unlicensed and so evidently lacking in skill, knowledge, and experience was an act of reckless disregard of the patient's safety and justified an award of punitive damages. Another example of incompetence rising to a level of egregiousness supporting a punitive damage claim was presented in a case where an osteopathic physician used an improper method to set a fracture and improperly applied a cast to the patient's leg. [13] The court viewed the negligence in this case as so gross as to warrant a punitive award.

Prescribing drugs that the physician knows are not approved for a particular use, or about which the physician knows he lacks sufficient knowledge to assess the proper use, has prompted courts to approve punitive damage claims. In *Short v. Downs*, [14] a physician injected liquid silicone into the patient's breasts even though he knew the silicone was labeled "not for human use." The doctor did not undertake to find out what risks and complications might result from human injection. Accordingly, the court held that punitive damages were justified. A summary judgment dismissing a punitive damage claim was reversed when the evidence showed that the physician had prescribed a drug that caused bleeding and death and that he did not attend the patient in a timely manner when notified of his worsening condition. [15]

The award of punitive damages has been allowed for consciously withholding critically needed care from a patient or consciously exposing the patient to a needless and unjustifiably risky procedure. The first type of situation is illustrated by a case where a physician knew that a child needed to be admitted to a hospital to be properly treated but assured the parents that the admission was not necessary because he did not have admitting privileges at the hospital. [16] The second type is illustrated by a case where a dentist knew that similar treatment had caused similar injuries in the past and nevertheless failed to disclose this information to the patient. [17]

In comparison, the cases where the courts have rejected the viability of the plaintiff's punitive damage claim usually involve mistakes in judgment or inadvertence—negligent acts that do not rise to the level of reckless indifference. Thus, for example, the Third Circuit held that the trial court erred in submitting a punitive damage claim to the jury where the evidence would support an inference that the defendant advised the plaintiff that she should have an impacted wisdom tooth removed to avoid a 9 percent risk of cancer but did not establish that the defendant knew his statement concerning the risk of cancer to be false. [18] The experts testified that there was a small risk of cancer from an impacted wisdom tooth but that the risk was substantially less than 9 percent. The defendant testified that he told the plaintiff that there was a 0.09 percent risk of cancer and that he always qualified his discussion of the risk by saying it was one in a million. He said he had attended a lecture where an expert had stated that the risk of cancer from an impacted wisdom tooth was another reason justifying its removal. The appellate court found an award of punitive damages improper in this situation because the dentist's statements did not resemble intentional fraud and there was insufficient evidence to support a conclusion that the dentist knew the statement he made to the plaintiff was false or that there was no basis for it.

In another case the plaintiffs sought punitive damages for the circumcision of their newborn child, performed without their permission and against explicit written instructions entered on the hospital admission chart.[19] The circumcision was performed by the resident after the attending physician delivered the child and left the delivery room. There was no evidence, however, that the resident knew that the circumcision was not authorized at the time that she performed it. The appellate court ruled that in the absence of proof that the physician knowingly disregarded the parents' wishes, punitive damages could not be awarded.

Other examples of negligent medical conduct that was held not to rise to the level of reckless or wanton conduct justifying punitive damages include failing to operate on one of the two hernias that plaintiff sought to have repaired,[20] performing a spinal puncture test on the wrong patient,[21] failing to warn a patient of the risk of fractures during electro-shock treatment and failing to administer a muscle relaxant as required,[22] and oversedating a patient during a dental procedure.[23]

Pleading, Discovery, and Burden-of-Proof Issues

The preceding discussion of goals and standards governing punitive damage awards reveals the heavy burden placed on a plaintiff who seeks to recover an award of punitive damages against a doctor, nurse, or other health care provider. The pleading, discovery, and burden-of-proof rules make the task even more difficult.

The standard of recovery requires proof of willful, wanton, or reckless conduct. To initiate a quest to meet this standard, a plaintiff is required to plead the facts that support the claim with specificity. But, since the essential facts involve the state of mind of the defendant, or what he knew or should have known about the likelihood that his conduct would cause harm to the plaintiff, it is difficult to plead the specific facts that support the claim before discovery. If no punitive damage claim is included in the complaint, the plaintiff will confront constant objections during discovery—particularly when taking the defendant's deposition—that the information sought has no relevance to the issues raised by the complaint. In other words, the defendant's lawyer will seek to use the absence of a punitive damage claim in the complaint as a basis for preventing the plaintiff from discovering the facts that may support a punitive damage claim. Finally, even if sufficient facts are discovered to support pleading a claim for punitive damages, the plaintiff will in some jurisdictions face a more difficult burden of proof, such as clear and convincing evidence.[24]

Edwards v. Our Lady of Lourdes Hospital,[25] discussed earlier, reflects the confusion a court experiences when it attempts to apply a special pleading burden for a punitive damage award in a medical malpractice case. In *Edwards*, as we recall, the court ruled that the plaintiffs could not rely on the same facts pleaded in their complaint as the basis of negligence to justify a punitive damage award. The plaintiffs' claim of willful, wanton, and reckless conduct was based on the hospital's failure to monitor the infant's endotracheal tube placement and his blood levels of a toxic drug. In addition, the plaintiffs contended that the hospital failed to ensure that trained nursing staff was present during the night shift. The court dismissed the punitive damage claim, reasoning that the allegations amounted to nothing more than recasting a claim of ordinary negligence into a claim of recklessness.

The *Edwards* decision rests on the erroneous assumption that the same specific facts that support a negligence claim may not support an allegation of reckless disregard of another's safety. The better approach recognizes that deciding whether the facts pleaded justify a punitive damage claim involves drawing reasonable inferences from the facts. Accordingly, a common set of facts may support allegations of both negligence and recklessness. For example, assume that a child was injured when he was struck by an automobile driven by the defendant at a speed of sixty miles per hour in a school zone. An allegation in a complaint against the defendant that he engaged in negligent conduct would certainly be meritorious. In addition, a count pleading the same facts and alleging that this conduct rose to the level of reckless disregard of the plaintiff's safety, justifying an award of punitive damages, would also be meritorious. Even if the defendant claimed that he did not know at the time that he was driving in a school zone, if signs indicating the school zone were present, the fact that he should have known would be enough to justify an award of punitive damages. Alternatively, the jury should be given the opportunity to determine whether he actually knew that he was driving in a school zone. If they conclude that he did or that there was no excuse for his not knowing, punitive damages should be permissible. The same reasoning should apply to a punitive damage claim against a health care provider.

Regardless of the ruling on this issue, discovery should be permitted that will allow the plaintiff to explore all the information that may support either claim. This broad scope of discovery relating to the defendant's state of mind is certainly justified on the basis of relevancy in that it either will relate to information bearing directly on the negligence claim or may lead to information that may bear on the appropriate award of damages.

On the other hand, unless the plaintiff can plead and discover facts that would allow a reasonable person to infer willful, wanton, or reckless conduct, she should not be allowed to discover information pertaining to the defendant's wealth, such as income tax returns and profit-and-loss statements. Of course, with a viable punitive damage claim, this information becomes critical to assessing the proper amount of money required to punish the defendant and deter him from engaging in such outrageous conduct in the future.

Insurance Considerations

If the plaintiff's punitive damage claim survives a motion to dismiss, counsel for the defendant faces a potential conflict of interest. Counsel must determine whether the defendant's liability insurance policy obligates his insurer to defend against the punitive damage claim and indemnify the defendant for any punitive damage award that the plaintiff wins. The answer to the question turns first on interpreting the language in the insurance policy and second on the law of the jurisdiction governing the insurance policy.

Jurisdictions disagree as to whether it is against public policy to allow a person to insure against a punitive damage award. Some take the view that to allow such insurance would defeat the primary purpose of the award, namely, punishing the defendant.[26] Others argue that as long as the conduct that gives rise to the claim does not amount to an intentional tort, the public policy of compelling a party to honor his contract prevails.[27]

Since the insurance company usually hires the attorney to defend against the medical malpractice claim, unless the insurance company is prepared to stipulate that the policy obligates it both to defend against the punitive damage claim and to indemnify the defendant if the plaintiff prevails on the claim, the insured health care provider is entitled to independent counsel; the attorney hired by the insurance company should so advise the insured. In the absence of independent counsel, the attorney representing the defendant will be burdened with a conflict in developing evidence and arguments to support the position that the insurance either does or does not cover the claim and that coverage either is or is not consistent with the state's public policy.[28]

From the plaintiff's perspective, the desirability of having the insurance policy cover the punitive damage claim would seem to turn on the nature of the case and the wealth of the defendant. Obviously, an award of punitive damages that cannot be collected is valuable to the plaintiff only in emotional terms. In some situations it may be enough for the plaintiff to see the defendant sweat and go into bankruptcy. In most cases, however, the plaintiff probably prefers the concrete vindication that comes with compensation to the emotional one that accompanies an uncollectible punitive damage award.

Constitutional Issues

The ultimate question posed by a request for punitive damages is whether the court should afford a jury an opportunity to express indignation at the conduct of the defendant by making him pay an amount beyond the cost of the damages he caused. The question takes on added significance in light of the limited control the court will have over the amount of punitive damages that the jury may award. Recently, concern over the broad discretion granted to juries in most states to assess punitive damages prompted a constitutional challenge that bestowing such power on the jury violates the due process clause of the Fourteenth Amendment to the U.S. Constitution. The case involved a large award against an insurance company and its agent, who had misappropriated health insurance premiums, leaving individuals without any health insurance. One woman discovered the fraud when she was hospitalized and the health insurance company denied coverage. She was required to make payments on her bill before the hospital would discharge her. Her physician later submitted his unpaid bill to a collection agency, and her credit was adversely affected. A jury awarded her and other claimants who were defrauded punitive damages. The trial court and the Alabama Supreme Court affirmed the awards.[29]

Dissatisfied with this result, the defendant who employed the guilty agent appealed to the U.S. Supreme Court. The Supreme Court held that punitive damages per se were not violative of the due process clause of the Fourteenth Amendment.[30] Noting that the Fourteenth Amendment does place some limits on an award of punitive damages, the court found that the award in this case withstood constitutional scrutiny. That was because the jury received adequate instructions regarding the basis and purposes of a punitive damage award, the trial court followed established posttrial procedures for scrutinizing the award, and the state supreme court provided an additional check on the jury's or trial court's discretion.

The Supreme Court decision upholding the constitutionality of the punitive damage award eliminates the uncertainty regarding a state's power to grant such awards in tort cases. The decision also sets forth guidelines for placing some limits on the discretion of juries and trial courts. The guidelines are quite general, however, and the extent to which punitive damages are allowed will turn on the policies and attitudes embraced by the individual states.[31]

Part III

Gathering Evidence and
Developing Strategies

Chapter 9

Obtaining and Reviewing Medical Records

Medical records present a lawyer with three recurring problems: acquiring a complete and legible copy in a timely manner, interpreting the medical terminology, evaluating the medical-legal significance of the information. Ordinarily, defense counsel has less difficulty obtaining a complete, legible copy of the records than plaintiff's counsel since the defendant usually has immediate access to the records reflecting the care rendered by him. If it becomes necessary to review the records of another doctor or a hospital, however, defense counsel will need an authorization from the plaintiff for release of the records. If the plaintiff refuses the requested authorization, a court order may be required.[1]

Defense counsel faces the same challenge as plaintiff's counsel in trying to make sense of the medical records. She can, however, turn to her client for help in understanding them. Plaintiff's counsel must depend on his own knowledge and experience and on the assistance of expert witnesses in interpreting the language of the records and evaluating their significance.

Medical records present the basic script for a medical malpractice case. Counsel for both sides must scrutinize the records for potential bombshells.

■ **Problem:** *Incomplete Medical Record*

Joy Jenkins has retained counsel to evaluate a potential medical malpractice case against the obstetrician who delivered her baby, who was stillborn. She has been advised by another obstetrician, who is a friend of her family, that her treating obstetrician may have unduly delayed the performance of a caesarean section, which could have saved the life of

149

her child. The merit of her case turns on an evaluation of the fetal monitor tape, however, which shows the status of the fetus's heartbeat during
the hour preceding delivery. Mrs. Jenkins's attorney has been supplied
the entire medical record, except for the fetal monitor tape. The hospital
claims the tape is either lost or destroyed. What remedies are available to
Mrs. Jenkins?

In reflecting on this problem, reconsider Problem Four in Chapter 1.

The issues raised here pose a significant challenge to all concerned. The
law requires a health care provider to complete an accurate medical record
in a timely manner. Specifically, the *Accreditation Manual for Hospitals (1992)*,
published by the Joint Commission on Accreditation of Healthcare Organizations, states: "The hospital is responsible for safeguarding both the record
and its informational content against loss, defacement, and tampering and
from use by unauthorized individuals" (MR3.1 at 52). The manual further
provides: "The length of time that medical records are to be retained is dependent on the need for their use in continuing patient care and for legal,
research, or educational purposes and on law and regulation" (MR.4.2). The
problem, from the perspective of an attorney evaluating a potential medical
malpractice case, is that the law is unclear concerning the remedy available to
the suspected malpractice victim who cannot fully evaluate his case because
the health care provider has breached his record-keeping obligations.

Clearly, the content of the medical records bears heavily on the health
care provider's credibility. One court, for example, held that a jury could
rely on the absence of an entry in the medical record to find that a physician
breached his duty to monitor carefully the administration of a drug (Pitocin)
during the delivery of the plaintiff's baby.[2] In that court's view the absence of
an entry noting the physician's presence during the critical period of the delivery allowed the jury to conclude that the physician was not present, despite
his trial testimony to the contrary. In other words, the jury could conclude
that the medical records presented more believable testimony on this issue
than the physician's trial testimony.

In another case a plaintiff sued a hospital alleging that the hospital
breached its duty to keep and maintain her late husband's medical records
and that the breach rendered her unable to prove that her husband's death
was caused by the negligence of the hospital and other health care providers.
The trial court dismissed her negligence claim based on inadequate record
keeping. But the appellate court reversed, holding that the hospital clearly
had a duty to maintain the records and that a breach of this duty would
support a traditional negligence claim.[3] The court's ruling implied that if the
plaintiff could prove that she lost her underlying medical malpractice claim

because of the hospital's failure to maintain the records, she could recover in her negligent record-keeping lawsuit all the damages that she otherwise could have recovered in the initial malpractice action. Though the theory of the case warrants further development, the decision demonstrates the importance of medical records in medical malpractice litigation.

The preceding decisions provide a basis for argument as to the appropriate remedy, but they are not squarely on point. The law on this subject is in its infancy. We will return to a consideration of the issues raised in the problem after an excursion through the basic procedures and standards applicable to the acquisition, retention, and review of medical records.

Acquiring the Records

As a general rule, the health care provider owns the actual medical records.[4] Many states, however, provide by statute[5] or case law[6] that the patient or her duly authorized representative has a right to a copy of the medical records on request and payment of a reasonable fee for identifying and reproducing them.[7] In most cases the medical records will be supplied to plaintiff's counsel only after submission of a written request accompanied by a properly executed authorization from the client. Though the procedure may not be legally necessary, to avoid a delay in the production of the documents counsel may also find it advantageous to have the client's signature notarized to bypass questions about the authenticity of her authorization.

A medical records custodian who has been presented with a request for records must take into account the patient's right to a copy of her records, her right of privacy, her health, and the public health. If the patient or her representative makes the request, the dominant consideration is the patient's right to her records, balanced against a paternalistic concern about whether the release of the records will be detrimental to the patient's well-being. The latter concern merits substantial weight in some situations, such as when a patient suffers from a mental illness. In the absence of mental illness or incompetency, however, the custodian cannot justify withholding the medical records from an adult patient on the ground that disclosing the information to the patient would be detrimental to her health.[8]

It is true that the method of disclosure warrants thought, particularly in a case where the plaintiff may be shocked by the information regarding her health, but such concern does not justify withholding the records. A 1986 appellate court decision in Pennsylvania awarded $2,500 in compensatory damages and $10,000 in punitive damages against physicians who repeatedly refused to provide a former mental patient with a copy of her medical records.[9] A New York court ruled in 1986 that a physician breached his duty of confidentiality to his patient by supplying a copy of her medical records to his medical malpractice insurer because he assumed the patient was preparing to sue him when she requested a copy of her medical records.[10] In effect, both decisions affirmed the patient's right to control and direct release of the information contained in the records.

Plaintiff's counsel will find that doctors and hospitals may deliberately delay reproducing and forwarding medical records to him. Even when they are sent, substantial portions of the records may be incomplete or illegible. If time is of the essence, a court order directing the health care provider to produce the records on or before a certain date may be required.[11] For example, in death cases it is often important to have an autopsy done to clarify the cause of the patient's death, and the patient's medical records may be needed to assist the pathologist's investigation.

For various reasons, in the absence of a court order, the health care provider commonly takes weeks to supply the patient's lawyer with a complete copy of the medical records. Sometimes the delay is due to the health care provider's inefficient system of managing and reproducing medical charts. In other instances the hospital or doctor may route the medical records to their risk managers or legal counsel for review before they are released. The problem is so prevalent that in some jurisdictions medical record copy services have found a viable market in retrieving medical records for patients and their attorneys.

Reviewing Medical Records

Before requesting and reviewing a client's medical chart, the attorney should become familiar with the typical components of a medical record so that he knows what to ask for and can be sure that he receives as much information as possible as quickly as possible. There is no substitute for a detailed review of every word in the medical record and every laboratory report and X ray. Before beginning the review, counsel should gain some familiarity with the ordinary format and contents of medical records, as well as accepted procedures for making entries into them. The *Accreditation Manual for Hospitals* is a useful reference source. Its basic provisions pertaining to medical records include the following standards:

> MR.1. The hospital maintains medical records that are documented accurately and in a timely manner, are readily accessible, and permit prompt retrieval of information, including statistical data.
> MR.2. The medical record contains sufficient information to identify the patient, support the diagnosis, justify the treatment, and document the course and results accurately.

MR.3. Medical records are confidential, secure, current, authenticated, legible, and complete.

MR.4. The medical record department is provided with adequate direction, staffing, and facilities to perform all required functions.

MR.5. The role of medical record personnel in the hospital's overall program for the assessment and improvement of quality and in committee functions is defined.

In addition to general standards, the *Accreditation Manual* lists specific requirements that may be useful in particular cases. The manual also contains provisions applicable to specialized services such as surgery, anesthesia, emergency care, and respiratory services.

It is the responsibility of counsel for both plaintiff and defendant to be sure that they have obtained all medical records that bear on an evaluation of the care rendered to the patient. In accordance with accreditation standards and customary practices, hospital records usually consist of the following components: the emergency room record or admission chart, the operative report, progress notes, nurses' notes, physicians' orders, consultants' reports, social workers' notes, laboratory reports, X rays and other radiological studies, and the discharge summary or autopsy report. Physicians' office records usually consist of physical examination records, laboratory reports, notes of consultations, and prescriptions.

In reviewing the medical records, the attorney should ascertain and verify the reason medical care was desired and/or required, the specific care actually rendered, the timeliness of the care rendered, the appropriateness of the care rendered, and the cause of the untoward result that has brought the patient or her representative to the attorney's office. A systematic review of the medical records will reveal many of the central facts needed for evaluating the potential of a meritorious medical malpractice case. Information gathered from each portion of the chart must be summarized, analyzed in detail, and compared. In addition, if the attorney is familiar with the contents of the medical record and has produced his own summary, the quality of the expert review will be increased and its cost decreased.

The emergency room record or admission chart presents the first part of the story. This chart usually contains a brief history of the patient's physical condition as reported by the patient or her representative, followed by a description of the patient's chief complaint and the admitting physician's observations about the patient's physical condition when she arrived at the hospital. The chart also usually reports the patient's vital signs: pulse rate, blood pressure, respiration, and temperature. In addition, the admitting note sets forth the physician's plan for treatment in light of the diagnosis of the patient's condition.

The next part of the story may appear in a variety of places. Nurses' notes report observations about the patient after admission and the treatment rendered by the nurses in following the physicians' orders. The physicians' orders appear in another part of the chart bearing the same name. If surgery is performed, the surgeon dictates a surgical note describing what occurred during the surgery from the surgeon's perspective, and an anesthesia chart describes the anesthetic administered and the patient's response to it. Laboratory reports set forth the results of all diagnostic tests performed, including such matters as blood cultures, studies of blood gases, and blood transfusions. Records of X rays, ultrasound studies, and CT scans contain important information about the patient's condition at various points in time. The physicians' observations about the patient's progress are set forth in the progress notes. If specialists have been called in, their consultation notes appear among the progress notes. Finally, overall observations about the patient's hospital course are set forth in the discharge summary.

The easiest section of the patient's chart for a layperson to read is generally the discharge summary, because it is usually typewritten and contains fewer abbreviations and complex medical terms than other parts of the chart. Nurses' notes come second. They are usually written legibly and describe the treatment with less medical jargon. The most difficult to read are the laboratory charts and the physicians' orders, which are the least legible and the most steeped in medical terminology. The attorney assessing a case may thus find it useful to begin with the discharge summary and the nurses' notes in order to get a basic understanding of the nature of the case and save a detailed review of the more difficult portions of the chart for the end. It is important to understand, however, that because the discharge summary merely reflects the effort of a physician to summarize what has occurred, it may contain significant errors.

Translating and Summarizing Medical Records

Most lawyers can remember how, during their first year of law school, they methodically plowed through a case in an attempt to understand it well enough to prepare a brief. In the early stages of legal training, an important first step to understanding the overall significance of a court's opinion is to use a legal dictionary to translate the meaning of particular words that are not commonly confronted outside the legal context. Guessing at the meaning of these words by looking at the context in which they appear often leads the student to misinterpret the passage and miss its true significance. A lawyer who is handling his first medical malpractice case must often relive this part of his law school experience if he is to evaluate and prosecute the case effectively.

There is no substitute for a painstaking translation and analysis of each page of the patient's medical record. It may not be necessary for the lawyer who will exercise the ultimate valuative judgment or who will try the case personally to translate and analyze each page of the record, but it must be done by someone retained by him, and he is ultimately obliged to understand it. A system for translating and summarizing the medical records is thus critical to evaluating a potential case. And, clearly, trained and disciplined personnel are key to running the system efficiently and reliably. The attorney who relies completely on outside experts to review the records and identify the important aspects of the case from a medical-legal perspective is not only paying too much money, but is also inviting errors and oversights that may haunt the evaluation and litigation of the case for years to come. If the expert is competent, she is likely to have many demands on her time and the particular case under review is not necessarily going to be her highest priority. If she does find the time for a thorough review, the cost per hour may be astounding. For all these reasons, alternatives to total reliance on an expert warrant careful attention.

The first decision is who should bear initial responsibility for organizing and translating the medical records. The characteristics and abilities of the person selected are more important than the person's particular background. Medical records do not by their nature grip the attention of the reader for long periods of time. To perform the task effectively, the reviewer must be patient, methodical, disciplined, and intelligent. These characteristics may be found in an individual secretary, paralegal, or attorney or in a person with no prior work experience in the law. Regardless of background, the person must take pride in having the perseverance to review an abundance of data until the relevant information is highlighted and organized. He must also be able to take what he has digested and communicate it intelligibly and constructively to facilitate reading and use by the attorney litigating the claim.

When the medical records are secured, they should be viewed as an especially important piece of evidence that will be needed for a long period of time. Maximizing effective use of medical records requires early recognition of their future use. Problems of identification, authentication, and admissibility must be anticipated. Because of the importance of the medical records and the central role assigned to them as evidence in the potential case, the first task of the reviewer should be to number the pages and copy the records as numbered. Numbering the pages at the outset allows counsel to be sure that all persons with whom he discusses the case are addressing the same information and that all relevant portions of the record are produced and retrieved at the various stages of the evaluation process and, later, during litigation. It also permits a careful comparison of the records supplied by the health care provider with the original records in the attorney's possession.

The next task is to translate the medical terms in the records so that the attorney can understand the diagnosis and treatment well enough to communicate with health care professionals and raise the right factual questions. The initial reviewer should highlight words that she does not understand because of their technical nature. She should also underline words or phrases that she finds illegible because of poor reproduction or poor writing. The tendency to ignore such words must be resisted, lest significant facts escape acknowledgment. To do this effectively will require the use of a medical dictionary and medical texts and the assistance of trained health care professionals.

It is important to organize the records in a manner that will allow fast retrieval of desired information. An index should be prepared identifying the pages of the medical records where a particular matter appears. If a theory of liability or causation has surfaced, the organizer of the document should also produce an index designating the location of the relevant information. In addition, if following a sequence of information (such as vital signs or daily doses of medication) over a period of time is important, a flow chart of some sort should be prepared to allow examination of the data at a glance.

Translating, organizing, and summarizing the medical records takes considerable time. If this task is done well in the first instance, however, it will not only save thousands of dollars in expert fees but will also enhance the validity of the case evaluation, allowing the attorney to screen and prosecute the case more effectively. Once the records have been reviewed and organized in this manner, the attorney is in a position to elicit some preliminary reactions from potential experts and to conduct a full-scale evaluation of the case if the initial reactions and other valuative factors support the investment.

The Altered or Missing Medical Record

Any attorney, whether for the plaintiff or for the defendant, who believes that the medical records produced have been altered should take immediate steps to resolve these concerns. If an alteration has indeed occurred, it is important to determine when it happened, who did it, and whether it involves material facts or seemingly insignificant data.

Clearly, the worst situation for a health care provider, and for his lawyer, is one where material information has been altered after the appropriateness of the care rendered has been questioned. Whoever altered the records in these circumstances faces a serious challenge to his or her credibility. The best thing for defense counsel to do in such a case is to bring the matter to the attention of the court and the plaintiff if litigation has already commenced. The rules of professional conduct mandate that the court and opposing counsel be advised. Moreover, since expert document examiners are able to identify altered records through a variety of methods, including ink analysis, the chance of an altered record escaping detection by experienced plaintiff's counsel is small. If the alteration was made to deceive, defense counsel will pay a high price for disclosing the fact, but she will pay an even higher price if the alteration is exposed to the jury in the form of a cover-up.

Medical records are generally admissible as substantive evidence in the trial of the case. Although the statements recorded in the record are hearsay, the Federal Rules of Evidence and many state rules allow the admission of medical records as an exception to the hearsay rule. The reason for admitting the records is that statements made by a patient for the purpose of receiving medical care are deemed trustworthy. The same is true of observations, findings, opinions, and diagnoses made by health care providers at the time they are treating a patient. The admissibility of the records as evidence sets the stage for dramatic trial confrontations when the records are missing or altered.

It is important to determine the motivation or fault of the health care provider in connection with lost or altered records. For evidentiary purposes, the law deals more harshly with the intentional or negligent alteration or destruction of records than it does with records innocently lost or destroyed. Courts have held that a person who deliberately or negligently destroys evidence should not benefit from that action. Accordingly, a doctrine known as *spoliation* has been embraced. This doctrine penalizes the spoiler of the evidence by either creating a rebuttable presumption or allowing a jury to draw an inference that the lost or altered evidence would have been unfavorable to the spoiler. In a medical malpractice trial such a charge to the jury could significantly influence the evaluation of the case. It should be noted, however, that the courts have not gone so far as to hold that the factfinder must find that the spoiler of evidence was guilty of malpractice. The plaintiff still must prove her prima facie case with evidence independent of the spoiled evidence.

To assess the potential impact of lost or spoiled evidence, counsel should carefully research the theoretical causes of action, remedies, and defenses, as recognized in the jurisdiction whose law will govern. Significant cases addressing the spoliation issue include the following.

1. Recognition of a Cause of Action: Underlying Theories
    a. Negligence
        In *Langager v. Lake Havasu Community Hospital*,[12] the plaintiff brought a two-count medical malpractice action against the hospital. The first count set forth a straightforward cause of action of medical malpractice "alleging gross negligence and carelessness on the part of the hospital and its employees in methods of record keeping adopted by the hospital."[13] The second count alleged that the hospital " 'spoliated, altered and fabricated the [deceased patient's] medical records . . . with the intent of concealing and misrepresenting certain facts about [the deceased patient's] condition, injury and the cause'. . . . Plaintiffs allege[d] this caused them severe mental and emotional distress."[14] As

to the negligence count, plaintiff alleges that the hospital breached its duty of care to the deceased patient." Plaintiff defined this duty of care as "the proper recordation of medical information, the preservation thereof, and its accurate maintenance for the purpose of rendering treatment to the plaintiff." [15] The court, in recognizing the validity of this cause of action for negligence, agreed with plaintiff that the hospital had a duty to maintain patient medical records.

The court affirmed the lower court's dismissal of the claim, however, because the action had been filed three years after the injury was known. [16] The court's treatment of the emotional distress claim, discussed more fully below, was also dismissed on the basis of the statute of limitations.

If the plaintiff in *Langager* had met the three-year statute of limitations, she might have faced another type of procedural problem, as discussed in *Fox v. Cohen*. [17] In *Fox*, the plaintiff filed, as one of three counts, a negligence action against the hospital and its employees for the "loss, destruction or misplacement" of the deceased patient's test results and reports. [18] Plaintiff based this claim on the theory that the hospital had a duty to exercise reasonable care in the custody, safekeeping, and maintenance of records related to patient care. [19] To establish the hospital's duty not to alter records, the plaintiff pointed to authority recognizing the existence of a common law duty [20] and a statutory law duty [21] for the maintenance of patient medical records. Based on a review of its jurisdiction's negligence cases, the court agreed that a duty existed. [22]

Next the court looked to pertinent legislative enactments, administrative regulations, and standards set forth by the American hospital Association to determine the standard of conduct. [23] It concluded that the hospital did indeed have a duty to use reasonable care to maintain a complete and accurate medical record on each patient.

Notwithstanding the finding of a duty, the *Fox* court affirmed the dismissal of the plaintiff's claim of negligent record keeping on the ground that it was premature. [24] Since the plaintiff's medical malpractice claim was still pending, [25] the court rejected as pure speculation plaintiff's contention that "she will sometime in the future lose the malpractice action because of the absence of [a test or record]." [26] Under this ruling, a plaintiff must wait until she has lost her medical malpractice claim and then bring an action alleging that she lost her medical malpractice suit as a direct result of the alteration or loss of medical records. [27]

b. Negligence Per Se

The plaintiff in *Bondu v. Gurvich* contended, among other things, that the hospital was negligent per se for failing its statutory duty to provide the plaintiff with the deceased patient's medical records. [28] The lower court granted the hospital's motion for summary judgment on the premise that the filing of this claim was premature. [29] In dismissing the claim, the lower court reasoned that "no cause of action lay for the failure of the hospital to provide plaintiff with the deceased patient's medical records which rendered the plaintiff unable to pursue certain proof which *may* be necessary to prove her related medical malpractice claims." [30]

Although the reviewing court concurred with the lower court's rationale for dismissing the original claim, it reversed the lower court's decision dismissing the claim on the basis that the plaintiff had filed an amended complaint after the entry of summary judgment against her medical malpractice claims.[31] As soon as the plaintiff's medical malpractice claims were dismissed, "the fact of damage became certain and her cause of action ripened."[32]

c. Emotional Distress

In *Langager*, the plaintiff alleged, among other things, that the defendant's intentional concealment and misrepresentation of certain facts regarding the deceased patient's condition caused her severe mental and emotional distress.[33] Citing *Fox* and *Bondu*, the plaintiff argued that the *Langager* court should recognize this new tort as "spoliation of evidence."[34] The court recognized the new tort but affirmed the lower court's decision dismissing the count because the two-year statute of limitations had expired.[35] The plaintiff, to no avail, first argued that the three-year statute of limitations should run, since the injury arose in the context of a health care provider–patient setting.[36]

The court acknowledged that in certain situations where there are duplicate causes of action arising out of the same set of facts, the longer statute of limitations is applicable.[37] For example, if in addition to the traditional medical malpractice claim a plaintiff is also alleging a count of battery, the three-year statute of limitations applies to the battery claim although such claims usually have a shorter statute of limitations.[38] But the court distinguished the plaintiff's situation from this type of situation on the basis that the set of facts leading to the claim of emotional distress arose out of a different set of facts removed from the traditional medical malpractice claim.[39]

In rejecting the plaintiff's additional arguments, the court noted that under the state's statutory scheme, the statute of limitations begins "upon the occurrence of the injury, not when the injury manifests itself."[40] The plaintiff argued that the statute of limitations should have begun from the moment she started to suffer from emotional distress as a result of her knowledge that the medical records had been altered. In the alternate the plaintiff contended that the statute of limitations should have begun when her unsuccessful medical malpractice suit was dismissed, because "the unsuccessful conclusion of her [s]tate court action against the treating physician was proximately caused by [the physician's] alteration of [the deceased patient's] medical records."[41] Neither one of these arguments was successful.

d. Intentional Fraud, Concealment, and Alteration

In *Jackson v. Julian*,[42] the plaintiff patient appealed the lower court's order dismissing her fraud allegations for failure to state a claim. Plaintiff alleged in her complaint that the physician deliberately did not tell her that he had injured one of her organs during surgery.[43] In addition, the plaintiff alleged that the physician deliberately did not tell her that he had, without her permission, removed one of her organs. He attempted to cover up this act by telling her that the organ was removed by another physician in an earlier operation.[44]

The first allegation concerned actual fraud. "To state a cause of action for actual fraud, the patient must allege that the doctor knowingly or recklessly made a false representation of material fact with the intention that the patient would act thereon, and that she acted in reliance on the representation to her injury."[45] The court dismissed the allegation by the plaintiff of actual fraud on the basis that she failed to allege that the physician, in attempting to cover up his mistakes, made material statements which he intended her to rely on or that she suffered damages through relying on them.[46]

As for constructive fraud, however, the court reversed the lower court's decision dismissing the claim, because it reasoned that the plaintiff need not claim that her physician intended that she rely on the material misrepresentations:[47]

> [C]onstructive fraud occurs when one breaches a legal or equitable duty. Even though this breach may be unintentional, the law considers it fraudulent because it misleads others, violates a confidence or injures a public interest. . . . Because of the doctor's superior medical knowledge and the nature of his relationship with a patient, the courts have applied this doctrine when a doctor makes inaccurate statements to his patient concerning treatment or diagnosis.[48]

e. Conspiracy

Conspiracy is an alternative theory to intentional fraud, concealment, and alteration when two or more defendants are involved in the alleged misconduct. In *Henry v. Deen,*[49] the plaintiff claimed that the deceased patient's physicians and a physician assistant had entered into a conspiracy to destroy the deceased patient's medical records and to falsify and fabricate medical records in an attempt to cover up their alleged negligence.[50] In reversing the lower court's decision to dismiss the claim, the *Henry* court found that the combination of the original complaint and amended complaints did indeed allege a civil conspiracy among the three defendants.[51]

To prove civil conspiracy in the state of North Carolina, the plaintiff must prove that there was a conspiracy among the defendants and that one of the defendants committed wrongful acts in furtherance of the conspiracy.[52] In addition, there must be an allegation that an injury occurred as a result of the conspiracy.[53] Finally, the complaint must allege that the conspiracy occurred before discovery proceedings.[54] The court found that the defendants had deliberately frustrated the plaintiff's ability to gather evidence by lying under oath regarding the content or existence of the deceased patient's medical records.[55] In this particular situation it was alleged that the defendants had agreed to create and did create false entries and misleading entries and also obliterated an entry to conceal the true facts of the diagnosis and treatment of the deceased patient.[56]

In some jurisdictions there is an important distinction between a negligence action and one of civil conspiracy: the plaintiff need not wait for the disposition of the traditional medical malpractice claim before alleging a claim for conspiracy.[57]

2. Maintaining the Action

    a. Presumptions and Burdens

If the plaintiff persuades the court that she has a viable claim of negligence, fraud, conspiracy, and so on, the court must decide what procedures are appropriate for resolving the claim and what remedies are available if the plaintiff prevails. In *Langager* and *Fox*, the courts recognized that a plaintiff has a right to file a subsequent suit alleging the alteration of medical records if the traditional medical malpractice claim is unsuccessful. As stated by the court in *Public Health Trust of Dade City v. Valcin*,[58] however, the mere fact of the existence of altered or missing medical records is not conclusive evidence or an irrebuttable presumption that the hospital or physician acted in a negligent manner.[59]

After determining that the defendant hospital had a duty to maintain patient medical records, the *Valcin* court affirmed in part and rejected in part the lower court's creation of rules allocating the burden of proof.[60] The lower court held that the initial burden of proof should be on the hospital. Once the evidence is brought forth by the hospital, the court's attention should turn to the hospital's conduct in maintaining the patient's medical records. This will determine whether the factfinder should judge the evidence using an irrebuttable presumption (if the hospital acts in an intentional, fraudulent, or conspiratorial manner) or a rebuttable presumption (if the hospital acts in a negligent manner).[61]

    (1) Conclusive Evidence or Irrebuttable Presumption

The *Valcin* court rejected the lower court's irrebuttable presumption on two bases: First, it violated due process "in its failure to provide the adverse party any opportunity to rebut the presumption of negligence."[62] Second, the court stated that such a presumption interferes with the factfinder's function, which is to determine if the defendants acted in an intentional, fraudulent, or conspiratorial manner.[63] Finally, the court stated that if the defendants intentionally interfered with the plaintiff's access to the necessary medical records, then the courts could impose sanctions under the governing rules of civil procedure.[64] The court held that regardless of the cause of action, the rebuttable presumption is to apply.[65]

    (2) Rebuttable Presumption

The lower court, in adopting its rebuttable presumption, placed the burden of proof initially on the hospital to show by the "greater weight of evidence 'that the records are not missing due to an intentional or deliberate act or omission' of the hospital or its employees."[66] If the hospital met its burden, then the " 'fact that the record is missing will merely raise the presumption that the surgical procedure was negligently performed, which presumption may be rebuttable by the hospital by the greater weight of the evidence.' "[67] On review the court affirmed the lower court's rebuttable presumption rule but modified its application.[68]

The court reasoned that unless the purposes of justice are being served, the rebuttable presumption is inapplicable since in certain situations not every missing medical notation or record is indicative of medical malpractice.[69] Once a determination is made by the court that a rebuttable presumption exists, however, the initial burden of proof rests with the plaintiff, who must demonstrate that the absence of evidence hinders the ability to establish a prima facie case.[70]

b. Proof, Evidence

Perhaps the most difficult aspect of this type of litigation for the plaintiff is not presenting the evidence but acquiring it. In these types of cases the plaintiff is forced to rely on the very parties who may have committed the medical malpractice to get evidence to prove his case. The issue of shifting burdens becomes irrelevant if the plaintiff cannot obtain the necessary medical records from the defendants.

The following cases illustrate the types of relief that may be available to a plaintiff who is unable to obtain the medical records. In *Hermann Hosp. v. Thu Nga Thi Tran*,[71] the plaintiff sought a temporary restraining order[72] and a temporary injunction to enjoin the hospital from "(1) destroying or altering medical records relating to the care of the patient; (2) making any notes or entries in the records without indicating the date of the note or entry,"[73] in an effort to ensure that he received all existing medical records necessary for the trial of his medical malpractice case.

The appellate court agreed with the hospital's contention that the trial court abused its discretion in issuing the injunction because "there was factually insufficient evidence to support a finding that [the hospital] intended to engage in the activities sought to be restrained."[74] In addition, the plaintiff was unable to convince the court that irreparable harm would be done if the injunction was not granted.[75]

Most likely, as in *Marsh v. Lake Forest Hospital*,[76] the court will wait until the plaintiff receives a negative response from the defendants regarding any request for the medical records before providing relief. The *Marsh* court ordered polygraph tests.[77] Furthermore, when the requested documents were not produced, a contempt order was issued against hospital's counsel.[78] The purpose of the polygraph tests was to determine if the requested medical records had been altered.[79]

If the plaintiff is unable to present before the factfinder direct evidence regarding the validity of the allegations of record tampering, the courts have allowed an eyewitness to the concealment or alteration of the records. As stated by the court in *May v. Moore*,[80] the plaintiff may establish fact by either direct or circumstantial evidence, and proof is sufficient if, from facts and circumstances adduced, it can be reasonably inferred.[81] In *May*, the court specifically allowed the use of testimony to show that the physician intentionally failed to produce evidence.[82] The testimony was allowed to impeach previous testimony of the physician, who denied that he ever possessed the patient's medical records.[83]

3. Defenses to Action

A procedural defense often used is the statute of limitations. As the cases indicate, the cause of action and the time of discovery of the concealment or alteration will determine the applicable statute of limitations. While the time barring of causes of action has been discussed in the context of access to medical records, at issue still is what happens when the plaintiff cannot initiate a traditional medical malpractice claim in a timely manner because the necessary medical records either are missing or have been altered.

Courts in some traditional medical malpractice cases have viewed the concealment of information as having an adverse impact on the plaintiff's ability to file a claim before the statute of limitations is up. For example, in *Harrison v. United States*,[84] the court held that the statute of limitations was tolled during the critical time that the defendant deliberately concealed the medical records.[85] In addition, the court placed a heavier burden on the defendant to show that the plaintiff possessed the level of knowledge required to commence accrual of the period of limitations.[86]

Summary

Because the review of medical records is so important to a case, and its conduct is so lengthy and laborious, it may be helpful to outline the stages we have examined above and list their components.

A. Acquiring a complete copy of the medical records
    1. Before filing lawsuit
        Request documents.
            Recent medical records of client
            Previous medical records of client
            Client authorization forms
        If request is denied, seek court order.
        Research causes of action.
            Negligence
            Negligence per se
            Emotional distress
            Intentional fraud, etc.
            Civil conspiracy
    2. After initiation of lawsuit:
        Seek order to compel document production.
        Seek temporary restraining order.
        Seek injunction.
B. Collecting reference materials
        Dictionary
        Dictionary of medical terms
        Human anatomy book

C. Reviewing medical records
>>> Count and number pages.
>>> Copy numbered record.
>>> Translate medical terms.
>>> Highlight unknown words.

D. Organizing records
>>> Index contents of record.
>>> Create data flow charts.

E. Selecting records to review in detail
>>> Emergency room or admission chart
>>> Operative report
>>> Progress notes
>>> Nurses' notes
>>> Physicians' orders
>>> Consultants' reports
>>> Social workers' notes
>>> Laboratory reports
>>> X ray reports, other radiological studies
>>> Discharge summary or autopsy report

F. Evaluating medical-legal significance
>> 1. Performing process of evaluation
>>> Know components of medical record.
>>>> Patient's history
>>>> Patient's condition
>>>> Description of patient's complaint
>>>> Admitting physician(s)' observations
>>>> Patient's vital signs
>>>> Physician's treatment plan
>>> Summarize contents in report.
>>>> Reason why treatment was sought
>>>> Specific care rendered
>>>> Timeliness of care
>>>> Appropriateness of care
>>>> Cause of problem
>> 2. Discussing significance with evaluation team
>>> Clients
>>> Medical experts

Successfully completing the stages of this process, and identifying and evaluating the items listed, should take counsel a long way toward approaching the litigation confidently so that she may devote her attention to attacking the weaknesses in her opponent's case rather than worrying about bombshells that may be hidden in the medical records.

Chapter 10

Choosing and Using an Effective Expert Witness

Most medical malpractice cases involve factual issues that are beyond the common knowledge of the jury. Accordingly, both parties must present expert testimony to explain and support their positions. To establish a case warranting submission to a jury, the plaintiff must present the testimony of a doctor or nurse to inform the jury of the standard of care customarily followed in the circumstances and the probable cause of the plaintiff's injuries. The defendant must counter the plaintiff's theories with the testimony of his experts concerning standard of care and causation.

Selecting and presenting the testimony of an expert is the most critical task that a medical malpractice attorney performs. In light of the complexity of medicine and the highly specialized nature of medical practice, a threshold consideration is the type of expert needed. Another issue is whether to use an expert from the local community or to disregard locality considerations. Of equal importance is the ability of the expert to communicate with laypersons. In short, fundamental criteria for selecting an expert include competency in skill and knowledge, the probability that the jury will identify with the expert, and the likelihood that the jury will understand and believe the expert's testimony.

If the lawyer cannot find an expert who is willing to testify, he must determine whether an exception exists that will allow the case to go to the jury in the absence of expert testimony. If he feels he can get by without expert testimony, he must assess the likelihood that the jury will believe his contentions without the support of an expert. This chapter discusses the necessity, admissibility, and sufficiency of expert testimony, giving special consideration to factors that may influence the selection of an expert and the effectiveness of her testimony in light of the particular issues and defendants involved in the case. The chapter concludes with reflections on the law and the process of resolving medical malpractice claims.

■ **Problem:** *Generalist vs. Specialist*

Carl Conrad suffered total loss of feeling in his lower lip after oral surgery. He says he was never advised by the oral surgeon that permanent loss of feeling was an inherent risk of the procedure. His attorney has retained a review of the case by a dentist, Joe Generalist, who has expressed the view that the loss of feeling was due to negligence on the part of the oral surgeon in cutting a nerve during the procedure. In his view the nature of the surgery posed a slight risk of damage to the nerve, but in most cases when the nerve is damaged during this procedure, the damage is due to negligence in surgical technique, such as occurred in this case. He further opines that the oral surgeon should have advised Carl of the risk of nerve damage before performing the procedure.

Dean Smith, the oral surgeon, responds by saying that Generalist does not know what he is talking about. He is not board certified in oral surgery, as is Dean, nor does he have the wealth of experience that Dean has in performing the procedure. Further, Dean swears that he advised Carl of the risk of loss of feeling in his lower lip. He specifically told Carl that in most cases such loss of feeling is temporary, but in rare cases it is permanent.

Does Carl have a viable claim against Dean Smith? If so, should Carl's expert—licensed in dentistry but not board eligible or certified in oral surgery—be allowed to testify concerning standards of informed consent and oral surgery applicable to this case?

Necessity of Expert Testimony

The initial inquiry a trial court makes when a plaintiff proffers expert testimony is whether the subject matter on which the expert offers an opinion is "so distinctly related to some science, profession, business or occupation as to be beyond the ken of the average layman."[1] If the answer is yes, the court must then determine whether the proffered witness possesses the requisite skill and knowledge to offer an opinion that will assist the judge and jury in arriving at a verdict.[2] To this extent, the expert presented by a plaintiff in a medical malpractice case must satisfy the requirements for experts generally.

Overwhelming authority supports the general rule that expert testimony is usually necessary to sustain a medical malpractice action.[3] This rule is founded on the presumption that neither courts nor jurors possess the requisite knowledge and experience to evaluate the conduct of medical practitioners adequately. Expert testimony assists the factfinder in ascertaining the level of skill and expertise customarily possessed and employed by physicians in diagnosing and treating illness under circumstances similar to those in the plaintiff's case.[4] In addition, expert testimony enables the factfinder to determine whether the defendant's alleged deviation from the standard of care caused the plaintiff's injury.[5]

A malpractice action based on lack of informed consent presents unique considerations regarding expert testimony. A majority of jurisdictions require expert testimony to establish the existence and scope of a physician's duty to disclose information concerning the treatment rendered[6] as well as the materiality of risks, benefits, or alternatives to that treatment.[7] In most jurisdictions customary medical practice defines the scope of the defendant's duty to disclose information. The factfinder's role is thus limited to determining whether the defendant conformed to customary medical practice in disclosing or failing to disclose information to the patient.[8] The focus of the expert's testimony varies according to each jurisdiction's views on locality rules, specializations, and schools of medicine. In addition to presenting testimony on customary disclosure practices, the plaintiff must present expert testimony that the physical harm she suffered was caused by the medical treatment rendered.[9]

A substantial number of courts, however, have held that expert testimony is not essential to establishing a physician's duty of disclosure.[10] The court in *Canterbury v. Spence,*[11] for example, distinguished between "medical facts" (requiring expert testimony) and "other facts" (requiring "any witness—expert or not—having sufficient knowledge and capacity to testify to them").[12] Using this distinction, the *Canterbury* court held that while expert testimony was required to establish medical risks, benefits, and alternatives, it was not required to establish which of those risks, benefits, or alternatives were material to a patient's decision.

Those courts not requiring expert testimony on the duty to disclose have cited three principal justifications. First, allowing the patient's physician to exercise unlimited discretion as to disclosure collides with the root premise of informed consent that the patient has the right to make the decision.[13] Second, the subjective nature of testimony on the duty to disclose, along with the corresponding difficulty in defining a community standard of disclosure, precludes meaningful expert testimony on the issue.[14] Finally, because the particular circumstances on which the claim of nondisclosure is based are necessarily fact-sensitive, no expert can honestly say that any customary disclosure practice governed the situation.[15]

While the broad access that today's attorney has to medical experts may persuade a court of the invalidity of the "community of silence"[16] justification for not requiring expert testimony,[17] the difficulty of eliciting meaningful testimony as to a customary disclosure standard may persuade the court to abandon the requirement for expert testimony on the issue. Nevertheless, even when the plaintiff need not produce expert testimony regarding the duty of disclosure, such testimony may be required to establish the materiality[18] or the incidence of certain risks associated with a particular treatment.[19] A medical expert's testimony may also be necessary to establish the existence and feasibility of alternative forms of treatment, the effect of disclosure on the patient, and/or the likely results of nontreatment.[20]

Moreover, variations on the rules regarding expert testimony in informed consent cases occur when the defendant physician discloses none or only some of the risks of a proposed treatment. For example, *Hamilton v. Hardy*[21] held that in light of evidence that the treating physician failed to inform the plaintiff of the risk of abnormal blood clotting associated with the birth-control pill he had prescribed for her, despite his testimony that he was aware of such a risk, there was no need for expert testimony on the medical community's disclosure practices in order to establish a prima facie case. Rather, such evidence made it incumbent on the defendant to introduce evidence that nondisclosure complied with the medical community's standards. In *Morgenroth v. Pacific Medical Center*,[22] on the other hand, the court held that expert testimony was required to establish whether nondisclosure of the risk of stroke in connection with a coronary arteriography was in accord with accepted medical practice. Moreover, since the defendant physician advised the plaintiff that the procedure carried the risk of death or serious disease, the court concluded that this disclosure sufficiently included the risk of a lesser complication such as a stroke.

Because views on the requirement of expert testimony in malpractice cases based on lack of informed consent diverge substantially, an attorney should carefully analyze the trend of her jurisdiction concerning the particular disclosure issue involved. Where such testimony is required, a challenge of the basis of the requirement may be in order. A fact-oriented challenge should focus on the basis of the expert's opinion as to what is customarily disclosed, the source of professional standards, and the rationale for any limitations placed on the disclosure duty. The attorney should also consider a policy-oriented challenge focused on patient autonomy.[23]

Exceptions to the Requirement of Expert Testimony

The most frequently cited exception to the general rule requiring expert testimony concerns nontechnical aspects of the malpractice case. Generally, these are matters readily comprehended and understood by the layperson or so patently obvious that expert testimony is deemed unnecessary. In *Chapman v.*

Pollack,[24] for example, the plaintiff alleged that the defendant negligently failed to diagnose and treat his appendicitis, resulting in a bowel obstruction caused by an infected and ruptured appendix. The court reasoned that while the precise test or means to use in diagnosing appendicitis is a medical matter not commonly known, it is commonly known that such a condition, left untreated, entails imminent and grave danger to life. Accordingly, expert testimony was not required to support a finding that a complete lack of treatment was improper in these circumstances. The court observed:

> Appendicitis is not an obscure medical problem unknown to people generally and the practices of physicians in undertaking to diagnose it are not known only to them. It is a matter of common knowledge, we believe, that the doctors who have patients with persistent, continuing abdominal pain and other symptoms of appendicitis usually attempt to ascertain the cause of the pain . . . and usually do not remain inactive for two or three days while the conditions are not only continuing, but getting worse. And it is also commonly known that when the condition is appendicitis, simple, usually effective means for . . . removing the diseased appendix before it ruptures and spreads infection throughout the body are available to the profession and usually employed.[25]

The court thus found that even in the absence of expert testimony about the proper standard of care for diagnosing and treating appendicitis, the evidence that the plaintiff's condition worsened substantially over three days was sufficient to show that the defendant had departed from medical standards requiring prompt diagnosis and treatment. A majority of jurisdictions support the common-knowledge exception to the rule generally requiring expert testimony.[26]

The doctrine of res ipsa loquitur, discussed in Chapter 3, may also provide grounds for an exception to the expert testimony requirement. Although generally inapplicable to a medical malpractice case, res ipsa loquitur applies if the accident that caused the plaintiff's injury is the kind that ordinarily does not occur unless someone is negligent. For example, a sponge is not usually left in a patient's body following surgery in the absence of negligence, nor is one's shoulder ordinarily injured in the course of a tonsillectomy. In such cases the doctrine of res ipsa loquitur is applied without the necessity of expert testimony. In other situations expert testimony may provide the basis for invoking the doctrine. In other words, even though the expert cannot identify the specific negligent act committed by the defendant, he may express an opinion to a reasonable medical certainty that the nature or extent of the injury that the plaintiff suffered does not ordinarily occur as a result of the medical treatment rendered in the absence of some negligent act on the part of the caregiver.

An interesting example of the invocation of res ipsa loquitur on the basis of expert testimony is found in *Wilkinson v. Vessey*, [27] where the court relied on the testimony of the defendant radiologists to support using the doctrine against them. The plaintiff, Ms. Wilkinson, had suffered serious skin damage as a result of radiation treatment and alleged that the injury was due to negligence in the manner in which the radiologists administered her X ray treatment. She did not present an expert witness to support her claim, however. The defendant radiologists, who testified on cross-examination, acknowledged that if the treatment had been given to Ms. Wilkinson as prescribed, she would not have been harmed. On the basis of this testimony the appellate court reasoned that the jury could conclude that the kind of injuries suffered by Ms. Wilkinson were the type that ordinarily would not occur during the course of the kind of radiation therapy she was undergoing in the absence of some mishap.

On the basis of cases such as *Wilkinson* the plaintiff's attorney who anticipates relying on the doctrine should prepare to offer expert medical opinion that the alleged harm does not usually occur in the absence of negligence. Such testimony is helpful even where the facts of a case appear clearly to warrant application of the doctrine.

Holmes v. Gamble [28] illustrates the difficulty entailed in relying on the doctrine in some jurisdictions, even when a plaintiff presents expert medical testimony. In *Holmes*, the plaintiff suffered a serious injury to his knee when a ditch caved in at his worksite. The injury required emergency surgery performed under general anesthesia. The plaintiff testified that on awakening from the operation, he experienced numbness and tingling in the last three fingers of both hands. He also testified that when he reported these sensations to the defendant orthopedic surgeon, the surgeon suggested they were caused by pressure on his elbows during the operation. A neurologist the plaintiff consulted after the operation diagnosed the sensations as symptoms of bilateral ulnar neuropathy, which can be caused by trauma to nerves in the elbow. The plaintiff underwent neurosurgery on one elbow and had regained some but not full use of both hands by the time of the trial.

Because he was unconscious during the entire operation, the plaintiff relied on the doctrine of res ipsa loquitur to create a presumption that his neural disorder was a proximate result of negligence on the part of the surgeon and anesthesiologist. Specifically, he alleged that his injury resulted from their negligent failure to position him properly on the operating table. In addition to circumstantial evidence, the plaintiff offered expert medical testimony. At the close of the plaintiff's evidence the trial court directed a verdict in favor of the anesthesiologist. After the presentation of the surgeon's evidence the court directed a verdict for the surgeon, ruling in part that the doctrine of res ipsa loquitur did not apply to the case. The court of appeals upheld this ruling. [29]

On appeal,[30] the Supreme Court of Colorado held that the plaintiff failed to establish a case based on res ipsa loquitur against either defendant: "Taking all of the evidence and inferences . . . in the light most favorable to [plaintiff], we find that it is at least equally likely that a cause other than the defendants' negligence was the basis of [plaintiff's] injury."[31] In the court's view the plaintiff failed to eliminate other possible causes of his injury, such as the original accident and the pressure on his elbows while he was being transported from a clinic to the hospital. Consequently, the court did not consider the sufficiency of the evidence to support the other elements of res ipsa loquitur.[32]

Thus, even when reliance on the doctrine of res ipsa loquitur appears warranted, it should be recognized that the court will apply stringent standards to determine whether the evidence offered is sufficient to support the claim. Exclusive reliance on res ipsa loquitur should therefore be a matter of last resort.

Competency

The law vests the trial court with the responsibility and discretion to determine whether a witness is competent to render an expert opinion in a medical malpractice case. The trial court's decision will be disturbed on appeal only where the court has abused its discretion or committed a clear error of law.[33] To qualify as an expert, a witness must have acquired specialized knowledge, through either academic study or practical experience, that will assist the trier of fact in arriving at a verdict. There is no one formulation that renders a witness competent to express an opinion. Beyond the trial court's determination of the competency of the witness, the jury is left to weigh the credibility and accuracy of his testimony.[34]

The qualifications of the expert medical witness are often closely related to the substantive impact of his testimony. Offering the testimony of an expert-physician who possesses significant professional credentials, for example, can help ensure the jury's belief in the opinion he renders. An evaluation of a potential witness's qualifications, therefore, should include consideration of academic credentials, professional affiliations, publications, licensure, awards, and practical experience in the subject on which testimony will be given.

Although possession of a license to practice medicine may be sufficient proof of a witness's competency to testify on medical matters, failure to possess such a license does not by itself disqualify a witness from offering an expert medical opinion.[35] Thus, a physician's assistant with more than ten years' experience was found properly qualified to testify in an action alleging the defendant-physician's negligence in permitting a gauze sponge to remain inside the plaintiff after an appendectomy.[36] On the other hand, a licensed witness who lacks recent practical experience, board certification in a particular specialty, or formal study in the subject under investigation may be deemed disqualified from testifying even though he possesses a valid license to practice medicine. In *Gilmore v. O'Sullivan*,[37] for example, the plaintiff's medical expert admitted he had not delivered a baby since 1959, had not studied obstetrics, and had no board certification in obstetrics. Based on these facts, the court held that he was not qualified to offer an opinion in an action against a defendant-obstetrician alleging negligent prenatal care and delivery. Of controlling importance, therefore, is the potential expert's occupational experience or practical knowledge of the standards customarily followed in the profession that would render him competent to testify.[38]

Familiarity with the Medical Matter in Question

It is unclear whether the requirement that the expert have practical knowledge on the area under consideration means that he must have personally diagnosed or treated patients under the circumstances of the case. Generally, the attorney ought to try to locate an expert who has at least some familiarity, through personal experience, observation, or consultation, with the medical matters at issue. This is particularly important in view of the rapid advances in medical technology, for what was standard practice in the recent past may now be outmoded as a result of research and clinical developments. Moreover, even where the expert's training and experience reveal familiarity with the technique or procedure alleged to have been performed negligently by the defendant, opinion testimony may be tempered by locality, academic, or specialization considerations.

As a general rule, most jurisdictions require the expert witness to have some familiarity with the care and treatment of the illness or injury in suit, although not necessarily personal experience.[39] This is especially so where the matter involved entails a unique or novel procedure.[40] Where the expert does have practical experience and has studied relevant medical data and materials, a trial court's exclusion of his opinion is likely to constitute reversible error.[41]

In considering the medical witness's purported familiarity with the medical matter in question, a court may further focus on the time period in which the witness's knowledge of the subject was acquired. The issues that may evolve from this consideration are typically fact-oriented. For instance, an expert offered by a plaintiff in a malpractice action alleging negligent performance of a vasectomy, who had not engaged in performing vasectomies for fifteen years before trial, was found by the trial court to be unqualified to render an opinion because this specialized field of medicine had undergone recent material developments. In affirming this decision, the Delaware

Supreme Court agreed with the lower court that "[a] professional is entitled to be judged according to the state of the art appropriate to the litigation."[42]

On the other hand, the Supreme Court of California found prejudicial error in a lower court's refusal to allow an expert to testify on the standard of care prevailing in 1949, when the operation on the plaintiff had taken place, even though the expert had not been admitted to practice until several years later.[43] The court observed that in preparing for his testimony, the expert had examined available literature on the topic and based his opinion not only on such literature but also on his personal training and experience. In finding no authority for the proposition that the "occupational experience" test of a witness's qualifications relates exclusively to the time of the alleged malpractice, the court held that "an invariable rule which would require in all cases that an expert must have acquired a personal working knowledge of the standard of care at the time when the alleged malpractice occurred would be untenable."[44] Noting that the defendant had the resources of intensive cross-examination and opposing experts to overcome any injustice involved in allowing the plaintiff's expert to testify, the court rejected a strict standard regarding testimonial qualifications of medical experts.[45]

The Locality Rule

The locality in which a physician practices can have significant impact on the expert witnesses' qualifications. In its most narrow sense the "locality rule" provides that a medical practitioner's conduct is to be assessed according to the standard in the community in which he practices. Strict application of this rule requires a plaintiff to present expert testimony only from a witness familiar with the standard of care exercised by physicians in the defendant's community.[46]

Modern decisions, however, lend little support to this rule.[47] Rather, the majority view supports the rule that the standard of care by which a physician's conduct is to be judged is determined by reference to the standard of care in effect in the defendant's community *or* in a similar locality.[48] To determine whether two localities are similar, courts generally focus on characteristics that have an impact on the medical care offered there, such as the nature and number of medical and research facilities, the medical population, and the availability of training and equipment.[49]

Although most jurisdictions apply a "same or similar locality" rule,[50] many use a "national standard" rule where the particular technique or procedure at issue is performed uniformly throughout the country.[51] This rule allows qualified witnesses not practicing in the defendant's community or even in a similar community to testify in a medical malpractice case.

Some courts apparently adopt a national standard while still allowing locality considerations to be taken into account in determining the degree of care and skill expected of a physician.[52] Generally, however, even where jurisdictions maintain the "same or similar" locality rule for assessing a medical practitioner's conduct, the rule is held inapplicable with respect to specialists. Thus, if a physician holds herself out as a specialist, a national standard for that specialty is applied.[53] Accordingly, an expert witness practicing in the same specialty as the defendant is typically found competent to testify regardless of locality considerations.

Same School of Learning

With certain exceptions, an expert medical witness must have acquired his knowledge and training in the context of the same school of medicine in which the defendant was schooled and trained.[54] This rule ensures that a physician's conduct is assessed according to the standards derived from the philosophical and technical teachings embraced by a particular school of medicine. Thus, for instance, an osteopath may not testify against an allopathic physician, nor may an allopathic physician testify against a chiropractor.[55] A notable and frequently cited exception to this rule occurs when the methods of treatment in the defendant's school and the witnesses' school are the same[56] or when they should be the same.[57] A witness from a school other than that of the defendant may also be permitted to testify where the witness is familiar with the practice of the defendant's school.[58]

Sufficiency of the Expert Opinion

The nature of the testimony presented by a medical expert can significantly affect the outcome of a malpractice case. Thus, it is important to select the expert carefully and give considerable thought to determining the kind of presentation she should make. Typically, sufficient testimony must be presented to establish the standard of care required of a physician under the circumstances, the defendant's adherence to or departure from that standard, and, where the causal relation issue is not within the common-knowledge exception, the cause in fact of the harm alleged. From the plaintiff's point of view, it is critically important to secure an expert whose opinion sufficiently shows that the defendant's action or omission was a proximate or contributing cause of the plaintiff's injuries. Without such testimony, a claim rests merely on conjecture, compelling a jury to speculate on how the injury related to the defendant's conduct.

The case of *Walton v. Jones*[59] illustrates the importance of sufficient expert testimony. In that case the plaintiff instituted an action for the wrongful death of her husband, alleging that the defendant's negligent treatment of her husband's fractured ankle resulted in his death from pulmonary emboli. Both her witnesses, an internist who treated her husband and the pathologist who supervised the autopsy,[60] as well as the defendant, testified that drugs are available that may arrest the formation of new blood clots. No testimony indicated, however, that treating the decedent with anticoagulant drugs would have reduced the likelihood of his death. Nor did any testimony identify the source of the fatal emboli. The trial court granted the defendant's motion for a directed verdict on the ground that the plaintiff had failed to introduce sufficient medical testimony to create a jury issue on the causal connection between the defendant's actions or omissions and the decedent's death.

On appeal the order was affirmed. In its review of the testimony the Minnesota Supreme Court observed that while the evidence could be consistent with the plaintiff's theory that the defendant's negligent treatment of the decedent resulted in his death and that his death would not have occurred had he been given proper treatment, consistency was not enough to justify that theory. In setting forth the standard by which expert testimony is assessed, the court stated: "[T]he expert testimony must demonstrate a reasonable probability that defendant's negligence was the proximate cause of the injury. Testimony must show that it was more likely that death occurred from defendant's negligence than from anything else."[61]

Walton thus illustrates that the absence of concise expert testimony on the applicable standard of care, the defendant's deviation therefrom, and, most important, the issue of causation will prove fatal to a plaintiff's case. In rejecting such claims, courts remain committed to preventing verdicts based on speculation. There are, however, cases in which courts recognize the fundamental unfairness of imposing this stringent burden of proof of causation on the plaintiff. Such cases typically involve a health care service that the defendant had a duty to render under the circumstances but nevertheless failed to render, often with fatal results. And because these courts relax the burden of proof on causation, the requirement that an expert testify to a reasonable medical certainty is also relaxed. The leading case representing this approach, *Hamil v. Bashline*,[62] relies on the provision of the *Restatement (2d) of Torts*, Section 323, that one who undertakes to render services for another that he should recognize as necessary for protecting the other is liable for the consequences that flow from his failure to exercise reasonable care to perform those services. This approach is based on the following reasoning of *Hicks v. United States:*[63] "It does not lie in the defendant's mouth to raise conjectures as to the measure of the chances that he has put beyond the possibility of realization."[64] Because of this reasoning, the courts have ruled that expert testimony that the defendant's failure to act increased the risk of harm to the plaintiff is sufficient to take the case to the jury on the issue of causation.

A narrowed variation of this rationale occurs in some jurisdictions in cases where there is a negligent treatment of a potentially fatal illness. In *Roberson v. Counselman,*[65] for example, the plaintiff-widow contended that the defendant-chiropractor was negligent in failing to recognize that her husband was experiencing symptoms consistent with those of acute heart disease and thus substantially reduced his chance of surviving a fatal heart attack that occurred shortly after he received treatment from the defendant. In sustaining the defendant's motion for summary judgment, the district court reasoned that there was insufficient proof that the defendant's conduct was a cause in fact of the plaintiff's injuries. At trial one of the plaintiff's expert witnesses testified that with prompt treatment the decedent would have had a 40 percent chance of survival, and another stated that he would have had a 6 percent chance of survival with such treatment. On review the Supreme Court of Kansas reversed, holding that the plaintiff's evidence on causation was indeed sufficient to withstand a summary judgment motion. Rejecting the stringent causation requirement espoused by other courts[66] as one that "declares open season on critically ill or injured persons,"[67] the court noted the harsh result inherent in requiring the plaintiff to prove that failure to treat a fatal illness resulted in a more than 50 percent reduction in one's chance of survival if given prompt treatment. Thus, in reviewing the evidence on causation in cases involving negligent treatment of potentially fatal conditions where evidence has established that a patient had an appreciable chance of survival with proper treatment, the court reasoned that "the finder of fact should take into account both the patient's chances of survival if properly treated and the extent to which the patient's chances of survival have been reduced by the claimed negligence."[68]

Reflection on these authorities reveals that effective preparation of a case for trial includes procuring an expert opinion that will show that the defendant's deviation from the standard of care was in fact the cause of the plaintiff's injury. If such testimony is unavailable, however, the plaintiff may still prevail in some jurisdictions if the defendant had assumed the responsibility of providing medical care and failed to do so under circumstances that permit an expert to state that the failure to act decreased substantially the plaintiff's chances of survival.

Reflections on Medical Experts and the Trial Process

Except in rare cases where the act of negligence speaks for itself, the best gauge of the merit of a medical malpractice case is the willingness or reluctance of qualified experts to express an opinion in private that the diagnosis, treatment, or follow-up care did not meet medical standards. If such an opinion is rendered, the plaintiff's lawyer at least has confirmation that the case is worth pursuing and then can concentrate on finding the most qualified and effective expert to express that opinion in court. If no qualified expert is willing to express that opinion in private, the case is, in all probability, without merit.

For this reason, the lawyer evaluating and litigating medical malpractice cases will benefit from forming relationships of mutual respect and trust with physicians. Access to informal medical opinions can save an attorney a lot of sweat and tears. Many physicians are willing to evaluate the care rendered by their colleagues if it does not require them to confront the colleague personally or take time from their primary professional responsibilities to testify in a hostile and often lethargic legal process. While it is ideal in the initial stage of evaluating a case to have an expert who is willing to testify, the ideal is not always attainable, and the less-than-ideal is often worth pursuing. An attorney's primary objective at this stage is to understand what caused the patient's injuries and whether better care could have prevented the injuries. If the medical treatment or failure to treat caused the injury, determining whether the better treatment corresponds to the required standard of care often calls for much research and much dialogue with knowledgeable persons. Both ventures are expensive in time, energy, and money.

If the case is going to trial, each side should strive to retain two experts to testify to the required standard of care and the cause of the plaintiff's injuries. At least one expert should have both academic and practice experience. The other should be a highly regarded clinician practicing in the community where the alleged malpractice occurred. Both should be board certified in the specialty of medicine most relevant to the plaintiff's case.

From the plaintiff's perspective, the ideal testimony elicited from each expert would be an expression of opinion to a reasonable medical certainty as to the standard of care applicable to the situation, an opinion that the health care provider deviated from this standard of care, and an opinion that the deviation caused the plaintiff's injuries. The defendant, on the other hand, seeks testimony that his treatment conformed to the existing standard of care, that there is no one standard of care applicable to the circumstances, or that any deviation from the required standard of care could not have caused the plaintiff's injuries.

Securing two experts is desirable for reasons of effectiveness and cost. Two experts expressing the same opinion concerning professional standards and complex technical matters are likely to be more persuasive than one. While having two experts presents the risk that cross-examination may elicit inconsistent statements, thus weakening the case, this possibility is usually outweighed by the risk inherent in relying on one expert to carry the entire case on liability. The one expert relied on may be unavailable to provide live testimony at trial for compelling personal or professional reasons, or her testimony may be shaken by a surprise approach or exceptionally skillful cross-examination. In addition, the number or complexity of factual and legal issues may prove too taxing for one expert in light of her expertise or available trial preparation time. For these reasons, the second expert is needed as a safety net.

On the other hand, having three experts testify to the same issues presents substantial disadvantages. First is the expense. An expert may charge anywhere from one to three hundred dollars an hour to prepare for and testify at trial, and this fee must be paid whatever the outcome of the litigation. Moreover, trying to prepare and present the testimony of three experts on the same questions can lead to a variety of problems. It is highly improbable that three experts will agree in their interpretations of the significance of every factual or medical issue involved in the case. Although many of the topics on which they will disagree may be insignificant to the basic claim or defense, the opposing party will undoubtedly attempt to capitalize on these inconsistencies and their meaning in the case. The plaintiff suffers a much greater harm from such disagreements than does the defendant: in the ordinary case the defendant benefits if the factfinder concludes that the issues concerning the standard of care or causation are so complex that a layperson cannot be certain which expert is right.

The plaintiff should support her experts' views with concurring opinions from authoritative sources. Learned treatises and published standards of professional associations may tip the balance of credibility where experts have expressed inconsistent views. If the jury is left to resolve the issues with the plaintiffs' experts saying one thing and the defendants' experts saying the opposite, and no other basis exists for choosing between the differing opinions, the plaintiff is at a decided disadvantage since she must carry the burden of proof.

In the end, both sides hope to find an expert who is honest and credible, with an ability to communicate with laypeople in a persuasive manner. Unless the medical care provided was grossly negligent, it is likely that honest and competent health care professionals will indeed hold different opinions concerning the acceptability of the defendant's conduct. When the dispute is resolved through the trial process, the winner may be determined by how well each side presents its case. But if the case is close, with competent experts on both sides, studies of medical malpractice litigation suggest that the defendant will prevail.

Chapter 11

Special Problems Related to Therapeutic Drug-induced Injuries

Modern medical therapy relies heavily on prescription drugs. This development began after World War II and reflects the impact of the so-called miracle drugs: antibiotics, vaccines, and local anesthetics. These therapeutic drugs radically changed the world's approach to medical care, providing new weapons to prevent diseases and to treat them if they occurred. Antibiotics enabled health care providers to fight infections before and after they developed. Vaccines provided protection against many crippling or fatal diseases. Safe and effective local and general anesthetics allowed the development of many new surgical procedures that had been unavailable earlier because of their inherent pain or because of the risk of fatality.[1]

Despite the benefits achieved through the use of these drugs, however, the world has recognized that the same drugs that produce miracles also produce tragedies. Adverse reactions to the new therapeutic drugs range from transient problems such as rashes and nausea to extreme horrors such as limb deformities and death.[2] Significant public policy issues thus have emerged regarding who should bear the costs of such accidents.[3]

From an economic or ethical perspective, complex issues arise regarding whether it is fair or economically efficient to permit an unlucky victim to bear the entire loss by herself. As an alternative, the economic costs of an adverse drug reaction could be shifted to health care providers, patients, the manufacturer of the drug, or the community at large. Questions concerning the proper distribution have percolated in the legal system since the early 1960s, producing widely varying answers that are often inconsistent even within the same jurisdiction.[4]

Consequently, the practicing attorney who is evaluating a potential medi-

179

cal malpractice case in which a drug is suspected to have contributed to the patient's injuries faces some difficult legal, ethical, and economic issues. He must not only assess the conduct of the health care provider under the customary standards governing negligence and informed consent claims, but also evaluate the conduct of third parties such as drug manufacturers, pharmacists, and the Food and Drug Administration (FDA). If he concludes that persons beyond the immediate health care providers may bear or share responsibility for the client's injuries, he must decide if and when to join such third parties in the lawsuit, taking into account legal issues regarding the standard of care required of a drug manufacturer and the potential applicability of product liability law. This chapter discusses the factual and legal issues that often require attention when a therapeutic drug has played a role in causing the plaintiff's injury.

■ **Problem:** *Adverse Reaction to a Drug*

Mary Kaye recently died at the age of eighty-two as a result of liver damage caused by the drug Miracle, which she took following her doctor's prescription in an effort to slow the progression of Alzheimer's disease. Miracle was approved by the FDA for treatment of Alzheimer's about a year before Ms. Kaye's death. Since the approval the drug has been prescribed by physicians to more than one million patients. The medical consensus is that the drug does not cure the disease but slows its progression in about 10 percent of the patients who take it as prescribed. While the drug company has received hundreds of reports of side effects such as drowsiness and headaches, it has received only five reports of liver damage. Because each of the reports involved patients whose liver damage may have resulted from other medication they were taking, Miracle's manufacturer, Dynamite Drug, Inc., decided to await further scientific studies before advising the medical community. The labeling that accompanies the drug when it is sold, which is approved by the FDA, does not warn of the risk of liver damage.

If representatives for Ms. Kaye and her family can prove that Miracle caused her liver damage and premature death, do they have a good medical malpractice case against the prescribing doctor? Do they have a meritorious claim of liability against Dynamite Drug, Inc.?

History of Drug Regulation

Before 1906 drugs could be sold in the United States for therapeutic purposes without being previously tested for safety or effectiveness. Indeed, before industrialization the United States government neither supervised nor restricted the chemical makeup of therapeutic drugs or the claims made about their effectiveness and safety. The salesman could arrive in town touting a magic potion that would cure everything from the common cold to cancer, sell the drug to any gullible consumer, and be on his way. Usually, the potion contained a high percentage of alcohol or a narcotic, leading the consumer to believe—at least temporarily—that the potion had relieved her symptoms.[5]

Efforts at significant regulation began in 1906 with the passage of the Pure Food and Drug Act, prohibiting the sale of misbranded or adulterated drugs and forbidding the making of false claims about the ingredients in food and drugs.[6] Although the statute represented a step forward in promoting public safety in the consumption of food and drugs, it had a limited effect. For one thing, it restricted the government's regulation to claims made about the ingredients of the drug. Thus, the statute was construed as not prohibiting the making of false claims about the therapeutic effects of drugs.[7] Under this construction, the statute prohibited the making of false claims about a drug's ingredients, but not false claims about its effectiveness.

In 1912 the Pure Food statute was amended to prohibit the seller of the drug from labeling it with false therapeutic claims with the intent to defraud a purchaser.[8] Even this amendment had a qualified impact, however, because it was interpreted as requiring an intent to defraud the purchaser, and thus a false claim negligently made was not a violation of the law. Moreover, the act did not require the seller to test the claims made on the label about the medicine's safety and effectiveness.

The requirement that the manufacturer of a drug test it for safety before selling it did not arise until the passage of the Federal Food, Drug and Cosmetic Act in 1938.[9] The decision by Congress to require safety testing followed more than one hundred deaths caused by a drug, sulfanilamide crystals dissolved in diethylene glycol, sold for the treatment of infections.[10] The drug had been examined for color and taste but not for safety before sale. The tragedy led policy makers to recognize the dangers of allowing the free market to determine the safety of therapeutic drugs with no governmental regulation of the product's safety before its entry into the market.

The 1938 act, passed in an effort to prevent the recurrence of such a disaster, required that a drug manufacturer test any new drug for safety and submit an application to the FDA for approval before selling it to the medical community.[11] The act did not contain a requirement that the drug be tested for effectiveness before its sale, however. Moreover, procedurally, the act provided that if the FDA did not affirmatively reject the new drug application (NDA) within six months of its submission, it would be automatically approved.

The danger inherent in the NDA procedure surfaced dramatically in 1961 with the thalidomide tragedy.[12] A drug manufacturer began selling the drug in Europe to be used by pregnant women as a sedative. The drug was, unfortunately, a teratogen, which caused a developmental defect in the limbs of the fetus—a condition known as phocomelia, in which the hands and feet are attached close to the body, resembling a seal's flippers. When reports of the drug's teratogenic effects surfaced in Europe, the FDA undertook to limit its impact in the United States. Luckily, at the time thalidomide had been released in the United States only for investigational use, which made the task of recalling the drug much easier.[13] It was soon learned, however, that determining who had been prescribed the drug for investigational or experimental use was no easy task. Record keeping by the physicians who had received the drug from the company for use in the investigation was often slack. The FDA did not have any regulations that required informed consent or detailed record-keeping standards for the testing of an experimental drug. Moreover, since the FDA was not involved in the distribution process, and the existing regulations did not require approval of the drug before distribution, determining how many women had received the drug was close to impossible.[14]

The thalidomide tragedy and the efforts to minimize its effects in this country provided the impetus for the passage of the 1962 amendments to the 1938 act. Central to the amendments was a new requirement that no "new drug" could be introduced into the market without affirmative approval of the FDA.[15] In addition, the amendments instituted a new standard for the approval of a new drug. The 1938 act required only that the drug be proven to be safe in order to receive marketing approval. The 1962 amendments added the explicit requirement that the drug also be proven to be effective for the treatment of the conditions for which it was marketed.[16] The amendments set forth an explicit provision that no experimentation with drugs could take place without an informed consent from the human subject, and they provided detailed definitions and standards for informed consent.[17] Finally, the amendments required the manufacturer of a new drug to maintain records about the processes used in making the drug and to file with the FDA periodic reports of any adverse reactions that the manufacturer receives after the drug has been approved and is being used for clinical purposes.[18] As we will see below, the 1962 amendments, with their focus on scientific evidence of the drug's safety *and* effectiveness before marketing, together with the requirement that the drug company closely monitor the drug's effects after it is marketed, have become central to much modern medical malpractice litigation.

The Regulatory Scheme: Drug Classification and Terminology

If a review of the medical records and other available references on the patient's history indicates that a drug may have contributed to the patient's injury, the attorney must seek a better understanding of the drug. Therapeutic drugs may be classified in several ways, depending on the purpose of the classification. For purposes of assessing the medical/legal implications of the therapy, three classifications are paramount: the therapeutic purpose of the drug; the drug's availability (that is, whether it is sold by prescription or over the counter), and its classification as a "new drug" or an "old drug" for purposes of the Federal Food, Drug and Cosmetic Act. Each of these classifications may significantly influence the ultimate assessment of responsibility of the prescribing physician, the drug company, the FDA, and the patient with respect to the safe use of the drug.

We first consider the therapeutic classification.[19] The purposes for which therapeutic drugs are most frequently prescribed are reduction or control of physical or mental pain and suffering, protection against viruses, treatment of infections, and anesthetization in connection with a surgical procedure.

Drugs aimed at controlling physical or mental pain are usually referred to as painkillers or sedatives. With any such drug, a primary concern if it is prescribed for women of childbearing age is whether it is teratogenic—having the capacity to cause malformations in a fetus. In addition to thalidomide, charges of teratogenic effects have been made in recent years against the drug Bendectin, marketed for morning sickness. The allegations that Bendectin caused a wide variety of limb defects in fetuses have produced mixed results in the cases tried to date.[20]

Drugs prescribed for the prevention of diseases caused by viruses are known as vaccines.[21] A vaccine is a preparation of a killed microorganism or a living weakened organism that produces immunity to a specific disease by causing the formation of antibodies when it is introduced into the body. Examples are the polio vaccine—perhaps the most widely recognized vaccine—and vaccines against such childhood diseases as mumps or whooping cough. Since the mechanism by which vaccines work involves actuating the body's response to the introduction of the virus that the physician is attempting to prevent, in a few unfortunate instances the individual contracts the very disease he or she is trying to avoid. In such cases an evaluation of the chemical makeup of the lot of the vaccine used is in order. In addition, the question of informed consent may be pivotal in assessing the merits of a potential claim against the doctor or clinic that prescribed or administered the vaccine.

Drugs prescribed to treat or prevent infections are known as antibiotics.[22]

Such drugs have the capacity to inhibit the growth of bacteria or microorganisms or to destroy them. Examples of antibiotics are penicillin, tetracycline, and streptomycin. Antibiotics have played a significant role in improving health and increasing life expectancy. The process by which they have been marketed and prescribed, however, has also played an important part in the development of legal principles governing the liability of sellers and prescribers of prescription drugs.

Drugs are also classified by the method by which the consumer gains access to the drug. A prescription drug is one that poses such a great risk to the consumer as a result of its chemical makeup that it cannot be safely used without the guidance of a physician.[23] In contrast, an over-the-counter drug presents a low enough risk that it can be sold to consumers without a doctor's intervention.[24] Consequently, tort claims based on reactions to prescription drugs may focus on the primary physician, while tort claims based on reactions to over-the-counter drugs usually focus on the manufacturer, since the consumer has ordinarily been induced to use the product by advertising.

Prescription drugs may be further classified as "new" or "old" for federal regulatory purposes.[25] This classification is somewhat misleading since most of the drugs that are prescribed for therapy today are considered new drugs.[26] The significance of the classification from a regulatory perspective is that an old drug is not subject to the detailed investigation and marketing standards embodied in the regulations issued by the FDA to enforce the Food, Drug and Cosmetic Act. The act defines a new drug as one that has not been used long enough or widely enough to be generally recognized as safe *and* effective by experts for treatment of the conditions for which it is marketed.[27]

In applying the definition, the critical date is 1962 and the critical findings are safety and efficacy.[28] Before 1962 a drug was considered new if it had not been marketed long enough to gain general recognition as safe under the standards of the act as passed in 1938. Since most antibiotics and vaccines were developed after 1938, this definition encompassed most of the therapeutic drugs relied on in modern medicine. The 1962 amendments expanded the definition of a new drug to include an evaluation of its effectiveness.[29] Thus, many manufacturers of drugs developed during World War II era took the position after the passage of the amendments that drugs manufactured and sold since the 1940s ought to be exempt from FDA regulation as "old drugs." In a quartet of companion cases, however, the U.S. Supreme Court held that unless a drug was exempted by the grandfather clause of the 1938 act as having been recognized as safe at the passage of that act, the drug remained subject to regulation under the act, notwithstanding the manufacturers' contention that such drugs should have been considered old drugs by 1962.[30]

The Supreme Court's interpretation of the scope of the act's applicability to drugs on the market is pivotal to the federal government's ability to monitor many of the therapeutic drugs being sold today. The act, as amended in 1962, enables the FDA to monitor therapeutic drugs intended for human consumption throughout the process of investigation, production, and marketing.[31] Before a drug is offered for use in humans, the act and implementing regulations require that it first be tested in animals.[32] If the evidence acquired through animal testing indicates that the drug may be safe and effective for particular uses, the manufacturer may submit an investigational new drug application (IND) for testing the drug in volunteer human subjects.[33] The act and its implementing regulations require that informed consent be obtained in writing for the testing of a drug in humans.[34]

If the investigation in humans suggests safety and effectiveness for certain therapeutic purposes, the manufacturer may seek approval of a new drug application.[35] Affirmative approval of the NDA is required before the drug may be marketed. In connection with the application, the sponsor of the drug must submit all the relevant data on animal testing, the investigation in humans, and proposed labeling. The proposed labeling must state, among other things, the therapeutic purposes for which the drug is effective, recommended dosages and routes of administration, any side effects, and warnings as to serious adverse reactions that have been encountered during testing or in clinical use.[36] Once approved, the labeling is known as a package insert and is included with each shipment of the drug.[37] The same labeling is published annually in the *Physician's Desk Reference*, often referred to as the *PDR*.[38]

The labeling of the drug is the principal means by which the drug company informs the medical community of the drug's risks and benefits. Drug companies also use other forms of communication. Their sales representatives, known in the industry as "detail men," both sell the drug—using free samples to doctors as a marketing device—and advise the medical community about the risks and benefits.[39] Companies also advertise in medical journals or directly to doctors' offices and hospitals.[40] Finally, in situations of serious risks that are newly discovered, a drug company sends out a direct mailing, called a "dear doctor letter," to alert physicians to the dangers.[41]

Drug companies sell their products under a trade name but are required to include the drug's established (or official) name on the drug's labeling.[42] After an NDA has been approved and the drug is marketed, the manufacturer is required to file with the FDA reports of adverse reactions that it receives from any source.[43] Other persons—including physicians, nurses, hospitals, and patients—may also report suspected adverse reactions to the FDA, but the manufacturer is the only entity required by law to do so. If the reaction reported was "unexpected," meaning that it was not encountered during clinical trials, or the incidence of such reactions is much higher than previously encountered, the drug company must file the report with the FDA within fifteen days of receipt.[44] If the reaction was expected, it must be recorded by the company and filed with the FDA on an annual basis.[45]

The filing of adverse reaction reports is essential to the regulatory scheme. It is recognized that animal testing and experimentation in humans produce useful but limited data regarding a drug's safety and effectiveness. A true appreciation of a drug's effects must await its widespread clinical use in a varied population. The adverse reaction reports thus serve as a critical source of scientific information about a drug. Based on the information regarding adverse reactions, the FDA may order that the drug's labeling be revised; in extreme cases, the agency may direct that the manufacturer cease marketing the drug.

A drug that is sold with false and misleading claims regarding its ingredients or effects is considered a "misbranded" drug within the meaning of the act.[46] A drug that is sold with impurities is considered an "adulterated" drug.[47] If the FDA determines that a drug on the market is misbranded or adulterated, it may order that the drug be withdrawn immediately and may, in appropriate cases, initiate criminal prosecution.[48]

The FDA's Role Today

The role played by the FDA in protecting consumers against the marketing of unsafe drugs is widely misunderstood. Many people believe that a drug is not permitted to be sold until the FDA has tested it and determined it to be safe. This is true only with respect to particular batches of antibiotics[49] and insulin.[50] Otherwise, the FDA does not ordinarily perform drug testing, either of new drugs or of a particular lot of a drug before it is shipped, to determine whether a drug contains contaminants or conforms to its package labeling with respect to ingredients. Rather, the FDA promulgates regulations setting forth the requirements for drug testing and labeling and then relies on the drug manufacturer to comply with the regulations. Nor does the FDA sell or administer the drug in a clinical setting.

Given the passive role assigned to the FDA with respect to protecting the public from unsafe drugs, the central questions raised in a medical malpractice case involving a drug-induced injury concern what a drug manufacturer knew or ought to have known about the drug's risks and benefits and what the medical community knew or should have known about those risks and benefits at the time the drug was prescribed or administered to the patient. As we will see, the answer to the first question may usually be found in the files of the drug company.

Responsibility of the Drug Company

The history of the act and the current regulatory scheme make it clear that consumer safety in the consumption of prescription drugs depends primarily on the honesty and good faith of the drug manufacturer. The manufacturer sponsors the experimental testing of the drug, musters the evidence to persuade the FDA that the drug is safe and effective for particular purposes, controls the actual manufacturing process, and receives most information regarding the risks and benefits of the drug in its clinical use.

For the reasons set forth earlier in this chapter, tort law not only charges the drug manufacturer with the duty to possess and employ the skill and knowledge required of an expert in the field but also provides that the drug manufacturer may be held strictly liable to the injured consumer if the drug is not properly prepared and marketed. Although the courts have had a great deal of difficulty in clarifying the standard for applying the doctrine of strict liability to prescription drugs, the strict liability claim is an integral part of many medical malpractice cases that involve drug-induced injuries. For this reason, the legal and strategic aspects of situations with multiple tortfeasors require careful consideration in medical malpractice cases involving drugs (see Chapter 12 for a discussion of multiple-party issues). The principal strategic decision that a drug company must make if the plaintiff has a claim that is likely to reach the jury is whether to point the finger at the prescribing physician, arguing that she was a learned intermediary[51] who made an independent decision regarding the drug's risks and benefits.

Responsibility of the Physician

As noted earlier, the act provides that the consumer may not gain access to some drugs without a prescription.[52] The act defines a prescription drug as a drug intended for human use that

(A) is a habit-forming drug . . .
(B) because of its toxicity or there potentially harmful effect, or the method of its use, or the collateral measures necessary to its use, is not safe for use except under the supervision of a practitioner licensed by law to administer such drug; or
(C) is limited by an approved application under section 355 of this title to use under the professional supervision of a practitioner licensed by law to administer such drug. . . .

The act aims to protect consumers by placing a trained physician between the consumer and the drug manufacturer. The vast majority of physicians have only a limited knowledge of the chemical properties of the drugs they prescribe, the true risks and benefits of the drugs, and the alternatives to the drug therapy, however. The complexity of modern medicine limits the amount of time that can be devoted to the study of drugs in medical school and residency. Unless the physician does a residency in a specialty such as anesthesiology, hematology, or infectious diseases that relies heavily on drug therapy, he is likely to treat therapeutic drugs as incidental to the skill and knowledge necessary to comply with the required standard of medical care. He is therefore likely to adopt the prevailing custom, habit, and routine practice for prescribing therapeutic drugs without giving much thought to studying the drug until an untoward event comes about. Even then the average physician frequently resists the conclusion that the drug caused the reaction or that he did not fully appreciate the risks of the drug. For example, in the early 1960s the medical community reacted with denial to reports that MER/29, an anticholesterol drug marketed from 1960 through 1962, caused cataracts in 80 percent of its users. One commentator observed that "the doctors appear to have lacked the normal scientific curiosity that should have led to an early realization that MER/29 was a toxic drug. Some continued to prescribe MER/29 even after a patient had developed cataracts and had been operated on! In fact, without the detective work of the Mayo Clinic in 1961, MER/29's side effects might have remained undetected even longer."[53]

In writing prescriptions, physicians often rely on the limited knowledge they gained about drugs during medical school and residency training. They then supplement this knowledge with information gathered from discussions with colleagues, articles in medical journals and information distributed by the drug companies, and conversations with drug company representatives. Once the practicing physician adopts a course of conduct that has not produced a serious untoward result, he ordinarily does not reconsider critical matters such as dosages, routes of administration, and therapeutic risks and benefits. A federal task force on prescription drugs noted in 1968 that "the most widely used source of prescribing information [for physicians] is essentially a compilation of the most widely advertised drugs."[54]

Moreover, the factors that the task force identified as contributing to inadequate physician knowledge and sophistication regarding prescription drugs remain relevant today:

> Inadequate training in the clinical application of drug knowledge during the undergraduate medical curriculum.
> Inadequate sources of objective information on both drug properties and drug costs.

Widespread reliance by prescribers for their continuing education upon the promotional materials distributed by drug manufacturers.

The exceedingly rapid rate of introduction and obsolescence of prescription drug specialties.

The limited time available to practicing physicians to examine, evaluate, and maintain currency with the claims for both old drugs and newly marketed products.

The constant insistence on the idea that the average physician, without guidance from expert colleagues, does in fact possess the necessary ability to make scientifically sound judgments in this complicated field.[55]

In the meantime, as a drug is being put to widespread clinical use, information continues to accumulate regarding the drug's true risks and benefits. Unless the clinical information reveals an extreme and pervasive danger, the drug company is not inclined to emphasize any newly discovered risks, lest it place itself at a competitive disadvantage with other companies. The sources most likely to bring newly discovered risks to the attention of the practicing physician, therefore, are colleagues, presentations at continuing medical education conventions, or the general news media. But by the time the practicing physician has heard about new developments through these channels, specialists usually will have published articles regarding the clinical experience of the drug.[56]

Tort law provides that a physician has a duty to keep abreast of the advanced state of medical knowledge.[57] Consequently, in a medical malpractice case involving a drug-induced injury the pivotal issues involve the true risks and benefits of the therapeutic drug that was prescribed, how much the prescribing physician knew about those risks and benefits, and how much he should have known in light of the information published in the literature and in the drug company's files. For just as a physician must keep abreast of developments in medicine, a drug company must keep abreast of scientific developments regarding adverse reactions to its drugs and must notify the medical profession of significant new information.[58]

Responsibility of the Patient

In the area of prescription drugs the patient is almost totally dependent on the physician, the drug company, the pharmacist, and the FDA. For this reason, defenses of contributory negligence and assumption of the risk, though available, are likely to be viable in only limited and rare situations.[59]

Nevertheless, the patient does have an important role that should not be overlooked in evaluating a medical malpractice case involving a prescription drug. The two critical responsibilities of the patient are to take the medicine in the manner and amount prescribed and to inform the health care provider of her physical and mental response to the medication. The patient's failure to act reasonably in fulfilling either of these responsibilities may defeat a claim of negligence on the part of the prescribing physician or provide an effective affirmative defense of either contributory negligence or assumption of the risk. In cases where the physician has invoked a meaningful process of informing the patient of the risks and benefits of the drug, the conduct of the patient may determine the viability of the medical malpractice claim.[60]

General Principles of Drug Therapy

In evaluating a medical malpractice case where a therapeutic drug is suspected to have played a role in producing the plaintiff's injury, the attorney is obliged to familiarize himself with basic pharmacological principles as well as the specific characteristics of the drugs involved.[61] The basic pharmacological principles requiring exploration are outlined in the package insert of a prescription drug. Fundamental considerations involved in selecting an appropriate drug for use in a patient include the chemical structure of the drug, the uses for which it has proven effective, safe and effective dosage ranges, preparation forms of the drug, routes of administration, and potential adverse reactions and side effects.

The drug's chemical structure has important implications for understanding the conditions under which a drug is safe and effective. Drugs sharing a common chemical structure are marketed under their proprietary names rather than their generic names. While it is true that the method of manufacture and preparation may affect a drug's safety and effectiveness, however, it is still expected that drugs with similar chemical structure will have common effects. In the assessment of a drug's safety and effectiveness, important physiological considerations include the manner in which the drug binds to tissue, the process and timing of its distribution throughout the body, and the route by which it is distributed throughout and eliminated from the body. Any of these considerations may prove pivotal in determining whether the drug was the cause of a particular adverse reaction or properly claimed as being effective in treating a certain condition. Moreover, identifying the chemical structure of the drug will tell the parties which other proprietary drugs may offer clinical experience that sheds light on the validity of the claim of adverse reaction in the particular case.

For example, if a patient was administered a local anesthetic in connection with dental work and one hour later suffered convulsions, determining whether the local anesthetic is likely to have caused the convulsions requires a factual determination of the dosage that was administered and the route of administration. The age and weight of the patient and her general physical condition are also important. These facts must then be viewed in light of the accumulated medical knowledge as to the time that it takes this local anesthetic to be distributed throughout the body and eliminated from it when administered to a patient with the same physical characteristics and health condition as the plaintiff. Then the likelihood that the drug was present in the plaintiff's body in sufficient quantity to produce the adverse reaction that caused the injuries can be determined. In investigating and evaluating this type of case, the lawyer may gain useful information from reviewing the literature and adverse reaction reports of the particular proprietary drug as well as other proprietary drugs that have related chemical structures. This process can be tedious, since company records are often poorly organized.

Each case presents its own challenge both as to the facts of the medical treatment actually rendered and as to the state of medical knowledge about the pharmacological properties of the drug involved. Occasionally, an attorney will find himself in the position of confronting the first instance of a suspected adverse reaction to a drug under the particular circumstances. Such a claim of an adverse reaction presents an exceptional challenge to attorneys, expert witnesses, the court, and the jury. In this kind of case the litigation process—while certainly limited in its ability to pursue scientific truth—may be the first forum that presents participants with sufficient economic incentives to invest the level of resources necessary to determine the validity of an adverse reaction claim. We turn now to a review of some illustrative cases of typical claims and defenses.

Antibiotics

The discovery of sulfanilamide during the late 1930s, followed by the mass production of penicillin in 1941 for clinical trials, ushered in the era of miracle drugs. The scientific community had long recognized the potential therapeutic use of bacteria that inhibit the growth of microorganisms, but it was not until the clinical trials of penicillin during the World War II that the medical community began a systematic effort to employ antibiotics. Today antibiotics in use number in the hundreds, including agents that are produced synthetically.[62]

In light of the tremendous therapeutic benefits of antibiotics, they rightfully earned the title of miracle drugs. Like every therapeutic drug, however, antibiotics can cause serious adverse reactions. The widespread use of antibiotics in modern medical therapy, the hundreds of antibiotics on the market, the heavy reliance on drug companies for honest and complete information about the risks and benefits of the drugs, and the limited knowledge of most physicians about the properties of the drugs have combined to produce a multitude of medical malpractice and strict liability claims against health care providers and drug companies.[63]

The most common medical malpractice claim related to the prescription of an antibiotic is that the prescribing physician failed to appreciate the true risks or limited benefits of the drug and that the drug manufacturer failed to apprise the physician adequately of the risks.[64] This lack of knowledge may take several forms. The drug may be prescribed to treat an infection that it cannot treat, because medical experimentation and clinical use of the drug have already demonstrated its ineffectiveness for this purpose—for example, diseases caused by viruses, which are not affected by antibiotics. Physicians are also inclined to prescribe antibiotics for fevers of unknown origin, neglecting to assess the cause of the fever and exposing the patient to a risk of adverse reaction to a drug that may not be able to alleviate the underlying cause of the fever anyway.[65]

In addition, as with other drugs, the antibiotic may be prescribed in an improper dosage or for an improper period of time—either too short or too long. The physician may rely on the antibiotic alone to treat the infection when surgical drainage may also be required. The antibiotic may be prescribed based solely on clinical judgment and without the support of bacterial cultures performed by the laboratory, when such tests might show that the microorganism that is causing the infection is not treatable by the antibiotic or would be better treated by some other medication. Finally, case law reveals two additional sources of medical malpractice claims related to antibiotics: the failure to prescribe an antibiotic when it is indicated for treatment of an infection, and the failure to monitor adequately the patient who is being treated with antibiotics.[66]

Of the risks that ensue when an antibiotic is misused, blood disorders are among the most frequent. The case law is replete with medical malpractice claims against prescribing physicians and strict liability claims against drug manufacturers seeking recovery for injuries flowing from some form of blood dyscrasia.[67] Even though the danger of blood dyscrasias may be included among the warnings on the drug's package insert, the risk may be consciously or unconsciously disregarded by the prescribing physician, who, as we have seen, may fall into a habit of prescribing a drug after its initial use.[68] In other instances the true risk of the drug is not effectively communicated in the drug's labeling, or the appreciation of the risk is defeated or diminished by other advertising conducted by the drug company or by in-person communications by the company's sales staff.[69]

Vaccines

Vaccines for deadly and crippling diseases are also rightfully characterized as miracle drugs. They too, pose serious dangers, however. The medical theory underlying a vaccine is that introduction of a small portion of the virus that causes the disease allows the body to develop antibodies to fight off the disease. Given the differences in individual tolerance levels, the risk exists that an individual receiving the vaccination will be unlucky enough to contract the very disease the medical community is seeking to immunize her against. In the case of polio, for example, the effort to eliminate the risk of contracting the disease led to tragic victimization.[70] The delicate risk-benefit assessment that supports the decision to administer a vaccine may vary with the individual's age, medical history, and geographic location. It is thus not surprising that many of the medical malpractice claims that follow adverse reactions to vaccines rely on the doctrine of the patient's right to an informed consent. The courts have held that if reasonable people may disagree as to whether the drug's risks are worth its potential benefits, then both the manufacturer and the prescribing physician or clinic may have a duty to inform the patient of the risks and benefits of the drug before it is administered.[71]

Local Anesthetics

The use of local anesthetics, though a relatively new practice, is now commonplace. Almost every adult has received a local anesthetic, if only in a dental office. Novocaine was the most commonly used anesthetic in dental offices until the development of amide-linked drugs such as lidocaine hydrochloride (marketed as Xylocaine) during the late 1940s and early 1950s. Today the amide-type anesthetics have claimed a greater share of the market than novocaine, apparently because they can achieve an anesthetic effect faster with a lower dose.[72]

Many physicians believe that local anesthetics do not cause serious adverse reactions unless the person administering the drug inadvertently injects it intravenously or administers an overdose. Although this belief finds some statistical support, in that systemic reactions to local anesthetics are rare when the drugs are properly administered, a cavalier attitude toward the risks associated with local anesthetics may lead to a needless tragedy. Like air travel, local anesthetics are ordinarily safe; but in those rare instances where a problem arises, disastrous results may follow if the persons in charge are not prepared and vigilant.

Explaining the unusual adverse reaction to a normal dose produces a variety of terms, such as *allergic, idiosyncratic,* and *anaphylactic*. The term *aller-*

gic reaction describes adverse responses to the drug such as urticaria or hives.[73] While these reactions are potentially fatal if the respiratory system is affected, usually allergic reactions that manifest themselves in terms of itching and the like are self-limiting. The term *idiosyncratic* describes an allergic reaction but is used to connote the view that a small portion of the population will manifest a reaction to the drug under similar circumstances. An *anaphylactic reaction* is extremely dangerous and often fatal.[74] It reflects a hypersensitive response that manifests itself in the form of shock or some other severe physical reaction only after a previous exposure to the substance. In a sense it is an allergic reaction, but it is often extremely serious because the effects may be systemic rather than local. Thus, the reaction may involve an immediate decrease in the heart rate or the respiratory rate. The response is often characterized by the contraction of smooth muscle and dilation of capillaries. In any event, the anaphylactic reaction presents an extreme emergency and is a recognized risk of the administration of a local anesthetic.

The facts of *Stanton v. Astra Pharmaceutical Products, Inc.*[75] illustrate many of the issues pertinent to assessing a medical malpractice claim based on the administration of a local anesthetic. A hematologist, investigating the cause of a mild hemolytic anemia in a nine-month-old infant, performed a bone marrow test on the infant while she was in the hospital treatment room. Before performing the test, he injected her with Xylocaine in her right posterior iliac crest. He then extracted the bone marrow. The student nurse who took care of the infant after the test asked the hematologist whether there was anything to be concerned about. He responded that she should not worry because he had done thousands of these procedures and "nothing ever happens."

The student nurse carried the baby to her room. Fifteen to thirty minutes later, while she was feeding the child orange juice from a bottle, the infant's extremities began to twitch and jerk. Thinking that the infant had choked on orange juice, the nurse removed the bottle and patted the child on her back. When the twitching and jerking did not cease, she placed the child on the bed and called for help. On arrival, the resident observed the infant and concluded that she was not choking but was having convulsions. Tragically, efforts to treat the infant were ineffective, and she experienced several incidents of respiratory and cardiac arrest, resulting in severe brain damage.

The lawsuit instituted on behalf of the infant alleged, among other things, that the hematologist was negligent in the manner in which he administered the drug and provided for aftercare, that the resident and intern who responded to the convulsions were negligent in the manner in which they treated the convulsions and performed cardiopulmonary resuscitation (CPR), and that the hospital was negligent in its failure to train its physician and nurse employees properly in recognizing and treating an adverse drug reaction and in performing CPR. The drug manufacturer was sued on the theory of negligence and strict liability in the sale of the local anesthetic without adequate warnings about the risks of an adverse reaction. The warning that resuscitative equipment and drugs should be immediately available was added in a supplement to the *PDR* in the year in which the incident occurred, but the physician who administered the drug was unaware of this new warning and the drug company had used no other means to advise him that the warning had been added to the drug's labeling.

The lawsuit was eventually tried three times, resulting in settlements with all the health care providers and a verdict against the drug company alone for sale of a local anesthetic without filing the adverse reaction reports with the FDA as required by law.[76] For our purposes, the salient point is that none of the health care providers responsible for caring for the infant understood or appreciated the risk that the local anesthetic could cause such a serious adverse reaction in the absence of an overdose or inadvertent intravenous injection. All the defendants defended the action on the theory that the drug did not cause the adverse reaction. Based on the testimony of expert anesthesiologists and pediatricians, a jury ultimately answered a special interrogatory (a specific question submitted in writing by the court) by determining that the drug did cause the adverse reaction. Moreover, discovery in the action uncovered numerous incidents of suspected adverse reactions to local anesthetics administered in small doses, most of which were in dentists' offices.

From the perspective of public health and litigation, the risks of local anesthetics must be scrupulously evaluated. Though local anesthetics are generally safe, a serious health problem is posed by the fact that many in the medical community continue to take such drugs for granted although their use is always fraught with a serious risk to life; the vigilance of a properly trained and alert professional is mandated by due care. If a local anesthetic is administered in an environment where a person properly trained to perform CPR is present along with equipment and drugs such as oxygen and short-acting barbiturates, a systemic adverse reaction can be controlled and treated without tragic consequences. Omitting these safety features can lead to death or severe neurological injury.

In evaluating a local anesthetic case, an attorney should review the evidence to determine with certainty the dosage of the drug administered, the route of administration, the time of administration, and any other drugs administered. Standard texts on anesthesiology and pharmacology should be reviewed to determine the recognized risks and medical standards for administering the drug and monitoring the patient. An expert should then be consulted to assess the causative role, if any, of the local anesthetic in producing the adverse result. If a positive causal link is determined, discovery should be planned to disclose the extent of knowledge about the drug's risks possessed by the health care providers who cared for the patient and their preparedness to diagnose and treat an adverse reaction. In addition, the drug's labeling and the marketing practices of the drug manufacturer should be reviewed to determine whether the patient has a potential claim against the manufacturer in negligence or strict liability.

Drugs and the Pregnant Woman

Drugs administered to a woman during pregnancy may have a teratogenic effect (that is, cause malformation in a fetus), and thus no drug should be prescribed for a pregnant woman unless it is essential to her health or well-being.[77] Thalidomide, prescribed as a sedative, proved disastrous.[78] Bendectin, prescribed for morning sickness but suspected to cause a variety of birth defects, spawned so many lawsuits that the manufacturer took it off the market.[79] The bottom line is that an attorney evaluating a medical malpractice case involving injury to a child while in utero or the mother during pregnancy should begin with the basic questions of whether the drug caused the injury and, if so, whether it was violative of the standard of care to prescribe or administer the drug in light of the generally recognized teratogenic risk.

Drugs for Infants and Children

Children are therapeutic orphans when it comes to drug therapy. Since it is considered unethical to perform experimentation on children, the initial use of a drug to treat a condition in a child is often experimental. The drug will have been tested in animals and then investigated in adults to support the grant of an NDA. Since a child may participate in drug testing only when the drug is the sole therapy available for potentially treating the child's disease, physicians first prescribing the drug for use in a child do so without the benefit of data derived from prior investigation. Since a drug may have a very different effect on a child than on an adult, the child who first consumes the drug for therapeutic purposes is viewed as an "orphan."[80]

The literature on pediatric pharmacology emphasizes to the clinician that children should not be viewed as little adults. The immaturity of a child's organs often causes a drug to affect a child differently than an adult. The drug may be distributed through the child's system at a different rate and metabolized and eliminated in a different manner. Moreover, the immaturity of the organs may make it difficult to compute the maximum dosage of the drug that will be safe and effective for the child. While the child's weight may serve as a guide in computing proper dosage, pediatric pharmacologists suggest use of the child's surface area as a guide.[81]

For these reasons, the labeling of a drug may state that the child should be regarded as a therapeutic orphan for purposes of use of the drug. Often the labeling says that the drug has not been tested for safe use in children and thus the manufacturer makes no representations regarding its safety and effectiveness when used in a child.

The physician treating a child with a serious illness may face a dilemma. The child may manifest an illness for which a drug has proven safe and effective when prescribed to an adult. Thus, withholding the drug may subject the child to risks of the illness that might be alleviated by the drug therapy. On the other hand, since reliable testing or clinical data may be unavailable to allow a reliable assessment of the drug's potential risks and benefits for children, prescribing the drug may be nothing short of an experiment with therapeutic goals.

When a child experiences an adverse reaction to a drug, the investigation of the potential tort case should begin with the drug's labeling and proceed to the literature on pediatric pharmacology to determine the state of medical knowledge regarding the drug's risks and benefits when used in a child or infant. The knowledge of the prescribing physician about the drug's risks and benefits must be probed, along with the adverse reaction reports in the files of the drug company and the FDA. Although the drug company may not have been able to obtain an investigation of the drug in children, it has a responsibility to monitor the adverse reaction reports and medical literature to determine whether its labeling should include specific directions or warnings about the use of the drug in children. The prescribing physician has a responsibility to review the drug's labeling and literature to assess the drug's risks and benefits before prescribing the drug for the child. Legal theories of strict liability, informed consent, and negligence must be explored in light of the attorney's appreciation of the recognized risks of the drug when used in children at the time it was prescribed to the client. If the drug is a vaccine, the child may be entitled to compensation on a no-fault basis under the National Childhood Vaccine Act.[82]

Drugs and the Elderly

In 1968 a federal task force on prescription drugs observed:

> There are now more than 19 million Americans over the age of 65. Among them, about 57 percent are women and 43 percent are men. This disproportion in sex dis-

tribution has been increasing steadily since about 1930—a trend of importance in any prescription drug study, since the use of these drugs by women is significantly higher than by men. . . . Approximately 80 percent of the elderly—in comparison with 40 percent of those under 65—suffer from one or more chronic diseases and conditions. Arthritis and rheumatism afflict 33 percent; heart disease, 17 percent; high blood pressure, 16 percent; other cardiovascular ailments, 7.5 percent; mental and nervous conditions, 10.5 percent; hearing impairments, 22 percent; and visual problems, 15 percent. Many of these conditions can be controlled or alleviated by modern medical care, especially by proper use of drugs. This is reflected in the heavy expenses of the elderly for health care, and particularly in their heavy expenses for drugs.[83]

Throughout the 1980s the percentage of the population over the age of sixty-five increased steadily, along with their need for and use of therapeutic drugs. It is thus no surprise that the elderly constitute a high percentage of the victims of adverse drug experiences. Two characteristics in all likelihood reduce the number of lawsuits that might be instituted by elderly persons against doctors and drug companies for the misuse of therapeutic drugs. First, a chronic illness makes it more difficult to prove to a reasonable medical certainty that a therapeutic drug was the cause of an untoward result. Second, the diminution in earning capacity is an important element of damages in a medical malpractice case, and the limited nature of the losses in this area may make the lawsuit not viable from an economic perspective, unless the case had a strong dignitary aspect or punitive damage potential.

It is likely, however, that medical malpractice litigation on behalf of the elderly population will play a central role in the future development of law in this area, especially as it relates to nursing homes and mental health specialists. In this regard it is significant that when the 1968 task force considered the frequency with which therapeutic drugs were prescribed for the elderly, it found cardiovascular preparations the most common, followed by tranquilizers, diuretics, sedatives, and antibiotics. The prevalence of drugs prescribed for treatment of chronic diseases will inevitably lead family members of the elderly to seek legal advice on the propriety of the drug therapy rendered.

Investigating Therapeutic Drug Cases

The first step for both sides in evaluating any medical malpractice case is to assess the potential causes of the patient's injuries. Consequently, unless the cause is readily apparent, some thought must to whether a therapeutic drug has played a role. If an affirmative answer is possible, the attorney must pursue the issue further in order to understand and evaluate the case properly.

The initial interview with the client or her representative should include questions aimed at eliciting information regarding any drugs consumed by the potential plaintiff. This inquiry should include prescription drugs, over-the-counter drugs, and illegal drugs. It makes little sense to rush into a costly investigation of a medical malpractice case without having as complete a picture as possible of the potential causes of the plaintiff's injuries as well as the damages that may be recovered if malpractice is established.

The medical records, once obtained, must be reviewed carefully to ascertain each drug that was administered, the dosage administered, and the route of administration. For a complete and accurate picture, a daily chart should be made reflecting the drugs administered in accordance with the medication chart, the physician's orders, and the nurses' notes. If an anesthetic is involved, the anesthetic chart must also be reviewed.

Having identified the drugs administered or consumed, the attorney should then consult the *PDR* and other basic pharmacological texts to determine the therapeutic purposes of the drugs, directions for use, warnings, and reported adverse reactions.

The expert witness retained to review the case should be asked about the likelihood that any of the drugs administered to the plaintiff contributed to the injuries. Unless the expert is engaged in the practice of a specialty that requires her to keep abreast of the advanced state of medical knowledge with respect to the drug, however, caution should be exercised in relying too heavily on the expert's initial responses regarding the effects and risks of the drugs administered. If the facts of the case do not provide a basis for concluding with certainty the cause of the plaintiff's injuries, an expert should be retained specifically to render an opinion concerning the role played by any of the drugs administered to the plaintiff in producing the injuries. The particular specialty depends on the case. One may need to retain a pharmacologist, an anesthesiologist, a hematologist, an infectious disease specialist, a cardiologist, a pediatric pharmacologist, and so on, depending on the nature of the case, the treatment rendered, and other particulars.

If a positive conclusion is drawn as to the causative role of a therapeutic drug, the next step is to determine whether the risk that has materialized was acknowledged by the drug company and effectively communicated to the medical community by way of the *PDR* or some other means that could be reasonably relied on effectively to reach the prescribing doctor. If an adequate warning was given to the prescribing doctor, the liability claim must focus solely on him, unless the drug company engaged in marketing or advertising practices that functionally diluted the warnings communicated in the *PDR* or package insert. In this type of case both the prescribing doctor and the drug manufacturer may be held liable.

If an adequate warning was not given, the tort claim may shift from medical malpractice to a claim of strict liability and/or negligence against the drug manufacturer. The pivotal facts that affect the merits of the claim against the manufacturer are what the drug company knew or should have known about the drug's safety and effectiveness based on its premarketing investigations, its subsequent investigation of the drug, the adverse reaction reports received after marketing the drug, and the literature published in the medical journals about the drug's clinical experience after it was marketed. Ascertaining what the drug company knew or should have known requires a painstaking and dogged review of the company's NDA file, its adverse reaction files, the medical literature, and the files of the FDA, which should contain information that is the same as or similar to the contents of the drug company's files. Exploring both files is necessary for several reasons. First, the attorney must determine whether the drug company has complied with the legal requirements of providing the FDA with the data required by the IND, the NDA, and the postmarketing surveillance reporting. Second, it is important to discover whether the FDA has additional information supplied to it by other marketers of the generic drug under different proprietary names. Finally, the correspondence between the drug company and the medical community, the drug company and the FDA, and the medical community and consumer groups and the FDA may permit a more complete picture of the state of medical knowledge about the drug than is provided by a review of only one source.

Based on this investigation, an attorney should be in a position to assess the strength of evidence that the drug caused the plaintiff's injuries and that the health care provider, the drug company, or both may be liable to the plaintiff. If the evidence supports a claim that both are liable, the strategic decisions discussed in Chapter 12 on multiple parties must be considered. In addition, litigation theories must be explored and unraveled.

Chapter 12

Multiple Parties: Issues, Concerns, and Strategies

━━━━━━

Today's health care system relies heavily on specialists providing medical care within a hospital setting. Medical care frequently involves the administration of therapeutic drugs as well as the use of a variety of devices and equipment for diagnostic and therapeutic purposes. This pattern of health care delivery makes it difficult to determine the person or persons who may be responsible for a particular act of malpractice. Extensive investigation must take place in most cases to support a reliable assessment of the roles played by each of the parties who treated the patient. Even then responsibility may be shared among multiple health care providers.

In conducting an initial evaluation of the case, the plaintiff's lawyer and his experts often have to rely on information contained in the medical records. As we have seen, this information frequently is incomplete and may not allow a final determination about all the parties who may have been responsible for the care rendered to the plaintiff. Clarifying ultimate responsibility often requires extensive discovery available only after a lawsuit has been initiated. Rather than risk overshooting the statute of limitations, which would bar a meritorious claim, plaintiff's lawyers are often inclined to name all persons potentially liable as determined from the medical records at the time the initial complaint is filed.

Defense counsel hesitate to point the finger at any health care provider lest the plaintiff gain the advantage of having someone on the other side agreeing that her injuries were caused by substandard medical care. Except in rare cases, for strategic reasons counsel for health care providers prefer to present a united defense.

This chapter explores the numerous problems involved in assessing a

medical malpractice case involving multiple parties. The ramifications of joinder and settlement decisions and alternative techniques and changes in the
law require careful consideration.

■ Problem: *Bad Result Following Surgery*

Peter Gervin underwent surgery on his back. After recovering from the
effects of anesthesia, he noticed that his right hand was so numb that he
could not hold anything in it. The next day he spoke with his surgeon, who
advised him that the numbness in his hand could not have been caused
by the surgery. In any event, he assured Peter that the numbness would
be temporary. Peter's roommate overheard the conversation, and after
the surgeon left the room, the roommate advised Peter that the nurse had
left his bedrail down when he was first placed in the bed, and that he had
fallen on the floor, landing on his right arm. When Peter asked the nurse
on duty, she said that she was not on duty when the nurse's aides brought
him from the recovery room, but she was sure no nurse would have left
his bedrail down then because he was expected to remain drowsy for
some time. She believed the problem with his hand resulted from the surgeons, anesthesiologists, nurse anesthetists, and other operating room
personnel improperly positioning him on his hand during the surgery.

A year later, despite physical therapy and numerous tests, Peter still
has a numb right hand and no one has definitively diagnosed the cause
of his hand injury. Peter consults counsel. If counsel cannot determine
the cause of the hand injury by having Peter examined and the medical
records reviewed, should she bring a lawsuit in Peter's behalf? If so, who
should be sued? If the hospital is sued alone, should it join any doctors or
nurses in the lawsuit? If the surgeon alone is sued, what should he do?

Sifting through Multiple-Party Issues

To facilitate an understanding of the issues that arise in multiple-party cases,
we can focus on one medical malpractice case involving multiple parties, a
case that lasted ten years.

In *Stanton v. Astra Pharmaceutical Products*,[1] a medical malpractice and
product liability case described in Chapter 11, seven defendants—five doctors, a hospital, and a drug manufacturer—were named. Only after three
trials and one appeal were all the plaintiffs' claims against all the defendants
finally resolved. Since the plaintiffs settled with the various parties at different points in the trial process, the case serves as an excellent vehicle for

describing and analyzing the legal issues and strategic ramifications of joinder and settlement decisions.

Stanton involved a child who suffered two incidents of cardiac and respiratory arrest fifteen minutes after a bone marrow test was performed on her in a hospital. Determining whether anyone was legally responsible for Harrikah Stanton's injuries required a review of the conduct of eight persons: the hematologist, the attending pediatrician, the resident, the intern, the head nurse, the hospital, the hospital's director of pediatric education, and the drug company. Essential to evaluating the merits of the claim was determining what precipitated the infant's convulsions. After their initial review of the medical records the physician-experts retained by the plaintiffs' lawyers identified three possible causes of the infant's convulsions: a preexisting condition, choking on the orange juice, or the local anesthetic. Plaintiffs' lawyers consulted with specialists in hematology and anesthesiology, the medical specialties best suited to assessing the cause of the convulsions and the standard of care applicable to Harrikah's treatment. The consultants agreed that the most likely cause of the convulsions was choking on the orange juice. They felt that there was no basis for concluding that a preexisting condition—blood or otherwise—caused the convulsions and that the small amount of Xylocaine (0.75 ml of a 1 percent solution) made the drug an unlikely causative agent.

On the other hand, the specialists saw a strong probability of negligence in connection with the cardiopulmonary resuscitation (CPR) performed on the infant, since prompt and effective CPR in a hospital setting is ordinarily expected to avoid the injuries Harrikah sustained. Because an expert could not assess the CPR effort on the basis of the information in the medical record, however, specific information obtained from the physicians and nurses involved was essential to a fair and honest evaluation of their conduct.

Provoked and guided by these initial medical opinions, plaintiffs' counsel conducted extensive medical research on their own. The research confirmed the need to investigate whether applicable CPR standards had been met in this case and gave counsel the names of several experts on CPR training and performance. But in looking at the anesthesiology literature, counsel came across some articles by a highly regarded anesthesiologist claiming that very small amounts of local anesthetics could cause convulsions even when properly administered.

Pursuing the authors of articles in the medical literature, counsel produced two internationally renowned anesthesiologists who expressed the opinion that the local anesthetic was the most probable cause of the infant's convulsions; an internationally renowned neonatologist who felt that the CPR effort employed in treating the infant was inadequate; an opinion from the anesthesiologists that the manufacturer of the local anesthetic had failed to warn the medical community effectively of the risk of adverse reactions associated with the administration of even a small amount of Xylocaine; and an opinion from each of these experts that the hematologist was negligent in failing to ensure that proper procedures, equipment, and personnel were available and employed to treat the infant's adverse drug reaction.

Once assertions of negligence in the administration of the drug and in the CPR effort were supported by expert opinions, the threshold question was, Who should be sued? General principles of tort law hold that a hospital or a drug company may or may not be responsible, depending on the skill and knowledge of the particular physicians and nurses involved in the patient's care and their system for allocating and sharing responsibilities. Suing all persons potentially liable poses the risk of confusing the issues and draining substantial resources because of the numerous collateral battles that multiple-party lawsuits engender. On the other hand, since the claims of negligence necessarily precipitate efforts to shift responsibility, a failure to join a potentially responsible party could prove fatal if blame is shifted to a person not named as a defendant in a lawsuit.

In addition to concern over the effect on the trial process of joining multiple parties in a lawsuit, considerable attention should be paid to the effect of negotiating a settlement with any of the parties. Settlement decisions must be made with an awareness of the applicable law governing releases and contribution. From a plaintiff's perspective, a small settlement with a subset of the tortfeasors may substantially diminish her ultimate recovery.[2] On the other hand, a defendant must also be cognizant of the law governing joinder, contribution, and indemnification to avoid making strategic decisions concerning settlement or release that may return to haunt him. Declining to join a potentially liable party may be desirable since it will avoid a trial where co-defendants point fingers at each other. In some jurisdictions, however, the failure to join a defendant who is available for joinder may preclude a later assertion of a right to contribution or indemnity.[3]

Before attempting to settle a case with any person who may be responsible for the plaintiff's injuries, the plaintiff's attorney must make an initial assessment as to which person or persons are most likely to be responsible and which persons must be joined to protect the plaintiff's recovery, even though the potential liability of some of the defendants is remote. Settlement decisions must also take into account insurance coverage, agency law, and the cost of the litigation. In short, joinder or settlement decisions made as a result of a focus on only one issue or consideration may produce a short-term benefit that is not worth the long-term cost.

A brief review of the law applicable to multiple-party tort cases is necessary to clarify and buttress these observations. Afterward we return to a discussion of *Stanton v. Astra* to illustrate and analyze further the ramifications of joinder and settlement considerations in multiple-party medical malpractice cases.

Classification of the Tortfeasor

The classification of a tortfeasor may have important ramifications. Multiple tortfeasors are classified in tort law as *joint, concurrent,* or *successive.* In addition, courts tend to use the term *joint tortfeasor* to mean different things in different contexts.[4] Procedurally, the term is sometimes used to refer to tortfeasors who may be properly joined in the same lawsuit.[5] Substantively, it is used to describe (1) persons who may be jointly and severally liable to the plaintiff for an indivisible injury, (2) persons whose liability to the plaintiff may be discharged if another tortfeasor pays for a release or if the tortfeasors satisfy a judgment or a release, or (3) persons who may be entitled to contribution or indemnity from another tortfeasor as a result of making payments to a plaintiff following a settlement or a judgment.[6] Since liberal joinder rules under modern rules of civil procedure have reduced the significance of the procedural questions,[7] this chapter concentrates on the substantive issues.

Under modern tort law, joint tortfeasors may be jointly and severally liable to the plaintiff on three different bases. The first basis is that the defendants have acted in concert to fulfill a common plan.[8] Such individuals may have either intended to commit a tort or intended to engage in conduct violative of the law. In many jurisdictions classifying a person as a joint tortfeasor on the basis of a common plan prevents this kind of joint tortfeasor from seeking contribution from another joint tortfeasor.[9] In other words, if the plaintiff can prove that each party was a joint tortfeasor and chooses to collect the entire judgment from one of the joint tortfeasors, that tortfeasor must bear the loss. The rationale behind such an approach is that, since contribution is based on considerations of equity, a person who has acted in concert with another with the intention of committing a tort is not entitled to any equitable consideration.[10]

Concurrent tortfeasors[11] are also sometimes referred to as joint tortfeasors. Concurrent tortfeasors are persons who act independently of each other and without a common plan or agreement, but whose actions concur in producing harm to the plaintiff around the same time.[12] If their conduct produces an indivisible injury to the plaintiff, the plaintiff may join all such tortfeasors in one lawsuit and may collect the entire judgment against any one of them—unless the common law has been changed by the adoption of comparative negligence principles.[13] Unlike joint tortfeasors, concurrent tortfeasors may seek contribution if they have paid more than their fair share of the plaintiff's damages.[14]

Many jurisdictions have adopted the Uniform Contribution among Tortfeasors Act.[15] Under this act, the fair share of a concurrent tortfeasor is based exclusively on the number of tortfeasors involved.[16] In other words, if a plaintiff obtains a $1 million judgment against four tortfeasors, each will be liable for the entire amount. But any tortfeasor who pays more than one-fourth of the judgment will be entitled to contribution from the other tortfeasors of one-fourth of the judgment.

The adoption of comparative negligence in some jurisdictions has produced a change in joint tortfeasor law.[17] Some jurisdictions now provide that the plaintiff is entitled to collect only that percentage of the judgment from a concurrent tortfeasor which is equal to his comparative responsibility for the accident.[18] Other jurisdictions allow the plaintiff to collect the entire judgment from any one tortfeasor and then allow that tortfeasor to seek contribution toward any overpayment as measured by the proportionate share of his responsibility.[19]

Concurrent tortfeasors who have not caused an indivisible injury receive different treatment. If there is a reasonable basis for determining the portion of the damage caused by each concurrent tortfeasor, each tortfeasor will be liable only for the amount of the damage that he has caused.[20] In such an event issues of contribution will not arise.

A third basis for classifying multiple tortfeasors as joint tortfeasors is the master-servant relationship. If the individual who has engaged in the tortious conduct was an employee of another and was carrying out his duties as an employee or was subject to the direction or control of another, these facts will make the other a joint tortfeasor on the basis of vicarious liability.[21] In such a case the parties will be found jointly and severally liable, and the person who is vicariously liable may be entitled to indemnification from the employee or servant for any amount that he pays toward the plaintiff's claim of damages.[22]

Successive tortfeasors require a different approach.[23] If one tortfeasor's conduct creates the risk of further harm to the plaintiff by a second tortfeasor, the parties will be classified as successive tortfeasors.[24] In such a case the tortfeasor who acted last in time would be responsible only for that harm that his action caused.[25] Whether the liability of the first tortfeasor is limited to the harm he caused in the first instance, however, depends on principles of proximate cause. If the action of the second tortfeasor is not deemed to be a superseding cause or a totally independent tort, the original tortfeasor may be held liable for all the harm caused, including that caused by the second tortfeasor.[26]

In light of the ramifications of these classifications, the plaintiff evaluating a potential multiple-party medical malpractice action must give considerable thought to the potential classifications of the tortfeasors. Failure to join a concurrent tortfeasor who caused an independent injury or a successive tortfeasor who caused a distinct injury, or to initiate an independent action before the statute of limitations runs out, may result in the plaintiff's not being able to recover for that injury. In addition, the failure to join such a tortfeasor may allow the tortfeasor who was joined in the suit to develop a defense aimed at shifting all the responsibility to the party who was not joined. Finally, since it is usually not possible for the plaintiff's attorney to determine in advance of filing the lawsuit the extent of a particular party's insurance coverage, deciding to exclude a potentially liable party may result in a judgment that is not collectible in full or at all.

Settlements

Under the common law, a settlement with a joint tortfeasor who has caused an indivisible injury results in the release of all tortfeasors responsible for the injury.[27] Most states, however, have now adopted statutes changing the effect of settling with one tortfeasor. The Uniform Contribution among Tortfeasors Act provides that a release of one tortfeasor is not a release of another unless the release expressly so provides.[28] Since a defendant who is prepared to settle a lawsuit usually demands assurance that a settlement will extinguish his liability, the most common release extinguishes the liability of the settling tortfeasor to the extent of his proportionate share. Because a plaintiff and one settling defendant cannot by their agreement eliminate or reduce a nonsettling defendant's right to contribution, the law provides that the release of a defendant to the extent of his proportionate share bestows a benefit on the nonsettling defendant if it is established that the settling defendant was indeed a joint or concurrent tortfeasor.[29] In other words, the nonsettling defendant gets to credit the money paid by the settling defendant to the plaintiff to any judgment that is rendered against him if the settling defendant is determined to be also responsible for the injuries.

Assume that a plaintiff settles with one defendant for $250,000. Later that defendant is found to be one of two defendants responsible for the injuries, and a verdict is rendered for $1 million. The defendant who did not settle will be faced with a judgment of $1 million. He would get credit, however, for the release entered into by the settling defendant—to the extent of the settling defendant's proportionate share. If we assume that the Uniform Contribution among Tortfeasors Act applies, unmodified by comparative negligence, this would mean that the nonsettling defendant would get credit for $500,000, since there are only two tortfeasors and the proportionate share of each would be one-half the judgment. The nonsettling defendant would be liable to the plaintiff for $500,000, making the plaintiff's total recovery $750,000. The plaintiff would thus lose the right to collect $250,000 of her $1 million judgment as a result of the earlier settlement.

On the other hand, if there was a $250,000 settlement and the plaintiff obtained a judgment of $300,000, with both defendants being found liable, the nonsettling defendant would be responsible only for payment of $50,000 to the plaintiff, since the plaintiff can collect only up to the full amount of her judgment. In this case a dispute would then arise concerning the right of the settling defendant to seek contribution from the nonsettling defendant.[30] In our example the settling defendant would prevail in his contribution claim because there would be no doubt that he paid more than his proportionate share of the judgment.[31]

If, however, the plaintiff, after settling for $250,000 with one defendant, went to trial, and the jury rendered a defense verdict, the settling defendant would not be entitled to any contribution. The rationale for this result would be that the defendant paid the settlement at his own risk. His settlement did not inure to the benefit of the nonsettling defendant, and thus the nonsettling defendant has not been enriched by the settlement. To demonstrate the issues of strategy that flow from these rather complicated legal principles, we return to a discussion of *Stanton*. We then review another case, *Washington et al. v. Washington Hospital Center*,[32] to consider the circumstances in which a defendant may desire to cross-claim or join another health care provider in the lawsuit to protect his right to contribution or indemnity.

Stanton v. Astra Revisited

As noted earlier in this chapter, in *Stanton*[33] the plaintiff's initial investigation disclosed the potential liability of numerous parties, including a hematologist, a pediatrician, the director of pediatric education, a pediatric resident, an intern, the head nurse, a hospital, and a drug company. Because it was impossible to determine in advance of discovery whether all or any of these parties were legally responsible for Harrikah Stanton's injuries, the plaintiff elected to sue all the defendants. In response the defendants elected to put on a joint defense, contending that no one was liable for the plaintiff's injuries. Each defendant, however, preserved the right to assert a contribution or indemnity claim.

Pretrial discovery disclosed facts that encouraged the hematologist to settle the case. In his first deposition he testified that he had administered 0.75 ml of a 1 percent solution of Xylocaine to the infant in connection with the bone marrow test he had performed. He also stated that in his view no special precautions were necessary to protect the child against injury following such a test because he had previously administered Xylocaine to the child, who had shown no allergic reaction to the drug, and because he had used the local anesthetic in connection with bone marrow tests approximately two thousand times and no adverse reaction had ever occurred. Indeed, it was his view that when the drug was administered in such a small dose, no adverse reaction would occur in the absence of an allergy or an inadvertent intravascular injection. He was sure that neither of these had occurred in connection with the infant plaintiff.

In his second deposition the hematologist was confronted with a supplement published in the *Physician's Desk Reference* (*PDR*) a few months before his administration of Xylocaine to the child. The supplement stated for the first time: "RESUSCITATIVE EQUIPMENT AND DRUGS SHOULD BE IMMEDIATELY AVAILABLE WHENEVER ANY LOCAL ANESTHETIC IS USED."[34] The hematologist acknowledged that he was unaware that this new warning had been added in the drug's labeling at the time he administered the drug. In addition, discovery revealed that the hematologist had unknowingly administered a 2 percent solution of the drug when he intended to administer a 1 percent solution. This mistake apparently occurred because the hematologist had been unaware that the hospital had changed its earlier practice of stocking a 1 percent solution in the area of the hospital from which the drug was secured for administration to the infant plaintiff. Thus he had administered twice as much of the drug as he had intended. Although the dose actually administered was still within an acceptable range, the mistake would undoubtedly affect his credibility at trial.

After considerable negotiation the hematologist offered $80,000 to settle the case before trial. On one hand, the plaintiffs feared that if he were found to be the sole tortfeasor, the plaintiff's recovery might be limited to this amount although the verdict expectancy was considerably higher. On the other hand, if he were found to be one of several parties responsible, the plaintiff's ability to collect on her ultimate judgment would be reduced to the extent of his proportionate share in light of Pennsylvania's adoption and construction of the Uniform Contribution among Tortfeasors Act.[35]

In favor of a pretrial settlement with the hematologist were several troublesome factors. First, the plaintiff had an immediate need for funds to obtain high-quality medical care and other support to address the devastating effects of the injury on the infant and her family. Second, litigation expenses were expected to exceed $100,000. Third, the hematologist was a highly competent physician with an outstanding reputation, locally and nationally. His reputation, the exceptional skill of his counsel, and the complexity of the medical aspects of the case made it far from certain that members of a jury would find him liable—particularly if they were convinced that the drug company and/ or hospital were at fault. Finally, the highest verdict that had been rendered in a personal injury action in the local jurisdiction in which the case would be tried was in the neighborhood of $300,000. These considerations in combination proved compelling to the plaintiffs, and they ultimately decided to accept the hematologist's settlement offer and take their chances on the effect of the settlement on the resolution of the claims against the other defendants.

The case went to trial in 1976, and the plaintiffs put on their case, introducing expert testimony supporting a claim of negligence against each of the named defendants and a claim of negligence and product liability against the drug company. After four weeks of trial, during which the plaintiffs completed their case, the court ordered a mistrial. The court reasoned that the case was too complex to be tried against all defendants in one action. The court expressed its intent to have a new trial in which the actions against the physicians and the hospital were severed from the action against the drug company.

After the order of mistrial the hospital and all the individual physicians who were arguably agents or servants of the hospital settled with the plaintiffs for approximately $385,000. The pediatrician, who was not an agent or servant of the hospital and who was responsible for the infant's care only after she sustained brain damage, settled for $20,000.[36] The sole defendant left in the case was thus the drug company. Since each defendant who settled was given a release to the extent of his proportionate share, the future trial was fraught with risks for both the plaintiffs and the drug company. The possibilities were that the drug company would not be found liable by the jury, would be found solely liable, or would be found a joint tortfeasor with some combination of the defendants who had settled.

The settlements compelled both the plaintiffs and the drug company to make critical strategic decisions. Over the plaintiffs' objections, the trial court ruled that the drug company had a right to keep the settling defendants in the trial of the case for the purpose of determining whether they were joint tortfeasors. An affirmative finding would reduce the plaintiffs' ability to collect on any judgment obtained against the drug company to the extent of the proportionate share of any settling defendant who was found liable.

At trial plaintiffs focused all their efforts on proving the liability of the drug company and offered no evidence as to the negligence of the defendants who had settled.[37] The settling defendants offered evidence and arguments supporting their contentions that they were not negligent but made no effort to prove that the drug company was liable to the plaintiffs. The drug company vigorously defended against the plaintiffs' claims that it was negligent or sold a defective product. The only settling defendant to whom the drug company sought to shift responsibility was the hematologist. It was the company's position that if the jury found that the infant suffered an adverse reaction to its drug, it should find that the company had given an adequate warning to the medical community about the risks associated with the drug. Strategically, the company decided to base its major defense on the position that the infant did not suffer an adverse reaction to its drug, but rather choked on the orange juice.

On January 10, 1980, after an eight-week trial, a jury returned inconsistent answers to special questions submitted by the court,[38] reconsidered their answers pursuant to the court's instructions, and ultimately rendered a verdict in the amount of $315,000 against the drug company alone.[39] Because of a change in Pennsylvania law after the verdict regarding the measurement of future losses,[40] a new trial on damages alone was conducted in 1982, and the jury rendered a verdict totaling $1,908,371. Molding the verdict to add delay damages, the court entered a judgment of $2,367,032.[41] An appeal to the U.S. Court of Appeals for the Third Circuit produced an opinion affirming the substantive rulings of the trial court but reversing on the basis of the trial court's abuse of discretion in ordering a new trial on damages alone. The case was ultimately settled with the drug company.

It is evident that all parties to the litigation faced complicated strategic issues due to the presence of multiple parties. No one could be certain at any stage of the proceeding that the various risks were worth taking or avoiding. The same is true in most complex medical malpractice cases involving multiple parties. At a minimum, however, clients in multiple-party litigation have a right to expect that the advice rendered and judgments made reflect an awareness of the potential consequences.

Washington v. Washington Hospital Center

The case of *Washington v. Washington Hospital Center*[42] further illustrates the potential opportunities and pitfalls for plaintiffs and defendants alike in multi-party medical malpractice cases. Briefly stated, the facts are as follows. In 1987 LaVerne Thompson, a healthy thirty-five-year-old mother of two, entered the Washington Hospital Center to undergo minor surgery under general anesthesia. Within a few minutes after the start of the operation Ms. Thompson's blood was observed to be dark. This is one of the signs that blood is insufficiently oxygenated. Thereafter it was observed that Ms. Thompson's vaginal mucosa were pale, another symptom of insufficient oxygenation.[43] Within ten to fifteen minutes after the beginning of the operation, the nurse anesthetist called a "code blue," and cardiopulmonary resuscitation began. During the course of the resuscitation efforts Ms. Thompson's endotracheal tube was replaced. After the reintubation the efforts to resuscitate Ms. Thompson began to achieve some limited success. But although her vital signs improved, she remained, and most likely will remain for the rest of her life, in a persistent vegetative state.

At trial plaintiffs contended that the nurse anesthetist, supervised by an anesthesiologist, had improperly intubated Ms. Thompson. Instead of entering the trachea, the oxygen supplied by the endotracheal tube entered Ms. Thompson's esophagus. Until this mistake was corrected, Ms. Thompson did not receive adequate oxygen, as a result of which she had suffered severe brain damage. The plaintiffs alleged that there had been a negligent delay in recognizing the improper intubation.

In recommending whether to file suit in their case, plaintiffs' counsel faced two initial decisions: who could file suit and who should be sued. By virtue of her physical incapacities, Ms. Thompson could not bring suit herself. Accordingly, by family agreement, Ms. Thompson's mother, Alma Washington, was appointed conservator for Ms. Thompson. Under the law in the District of Columbia, Ms. Washington was thereby empowered to file suit on behalf of her daughter. In addition, Ms. Thompson's husband had a loss of consortium claim. Accordingly, Mr. Thompson, in his own behalf, and Ms. Washington, on behalf of her daughter, were appropriate plaintiffs.

In addition, Ms. Thompson's children had possible legally cognizable claims. Although thirty-year-old case law in the District of Columbia holds that children do not have legally recognized claims for loss of parental consortium of a living parent,[44] the emerging trend across the country is to recognize such claims.[45] Accordingly, in an effort to bring the law of the District of Columbia into accord with those states that have recognized the right of a child to sue for loss of parental consortium, counsel recommended that Ms. Thompson's two children also bring suit. Finally, noting that there may be a similar trend permitting parents to recover for the loss of their children's consortium,[46] counsel recommended that Ms. Washington's claims also include a claim on her own behalf.

Counsel's decision to include Ms. Thompson's children and mother as plaintiffs in their own right aimed to protect their rights and effect a change in the law in the District of Columbia.[47] Counsel also wanted to obtain as much leverage as possible for settlement discussions.

In deciding whom to sue, counsel's analysis was similar to that employed in the *Stanton* case. Potential defendants included the anesthesiologist, the nurse anesthetist, the obstetrician-gynecologist who performed the surgery, and the hospital. Counsel's pre-filing investigation discovered an additional potential defendant. The nurse anesthetist and the anesthesiologist were employed by an independent contractor charged by the hospital with performing anesthesia services. Accordingly, the independent contractor and not the hospital could be held responsible for the negligent acts of the nurse anesthetist and the anesthesiologist.

Nevertheless, counsel's investigation discovered a separate basis for proceeding against the hospital. Under an agreement entered into between the hospital and the independent contractor, the hospital was responsible for furnishing the anesthesia equipment. Counsel also learned that the hospital had failed to provide either an end-tidal CO_2 monitor (apnograph) or a pulse oximeter for use during Ms. Thompson's surgical procedures.[48] Based on counsel's consultations with several renowned anesthesiologists, the plaintiff alleged that the applicable standard of care required that the hospital make available one or both of these machines, either of which would have detected the improper intubation long before Ms. Thompson's condition became imperiled.

Accordingly, Mr. Thompson, on his own behalf, and Ms. Washington, on behalf of herself and her daughter, Ms. Thompson, and Ms. Thompson's two children filed suit against the hospital, the anesthesia independent contractor, the anesthesiologist, the nurse anesthetist, and the obstetrician-gynecologist. Early in discovery it became evident that the obstetrician-gynecologist did not have any legal responsibility for this tragedy. Accordingly, plaintiffs successfully moved to dismiss him from the case. At about the same time, the defendants moved to dismiss the children's claims as well as Ms. Washington's individual claims. These motions were granted.

Trial commenced amid a great deal of talk regarding settlement. Partially through plaintiffs' presentation of evidence, plaintiffs' counsel received two settlement offers: the anesthesia defendants—that is, the independent contractor, the anesthesiologist, and the nurse anesthetist—offered to settle the claims against them for $2,000,000; all the defendants—that is, the anesthesia defendants and the hospital—offered to settle for $2,400,000. For a variety of reasons, both counsel and the plaintiffs believed the $2,400,000 figure was too low. On the other hand, accepting the partial settlement offered several advantages. First and most important, the partial settlement ensured that regardless of what happened at trial, Ms. Thompson would receive high-quality medical care and treatment for the rest of her life. Second, the partial settlement provided sufficient compensation for Ms. Thompson's children to improve substantially their material standard of living and to ensure that they would be adequately protected, financially at least, in the future. Third, the partial settlement eased the financial burden incurred in litigating the case.

Although accepting the partial settlement presented these advantages, it also posed some disadvantages. Chief among them was that accepting the offer meant that the plaintiffs' theory of the case would have to change in the middle of the trial. In addition, accepting the partial settlement presented several multiple-tortfeasor problems. In the end, the plaintiffs elected to accept the partial settlement and to proceed against the hospital. The jury found the hospital to have been negligent and awarded Ms. Thompson $4,586,278.

The hospital's posttrial motions demonstrate the importance of carefully considering partial settlements in multiple-tortfeasor situations. The hospital urged the court to credit it with a *pro rata* (prorated) credit. Since there were essentially three defendants (the anesthesiologist, the nurse anesthetist, and the hospital), the hospital contended that the court should reduce the hospital's portion of the verdict by two-thirds. Such a reduction would have resulted in the plaintiffs' recovering less than the jury had awarded. The hospital argued that even if a *pro tanto* (dollar for dollar) credit were applied, the hospital should receive a credit for the entire $2,000,000 partial settlement.

The plaintiffs disputed the hospital's argument on both points. In the District of Columbia, as in many jurisdictions, where both the settling and nonsettling defendants are found to be liable, the verdict should be reduced by the settling party's *pro rata* share.[49] Where a settling party is exonerated, however, the remaining party is entitled only to a *pro tanto* credit.[50] In Ms. Thompson's case there had been no finding regarding the anesthesia defendants' liability. In the settlement agreement the anesthesia defendants specifically disclaimed all liability. In *Hall v. General Motors Corp.*[51] and in *Crooks v. Williams*,[52] the courts, following the general law in most jurisdictions, held that where the settling defendant's liability has not been determined, the granting of a *pro tanto* credit is proper.[53] The court agreed and granted the hospital only a *pro tanto* credit.

The next issue concerned the amount of the *pro tanto* credit. Although the partial settlement amounted to $2,000,000, Ms. Thompson received only $1,328,148 of it. Thus, the settlement encompassed claims (or potential claims) that were not before the court. Under the settlement, each of the putative plaintiffs received compensation totaling $597,778. This compensation included a *pro rata* allocation of the settlement's court-approved attorneys' fees. Accordingly, the plaintiffs argued that the jury's award to Ms. Thompson should be reduced only by the amount of the settlement actually allocated to Ms. Thompson ($1,328,148), rather than by the full amount of the settlement ($2,000,000).

The court agreed, reasoning that there is no justification for applying the $671,852 that the settling defendants had paid to the putative plaintiffs and to Ms. Thompson's husband for their own individual claims as a set-off against the amount the jury awarded to Ms. Thompson for her claims. Credits such as the one to which the hospital is entitled are justified to prevent plaintiffs from recovering a total amount greater than what the jury awards as damages.

The court reasoned that this purpose is not served by crediting what one plaintiff receives in settlement against what another plaintiff receives from a jury.

Moreover, in this case the jury award included only those amounts necessary to compensate Ms. Thompson for her injuries. The jury never heard any evidence regarding the individual claims of Ms. Thompson's children or her mother. Careful drafting of the settlement instrument therefore resulted in the maximization of the plaintiffs' recovery.

Tactical Considerations

Ideally, a plaintiff wants to prosecute her claims against all parties who may be legally responsible for her injuries. She also wants to avoid entering into any settlement that will preclude her from collecting the highest award possible. On the other hand, each defendant wants to contest every claim of negligence made against him that he believes lacks merit. To the extent that any claim has merit, the defendant wants to settle as quickly as possible for the lowest amount of money that the plaintiff will accept and to have any other party who was at fault contribute his fair share to the settlement.

Realistically, neither plaintiff nor defendant can achieve the ideal in every case, and blind pursuit of the ideal may do more harm than good to the litigants. Each case involving multiple parties must be evaluated in light of the many interrelated factors that may influence the verdict and the psychological and financial costs to the parties of protracted litigation whose outcome cannot be guaranteed.

When the medical care that gives rise to a medical malpractice claim is rendered in a hospital and involves the administration or prescription of therapeutic drugs, the plaintiff's attorney is confronted with exceptionally complicated strategic decisions that are not susceptible to uniform guidelines. Suing only the plaintiff's primary physician simplifies the case, reduces the cost of the litigation, and places pressure on the physician to attempt to shift responsibility for the untoward result to a third party, such as the drug manufacturer or hospital personnel. If the physician elects to shift responsibility without joining the responsible third party, however, the plaintiff risks a jury's finding that the doctor is not liable but that it was the nonjoined third party who was really at fault.

Suing the hospital offers the advantage that jurors are likely to be much less sympathetic to a depersonalized corporate entity than they are to a physician. But there are two significant disadvantages to this approach. First, the treating physician is likely to be an independent contractor for whom the hospital is not vicariously liable. If the treatment that produced the injury falls exclusively within the province of the treating physician, the court may direct a verdict in favor of the hospital. Second, some jurisdictions still provide a full or limited charitable immunity for hospitals. In these jurisdictions it obviously makes no sense to sue the hospital alone. Moreover, in these cases it may be advisable not to sue the hospital at all to avoid the risk that the jury may find the hospital solely liable—letting the physician off the hook—and leave the plaintiff with a judgment that cannot be fully collected from the hospital.

The advantage to suing a drug company is that local jurors are unlikely to sympathize with such a remote entity. The principal disadvantage is that therapeutic drug cases present exceptionally complex medical questions that are difficult for jurors to decipher. Moreover, a drug company has both the incentive and the resources to engage in a fight to the death to prove that its drug did not cause the plaintiff's injuries. If it cannot prevail on the causation issue, it may attempt to exhaust the resources of the plaintiff's attorney and his client in order to diminish substantially their ability and will to press forward with a protracted and complex case that will take years to resolve. Finally, if all else fails, the drug company may attempt to shift responsibility for the accident to the treating physician. Defense counsel must treat this approach with caution because of the risk of jeopardizing the drug company's relationship with the medical community, but if extensive discovery has made the company feel vulnerable, counsel may recommend the option as a last resort.

Co-defendants should avoid pointing fingers at one another until such time as this approach is no longer self-defeating. Ideally, a defendant in a multiple-tortfeasor case wants to preserve his rights to seek contribution or indemnity without helping the plaintiff prove her case. If the law of the jurisdiction allows delaying the proof essential to the third-party claim until after the plaintiff's claim is resolved, rarely will a defendant find it advantageous to offer evidence and make arguments that prove that a co-defendant engaged in tortious conduct. On the other hand, if the jurisdiction takes the view that claims of contribution and indemnity must be resolved by the jury in the trial of the plaintiff's claims, the defendant faces the choice of asserting the cross-claim or losing the right to assert it forever.

The cases and problems explored in this chapter offer an important lesson to counsel for both plaintiffs and defendants. It is risky, and in some cases foolhardy, to remain locked into one strategy in multiple-party situations. General strategic principles should be used as a guide and not as a mandate. As the case develops, counsel for each party must remain flexible and prepared to add or drop parties, claims, and defenses to comport with a realistic evaluation of the evidence in the case and the likely outcome of the trial.

Chapter 13

Preparing for Trial: Integrating Law and Medicine

Preparing for trial requires a systematic review of the information and legal theories developed during the discovery process and careful construction of a trial strategy in light of this information. Equally important is psychological preparation. Counsel and parties must expect to try the case rather than settle it. In addition, to prepare for trial effectively, counsel needs to step away from the mountain of factual, legal, and medical information and attempt to gain a perspective on how the case will look to someone who has not lived with it for years.

One of the most difficult challenges for trial counsel in a medical malpractice case is to keep in mind that judges and jurors are likely to view the case through biased eyes. People have strong feelings about medical malpractice claims, and these feelings significantly influence their willingness to accept the different constructions of reality presented in counsel's version of the facts or legal and medical theories. In selecting the jury and presenting the case, counsel should anticipate those biases. As the date for trial approaches, it is helpful to solicit responses from as many different people as possible to the core facts of the case.

For example, in preparing for the trial of a case involving a failure to detect cancer, I visited the courtroom where a similar case was being tried. During the recess I asked the court clerk about the issues in the case and about how he felt the case was going. After reciting some of the claims made in the case, the clerk pulled me a little closer and whispered that the plaintiff was likely to lose. When I asked why, he said that it was his view that God caused cancer in response to evil conduct and that therefore one could not hold a physician responsible for the harm that the cancer victim suffered.

This clerk, however unique his perspective, could well be sitting in a jury box deciding a case if his religious views were not uncovered during the voir dire. All the medical experts and texts in the world will have little effect on such a person's view of legal responsibility. Similarly, some people feel that they owe their lives to the medical profession. Others feel that the medical profession is fundamentally corrupt, greedy, and incompetent. Most potential jurors hold views somewhere in between. To be ready for trial, counsel must acknowledge the wide differences in perspectives, values, education, and intellectual capacities of the potential decision makers and critically assess how the case is likely to be received by the individuals who are likely to evaluate it. In view of the wide variety of publications discussing trial preparation generally in civil cases, this chapter attempts to highlight only the important considerations unique to medical malpractice cases.

Discovery

The outcome of a medical malpractice case turns as much or more on trial preparation as it does on the trial itself. The ordinary mechanisms that the law provides for ascertaining facts before trial must be vigorously employed in a medical malpractice case. Some mechanisms are more useful than others, but most serve a meaningful role. The following discussion illustrates some approaches to discovery in medical malpractice cases.

Interrogatories

Interrogatories (written questions) serve a limited but useful purpose to a plaintiff in a medical malpractice case. They are employed in such cases principally to identify the names and addresses of all potential parties and witnesses to the lawsuit, along with the basic facts about the relationships among the parties. In addition, in cases where the standard of care is embodied in documents, interrogatories may help uncover the author and present location of a document.

Interrogatories generally are not useful in proving that the defendant was negligent. In most cases asking a question on standard of care in the interrogatories will trigger deep reflection on the part of the defendant and his counsel and elicit an artfully phrased response to a pivotal issue in the case. Consequently, in the ordinary medical malpractice case the plaintiff is ill advised to use interrogatories to evoke answers to standard-of-care questions before the defendant is deposed. Doing so will enable the defendant to anticipate the plaintiff's theories of the case for use in his deposition without disclosing any useful information in return.

Defendants will find interrogatories more productive. Since the plaintiff begins the case with the advantage of a pretrial factual investigation and expert review, defendants may use interrogatories to gain more specific information regarding the plaintiff's theories of liability and damages. Interrogatories are also useful in obtaining information regarding the factual investigation that the plaintiff has conducted in terms of witnesses and documents.

The tension that inevitably develops between counsel for the plaintiff and counsel for the defendant concerning interrogatories concerns the timing of the disclosure of the identity of experts, their theories of liability, and the specific bases on which they will rest their opinions. Rules of discovery require the disclosure of such matters only as they relate to experts the parties will use at trial as distinguished from experts consulted solely for investigative and evaluative purposes. Consequently, the plaintiff should reserve decisions as to which experts will be used at trial until all material witnesses, including the defendants, have been deposed. Otherwise, defendants and their experts will develop their testimony, factual investigation, and research toward those issues. This is not to say that perjury will occur. Rather, it is human nature to adjust one's position to support a favorable view of oneself and the persons with whom one is aligned. For the same reasons, the goal of the defense is to learn as much as possible about the plaintiff's version of the facts and the medical theories before taking the depositions of the key fact and expert witnesses.

Requests for Production of Documents

In a case against a hospital or a drug company, understanding what documents to secure and how to secure them may be pivotal in the plaintiff's effort to prove that the defendant has engaged in negligent conduct or has sold a defective product (see Chapter 9 for a full discussion). But it bears emphasizing that, even if counsel believes he has secured a complete and accurate record through a request served before filing the complaint, he should still serve a formal request for production of documents on the doctor or hospital. If a health care provider who has relevant medical records is not a party to the action, counsel should subpoena the records. The objective is to secure a response to the document request that will be under oath and will thus subject the hospital to legal sanctions if it fails to supply the plaintiff with a complete and accurate medical record.

If the hospital from which medical records are sought is accredited by the Joint Commission for the Accreditation of Hospitals, JCAH standards may be admissible into evidence. Accordingly, if the hospital claims that it does not have in its possession, custody, or control a particular record that plaintiff's counsel believes should be in the hospital's possession, counsel should determine whether failure to complete the document or preserve it violates

JCAH's record-keeping requirements. In addition, counsel should determine whether the state or local government has promulgated any standards for record keeping that may have been violated.

The complex regulatory process governing the development and marketing of therapeutic drugs, including the requirements for record keeping and reporting, is discussed in detail in Chapter 11. If a therapeutic drug or anesthetic is suspected of having played a role in causing the plaintiff's injuries, counsel should secure a copy of the relevant documents from the drug manufacturer and the FDA. Documents that do not contain trade secret information may be obtained from the FDA through a request submitted under the Freedom of Information Act. If the evaluation of the initial data suggests that a drug was causally connected with the plaintiff's injuries and there is a basis to support the assertion of a strict liability or negligence claim against the drug company, counsel for the plaintiff and the defendant must decide whether to join the drug company in the lawsuit. Many of the relevant considerations are discussed in Chapter 12 on multiple parties and in Chapter 11 on therapeutic drugs.

Where the relevant documents are voluminous, it is important for counsel to employ a system of identifying, logging, and retrieving them. The important information needed by an expert to formulate her opinion or needed by counsel for cross-examination must be retrievable on request. In addition, counsel should secure stipulations—agreements not to contest—from the opposing attorney regarding the authenticity and admissibility of a copy of the relevant records before trial. If the stipulation is not forthcoming, counsel should subpoena the appropriate custodian of records to testify to the accuracy and authenticity of the records. Defense counsel should painstakingly review all relevant documents to determine whether they contain any privileged information that warrants protection from plaintiff's discovery efforts. In addition, counsel must decide whether to protect documents from discovery and may choose instead to comply with requests in order to minimize fishing expeditions and the imposition of undue costs and burdens on her client.

Inspection of Premises

If the plaintiff is claiming an untimely response to an emergency, plaintiff's counsel should serve on the defendant a request for inspection of premises and also request blueprints of the relevant areas in the hospital where the plaintiff was treated. The purpose of these requests is to allow the attorney to assess the credibility of the claims of the witnesses as to what was done and how quickly it was done. In addition, counsel should secure the assistance of an appropriate expert—draftsperson, photographer, or other professional—

to assist him in preparing demonstrative evidence that will allow the jury to assess the credibility of the witnesses concerning the timeliness of various responses.

Moreover, since most responses in emergency situations include securing appropriate equipment and drugs, counsel should request the production of documents that will verify or refute the claims of the witnesses about where they got particular pieces of equipment and drugs at the time the emergency occurred.

Depositions of Fact Witnesses

Before the trial of a medical malpractice case plaintiff's counsel will find it necessary to interview and depose many persons who are witnesses to the events leading up to the plaintiff's injury or the impact of these injuries on the plaintiff. Since it is to the plaintiff's advantage to know before taking depositions whether particular witnesses will be neutral, friendly, or hostile, plaintiff's counsel should interview each prospective witness who is willing to speak with him before the deposition. The rules of procedure and professional ethics prevent counsel from speaking to opposing parties without the permission of opposing counsel. But there is no prohibition against interviewing persons who are not parties. This includes former employees of the defendant as well as present employees who are not managing agents.

Whether counsel gains an interview with any such fact witnesses depends on the willingness of the witness to speak with him and counsel's powers of persuasion. Many health care personnel will agree to speak with plaintiff's counsel and tell him what they know if they are assured that there is nothing unethical in doing so and that they are not targets of the lawsuit. Counsel should advise the witness that she is not compelled to discuss the events with him in the absence of a subpoena but that a preliminary discussion will assist counsel not only in ascertaining the truth—which is the purpose of the trial—but in determining whether the witness is familiar enough with the relevant facts to warrant her testimony at trial. If the witness replies that she is unwilling to discuss the case because of threats from her present or former employer, counsel should pursue the facts with opposing counsel as well as the court, if necessary. Neither side has a legal right to direct or restrict the testimony of a nonparty fact witness.

If a witness has relevant information, counsel must make a strategic decision whether to depose her. Obviously, if the testimony of the witness is favorable to counsel's claims, counsel will want to ensure that the testimony gets before the court. But he will not be eager to bring to the attention of opposing counsel facts that she does not know and shows no interest in ascertaining. The risk of not taking the deposition is that the witness may die, become ill, or disappear by the time of the trial. Moreover, a possibility exists that the witness will lose her grasp of important details or that her testimony cannot withstand pointed cross-examination. For these reasons, it is probably advisable to take the deposition of any witness who has firsthand knowledge of any of the critical facts that support counsel's claim or defense.

Initiating the discovery process as quickly as possible after filing the lawsuit is important in medical malpractice cases. Doctors and nurses frequently move or change their place of employment. Locating witnesses becomes more difficult with the passage of time. Health care professionals are involved in the treatment of numerous persons, and while they are not likely to forget the occurrence of tragic events, they will fail to remember important details associated with the medical care rendered to the victim as time goes on. These same considerations apply to the individual defendant physicians and nurses who, for purposes of describing the facts underlying the claims or defenses in the lawsuit, are fact witnesses rather than expert witnesses.

Depositions of Defendants

Absent some unusual circumstance that requires a different strategy, plaintiff's counsel should defer deposing the defendants until he has a good grasp of the facts, medical theories, and legal theories that he must prove in order to prevail on his claim. He will gain some of the basic facts from his client or her representative. He will then have secured and carefully analyzed all the relevant medical records. Ideally, he will have submitted the medical records, along with his factual summary, to an expert who, after reviewing the matter, has agreed to testify at trial. Plaintiff's counsel, if he follows this suggested approach, will also conduct his own medical research and become intimately familiar with the medical literature and authorities in the field. Familiarity with both the facts of the case and the medical issues involved will allow him the opportunity to engage in meaningful dialogue with his expert and formulate a plan for deposing the defendants.

Plaintiff's counsel should pursue several goals in deposing defendants who are health care professionals. First, he should identify and assess the defendant's version of the facts surrounding the medical care rendered to the plaintiff and the cause of the plaintiff's injuries. Second, he wants to probe the defendant's knowledge of the medical issues and assess whether the defendant possessed the degree of skill and knowledge required to treat the plaintiff properly. Third, he can assess the defendant's general style and demeanor and evaluate how he is likely to influence the judge and the jury.

To accomplish these objectives requires a detailed grasp of the facts and the medical issues and a plan for conducting the deposition. Though it is not possible to describe a deposition plan that serves all cases, certain strategies warrant general recommendation. First, it serves no constructive purpose to argue with the defendant or attempt to show him where he is wrong during the course of his deposition. If the parties are really preparing for trial, it is best simply to allow the defendant to answer the questions as fully and completely as he can. Incorrect assertions regarding medicine or science can be dealt with better at trial, when the defendant will lack the comfort that his lawyer may provide at the deposition by way of spoken objections or timely interruptions of the questions or the answers. Moreover, if the defendant is stating matters that are flatly wrong, this sworn testimony will bear on his credibility at trial. Rather than attempt to impeach the defendant at his deposition on facts or principles of medicine, it is better to probe him about why he holds the view he has expressed and about authorities that concur in this view.

If the defendant makes misstatements of facts as well as medical principles, it may mean that he is unprepared, untruthful, or simply lacking an accurate recall. Whatever the explanation, plaintiff's counsel is probably better off simply making a note of the misstatement for later exploration and use. Of course, if the defendant is simply incorrectly recalling an immaterial fact, it is probably better to inform him of the mistake and allow the questioning and answers to focus on material issues. The bottom line, however, is that the deposition of the defendant health care provider should be used as a true discovery deposition in uncovering the truth as the defendant sees it so that the relative strengths of the parties' factual, medical, and legal claims can be evaluated.

In light of the tactics that plaintiff's counsel will likely employ at the deposition, it behooves defense counsel to thoroughly prepare the health care provider for the deposition, emotionally and intellectually. It is a good idea to prepare the doctor in the attorney's office to get his full-time attention and to assess how he acts in a nonmedical environment. In addition to the usual instructions to limit answers to the questions asked, the defendant should be educated about the rules of the game governing depositions and the likely tack of plaintiff's counsel. In particular, the defendant should be advised of the purpose of plaintiff's counsel's questions regarding learned treatises and other sources that plaintiff will attempt to use to establish the standard of care. Most important, the doctor or nurse should review his medical records, refresh his recall about all relevant facts, and be prepared to acknowledge his inability to recall every detail about the case. On important matters that cannot be remembered, the doctor should discuss his ordinary habit and routine practice.

Depositions of Plaintiffs

Unless the case involves an informed consent claim, the deposition that the defendant takes of the plaintiff is likely to focus almost exclusively on damages. Plaintiffs usually have little relevant knowledge about facts pertaining to the defendant's liability, other than the directions or warnings that the defendant communicated to them. In some cases, however, defenses of statute of limitations, contributory negligence, or assumption of the risk may depend on a thorough exploration of the plaintiff's knowledge and conduct at relevant times before, during, and after the defendant rendered medical care to the plaintiff. Moreover, defense counsel should attempt to evaluate how the plaintiff is likely to appear in court and how effective she is likely to be in helping her case.

The importance of preparing the plaintiff for her deposition should not be underestimated by plaintiff's counsel. Not only will the plaintiff's presentation have an impact on defense counsel's assessment of the risks of the litigation; it will also have a substantial influence on the judge and the jury as they assess the propriety of a large damage award.

Helping his client put her best foot forward requires that plaintiff's counsel make a substantial effort to prepare her for the deposition. Preparing the plaintiff's deposition and trial testimony should actually begin at the initial interview, when counsel is evaluating the case. As we saw in Chapter 1, it is important to assess the plaintiff's potential to help or hurt the case by her appearance, demeanor, and ability to articulate what occurred and the injuries flowing from the tortious conduct. At the initial interview both concerns are addressed: counsel discusses with the client the importance of presenting to the court a good physical appearance in terms of dress and also suggests that she begin to keep a diary in order to record the dates of visits to doctors and physical therapists, dates of missed work or other activities because of the effects of the accident, and dates of exceptionally painful or embarrassing experiences.

If the client has followed counsel's advice in this regard, preparation for her deposition is made a lot easier. Counsel reviews her diary and uses it to identify matters that need emphasis or clarification. The client must be given the usual instructions about answering the questions posed to her by the opposing counsel and not volunteering information. Most important, however, is to establish a level of comfort and confidence on the part of the client that she can participate in this unfamiliar process and help her case. The best way to accomplish this is to spend time with the client familiarizing her with the details of the deposition procedure and the tack that opposing counsel is likely to take in her questioning. If the client feels that she is prepared and that her attorney has confidence in her and will protect her from unfair surprises or abuse, her responses to the deposition questions will probably demonstrate this self-assurance and will promote a favorable evaluation of the case.

Depositions of Experts

Unless the claim of medical malpractice involves the rare fact situation where res ipsa loquitur applies or where a guarantee was made by the physician, the ultimate resolution of the liability question will probably turn on the credibility of each side's expert witnesses. Consequently, if the applicable rules of civil procedure allow it, the deposition of the opposing expert is one of the most important pretrial discovery events. At that deposition the parties have an opportunity to evaluate the substance of the expert's opinion, the factual and medical basis on which the opinion rests, and the manner in which the expert communicates with laypeople.

It is thus crucial that counsel be well prepared and well organized when taking the discovery deposition of the expert witness on the other side of the case. As in deposing the defendant doctor or nurse, the discovery deposition of the opposing expert should not be viewed as a chance to impeach the expert. The opportunity and time for impeachment is at trial. Efforts to impeach at the deposition only educate the expert about her points of vulnerability and enable her to prepare for her trial testimony better. The success of the deposition should be judged in terms of how thorough counsel is in gathering information about the opinions the expert will express to a reasonable medical certainty as to liability and causation, the facts of the case on which the expert's opinion rests, the medical principles that the expert believes support her opinion, and other medical authorities that the expert relies on.

Before the deposition the deposing party's counsel should have conducted an investigation through formal and informal discovery to learn as much as possible about the expert and her professional reputation. Some of the information should be obtained through expert interrogatories. Other information can be obtained by normal investigative processes, particularly through inquiries of the deponent's past and present professional colleagues and examining her research and professional publications.

Depositions for Use at Trial

Thus far, the discussion in this chapter has assumed that the depositions being taken are for discovery purposes only. There is always the possibility, however, that a deposition of a fact witness or an opposing party will be used at trial to the extent permitted by the applicable rules of civil procedure. Under the Federal Rules of Civil Procedure, the deposition of a party may be used at trial for any purpose, and the deposition of a fact witness may be used if the fact witness is unavailable for trial or resides outside the court's subpoena power. Moreover, the practice and procedure in some jurisdictions allow counsel to take an expert's deposition for use at trial if the opponent is properly notified of such intent before the witness is deposed.

If there is a probability that a deposition will be offered at trial as substantive evidence, each side must approach the deposition accordingly. The deposition practice of reserving all objections until the time of trial except for objections to the form of the question cannot be employed, and the opposing party must use any weapons he has to impeach the witness.

Strategically, I prefer to present my expert testimony live at trial and choose to depose my own expert for use at trial only where there is a high probability that she will be unavailable for live trial testimony. Experts who are testifying to damages only are, however, a different story. Unless there is a need for the expert to testify as to the plaintiff's actual condition as of the date of trial, it is often effective to depose a damage expert witness by means of videotape. Doing so will ordinarily not be objected to by the opponent unless the expert's testimony is significantly controverted.

Requests for Admissions of Fact

Litigants often overlook serving requests for admissions of fact. Perhaps this is because lawyers rarely admit anything that has the potential of hurting their claim or defense and thus view the requests as a waste of time. Notwithstanding the general validity of assuming that requests for admissions have limited value, they can be profitably used by plaintiffs in medical malpractice cases for several reasons. First, drafting requests for admissions is a process that allows plaintiff's counsel to clarify the factual issues in the case and the proof that he and his opponent are relying on to support their respective versions of the facts. Second, serving artfully drafted requests will compel one's opponent to focus on and acknowledge factual weaknesses in her case. Third, the requests may enable the parties to agree on some stipulations that may be used at trial. Fourth, a party's failure to admit a fact that he truly has no evidence to controvert will educate the court concerning the relative strengths and weaknesses of the parties' claims and defenses. Finally, in light of the tremendous cost of litigating medical malpractice cases, a party's refusal to admit a fact that he has no evidence to controvert will enable the party making the request to pass on to his opponent the cost of bringing in an expert or fact witness to prove an uncontroverted fact.

It should be noted that the more specifically a request is limited to facts as distinguished from standard-of-care questions that arguably pose mixed questions of fact and law, the more difficult it will be for the opposing side to offer an acceptable justification to the court as to why she should not be compelled to answer the requests.

Demonstrative Evidence

In Chapter 7 we discussed the importance of demonstrative evidence in promoting a better appreciation of the plaintiff's damages. We focused on the day-in-the-life film as a particularly effective form of demonstrative evidence. But there are many other ways in which such evidence may be useful to both parties in helping the jury to understand the issues arising out of the negligence claim. We have already mentioned charts and graphs that illustrate cost considerations. In addition, almost every medical malpractice case will present a need to educate the court and jury on anatomy to some extent. For this purpose, anatomical drawings or models may prove helpful. In appropriate cases the parties may find it worth the cost to have drawings enlarged or reproduced for showing on an overhead projector. The point is to view the case from the perspective of someone who is totally unexposed to the medical issues and ascertain the best techniques for teaching him about those issues.

Insurance Considerations

Plaintiff's first set of interrogatories should include questions concerning relevant insurance policies and the amount of coverage applicable to the present claim. Most states have statutes mandating that health care providers carry a specified minimum amount of liability coverage. Moreover, prudent health care providers purchase more than the required minimum insurance coverage to protect their personal assets. It is useful early in the litigation process to discover the total amount of insurance coverage available so that a realistic assessment may be made about how much of any potential judgment is collectible from an insurance company and how much of the excess verdict, if any, is collectible from the defendant or defendants. Learning the amount and sources of the coverage allows the plaintiff also to gain some appreciation of the true decision makers in the litigation and the pressures and potential conflicts that may exist or arise among these decision makers.

Often the health care provider has liability insurance coverage with one insurance company for the statutorily mandated minimum coverage and insurance with another company for excess liability. Moreover, the policy may provide for a deductible, requiring the health care provider to pay a certain amount of the claim before the insurance company is required to cover the loss. It is important for plaintiff and defense to know all the parties who are potentially responsible for paying the judgment, because each is likely to have some influence on litigation and settlement decisions.

In the same vein it is helpful to know whether the policy has a provision that reserves to the insured health care provider the right to approve any proposed settlement. The health care provider obviously has considerations and concerns that both overlap with and depart from the concerns of the insurer. Foremost among them is the impact of the various potential litigation outcomes on his professional reputation and his ability to earn income and respect in the future. The existence or nonexistence of a right to approve the settlement indicates whether the settlement considerations are likely to be dominated by economic and legal concerns as opposed to psychological and emotional ones. Disclosure relative to such an approval clause also sensitizes the plaintiff's attorney to potential conflicts of interest between the health care provider and the insurance company.

It is equally important to discover what claims are covered by the insurance policy and whether the company is defending the case while at the same time reserving its right to contest the insured's claim of coverage under the policy. Evaluating the scope of insurance coverage intelligently in regard to claims requires examining the entire policy, and plaintiff's counsel should request the production of the policy for this purpose. Determining whether the insurance company is defending under a reservation of rights assertion can be discovered through an interrogatory.

The language of some medical malpractice insurance policies attempts to limit the liability coverage to claims of negligence based on professional negligence. Thus, if the jurisdiction characterizes an informed consent violation as a battery rather than negligence, a question may arise if the plaintiff prevails on the informed consent claim as to whether it is covered by insurance for "professional negligence." The issue of coverage may be relevant if the plaintiff's claim of liability rests on an assertion of breach of contract or some form of misrepresentation. Anticipating such coverage issues may be helpful to the plaintiff and the insured so that protective action or alternative liability theories may be pursued at an early stage of the litigation.

Along with concern about the types of claims covered by the insurance policy, both parties should ascertain the types of damages it covers. The parties should attempt to anticipate defenses by the insurer that pure emotional harm or economic harm is not covered by insurance for "bodily injuries." Although it may not always be possible to restructure the claims in a way that ensures coverage, the parties have a mutual interest that conflicts with the interests of the insurance company in litigating the claim in a manner that makes the maximum coverage available.

Punitive damage claims merit particular attention when insurance is considered. A substantial number of jurisdictions embrace the view that it is against public policy to allow insurance against a punitive damage award. Since the objectives of a punitive damage award are to punish a person for outrageous or egregious conduct and to deter similar conduct in the future, it is thought that allowing an insurance company to pay such an award defeats its purpose. Not all jurisdictions agree. In addition, even in a jurisdiction that considers insurance against punitive damages to be counter to public policy, the court may allow a health care provider who is liable for punitive damages only on a basis of vicarious liability to cover this liability with an insurance policy.

Defense counsel should usually fight vigorously to obtain an order dismissing the punitive damage claim from the pleadings. If the punitive damage claim is not stricken from the complaint, counsel must explore two considerations: the insured and the insurer. First, does the insured now require independent counsel? In the presence of a punitive damage claim, it will not be possible for the attorney hired by the insurance company to direct the litigation in the interests of both the insured and the insurer. Second, is the case worth defending in light of the potential exposure of the health care provider's assets? The potential conflict of interest lies in assessing both the legal defenses and the strategies used to pursue the defense as well as in the judgment as to whether to settle within the policy limits. Lurking in the background is a potential suit by the insured against the insurer for a bad-faith refusal to settle within the policy limits. A developing body of law, in the form of court decisions and statutes, provides that an insurance company may be held liable to a claimant or the insured for an award above the policy limits if it fails in bad faith to accept an offer for settlement within the policy limits.

Other considerations relevant to the extent of liability coverage are whether the insurance policy provides for payments on a "claims made" or "occurrence" basis and how the claim or occurrence is to be defined. These are important questions for purposes of determining which insurance policy is applicable and the amount of liability insurance available. A "claims made" policy obligates the insurance company to defend and pay any claim that is made during the policy period regardless of when the tort occurred. An "occurrence" policy obliges the company to defend and pay a claim made within the applicable period of the statute of limitations, provided that the conduct giving rise to the claim occurred within the period during which the policy was in effect.

In addition, how the terms *claim* or *occurrence* are defined will determine the applicable deductible and the upper limits of the available coverage. Many policies provide that the insured is responsible for a set dollar amount of each claim, accident, or occurrence before the insurance coverage takes effect. Also, many policies define the maximum liability under the policy by reference to a certain amount for each person, a higher amount for each occurrence, and an absolute ceiling for an aggregate of claims during the policy period. In some policies terms such as *claim* or *occurrence* are not defined or the definition is unclear.

Where important terms such as *claim* or *occurrence* are not clearly defined, the court will be required to provide a definitive interpretation. Most courts begin their interpretation by acknowledging that where a policy provision is ambiguous, the court should construe the ambiguous term in favor of the insured to maximize the available coverage. The rationale for this approach is that the insurance company is in the best position to clarify the terms in the policy and that, in any event, the definitions of terms in most insurance contracts are not subject to real negotiation.

In most jurisdictions—Wisconsin being a noteworthy exception—the plaintiff does not have a direct action against the defendant's liability insurer. Thus she cannot become directly involved in any dispute regarding the coverage provided by the policy until she has either settled her claim or had a judgment entered in her favor. Nevertheless, it is likely that the plaintiff and the defendant will take the same position on the available coverage; both want the policy to be interpreted in a way that provides maximum coverage. Since the plaintiff cannot become directly involved in the coverage dispute before the verdict stage of the proceedings, her best way of staying apprised of the upcoming dispute is to submit the appropriate questions to the defendant through interrogatories or at his deposition. The questions will ask whether the insurance company is defending the claim under a reservation of rights to contest the coverage and what the defendant contends to be the scope of the coverage and its monetary limit.

Statutory Immunity and Ceilings on Damage Awards

Just as the available insurance coverage may place a ceiling on the amount of money that the plaintiff can realistically expect to recover, statutes and court decisions providing special protection to certain governmental or nonprofit health care providers may also define the upper limit of the value of the case. A comprehensive discussion of the statutory trends and the constitutional challenges to damage caps is presented in Chapter 6. In addition to the considerations raised there, counsel should note that in some jurisdictions medical care may be provided by a hospital owned and operated by the state or local government or by a health care professional who is employed by the government. Moreover, dependents of persons on active duty in the armed forces may receive medical care from entities owned or persons employed by the federal government. Generally, the federal government's liability under the Federal Torts Claim Act is determined in accordance with the same criteria employed by the state jurisdiction in which the treatment was rendered. In other words, the federal government has waived immunity from tort claims to the extent that a private person would be held liable for the same conduct. The liability of state and local government employees and entities depends on the extent of waiver of immunity under state law and the particular criteria promulgated in the state statute or court decision waiving sovereign immunity.

Finally, though the trend is definitely against providing a hospital with protection from tort claims based on the doctrine of charitable immunity, counsel should not assume that all jurisdictions have abolished such immunity for hospitals. For example, New Jersey still provides protection to hospitals within the state by a statute that sets a ceiling of $10,000 on the amount for which a hospital may be held liable. Litigation where a New Jersey hospital is one of the defendants is obviously very different from litigation in states that have abrogated the charitable immunity protection. In venues like New Jersey, if the plaintiff has a serious injury and the case presents a dispute as to whether the hospital or an individual health care provider is responsible, the plaintiff is probably better off dropping the hospital from the case as a defendant. That reduces the risk that the jury verdict may be influenced by a comparative fault assessment that lets the individual, who is insured, off the hook and places all the blame on the hospital, against which plaintiff can collect no more than $10,000.

The Pretrial Conference

The scheduling of a pretrial conference usually compels all parties in the litigation to focus on the case and make a realistic assessment of the relative strengths and weaknesses of their positions. In most jurisdictions the date of the conference signals that the time for trial is near and the time for posturing will soon pass. Attorneys for all parties must now review the evidence and legal theories with a view toward bargaining for an acceptable settlement or trying the case effectively. In my opinion, if the defendant has not made an offer of settlement that comes close to being acceptable before the pretrial conference, the plaintiff should eliminate settlement considerations from serious discussion and prepare to try the case. The best way to obtain an acceptable settlement at this stage of the proceedings is to demonstrate to the defense and the court that the plaintiff and her attorney have both the will and the resources necessary to present the case effectively. Preparation for the pretrial conference should thus focus on the tasks that a courtroom trial entails.

In federal court and in state courts having a pretrial conference rule similar to Rule 16 of the Federal Rules of Civil Procedure, both sides to the litigation may be restricted significantly to, if not totally locked into, the evidence and legal theories incorporated in the pretrial order issued at or after the pretrial conference. A thorough review and critical assessment of the evidence and the law is compelled by the impact that the pretrial order is likely to have on the presentation of the case. Among the tasks requiring the attorney's careful attention are preparing a trial exhibit list, extracting the relevant portions of the depositions, preparing a witness list, touching base with important fact witnesses and all the client's expert witnesses, and preparing the client for the battle ahead. Finally, while settlement considerations should not be allowed to influence counsel's approach to the pretrial conference unduly, it would be foolish to attend the conference without having determined the range of an acceptable settlement and adopted a strategy toward any settlement discussions that may occur.

The checklist that follows reviews the main tasks of the discovery stage and indicates those leading up to the pretrial conference and the trial itself.

> *Checklist of Considerations*
> > Discovery
> > > Interrogatories
> > > Documents
> > > Inspections of premises
> > > Depositions of fact witnesses
> > > Depositions of defendants
> > > Depositions of plaintiffs
> > > Depositions of experts
> > > Requests for admissions of fact
> > > Depositions for use at trial
> > > Demonstrative evidence
> > > Insurance considerations
> > > Statutory immunity and damages award ceilings
> > > Settlement discussions
>
> > *The Pretrial Conference*
> > > Preparing exhibit list
> > > Extracting depositions
> > > Preparing witness list
> > > Communicating with fact witnesses
> > > Communicating with expert witnesses

Communicating with client
Developing a strategy for settlement discussions
Reviewing the pretrial order

Trial Preparation
Reviewing pretrial order
Reviewing exhibit list and preparing exhibits
Reviewing witness list
Contacting witnesses
Contacting client
Preparing to select jury
   Community survey
   Voir dire questions
   Developing selection strategy
   Writing jury instructions
Preparing medical brief
Preparing trial briefs
Preparing for trial before judge
   Reviewing fundamental considerations
   Preparing medical brief
   Preparing trial brief
   Preparing proposed findings of fact and conclusions of law
   Preparing trial notebook
   Writing opening statement
   Establishing order of proof
   Writing closing statement
   Writing jury instructions
   Assessing form of jury verdict
   Posing special verdict questions
   Posing special interrogatories
   Polling jury

Conclusion

From the perspective of both the plaintiff and the defendant, preparing for trial in a medical malpractice case is a consuming task, emotionally and financially. Once plaintiff's counsel has started intense preparation, it sometimes is necessary for him to remind himself, if a serious settlement offer is made, that his job is to obtain an acceptable monetary result and that a trial is a means, but only one means, toward that end. At the same time, if the plaintiff has suffered catastrophic injuries and the verdict potential is high, counsel must realize that taking the case to verdict may be the only way of obtaining a just result for his client.

Defense counsel must remain sensitive to the potential impact of a settlement or a trial on her client. There is no pat answer as to what makes the most sense in every case. Each case and client commands and deserves careful individual evaluation.

If counsel and their respective clients are not prepared, emotionally and financially, to engage in an intense battle that may take years for final resolution, they should avoid getting involved in the litigation of complex medical malpractice cases. The most propitious time to resolve the case may be when it receives its first critical evaluation in the early stages. After that many cases tend to gather a momentum that makes them difficult to control. Any attorney who takes on a medical malpractice case had better be ready to try it.

Appendix

Notes

*Suggested Readings
in Case Law*

Indexes

Appendix

Certain ethical issues repeatedly confront attorneys representing plaintiffs and defendants in medical malpractice cases. Less routinely, health care professionals must deal with these issues and others involving professional standards and collegial relations. The American Bar Association (ABA) *Model Rules of Professional Conduct* offer one approach to these issues. They were adopted by the ABA House of Delegates on August 2, 1983, and amended in 1987, 1989, 1990, 1991, and 1992. For easy reference, the Rules are printed here, but without the accompanying comments and model code comparisons.

Following the Rules, this Appendix also presents a series of problems that encourage the reader to reflect on the ethical standards and rules of professional conduct applicable to a wide range of practices. These include soliciting clients, accepting cases, resolving conflicts among lawyers and clients, resolving conflicts among clients, contacting fact and expert witnesses, representing the impaired professional, responding to knowledge of altered records or concealed evidence, and settling cases.

Rules of Professional Conduct

Preamble, Scope and Terminology

Preamble: A Lawyer's Responsibilities

A lawyer is a representative of clients, an officer of the legal system and a public citizen having special responsibility for the quality of justice.

As a representative of clients, a lawyer performs various functions. As advisor, a lawyer provides a client with an informed understanding of the client's legal rights and obligations and explains their practical implications. As advocate, a lawyer zealously asserts the client's position under the rules of the adversary system. As negotiator, a lawyer seeks a result advantageous to the client but consistent with requirements of honest dealing with others. As intermediary between clients, a lawyer seeks to reconcile their divergent interests as an advisor and, to a limited extent, as a spokesperson for each client. A lawyer acts as evaluator by examining a client's legal affairs and reporting about them to the client or to others.

In all professional functions a lawyer should be competent, prompt and diligent. A lawyer should maintain communication with a client concerning the representation. A lawyer should keep in confidence information relating to representation of a client except so far as disclosure is required or permitted by the Rules of Professional Conduct or other law.

A lawyer's conduct should conform to the requirements of the law, both in professional service to clients and in the lawyer's business and personal affairs. A lawyer should use the law's procedures only for legitimate purposes and not to harass or intimidate others. A lawyer should demonstrate respect for the legal system and for those who serve it, including judges, other lawyers and public officials. While it is a lawyer's duty, when necessary, to challenge the rectitude of official action, it is also a lawyer's duty to uphold legal process.

As a public citizen, a lawyer should seek improvement of the law, the administration of justice and the quality of service rendered by the legal profession. As a member of a learned profession, a lawyer should cultivate knowledge of the law beyond its use for clients, employ that knowledge in reform of the law and work to strengthen legal education. A lawyer should be mindful of deficiencies in the administration of justice and of the fact that the poor, and sometimes persons who are not poor, cannot afford adequate legal assistance, and should therefore devote professional time and civic influence in their behalf. A lawyer should aid the legal profession in pursuing these objectives and should help the bar regulate itself in the public interest.

Many of a lawyer's professional responsibilities are prescribed in the Rules of Professional Conduct, as well as substantive and procedural law. However, a lawyer is also guided by personal conscience and the approbation of professional peers. A lawyer should strive to attain the highest level of skill, to improve the law and the legal profession and to exemplify the legal profession's ideals of public service.

A lawyer's responsibilities as a representative of clients, an officer of the legal system and a public citizen are usually harmonious. Thus, when an opposing party is well represented, a lawyer can be a zealous advocate on behalf of a client and at the same time assume that justice is being done. So also, a lawyer can be sure that preserving client confidences ordinarily serves the public interest because people are more likely to seek legal advice, and thereby heed their legal obligations, when they know their communications will be private.

In the nature of law practice, however, conflicting responsibilities are encountered. Virtually all difficult ethical problems arise from conflict between a lawyer's responsibilities to clients, to the legal system and to the lawyer's own interest in remaining an upright person while earning a satisfactory living. The Rules of Professional Conduct prescribe terms for resolving such conflicts. Within the framework of these Rules, many difficult issues of professional discretion can arise. Such issues must be resolved through the exercise of sensitive professional and moral judgment guided by the basic principles underlying the Rules.

The legal profession is largely self-governing. Although other professions also have been granted powers of self-government, the legal profession is unique in this respect because of the close relationship between the profession and the processes of government and law enforcement. This connection is manifested in the fact that ultimate authority over the legal profession is vested largely in the courts.

To the extent that lawyers meet the obligations of their professional calling, the occasion for government regulation is obviated. Self-regulation also helps maintain the legal profession's independence from government domination. An independent legal profession is an important force in preserving government under law, for abuse of legal authority is more readily challenged by a profession whose members are not dependent on government for the right to practice.

The legal profession's relative autonomy carries with it special responsibilities of self-government. The profession has a responsibility to assure that its regulations are conceived in the public interest and not in furtherance of parochial or self-interested concerns of the bar. Every lawyer is responsible for observance of the Rules of Professional Conduct. A lawyer should also aid in securing their observance by other lawyers. Neglect of these responsibilities compromises the independence of the profession and the public interest which it serves.

Lawyers play a vital role in the preservation of society. The fulfillment of this role requires an understanding by lawyers of their relationship to our legal system. The Rules of Professional Conduct, when properly applied, serve to define that relationship.

Scope

The Rules of Professional Conduct are rules of reason. They should be interpreted with reference to the purposes of legal representation and of the law itself. Some of the Rules are imperatives, cast in the terms "shall" or "shall not." These define proper conduct for purposes of professional discipline. Others, generally cast in the term "may," are permissive and define areas under the Rules in which the lawyer has professional discretion. No disciplinary action should be taken when the lawyer chooses not to act or acts within the bounds of such discretion. Other Rules define the nature of relationships between the lawyer and others. The Rules are thus partly obligatory and disciplinary and partly constitutive and descriptive in that they define a lawyer's professional role. . . .

The Rules presuppose a larger legal context shaping the lawyer's role. That context includes court rules and statutes relating to matters of licensure, laws defining specific obligations of lawyers and substantive and procedural law in general. Compliance with the Rules, as with all law in an open society, depends primarily upon understanding and voluntary compliance, secondarily upon reinforcement by peer and public opinion and finally, when necessary, upon enforcement through disciplinary proceedings. The Rules do not, however, exhaust the moral and ethical considerations that should inform a lawyer, for no worthwhile human activity can be completely defined by legal rules. The Rules simply provide a framework for the ethical practice of law.

Furthermore, for purposes of determining the lawyer's authority and responsibility, principles of substantive law external to these Rules determine whether a client-lawyer relationship exists. Most of the duties flowing from the client-lawyer relationship attach only after the client has requested the lawyer to render legal services and the lawyer has agreed to do so. But there are some duties, such as that of confidentiality under Rule 1.6, that may attach when the lawyer agrees to consider whether a client-lawyer relationship shall be established. Whether a client-lawyer relationship exists for any specific purpose can depend on the circumstances and may be a question of fact.

Under various legal provisions, including constitutional, statutory and common law, the responsibilities of government lawyers may include authority concerning legal matters that ordinarily reposes in the client in private client-lawyer relationships. For example, a lawyer for a government agency may have authority on behalf of the government to decide upon settlement or whether to appeal from an adverse judgment. Such authority in various respects is generally vested in the attorney general and the state's attorney in state government, and their federal counterparts, and the same may be true of other government law officers. Also, lawyers under the supervision of these officers may be authorized to represent several government agencies in intragovernmental legal controversies in circumstances where a private lawyer could not represent multiple private clients. They also may have authority to represent the "public interest" in circumstances where a private lawyer would not be authorized to do so. These Rules do not abrogate any such authority.

Failure to comply with an obligation or prohibition imposed by a Rule is a basis for invoking the disciplinary process. The Rules presuppose that disciplinary assessment of a lawyer's conduct will be made on the basis of the facts and circumstances as they existed at the time of the conduct in question and in recognition of the fact that a lawyer often has to act upon uncertain or incomplete evidence of the situation. Moreover, the Rules presuppose that whether or not discipline should be imposed for a violation, and the severity of a sanction, depend on all the circumstances, such as the willfulness and seriousness of the violation, extenuating factors and whether there have been previous violations.

Violation of a Rule should not give rise to a cause of action nor should it create any presumption that a legal duty has been breached. The Rules are designed to provide guidance to lawyers and to provide a structure for regulating conduct through disciplinary agencies. They are not designed to be a basis for civil liability. Furthermore, the purpose of the Rules can be subverted when they are invoked by opposing parties as procedural weapons. The fact that a Rule is a just basis for a lawyer's self-assessment, or for sanctioning a lawyer under the administration of a disciplinary authority, does not imply that an antagonist in a collateral proceeding or transaction has standing to seek enforcement of the Rule. Accordingly, nothing in the Rules should be deemed to augment any substantive legal duty of lawyers or the extra-disciplinary consequences of violating such a duty.

Moreover, these Rules are not intended to govern or affect judicial application of either the attorney-client or work product privilege. Those privileges were developed to promote compliance with law and fairness in litigation. In reliance on the attorney-client privilege, clients are entitled to expect that communications within the scope of the privilege will be protected against compelled disclosure. The attorney-client privilege is that of the client and not of the lawyer. The fact that in exceptional situations the lawyer under the Rules has a limited discretion to disclose a client confidence does not vitiate the proposition that, as a general matter, the client has a reasonable expectation that information relating to the client will not be voluntarily disclosed and that disclosure of such information may be judicially compelled only in accordance with recognized exceptions to the attorney-client and work product privileges.

The lawyer's exercise of discretion not to disclose information under Rule 1.6 should not be subject to reexamination. Permitting such reexamination would be incompatible with the general policy of promoting compliance with law through assurances that communications will be protected against disclosure. . . .

Terminology

"Belief" or "believes" denotes that the person involved actually supposed the fact in question to be true. A person's belief may be inferred from circumstances.

"Consult" or "consultation" denotes communication of information reasonably sufficient to permit the client to appreciate the significance of the matter in question.

"Firm" or "law firm" denotes a lawyer or lawyers in a private firm, lawyers employed in the legal department of a corporation or other organization and lawyers employed in a legal services organization. . . .

"Fraud" or "fraudulent" denotes conduct having a purpose to deceive and not merely negligent misrepresentation or failure to apprise another of relevant information.

"Knowingly," "known" or "knows" denotes actual knowledge of the fact in question. A person's knowledge may be inferred from circumstances.

"Partner" denotes a member of a partnership and a shareholder in a law firm organized as a professional corporation.

"Reasonable" or "reasonably" when used in relation to conduct by a lawyer denotes the conduct of a reasonably prudent and competent lawyer.

"Reasonable belief" or "reasonably believes" when used in reference to a lawyer denotes that the lawyer believes the matter in question and that the circumstances are such that the belief is reasonable.

"Reasonably should know" when used in reference to a lawyer denotes that a lawyer of reasonable prudence and competence would ascertain the matter in question.

"Substantial" when used in reference to degree or extent denotes a material matter of clear and weighty importance.

CLIENT-LAWYER RELATIONSHIP

Rule 1.1 Competence

A lawyer shall provide competent representation to a client. Competent representation requires the legal knowledge, skill, thoroughness and preparation reasonably necessary for the representation.

Rule 1.2 Scope of Representation

(a) A lawyer shall abide by a client's decisions concerning the objectives of representation, subject to paragraphs (c), (d) and (e), and shall consult with the client as to the means by which they are to be pursued. A lawyer shall abide by a client's decision whether to accept an offer of settlement of a matter. In a criminal case, the lawyer shall abide by the client's decision, after consultation with the lawyer, as to a plea to be entered, whether to waive jury trial and whether the client will testify.

(b) A lawyer's representation of a client, including representation by appointment, does not constitute an endorsement of the client's political, economic, social or moral views or activities.

(c) A lawyer may limit the objectives of the representation if the client consents after consultation.

(d) A lawyer shall not counsel a client to engage, or assist a client, in conduct that the lawyer knows is criminal or fraudulent, but a lawyer may discuss the legal consequences of any proposed course of conduct with a client and may counsel or assist a client to make a good faith effort to determine the validity, scope, meaning or application of the law.

(e) When a lawyer knows that a client expects assistance not permitted by the Rules of Professional Conduct or other law, the lawyer shall consult with the client regarding the relevant limitations on the lawyer's conduct.

Rule 1.3 Diligence

A lawyer shall act with reasonable diligence and promptness in representing a client.

Rule 1.4 Communication

(a) A lawyer shall keep a client reasonably informed about the status of a matter and promptly comply with reasonable requests for information.

(b) A lawyer shall explain a matter to the extent reasonably necessary to permit the client to make informed decisions regarding the representation.

Rule 1.5 Fees

(a) A lawyer's fee shall be reasonable. The factors to be considered in determining the reasonableness of a fee include the following:

(1) the time and labor required, the novelty and difficulty of the questions involved, and the skill requisite to perform the legal service properly;

(2) the likelihood, if apparent to the client, that the acceptance of the particular employment will preclude other employment by the lawyer;

(3) the fee customarily charged in the locality for similar legal services;

(4) the amount involved and the results obtained;

(5) the time limitations imposed by the client or by the circumstances;

(6) the nature and length of the professional relationship with the client;

(7) the experience, reputation, and ability of the lawyer or lawyers performing the services; and

(8) whether the fee is fixed or contingent.

(b) When the lawyer has not regularly represented the client, the basis or rate of the fee shall be communicated to the client, preferably in writing, before or within a reasonable time after commencing the representation.

(c) A fee may be contingent on the outcome of the matter for which the service is rendered, except in a matter in which a contingent fee is prohibited by paragraph (d) or other law. A contingent fee agreement shall be in writing and shall state the method by which the fee is to be determined, including the percentage or percentages that shall accrue to the lawyer in the event of settlement, trial or appeal, litigation and other expenses to be deducted from the recovery, and whether such expenses are to be deducted before or after the contingent fee is calculated. Upon conclusion of a contingent fee matter, the lawyer shall provide the client with a written statement stating the outcome of the matter and, if there is a recovery, showing the remittance to the client and the method of its determination.

(d) A lawyer shall not enter into an arrangement for, charge, or collect:

(1) any fee in a domestic relations matter, the payment or amount of which is contingent upon the securing of a divorce or upon the amount of alimony or support, or property settlement in lieu thereof; or

(2) a contingent fee for representing a defendant in a criminal case.

(e) A division of a fee between lawyers who are not in the same firm may be made only if:

(1) the division is in proportion to the services performed by each lawyer or, by written agreement with the client, each lawyer assumes joint responsibility for the representation;

(2) the client is advised of and does not object to the participation of all the lawyers involved; and

(3) the total fee is reasonable.

Rule 1.6 *Confidentiality of Information*

(a) A lawyer shall not reveal information relating to representation of a client unless the client consents after consultation, except for disclosures that are impliedly authorized in order to carry out the representation, and except as stated in paragraph (b).

(b) A lawyer may reveal such information to the extent the lawyer reasonably believes necessary:

(1) to prevent the client from committing a criminal act that the lawyer believes is likely to result in imminent death or substantial bodily harm; or

(2) to establish a claim or defense on behalf of the lawyer in a controversy between the lawyer and the client, to establish a defense to a criminal change or civil claim against the lawyer based upon conduct in which the client was involved, or to respond to allegations in any proceeding concerning the lawyer's representation of the client.

Rule 1.7   *Conflict of Interest: General Rule*

(a) A lawyer shall not represent a client if the representation of that client will be directly adverse to another client, unless:

(1) the lawyer reasonably believes the representation will not adversely affect the relationship with the other client; and

(2) each client consents after consultation.

(b) A lawyer shall not represent a client if the representation of that client may be materially limited by the lawyer's responsibilities to another client or to a third person, or by the lawyer's own interests, unless:

(1) the lawyer reasonably believes the representation will not be adversely affected; and

(2) the client consents after consultation. When representation of multiple clients in a single matter is undertaken, the consultation shall include explanation of the implications of the common representation and the advantages and risks involved.

Rule 1.8   *Conflict of Interest: Prohibited Transactions*

(a) A lawyer shall not enter into a business transaction with a client or knowingly acquire an ownership, possessory, security or other pecuniary interest adverse to a client unless:

(1) the transaction and terms on which the lawyer acquires the interest are fair and reasonable to the client and are fully disclosed and transmitted in writing to the client in a manner which can be reasonably understood by the client;

(2) the client is given a reasonable opportunity to seek the advice of independent counsel in the transaction; and

(3) the client consents in writing thereto.

(b) A lawyer shall not use information relating to representation of a client to the disadvantage of the client unless the client consents after consultation, except as permitted or required by Rule 1.6 or Rule 3.3.

(c) A lawyer shall not prepare an instrument giving the lawyer or a person related to the lawyer as parent, child, sibling, or spouse any substantial gift from a client, including a testamentary gift, except where the client is related to the donee.

(d) Prior to the conclusion of representation of a client, a lawyer shall not make or negotiate an agreement giving the lawyer literary or media rights to a portrayal or account based in substantial part on information relating to the representation.

(e) A lawyer shall not provide financial assistance to a client in connection with pending or contemplated litigation, except that:

    (1) a lawyer may advance court costs and expenses of litigation, the repayment of which may be contingent on the outcome of the matter; and

    (2) a lawyer representing an indigent client may pay court costs and expenses of litigation on behalf of the client.

(f) A lawyer shall not accept compensation for representing a client from one other than the client unless:

    (1) the client consents after consultation;

    (2) there is no interference with the lawyer's independence of professional judgment or with the client-lawyer relationship; and

    (3) information relating to representation of a client is protected as required by Rule 1.6.

(g) A lawyer who represents two or more clients shall not participate in making an aggregate settlement of the claims of or against the clients, or in a criminal case an aggregated agreement as to guilty or *nolo contendere* pleas, unless each client consents after consultation, including disclosure of the existence and nature of all the claims or pleas involved and of the participation of each person in the settlement.

(h) A lawyer shall not make an agreement prospectively limiting the lawyer's liability to a client for malpractice unless permitted by law and the client is independently represented in making the agreement, or settle a claim for such liability with an unrepresented client or former client without first advising that person in writing that independent representation is appropriate in connection therewith.

(i) A lawyer related to another lawyer as parent, child, sibling or spouse shall not represent a client in a representation directly adverse to a person whom the lawyer knows is represented by the other lawyer except upon conset by the client after consultation regarding the relationship.

(j) A lawyer shall not acquire a proprietary interest in the cause of action or subject matter of litigation the lawyer is conducting for a client, except that the lawyer may:

    (1) acquire a lien granted by law to secure the lawyer's fee or expenses; and

    (2) contract with a client for a reasonable contingent fee in a civil case.

Rule 1.9   *Conflict of Interest: Former Client*

(a) A lawyer who has formerly represented a client in a matter shall not thereafter represent another person in the same or a substantially related matter in which that person's interests are materially adverse to the interests of the former client unless the former client consents after consultation.

(b) A lawyer shall not knowingly represent a person in the same or a substantially related matter in which a firm with which the lawyer formerly was associated had previously represented a client

(1) whose interests are materially adverse to that person; and

(2) about whom the lawyer had acquired information protected by Rules 1.6 and 1.9(c) that is material to the matter;
    unless the former client consents after consultation.

(c) A lawyer who has formerly represented a client in a matter or whose present or former firm has formerly represented a client in a matter shall not thereafter:

(1) use information relating to the representation to the disadvantage of the former client except as Rule 1.6 or Rule 3.3 would permit or require with respect to a client, or when the information has become generally known; or

(2) reveal information relating to the representation except as Rule 1.6 or Rule 3.3 would permit or require with respect to a client.

Rule 1.10   Imputed Disqualification: General Rule

(a) While lawyers are associated in a firm, none of them shall knowingly represent a client when any one of them practicing alone would be prohibited from doing so by Rules 1.7, 1.8(c), 1.9 or 2.2.

(b) When a lawyer has terminated an association with a firm, the firm is not prohibited from thereafter representing a person with interests materially adverse to those of a client represented by the formerly associated lawyer and not currently represented by the firm, unless:

(1) the matter is the same or substantially related to that in which the formerly associated lawyer represented the client; and

(2) any lawyer remaining in the firm has information protected by Rules 1.6 and 1.9(c) that is material to the matter.

(c) A disqualification prescribed by this rule may be waived by the affected client under the conditions stated in Rule 1.7.

Rule 1.11   Successive Government and Private Employment

(a) Except as law may otherwise expressly permit, a lawyer shall not represent a private client in connection with a matter in which the lawyer participated personally and substantially as a public officer or employee, unless the appropriate government agency consents after consultation. No lawyer in a firm with which that lawyer is associated may knowingly undertake or continue representation in such a matter unless:

(1) the disqualified lawyer is screened from any participation in the matter and is apportioned no part of the fee therefrom; and

(2) written notice is promptly given to the appropriate government agency to enable it to ascertain compliance with the provisions of this Rule.

(b) Except as law may otherwise expressly permit, a lawyer having information that the lawyer knows is confidential government information about a person acquired when the lawyer was a public officer or employee, may not represent a private client whose interests are adverse to that person in a matter in which the information could be used to the material disadvantage of that person. A firm with which that lawyer is associated may undertake or continue representation in the matter only if the disqualified lawyer is screened from any participation in the matter and is apportioned no part of the fee therefrom.

(c) Except as law may otherwise expressly permit, a lawyer serving as a public officer or employee shall not:

    (1) participate in a matter in which the lawyer participated personally and substantially while in private practice or nongovernmental employment, unless under applicable law no one is, or by lawful delegation may be, authorized to act in the lawyer's stead in the matter; or

    (2) negotiate for private employment with any person who is involved as a party or as attorney for a party in a matter in which the lawyer is participating personally and substantially, except that a lawyer serving as a law clerk to a judge, other adjudicative officer or arbitrator may negotiate for private employment as permitted by Rule 1.12(b) and subject to the conditions stated in Rule 1.12(b).

(d) As used in this Rule, the term "matter" includes:

    (1) any judicial or other proceeding, application, request for a ruling or other determination, contract, claim, controversy, investigation, charge, accusation, arrest or other particular matter involving a specific party or parties, and

    (2) any other matter covered by the conflict of interest rules of the appropriate government agency.

(e) As used in this Rule, the term "confidential government information" means information which has been obtained under governmental authority and which, at the time this Rule is applied, the government is prohibited by law from disclosing to the public or has a legal privilege not to disclose, and which is not otherwise available to the public.

Rule 1.12   *Former Judge or Arbitrator*

(a) Except as stated in paragraph (d), a lawyer shall not represent anyone in connection with a matter in which the lawyer participated personally and substantially as a judge or other adjudicative officer, arbitrator or law clerk to such a person, unless all parties to the proceeding consent after consultation.

(b) A lawyer shall not negotiate for employment with any person who is involved as a party or as attorney for a party in a matter in which the lawyer is participating personally and substantially as a judge or other adjudicative officer or arbitrator. A lawyer serving as a law clerk to a judge, other adjudicative officer or arbitrator may negotiate for employment with a party or attorney involved in a matter in which the clerk is participating personally and substantially, but only after the lawyer has notified the judge, other adjudicative officer or arbitrator.

(c) If a lawyer is disqualified by paragraph (a), no lawyer in a firm with which that lawyer is associated may knowingly undertake or continue representation in the matter unless:

 (1) the disqualified lawyer is screened from any participation in the matter and is apportioned no part of the fee therefrom; and

 (2) written notice is promptly given to the appropriate tribunal to enable it to ascertain compliance with the provisions of this Rule.

(d) An arbitrator selected as a partisan of a party in a multimember arbitration panel is not prohibited from subsequently representing that party.

Rule 1.13 Organization as Client

(a) A lawyer employed or retained by an organization represents the organization acting through its duly authorized constituents.

(b) If a lawyer for an organization knows that an officer, employee or other person associated with the organization is engaged in action, intends to act or refuses to act in a matter related to the representation that is a violation of a legal obligation to the organization, or a violation of law which reasonably might be imputed to the organization, and is likely to result in substantial injury to the organization, the lawyer shall proceed as is reasonably necessary in the best interest of the organization. In determining how to proceed, the lawyer shall give due consideration to the seriousness of the violation and its consequences, the scope and nature of the lawyer's representation, the responsibility in the organization and the apparent motivation of the person involved, the policies of the organization concerning such matters and any other relevant considerations. Any measures taken shall be designed to minimize disruption of the organization and the risk of revealing information relating to the representation to persons outside the organization. Such measures may include among others:

 (1) asking reconsideration of the matter;

 (2) advising that a separate legal opinion on the matter be sought for presentation to appropriate authority in the organization; and

 (3) referring the matter to higher authority in the organization, including, if warranted by the seriousness of the matter, referral to the highest authority that can act in behalf of the organization as determined by applicable law.

(c) If, despite the lawyer's efforts in accordance with paragraph (b), the highest authority that can act on behalf of the organization insists upon action, or a refusal to act, that is clearly a violation of law and is likely to result in substantial injury to the organization, the lawyer may resign in accordance with Rule 1.16.

(d) In dealing with an organization's directors, officers, employees, members, shareholders or other constituents, a lawyer shall explain the identity of the client when it is apparent that the organization's interests are adverse to those of the constituents with whom the lawyer is dealing.

(e) A lawyer representing an organization may also represent any of its directors, officers, employees, members, shareholders or other constituents, subject to the provisions of Rule 1.7. If the organization's consent to the dual representation is required by Rule 1.7, the consent shall be given by an appropriate official of the organization other than the individual who is to be represented, or by the shareholders.

Rule 1.14   Client under a Disability

(a) When a client's ability to make adequately considered decisions in connection with the representation is impaired, whether because of minority, mental disability or for some other reason, the lawyer shall, as far as reasonably possible, maintain a normal client-lawyer relationship with the client.

(b) A lawyer may seek the appointment of a guardian or take other protective action with respect to a client only when the lawyer reasonably believes that the client cannot adequately act in the client's own interest.

Rule 1.15   Safekeeping Property

(a) A lawyer shall hold property of clients or third persons that is in a lawyer's possession in connection with a representation separate from the lawyer's own property. Funds shall be kept in a separate account maintained in the state where the lawyer's office is situated, or elsewhere with the consent of the client or third person. Other property shall be identified as such and appropriately safeguarded. Complete records of such account funds and other property shall be kept by the lawyer and shall be preserved for a period of [five years] after termination of the representation.

(b) Upon receiving funds or other property in which a client or third person has an interest, a lawyer shall promptly notify the client or third person. Except as stated in this Rule or otherwise permitted by law or by agreement with the client, a lawyer shall promptly deliver to the client or third person any funds or other property that the client or third person is entitled to receive and, upon request by the client or third person, shall promptly render a full accounting regarding such property.

(c) When in the course of representation a lawyer is in possession of property in which both the lawyer and another person claim interests, the property shall be kept separate by the lawyer until there is an accounting and severance of their interests. If a dispute arises concerning their respective interests, the portion in dispute shall be kept separate by the lawyer until the dispute is resolved.

Rule 1.16   Declining or Terminating Representation

(a) Except as stated in paragraph (c), a lawyer shall not represent a client or, where representation has commenced, shall withdraw from the representation of a client if:

(1) the representation will result in violation of the Rules of Professional Conduct or other law;

    (2) the lawyer's physical or mental condition materially impairs the lawyer's ability to represent the client; or

    (3) the lawyer is discharged.

(b) except as stated in paragraph (c), a lawyer may withdraw from representing a client if withdrawal can be accomplished without material adverse effect on the interests of the client, or if:

    (1) the client persists in a course of action involving the lawyer's services that the lawyer reasonably believes is criminal or fraudulent;

    (2) the client has used the lawyer's services to perpetrate a crime or fraud;

    (3) a client insists upon pursuing an objective that the lawyer considers repugnant or imprudent;

    (4) the client fails substantially to fulfill an obligation to the lawyer regarding the lawyer's services and has been given reasonable warning that the lawyer will withdraw unless the obligation is fulfilled;

    (5) the representation will result in an unreasonable financial burden on the lawyer or has been rendered unreasonably difficult by the client; or

    (6) other good cause for withdrawal exists.

(c) When ordered to do so by a tribunal, a lawyer shall continue representation notwithstanding good cause for terminating the representation.

(d) Upon termination of representation, a lawyer shall take steps to the extent reasonably practicable to protect a client's interests, such as giving reasonable notice to the client, allowing time for employment of other counsel, surrendering papers and property to which the client is entitled and refunding any advance payment of fee that has not been earned. The lawyer may retain papers relating to the client to the extent permitted by other law.

Rule 1.17   Sale of Law Practice

A lawyer or a law firm may sell or purchase a law practice, including good will, if the following conditions are satisfied:

(a) The seller ceases to engage in the private practice of law [in the geographic area] [in the jurisdiction] (a jurisdiction may elect either version) in which the practice has been conducted;

(b) The practice is sold as an entirety to another lawyer or law firm;

(c) Actual written notice is given to each of the seller's clients regarding:

    (1) the proposed sale;

    (2) the terms of any proposed change in the fee arrangement authorized by paragraph (d);

    (3) the client's right to retain other counsel or to take possession of the file; and

    (4) the fact that the client's consent to the sale will be presumed if the client does not take any action or does not otherwise object within ninety (90) days of receipt of the notice.

If a client cannot be given notice, the representation of that client may be transferred to the purchaser only upon entry of an order so authorizing by a court having jurisdiction. The seller may disclose to the court *in camera* information relating to the representation only to the extent necessary to obtain an order authorizing the transfer of a file.

(d) The fees charged clients shall not be increased by reason of the sale. The purchaser may, however, refuse to undertake the representation unless the client consents to pay the purchaser fees at a rate not exceeding the fees charged by the purchaser for rendering substantially similar services prior to the initiation of the purchase negotiations.

Counselor

Rule 2.1   Advisor

In representing a client, a lawyer shall exercise independent professional judgment and render candid advice. In rendering advice, a lawyer may refer not only to law but to other considerations such as moral, economic, social and political factors, that may be relevant to the client's situation.

Rule 2.2   Intermediary

(a) A lawyer may act as intermediary between clients if:
   (1) the lawyer consults with each client concerning the implications of the common representation, including the advantages and risks involved, and the effect on the attorney-client privileges, and obtains each client's consent to the common representation;
   (2) the lawyer reasonably believes that the matter can be resolved on terms compatible with the clients' best interests, that each client will be able to make adequately informed decisions in the matter and that there is little risk of material prejudice to the interests of any of the clients if the contemplated resolution is unsuccessful; and
   (3) the lawyer reasonably believes that the common representation can be undertaken impartially and without improper effect on other responsibilities the lawyer has to any of the clients.
(b) While acting as intermediary, the lawyer shall consult with each client concerning the decisions to be made and the considerations relevant in making them, so that each client can make adequately informed decisions.
(c) A lawyer shall withdraw as intermediary if any of the clients so requests, or if any of the conditions stated in paragraph (a) is no longer satisfied. Upon withdrawal, the lawyer shall not continue to represent any of the clients in the matter that was the subject of the intermediation.

Rule 2.3   Evaluation for use by Third Persons

(a) A lawyer may undertake an evaluation of a matter affecting a client for the use of someone other than the client if:
   (1) the lawyer reasonably believes that making the evaluation is compatible with other aspects of the lawyer's relationship with the client; and
   (2) the client consents after consultation.

(b) Except as disclosure is required in connection with a report of an evaluation, information relating to the evaluation is otherwise protected by Rule 1.6.

ADVOCATE

Rule 3.1   Meritorious Claims and Contentions

A lawyer shall not bring or defend a proceeding, or assert or controvert an issue therein, unless there is a basis for doing so that is not frivolous, which includes a good faith argument for an extension, modification or reversal of existing law. A lawyer for the defendant in a criminal proceeding, or the respondent in a proceeding that could result in incarceration, may nevertheless so defend the proceeding as to require that every element of the case be established.

Rule 3.2   Expediting Litigation

A lawyer shall make reasonable efforts to expedite litigation consistent with the interests of the client.

Rule 3.3   Candor Toward the Tribunal

(a) A lawyer shall not knowingly:
   (1) make a false statement of material fact or law to a tribunal;
   (2) fail to disclose a material fact to a tribunal when disclosure is necessary to avoid assisting a criminal or fraudulent act by the client;
   (3) fail to disclose to the tribunal legal authority in the controlling jurisdiction known to the lawyer to be directly adverse to the position of the client and not disclosed by opposing counsel; or
   (4) offer evidence that the lawyer knows to be false. If a lawyer has offered material evidence and comes to know of its falsity, the lawyer shall take reasonable remedial measures.
(b) The duties stated in paragraph (a) continue to the conclusion of the proceeding, and apply even if compliance requires disclosure of information otherwise protected by Rule 1.6.
(c) A lawyer may refuse to offer evidence that the lawyer reasonably believes is false.
(d) In an *ex parte* proceeding, a lawyer shall inform the tribunal of all material facts known to the lawyer which will enable the tribunal to make an informed decision, whether or not the facts are adverse.

Rule 3.4   Fairness to Opposing Party and Counsel

A lawyer shall not:
(a) unlawfully obstruct another party's access to evidence or unlawfully alter, destroy or conceal a document or other material having potential evidentiary value. A lawyer shall not counsel or assist another person to do any such act;
(b) falsify evidence, counsel or assist a witness to testify falsely, or offer an inducement to a witness that is prohibited by law;

(c) knowingly disobey an obligation under the rules of a tribunal except for an open refusal based on an assertion that no valid obligation exists;

(d) in pretrial procedure, make a frivolous discovery request or fail to make reasonably diligent effort to comply with a legally proper discovery request by an opposing party;

(e) in trial, allude to any matter that the lawyer does not reasonably believe is relevant or that will not be supported by admissible evidence, assert personal knowledge of facts in issue except when testifying as a witness, or state a personal opinion as to the justness of a cause, the credibility of a witness, the culpability of a civil litigant or the guilt or innocence of an accused; or

(f) request a person other than a client to refrain from voluntarily giving relevant information to another party unless:

(1) the person is a relative or an employee or other agent of a client; and

(2) the lawyer reasonably believes that the person's interests will not be adversely affected by refraining from giving such information.

Rule 3.5   *Impartiality and Decorum of the Tribunal*

A lawyer shall not:

(a) seek to influence a judge, juror, prospective juror or other official by means prohibited by law;

(b) communicate *ex parte* with such a person except as permitted by law; or

(c) engage in conduct intended to disrupt a tribunal.

Rule 3.6   *Trial Publicity*

(a) A lawyer shall not make an extrajudicial statement that a reasonable person would expect to be disseminated by means of public communication if the lawyer knows or reasonably should know that it will have a substantial likelihood of materially prejudicing an adjudicative proceeding.

(b) A statement referred to in paragraph (a) ordinarily is likely to have such an effect when it refers to a civil matter triable to a jury, a criminal matter, or any other proceeding that could result in incarceration, and the statement relates to:

(1) the character, credibility, reputation or criminal record of a party, suspect in a criminal investigation or witness, or the identity of a witness, or the expected testimony of a party or witness;

(2) in a criminal case or proceeding that could result in incarceration, the possibility of a plea of guilty to the offense or the existence or contents of any confession, admission or statement given by a defendant or suspect or that person's refusal or failure to make a statement;

(3) the performance or results of any examination or test or the refusal or failure of a person to submit to an examination or test, or the identity or nature of physical evidence expected to be presented;

(4) any opinion as to the guilt or innocence of a defendant or suspect in a criminal case or proceeding that could result in incarceration;

(5) information the lawyer knows or reasonably should know is likely to be inadmissible as evidence in a trial and would if disclosed create a substantial risk of prejudicing an impartial trial; or

(6) the fact that a defendant has been charged with a crime, unless there is included therein a statement explaining that the charge is merely an accusation and that the defendant is presumed innocent until and unless proven guilty.

(c) Notwithstanding paragraphs (a) and (b)(1–5), a lawyer involved in the investigation or litigation of a matter may state without elaboration:

(1) the general nature of the claim or defense;

(2) the information contained in a public record;

(3) that an investigation of the matter is in progress, including the general scope of the investigation, the offense or claim or defense involved and, except when prohibited by law, the identity of the persons involved;

(4) the scheduling or result of any step in litigation;

(5) a request for assistance in obtaining evidence and information necessary thereto;

(6) a warning of danger concerning the behavior of a person involved, when there is reason to believe that there exists the likelihood of substantial harm to an individual or to the public interest; and

(7) in a criminal case:

(i) the identity, residence, occupation and family status of the accused;

(ii) if the accused has not been apprehended, information necessary to aid in apprehension of that person;

(iii) the fact, time and place of arrest; and

(iv) the identity of investigating and arresting officers or agencies and the length of the investigation.

Rule 3.7 *Lawyer as Witness*

(a) A lawyer shall not act as advocate at a trial in which the lawyer is likely to be a necessary witness except where:

(1) the testimony relates to an uncontested issue;

(2) the testimony relates to the nature and value of legal services rendered in the case; or

(3) disqualification of the lawyer would work substantial hardship on the client.

(b) A lawyer may act as advocate in a trial in which another lawyer in the lawyer's firm is likely to be called as a witness unless precluded from doing so by Rule 1.7 or Rule 1.9.

Rule 3.8 *Special Responsibilities of a Prosecutor*

The prosecutor in a criminal case shall:

(a) refrain from prosecuting a charge that the prosecutor knows is not supported by probable cause;

(b) make reasonable efforts to assure that the accused has been advised of the right to, and the procedure for obtaining, counsel and has been given reasonable opportunity to obtain counsel;

(c) not seek to obtain from an unrepresented accused a waiver of important pre-trial right, such as the right to a preliminary hearing;

(d) make timely disclosure to the defense of all evidence or information known to the prosecutor that tends to negate the guilt of the accused or mitigates the offense, and, in connection with sentencing, disclose to the defense and to the tribunal all unprivileged mitigating information known to the prosecutor, except when the prosecutor is relieved of this responsibility by a protective order of the tribunal; and

(e) exercise reasonable care to prevent investigators, law enforcement personnel, employees or other persons assisting or associated with the prosecutor in a criminal case from making an extrajudicial statement that the prosecutor would be prohibited from making under Rule 3.6.

(f) not subpoena a lawyer in a grand jury or other criminal proceeding to present evidence about a past or present client unless:

   (1) the prosecutor reasonably believes:

      (i) the information sought is not protected from disclosure by any applicable privilege;

      (ii) the evidence sought is essential to the successful completion of an ongoing investigation or prosecution;

      (iii) there is no other feasible alternative to obtain the information; and

   (2) the prosecutor obtains prior judicial approval after an opportunity for an adversarial proceeding.

Rule 3.9   Advocate in Nonadjudicative Proceedings

A lawyer representing a client before a legislative or administrative tribunal in a nonadjudicative proceeding shall disclose that the appearance is in a representative capacity and shall conform to the provisions of Rules 3.3(a) through (c), 3.4(a) through (c), and 3.5.

TRANSACTIONS WITH PERSONS OTHER THAN CLIENTS

Rule 4.1   Truthfulness in Statements to Others

In the course of representing a client a lawyer shall not knowingly:

(a) make a false statement of material fact or law to a third person; or

(b) fail to disclose a material fact to a third person when disclosure is necessary to avoid assisting a criminal or fraudulent act by a client, unless disclosure is prohibited by Rule 1.6.

Rule 4.2   Communication with Person Represented by Counsel

In representing a client, a lawyer shall not communicate about the subject of the representation with a party the lawyer knows to be represented by another lawyer in the matter, unless the lawyer has the consent of the other lawyer or is authorized by law to do so.

Rule 4.3   *Dealing with Unrepresented Person*

In dealing on behalf of a client with a person who is not represented by counsel, a lawyer shall not state or imply that the lawyer is disinterested. When the lawyer knows or reasonably should know that the unrepresented person misunderstands the lawyer's role in the matter, the lawyer shall make reasonable efforts to correct the misunderstanding.

Rule 4.4   *Respect for Rights of Third Persons*

In representing a client, a lawyer shall not use means that have no substantial purpose other than to embarrass, delay or burden a third person, or use methods of obtaining evidence that violate the legal rights of such a person.

LAW FIRMS AND ASSOCIATIONS

Rule 5.1   *Responsibilities of a Partner or Supervisory Lawyer*

(a) A partner in a law firm shall make reasonable efforts to ensure that the firm has in effect measures giving reasonable assurance that all lawyers in the firm conform to the Rules of Professional Conduct.

(b) A lawyer having direct supervisory authority over another lawyer shall make reasonable efforts to ensure that the other lawyer conforms to the Rules of Professional Conduct.

(c) A lawyer shall be responsible for another lawyer's violation of the Rules of Professional Conduct if:

(1) the lawyer orders or, with knowledge of the specific conduct, ratifies the conduct involved; or

(2) the lawyer is a partner in the law firm in which the other lawyer practices, or has direct supervisory authority over the other lawyer, and knows of the conduct at a time when its consequences can be avoided or mitigated but fails to take reasonable remedial action.

Rule 5.2   *Responsibilities of a Subordinate Lawyer*

(a) A lawyer is bound by the Rules of Professional Conduct notwithstanding that the lawyer acted at the direction of another person.

(b) A subordinate lawyer does not violate the Rules of Professional Conduct if that lawyer acts in accordance with a supervisory lawyer's reasonable resolution of an arguable question of professional duty.

Rule 5.3   *Responsibilities Regarding Nonlawyer Assistants*

With respect to a nonlawyer employed or retained by or associated with a lawyer:

(a) a partner in a law firm shall make reasonable efforts to ensure that the firm has in effect measures giving reasonable assurance that the person's conduct is compatible with the professional obligations of the lawyer;

(b) a lawyer having direct supervisory authority over the nonlawyer shall make reasonable efforts to ensure that the person's conduct is compatible with the professional obligations of the lawyer; and

(c) a lawyer shall be responsible for conduct of such a person that would be a violation of the Rules of Professional Conduct if engaged in by a lawyer if:

   (1) the lawyer orders or, with the knowledge of the specific conduct, ratifies the conduct involved; or

   (2) the lawyer is a partner in the law firm in which the person is employed, or has direct supervisory authority over the person, and knows of the conduct at a time when its consequences can be avoided or mitigated but fails to take reasonable remedial action.

Rule 5.4   Professional Independence of a Lawyer

(a) A lawyer or law firm shall not share legal fees with a nonlawyer, except that:

   (1) an agreement by a lawyer with the lawyer's firm, partner or associate may provide for the payment of money, over a reasonable period of time after the lawyer's death, to the lawyer's estate or to one or more specified persons;

   (2) a lawyer who purchases the practice of a deceased, disabled or disappeared lawyer may, pursuant to the provisions of Rule 1.17, pay to the estate or other representative of that lawyer the agreed-upon purchase price; and

   (3) a lawyer or law firm may include nonlawyer employees in a compensation or retirement plan, even though the plan is based in whole or in part on a profit-sharing arrangement.

(b) A lawyer shall not form a partnership with a nonlawyer if any of the activities of the partnership consist of the practice of law.

(c) A lawyer shall not permit a person who recommends, employs or pays the lawyer to render legal services for another to direct or regulate the lawyer's professional judgment in rendering such legal services.

(d) A lawyer shall not practice with or in the form of a professional corporation or association authorized to practice law for a profit, if:

   (1) a nonlawyer owns any interest therein, except that a fiduciary representative of the estate of a lawyer may hold the stock or interest of the lawyer for a reasonable time during administration;

   (2) a nonlawyer is a corporate director or officer thereof; or

   (3) a nonlawyer has the right to direct or control the professional judgment of a lawyer.

Rule 5.5   Unauthorized Practice of Law

A lawyer shall not:

(a) practice law in a jurisdiction where doing so violates the regulation of the legal profession in that jurisdiction; or

(b) assist a person who is not a member of the bar in the performance of activity that constitutes the unauthorized practice of law.

Rule 5.6   *Restrictions on Right to Practice*

A lawyer shall not participate in offering or making:
(a) a partnership or employment agreement that restricts the right of a lawyer to practice after termination of the relationship, except an agreement concerning benefits upon retirement; or
(b) an agreement in which a restriction on the lawyer's right to practice is part of the settlement of a controversy between private parties.

PUBLIC SERVICE

Rule 6.1   Pro Bono Publico *Service*

A lawyer should render public interest legal service. A lawyer may discharge this responsibility by providing professional services at no fee or a reduced fee to persons of limited means or to public service or charitable groups or organizations, by service in activities for improving the law, the legal system or the legal profession, and by financial support for organizations that provide legal services to persons of limited means.

Rule 6.2   *Accepting Appointments*

A lawyer shall not seek to avoid appointment by a tribunal to represent a person except for good cause, such as:
(a) representing the client is likely to result in violation of the Rules of Professional Conduct or other law;
(b) representing the client is likely to result in an unreasonable financial burden on the lawyer; or
(c) the client or the cause is so repugnant to the lawyer as to be likely to impair the client-lawyer relationship or the lawyer's ability to represent the client.

Rule 6.3   *Membership in Legal Services Organization*

A lawyer may serve as a director, officer or member of a legal services organization, apart from the law firm in which the lawyer practices, notwithstanding that the organization serves persons having interests adverse to a client of the lawyer. The lawyer shall not knowingly participate in a decision or action of the organization:
(a) if participating in the decision or action would be incompatible with the lawyer's obligations to a client under Rule 1.7; or
(b) where the decision or action could have a material adverse effect on the representation of a client of the organization whose interests are adverse to a client of the lawyer.

Rule 6.4   Law Reform Activities Affecting Client Interests

A lawyer may serve as a director, officer or member of an organization involved in reform of the law or its administration notwithstanding that the reform may affect the interests of a client of the lawyer. When the lawyer knows that the interests of a client may be materially benefitted by a decision in which the lawyer participates, the lawyer shall disclose that fact but need not identify the client.

INFORMATION ABOUT LEGAL SERVICES

Rule 7.1   Communications Concerning a Lawyer's Services

A lawyer shall not make a false or misleading communication about the lawyer or the lawyer's services. A communication is false or misleading if it:
   (a) contains a material misrepresentation of fact or law, or omits a fact necessary to make the statement considered as a whole not materially misleading;
   (b) is likely to create an unjustified expectation about results the lawyer can achieve, or states or implies that the lawyer can achieve results by means that violate the Rules of Professional Conduct or other law; or
   (c) compares the lawyer's services with other lawyers' services, unless the comparison can be factually substantiated.

Rule 7.2   Advertising

   (a) Subject to the requirements of Rules 7.1 and 7.3, a lawyer may advertise services through public media, such as a telephone directory, legal directory, newspaper or other periodical, outdoor advertising, radio or television, or through written or recorded communication.
   (b) A copy or recording of an advertisement or communication shall be kept for two years after its last dissemination along with a record of when and where it was used.
   (c) A lawyer shall not give anything of value to a person for recommending the lawyer's services except that a lawyer may
      (1) pay the reasonable costs of advertisements or communications permitted by this Rule;
      (2) pay the usual charges of a not-for-profit lawyer referral service or legal service organization; and
      (3) pay for a law practice in accordance with Rule 1.17.
   (d) Any communication made pursuant to this Rule shall include the name of at least one lawyer responsible for its content.

Rule 7.3   Direct Contact with Prospective Clients

   (a) A lawyer shall not by in-person or live telephone contact solicit professional employment from a prospective client with whom the lawyer has no family or prior professional relationship when a significant motive for the lawyer's doing so is the lawyer's pecuniary gain.

(b) A lawyer shall not solicit professional employment from a prospective client by written or recorded communication or by in-person or telephone contact even when not otherwise prohibited by paragraph (a), if:
   (1) the prospective client has made known to the lawyer a desire not to be solicited by the lawyer; or
   (2) the solicitation involves coercion, duress or harassment.

(c) Every written or recorded communication from a lawyer soliciting professional employment from a prospective client known to be in need of legal services in a particular matter, and with whom the lawyer has no family or prior professional relationship, shall include the words "Advertising Material" on the outside envelope and at the beginning and ending of any recorded communication.

(d) Notwithstanding the prohibitions in paragraph (a), a lawyer may participate with a prepaid or group legal service plan operated by an organization not owned or directed by the lawyer which uses in-person or telephone contact to solicit memberships or subscriptions for the plan from persons who are not known to need legal services in a particular matter covered by the plan.

Rule 7.4   Communication of Fields of Practice and Certification

A lawyer may communicate the fact that the lawyer does or does not practice in particular fields of law. A lawyer shall not state or imply that the lawyer has been recognized or certified as a specialist in a particular field of law except as follows:

(a) a lawyer admitted to engage in patent practice before the United States Patent and Trademark Office may use the designation "Patent Attorney" or a substantially similar designation;

(b) a lawyer engaged in Admiralty practice may use the designation "Admiralty," "Proctor in Admiralty" or a substantially similar designation; and

(c) [for jurisdictions where there is a regulatory authority granting certification or approving organizations that grant certification] a lawyer may communicate the fact that the lawyer has been certified as a specialist in a field of law by a named organization or authority but only if:
   (1) such certification is granted by the appropriate regulatory authority or by an organization which has been approved by the appropriate regulatory authority to grant such certification; or
   (2) such certification is granted by an organization that has not yet been approved by, or has been denied the approval available from, the appropriate regulatory authority, and the absence or denial of approval is clearly stated in the communication, and in any advertising subject to Rule 7.2, such statement appears in the same sentence that communicates the certification.

(d) [for jurisdictions where there is no procedure either for certification of specialities or for approval of organizations granting certification] a lawyer may communicate the fact that the lawyer has been certified as a specialist in a field of law by a named organization, provided that the communication clearly states that there is no procedure in this jurisdiction for approving certifying organizations.

Rule 7.5 *Firm Names and Letterheads*

(a) A lawyer shall not use a firm name, letterhead or other professional designation that violates Rule 7.1. A trade name may be used by a lawyer in private practice if it does not imply a connection with a government agency or with a public or charitable legal services organization and is not otherwise in violation of Rule 7.1

(b) A law firm with offices in more than one jurisdictionmay use the same name in each jurisdiction, but identification of the lawyers in an office of the firm shall indicate the jurisdictional limitations on those not licensed to practice in the jurisdiction where the office is located.

(c) The name of a lawyer holding a public office shall not be used in the name of a law firm, or in communications on its behalf, during any substantial period in which the lawyer is not actively and regularly practicing with the firm.

(d) Lawyers may state or imply that they practice in a partnership or other organization only when that is the fact.

MAINTAINING THE INTEGRITY OF THE PROFESSION

Rule 8.1 *Bar Admission and Disciplinary Matters*

An applicant for admission to the bar, or a lawyer in connection with a bar admission application or in connection with a disciplinary matter, shall not:

(a) knowingly make a false statement of material fact; or

(b) fail to disclose a fact necessary to correct a misapprehension known by the person to have arisen in the matter, or knowingly fail to respond to a lawful demand for information from an admissions or disciplinary authority, except that this rule does not require disclosure of information otherwise protected by Rule 1.6.

Rule 8.2 *Judicial and Legal Officials*

(a) A lawyer shall not make a statement that the lawyer knows to be false or with reckless disregard as to its truth or falsity concerning the qualifications or integrity of a judge, adjudicatory officer or public legal officer, or of a candidate for election or appointment to judicial or legal office.

(b) A lawyer who is a candidate for judicial office shall comply with the applicable provisions of the Code of Judicial Conduct.

Rule 8.3 *Reporting Professional Misconduct*

(a) A lawyer having knowledge that another lawyer has committed a violation of the Rules of Professional Conduct that raises a substantial question as to that lawyer's honesty, trustworthiness or fitness as a lawyer in other respects shall inform the appropriate professional authority.

(b) A lawyer having knowledge that a judge has committed a violation of applicable rules of judicial conduct that raises a substantial question as to the judge's fitness for office shall inform the appropriate authority.

(c) This rule does not require disclosure of information otherwise protected by Rule 1.6 or information gained by a lawyer or judge while serving as a member of an approved lawyers assistance program to the extent that such information would be confidential if it were communicated subject to the attorney-client privilege.

Rule 8.4 *Misconduct*

It is professional misconduct for a lawyer to:

(a) violate or attempt to violate the Rules of Professional Conduct, knowingly assist or induce another to do so or do so through the acts of another;

(b) commit a criminal act that reflects adversely on the lawyer's honesty, trustworthiness or fitness as a lawyer in other respects;

(c) engage in conduct involving dishonesty, fraud, deceit or misrepresentation;

(d) engage in conduct that is prejudicial to the administration of justice;

(e) state or imply an ability to influence improperly a government agency or official; or

(f) knowingly assist a judge or judicial officer in conduct that is a violation of applicable rules of judicial conduct or other law.

Rule 8.5 *Jurisdiction*

A lawyer admitted to practice in this jurisdiction is subject to the disciplinary authority of this jurisdiction although engaged in practice elsewhere.

Problems Related to Ethical Issues

Problem One

Barbara Trentalange, Esq., receives a telephone call from Alice Walker, a social worker in a local hospital, advising her that Paul Gerritt, who underwent surgery that day for appendicitis, is now unconscious and on a respirator. Trentalange is unfamiliar with Mr. Gerritt and has never represented him. Walker called Trentalange because the two are social friends and she is aware of Trentalange's reputation as an outstanding personal injury attorney. Walker tells Trentalange that Gerritt is separated from his wife and living with his mother. The patient's mother, Molly, is now in the hospital waiting room and appears overwhelmed. Walker has advised Molly to call Trentalange but doesn't think she will do so: Molly told Walker that she would probably call Leo Bailey, a criminal law attorney who represented her son five years ago when he was charged with a minor criminal offense.

What, if anything, may Trentalange do to get the case? What action may she take directly? What action may she take through Walker or some other third party not employed by her?

Consider Rules 7.3, 7.4, and 8.4 (a). Are any other Rules applicable?

PROBLEM TWO

Molly has called Leo Bailey and asked him to represent her son and her. Bailey has never handled a medical malpractice case, but has a lot of criminal law trial experience. May he accept the case without obtaining the help of another attorney? If he obtains the help of another attorney, what are their relative responsibilities? If he refers the case to another attorney, may he accept a referral fee and, if so, how much? See Rules 1.1, 1.5 (e), 5.1, and 5.2.

PROBLEM THREE

The next week, Esther, Gerritt's estranged wife, calls Bailey and says she wants him to represent her in connection with any rights she may have to recover in a potential medical malpractice case. She states that she and the patient had been intimately involved again over the past three months and planned to resume living together in the near future. She also states that she is pregnant with Gerritt's child.

May Bailey represent Esther and/or her child? See Rule 1.7.

PROBLEM FOUR

Assume that Bailey has referred Esther to Trentalange for representation. May Bailey accept a referral fee? See Rule 1.5 (e).

PROBLEM FIVE

Bailey represents Gerritt and his mother. Trentalange represents Esther. Gerritt dies after remaining in a coma for three weeks. Esther rejects an autopsy because she says Gerritt instructed her that he would not want an autopsy done on him; he wanted to be cremated as quickly as possible. Both attorneys believe that an autopsy would be helpful in proving the medical malpractice case. The mother has authorized Bailey to get an autopsy done at once. What should Bailey do? What should Trentalange do? What should the hospital's counsel advise his client to do? Do the *Model Rules of Professional Conduct* provide any guidance?

PROBLEM SIX

Nancy Price, a nurse, has called Bailey and advised him that she saw Anthony Smith, an anesthesiologist, making additions to Gerritt's medical record after it had been completed and transferred to the hospital's risk manager. May Bailey interview Price without advising counsel for the hospital in advance? See Rules 4.2 and 4.3.

PROBLEM SEVEN

Dan Patton represents the hospital, Dr. Anthony South, and Sam McManus, a surgeon. Dr. McManus advises Patton that he has become so depressed by Gerritt's death that he is consuming large amounts of alcohol. He further states that he believes Dr. South did not properly intubate Gerritt and that South's negligence was the cause of Gerritt's brain damage. What *may* Patton do? What *must* he do? See Rules 1.4 and 1.7.

PROBLEM EIGHT

Patton advises Dr. South that he should retain his own counsel because Patton has a potential conflict of interest. South interrupts: "Nancy Price told you that I altered Gerritt's medical record, didn't she?" What should Patton do? See Rule 3.3.

PROBLEM NINE

Carl Wilder is vice president and general counsel to MIC, the medical insurance company that issued the professional liability insurance covering Dr. South and Dr. McManus. The company's vice president for risk management comes to Wilder expressing outrage because he has just learned that E. D. Warrington, who carries professional liability insurance with MIC, is serving as an expert witness for the plaintiffs in their medical malpractice action. He wants to write Warrington a letter threatening to cancel his policy if he continues to serve as an expert for the plaintiffs. What should Wilder's advice be? Is there an applicable rule of professional conduct? Cf. *L'Orange v. The Medical Protective Company*, 394 F.2d 57 (6th Cir. 1968); *McDonnell v. Commission on Medical Discipline*, 301 Md. 426, 483 A.2d 76 (1984).

PROBLEM TEN

MIC has authorized defense counsel Patton to settle the Gerritts' claim against Dr. McManus for $50,000. McManus adamantly objects to settling because he says he did nothing wrong. The insurance policy does not expressly require his consent to settle a claim. Is Patton facing any ethical dilemmas? May Patton settle without violating any rules of professional conduct? See Rules 1.2, 1.4, and 1.16.

Notes

Chapter 1

1. For a discussion of the medical profession from a social perspective, see Paul Starr, *The Social Transformation of American Medicine* (1982). For a discussion of surgeons from an anthropological perspective, see Joan Cassell, *Expected Miracles: Surgeons at Work* (1991).

2. 66 Cal. 2d 399, 58 Cal. Rptr. 125, 426 P.2d 525 (1967).

3. 394 F.2d 57 (6th Cir. Ohio 1968).

4. 394 F.2d at 62.

5. 301 Md. 426, 483 A.2d 76 (1984).

6. 392 A.2d 1129 (1978).

7. 392 A.2d at 1134.

8. For thoughtful discussions of the fundamental ethical dilemma of a zealous advocate in an adversarial system, see generally "Teaching Legal Ethics: A Symposium," 41 *Journal of Legal Education* 1 (1991). For a comprehensive discussion of medical records and some legal and ethical issues that arise out of completing, maintaining, and producing medical records, see Chapter 9.

Chapter 2

1. See generally Paul Weiler, *Medical Malpractice on Trial* (1991).

2. 313 N.C. 338, 329 S.E.2d 355 (1985).

3. See Chapter 3 for a discussion of causation standards.

4. Id. 329 S.E.2d at 365.

5. Id. 329 S.E.2d at 367.

6. See Chapter 3.

7. See Annotation, "Legal Malpractice in Handling or Defending Medical Malpractice Claims," 78 *American Law Reports* 4th 725 (1990).

8. 535 So. 2d 308 (Fla. App. 1988).

9. For an excellent overview of peer-review issues, see Comment, "Medical Peer

Review Protection in the Health Care Industry," 52 *Temple Law Quarterly* 552 (1979).

10. Morrow, "Doctors Helping Doctors," *The Hastings Center Report* 32 (Dec. 1984), citing in note 1 Stephen C. Scheiber, "Emotional Problems of Physicians: Nature and Extent of Problems," in *The Impaired Physician* (Stephen C. Scheiber and Brian B. Doyle, eds., 1983).

11. See generally Comment, "The Impaired Physician: An Old Problem Creates the Need for New Legislation," 26 *St. Louis University Law Journal* 727 (1982); McAuliffe et al., "Psychoactive Drug Use among Practicing Physicians and Medical Students," 315 *New England Journal of Medicine* 895 (Sept. 25, 1986).

12. See American Bar Association, *Model Rules of Professional Conduct*, particularly Rule 1.14 (client under a disability), and Rule 1.6 (confidentiality of information). For cases addressing an attorney's potential liability to third persons see Annotation, "Attorney's Liability, to One Other Than His Immediate Client, For Consequences of Negligence in carrying out Legal Duties," 45 *American Law Reports* 3d 1181 (1972).

13. See Comment, "The Chemically Dependent Physician: Liability for Colleagues and Hospitals in California," 21 *San Diego Law Review* 431 (1984). See also the discussion of the corporate liability of a hospital in Chapter 3.

14. 30 Ill. Dec. 320, 392 N.E.2d 1365 (1979), *aff'd*, 81 Ill. 2d 201, 407 N.E.2d 47 (1980).

15. 735 S.W.2d 729 (Mo. App. 1987).

Chapter 3

1. 281 Md. 269, 378 A.2d 1121 (1977).

2. *Roach v. Hockey*, 53 Or. App. 710, 634 P.2d 249 (1981).

3. See e.g. *Naccarato v. Grob*, 384 Mich. 248, 180 N.W.2d 788 (1970) (pediatrician judged by a national standard).

4. See *Fiske v. Soland*, 8 Ariz. App. 585, 448 P.2d 429 (Ariz. App. 1968); *Shoumatoff v. Wiltbank*, 226 N.Y.S.2d 576 (N.Y. Supp. 1962).

5. See *Zills v. Brown*, 382 So. 2d 528 (Ala. 1980); *Schliesman v. Fisher*, 158 Cal. Rptr. 527 (Cal. App. 1979); *Bly v. Rhoads*, 216 Va. 645, 222 S.E.2d 783 (Va. 1976), *Superseded by Statute as Stated in Henning v. Thomas*, 235 Va. 181, 366 S.E.2d 109 (Va. 1988).

6. See e.g. *Brune v. Belinkoff*, 354 Mass. 102, 235 N.E.2d 793 (1968).

7. See e.g. *Incollingo v. Ewing*, 444 Pa. 263, 444 Pa. 299, 282 A.2d 206 (Pa. 1971).

8. See e.g. *Glicklich et al. v. Spievak*, 16 Mass. App. 488, 452 N.E.2d 287 (Mass. App. 1983); *Dornon v. Johnston*, 421 Pa. 58, 218 A.2d 808 (Pa. 1966).

9. *Schuler v. Berger*, 275 C. Supp. 120 (E.D. Pa. 1967), *aff'd* 395 F.2d 212 (3rd Cir. Pa. 1968) (pathologist competent to testify as to standard of care of obstetrician-gynecologist); *Hamil v. Bashline*, 224 Pa. Super. 407, 307 A.2d 57 (Pa. Super. 1973) (pathologist could testify regarding standard applicable to treatment of cardiac patient), *overruled by Hamil v. Bashline*, 243 Pa. Super. 227, 364 A.2d 1366 (1976).

10. 444 Pa. 263, 444 Pa. 299, 282 A.2d 206 (Pa. 1971).

11. 444 Pa. at 276–277, 282 A.2d at 214.

12. 444 Pa. at 275, 282 A.2d at 213.

13. 444 Pa. at 282, 282 A.2d at 217.

14. 444 Pa. at 283, 282 A.2d at 218.

15. 464 F.2d, 772/150 U.S. App. D.C. 263 (D.C. Cir. 1972).

16. For an analysis of *Canterbury* and its influence on the law, see Katz, "Informed Consent—A Fairy Tale? Law's Vision," 39 *University of Pittsburgh Law Review* 137 (1977).

17. 464 F.2d at 779–783.

18. 464 F.2d at 787.

19. 464 F.2d at 791.

20. 464 F.2d at 792.

21. *Nathanson v. Kline*, 186 Kan. 393, 350 P.2d 1093, *reh'g denied*, 187 Kan. 186, 354 P.2d 670 (Kan. 1960), is the leading case adopting the professional custom for defining the standard of disclosure. *Scott v. Bradford*, 606 P.2d 554 (Okla. 1979), held that a physician must disclose all the information that the particular patient would regard as material. For an overview of specific jurisdictional approaches, see Meisel and Kabnik, "Informed Consent to Medical Treatment: An Analysis of Recent Legislation," 41 *University of Pittsburgh Law Review* 407 (1980) (finding the professional standard of disclosure to be adopted by the majority of jurisdictions).

22. For an insightful exploration of the informed consent issue, see Jay Katz, *The Silent World of Doctor and Patient* (1984).

23. See Davis, "*Canterbury v. Spence* et al.—And Informed Consent, Revisited, Three Years Later," 11 *Forum* 708 (1975–76); Laskey, "*Canterbury v. Spence*— Informed Consent Revisited," 11 *Forum* 713 (1975–76).

24. See Katz, supra note 22.

25. For an insightful assessment of surgeons from an anthropoligical perspective, see Joan Cassell, *Expected Miracles: Surgeons at Work* (1991).

26. Restatement (2d), Torts 328.

27. See e.g. *Brown v. Keaveny*, 326 F.2d 660 (D.C. Cir. 1963), 117 U.S. App. D.C. 117 (broken jaw produced during removal of diseased and impacted teeth insufficient to warrant application of res ipsa loquitur doctrine).

28. See e.g. *Burke v. Washington Hospital Center*, 475 F.2d 364 (D.C. Cir. 1973), 154 U.S. App. D.C. 293 (res ipsa applied to case against surgeon who left surgical sponge in abdominal cavity); cf. *Smith v. Yohe*, 412 Pa. 94, 194 A.2d 167 (Pa. 1963) (lack of care may be so obvious that it is within range of common knowledge of laypersons, e.g., the failure to x-ray elderly patient complaining of hip pain after a fall).

29. 25 Cal. 2d 486, 154 P.2d 687 (1944).

30. 25 Cal. 2d at 494, 154 P.2d at 691.

31. *Ybarra v. Spangard*, 93 Cal. App. 2d 43, 208 P.2d 445 (Cal. App. 2 Dist. 1949).

32. Compare the following jurisdictions:

Ala.: *Powell v. Mullins*, 479 So. 2d 1119 (Ala. 1985)

Ariz.: *Carranza v. Tuscon Medical Center*, 135 Ariz. 490, 662 P.2d 455 (Ariz. App. 1983);
    Faris v. Doctor Hospital, Inc., 18 Ariz. App. 264, 501 P.2d 440 (Ariz. App. 1972)

Cal.: *Sheffield v. Eli Lilly Co.*, 144 Cal. App. 3d 583, 192 Cal. Rptr. 870 (Cal. App. 1

Dist. 1983); *Hale v. Venuto*, 137 Cal. App. 3d 910, 187 Cal. Rptr. 357 (1982); *Tri-bitte v. French Hospital*, 128 Cal. App. 3d 332, 180 Cal. Rptr. 152 (1982); *Sanchez v. Bay General Hospital*, 116 Cal. App. 3d 776, 172 Cal. Rptr. 342 (1981)

Conn.: *Cristini v. Griffin Hospital*, 134 Conn. 282, 57 A.2d 262 (Conn. 1948).

Fla.: *Marrero v. Goldsmith*, 486 So. 2d 530, (Fla. 1986); *West Coast Hospital Assoc. v. Webb*, 52 So. 2d 803 (Fla. 1951)

Haw.: *Kopa v. U.S.*, 236 F. Supp. 189 (D.C. Hawaii 1964)

Ill.: *Loizzo v. St. Francis Hospital*, 121 Ill. App. 3d 172, 76 Ill. Dec. 677, 459 N.E.2d 314 (1984); *Kolakowski v. Voris*, 83 Ill. 2d 388, 47 Ill. Dec. 392, 415 N.E.2d 397 (Ill. 1980); *Ybarra v. Cross*, 22 Ill. App. 3d 638, 317 N.E.2d 621 (Ill. App. 1974)

Iowa: *Frost v. Des Moines Still College of Osteopathy and Surgery*, 248 Iowa 294, 79 N.W.2d 306 (Iowa 1956)

Kan.: *Tatro v. Lucken*, 212 Kan. 606, 512 P.2d 529 (Kan. 1973); *Voss v. Bridwell*, 188 Kan. 643, 364 P.2d 955 (Kan. 1961)

Ky.: *Somerset v. Hart*, 549 S.W.2d 814 (Ky. 1977)

La.: *Andrepont v. Ochsner*, 84 So. 2d 63 (La. App. 1955)

Mich.: *Wilson v. Stilwell*, 411 Mich. 587, 309 N.W.2d 898 (1981)

N.J.: *Anderson v. Somberg*, 67 N.J. 291, 338 A.2d 1 (1975), *cert. denied*, 423 U.S. 929, 96 S. Ct. 279, 46 L. Ed. 2d 258 (1975)

Nev.: *Las Vegas Hospital Assoc. v. Gattney*, 64 Nev. 225, 180 P.2d 594 (Nev. 1947)

N.C.: *Schaffner v. Cumberland County Hospital System, Inc.*, 77 N.C. App. 689, 336 S.E.2d 116 (1985), *review denied*, 316 N.C. 195, 341 S.E.2d 578 (1986)

Okla.: *St. Johns Hospital & School of Nursing, Inc. v. Chapman*, 434 P.2d 160 (Okla. 1967), *superseded by statute as stated in Sisson By and Through Allen v. Elkins*, 801 P.2d 722 (Okla. 1990)

Or.: *Barrett v. Emanuel Hospital*, 64 Or. App. 635, 669 P.2d 835 (1983), review denied, 296 Or. 237, 675 P.2d 491 (1983)

Pa.: *Jones v. Harrisburg Polyclinic Hospital*, 269 Pa. Super. 373, 410 A.2d 303 (1979), *order reversed*, by 496 Pa. 465, 437 A.2d 1134 (1981)

Utah: *Talbot v. Dr. W. H. Groves Latter Day Saints Hospital, Inc.*, 21 Utah 2d 73, 440 P.2d 872 (Utah 1968)

Va.: *Danville Community Hospital v. Thompson*, 186 Va. 746, 43 S.E.2d 882 (Va. 1947)

Wis.: *Hoven v. Kelble*, 79 Wis. 2d 444, 256 N.W.2d 379 (Wis. 1977); *Beaudin v. Water-town Memorial Hospital*, 32 Wis.2d 132, 145 N.W. 166 (1966)

   33. 83 Wash. 2d 514, 519 P.2d 981 (1974), *superseded by statute as stated in Gates v. Jensen*, 20 Wash. App. 81, 579 P.2d 374 (1978).

   34. 444 Pa. 263, 282 A.2d 206 (1971).

   35. Following the decision in *Helling*, the Washington State legislature mandated that in actions for "professional" negligence the plaintiff must prove "that the defendant failed to exercise that degree of skill, care and learning possessed by other persons in the same profession and that as a proximate result of such failure, the plaintiff suffered damages." Wash. Rev. Code Ann. Sec. 4.24.290. Citing this statute, the court of appeals in *Gates v. Jensen*, 20 Wash. App. 81, 579 P.2d 374 (1978) found that the legislature's intent was to avoid decisions such as *Helling*. The Washington Supreme Court,

however, construed the statute's language differently and subsequently reversed the lower court's decision. *Gates v. Jensen*, 92 Wash. 2d 246, 595 P.2d 919 (1979). As a result, the basic principle adopted in *Helling* remains intact.

36. *Texas & Pacific Railway Co. v. Behymer*, 189 U.S. 468, 23 S. Ct. 622, 47 L. Ed. 905 (1903).

37. *Sullivan v. O'Connor*, 363 Mass. 579, 296 N.E.2d 183 (1973); *Guilmet v. Campbell*, 385 Mich. 57, 188 N.W.2d 601 (Mich. 1971), *superseded by statute as stated in Bucalo v. Board of Regents of University of Michigan*, 432 Mich. 859, 434 N.W.2d 413 (Mich. 1989); *Powers v. People's Community Hospital Authority*, 437 Mich. 910, 465 N.W.2d 566 (Mich. 1991).

38. *Dorney v. Harris*, 482 F. Supp. 323 (D. Colo. 1980); *Rogala v. Silva*, 16 Ill. App. 3d 63, 305 N.E.2d 571 (Ill. App. 1 Dist. 1973).

39. Ind. Code Ann. 16-9.5-1-4 (Burns 1975); Mich. Comp. Laws Ann. 566–132(g) (West 1975).

40. *Doerr v. Villate*, 74 Ill App. 2d 332, 220 N.E.2d 767 (1966).

41. *Robins v. Finestone*, 308 N.Y. 543, 127 N.E.2d 330 (N.Y. 1955).

42. *Taylor v. Baptist Medical Center Inc.*, 400 So. 2d 369 (Ala. 1981).

43. *Pearl v. Lesnick*, 20 A.D.2d 761, 247 N.Y.S.2d 561 (N.Y.A.D. 1964).

44. *Stephens v. Spiwak*, 61 Mich. 647, 233 N.W.2d 124 (1975).

45. *McKinney v. Nash*, 120 Cal. App. 3d 428, 174 Cal. Rptr. 642 (Cal. App. 3 Dist. 1981).

46. *Verra v. Koluksuz*, 74 A.D.2d 932, 426 N.Y.S.2d 151 (N.Y.A.D. 1980).

47. See *Zepeda v. Zepeda*, 41 Ill. App. 2d 240, 190 N.W.2d 849 (Ill. App. 1963) (coining phrase *wrongful birth* in suit brought by child against father for illegitimate birth), *cert. denied*, 379 U.S. 945, 85 S. Ct. 444, 13L. Ed. 2d 545 (1964).

48. See *Curlender v. Bio Science Labs*, 106 Cal. App. 3d 811, 165 Cal. Rptr. 477 (Cal. App. 2 Dist. 1980).

49. See e.g. *Gleitman v. Cosgrove*, 49 N.J. 22, 227 A.2d 689 (1967) (rejecting wrongful birth and wrongful life claims).

50. See *Turpin v. Sortini*, 31 Cal. 3d 220, 182 Cal. Rptr. 337, 643 P.2d 954 (Cal. 1982).

51. See e.g. *Becker v. Schwartz*, 46 N.Y.2d 401, 413 N.Y.S.2d 895, 386 N.E.2d 807 (N.Y. 1979); *Jacobs v. Theimer*, 519 S.W.2d 846 (Tex. 1975).

52. Cf. *Sorkin v. Lee*, 78 A.D. 2d 180, 434 N.Y.S.2d 300 (N.Y.A.D. 1980) (denying recovery); *Troppi v. Scarf*, 31 Mich. App. 240, 187 N.W.2d 511 (Mich. App. 1971) (permitting recovery).

53. Cf. *Jones v. Malinowski*, 299 Md. 257, 473 A.2d 429 (1984); *University of Arizona Health Services Center v. Superior Court*, 136 Ariz. 579, 667 P.2d 1294 (Ariz. 1982) (allowing recovery for cost of raising healthy child offset by intangible benefits derived from having a child); and *Cockrum v. Buumgartner*, 95 Ill. 2d 193, 69 Ill. Dec. 168, 447 N.E.2d 385 (Ill. 1983) (denying recovery for birth of healthy child); *Procanik v. Cillo*, 97 N.J. 339, 478 A.2d 755 (N.J. 1984), and *Harbeson v. Parke-Davis, Inc.*, 98 Wash. 2d 260, 656 P.2d 483 (1983) (allowing recovery for profoundly ill child where physician failed to disclose risk or conduct diagnostic tests).

54. See e.g. *Bing v. Thunig*, 2 N.Y.2d 656, 163 N.Y. S.2d 3, 143 N.E.2d 3 (N.Y. 1957) (ending the charitable immunity for hospitals, adopted more than forty years earlier in *Schloendorff v. Society of New York Hospital*, 211 N.Y. 125, 105 N.E. 92 (N.Y. 1914), *Superseded by statute as stated in Retkway v. Orentreich*, 584 N.Y.S.2d 710 (N.Y. Sup. 1992)

55. Southwick, "The Hospital as an Institution—Expanding Responsibilities Change Its Relationship with the Staff Physician," 9 *California Western Law Review* 429 (1973).

56. For a detailed hospital organization chart, see Perdue, "Direct Corporate Liability of Hospital: A Modern Day Concept of Liability for Injury Occurring in the Modern Day Hospital," 24 *South Texas Law Journal* 773, Appendix (1983).

57. *Bader v. United Orthodox Synagogue*, 148 Conn. 449, 453, 172 A.2d 192, 194 (Conn. 1961).

58. Holbrook and Dunn, "Medical Malpractice Litigation: The Discover-ability and Use of Hospitals' Quality Assurance Committee Records," 16 *Washburn Law Journal* 54, 57 (1976).

59. Thirteen years after the JCAH's inception, 85 percent of hospital beds in the United States were accredited. Id. at 58.

60. 33 Ill. 2d 326, 211 N.E.2d 253 (Ill. 1965), *Cert. Denied by Charleston Community v. Darling*, 383 U.S. 946, 86 S. Ct. 1204, 16 L.Ed. 2d 209 (1966).

61. 33 Ill. 2d at 333, 211 N.E.2d at 258.

62. Id.

63. 33 Ill. 2d at 332, 211 N.E.2d at 257.

64. See Perdue, supra note 55, at 809, 810.

65. Southwick, "The Hospital's New Responsibility," 17 *Cleveland Marshall Law Review* 146, 152 (1968).

66. The following jurisdictions have specifically adopted the doctrine of corporate negligence.

Ariz.: *Tucson Medical Center, Inc. v. Misevch*, 113 Ariz. 34, 545 P.2d 958 (Ariz. 1976); *Fridena v. Evan*, 127 Ariz. 516, 622 P.2d 463 (Ariz. 1980); *Purcell v. Zimbelman*, 18 Ariz. App. 75, 500 P.2d 335 (1972)

Ill.: *Darling v. Charleston Community Memorial Hospital*, 33 Ill. 2d 326, 211 N.E.2d 253 (Ill. 1965), *cert. denied*, 383 U.S. 946, 86 S. Ct. 1204, 16 L.Ed. 2d 209 (1966)

La.: *Sibley v. Board of Supervisors Louisiana State University*, 462 So. 2d 149, 53 U.S.L.W. 2384 (La. 1985)

N.Y.: *Felice v. St. Agnes Hospital*, 65 App. Div. 2d 388, 411 N.Y.S.2d 901 (N.Y.A.D. 1978)

N.C.: *Bost v. Riley*, 44 N.C. App. 638, 262 S.E.2d 391 (N.C. App. 1980), *cert. denied*, 300 N.C. 194, 269 S.E.2d 621 (N.C. 1980)

Wash.: *Pedroza v. Bryant*, 101 Wash. 2d 226, 677 P.2d 166 (Wash. 1984)

67. The six areas of direct corporate liability were compiled in Perdue, supra note 56, at 789.

68. 104 Cal. App. 3d 219, 163 Cal. Rptr. 513 (Cal. App. 1 Dist. 1980), *Opin. vacated by* 33 Cal. 3d 674, 190 Cal. Rptr. 371, 660 P.2d 829 (1983).

69. 510 S.W.2d 94 (Tex. Civ. App. 1974).

70. 255 Pa. Super. 381, 387 A.2d 480 (1978).

71. 99 Wis. 2d 708, 301 N.W.2d 156 (Wis. 1980).

72. See also *Purcell v. Zimbelman*, 18 Ariz. App. 75, 500 P.2d 335 (1972) (negligent supervision); *Hull v. North Valley Hospital*, 159 Mont. 375, 498 P.2d 136 (Mont. 1972) (need for actual and constructive knowledge of physician's lack of skill or incompetency); *Corleto v. Shore Memorial Hospital*, 138 N.J. Super. 302, 350 A.2d 534 (1975); and *Elam v. College Park Hospital*, 132 Cal. App. 3d 332, 183 Cal. Rptr. 156 (1982) (hospital's failure to ensure competence of medical staff through careful selection and review creates an unreasonable risk of harm to patients). Cf. *Harnish v. Children's Hospital Medical Center*, 387 Mass. 152, 439 N.E.2d 240 (1982) (no liability where offer of proof did not show that hospital had power to control surgeon's professional conduct).

73. 18 Ariz. App. 75, 500 P.2d 335 (1972).

74. 44 N.C. App. 638, 262 S.E.2d 391 (N.C. App. 1980).

75. 160 W. Va. 703, 236 S.E.2d 213 (W. Va. 1977).

76. 368 N.E.2d 264 (Ind. App. 1977).

77. 134 Ariz. 390, 656 P.2d 1251 (1982).

78. 435 N.E.2d 305 (Ind. 1982).

79. 590 S.W.2d 574 (Tex. Civ. App. 1979).

80. 233 Pa. Super. 136, 336 A.2d 351 (Pa. Super. 1975).

81. 60 A.D.2d. 647, 400 N.Y.S.2d 552 (N.Y.A.D. 1977).

82. 72 Wash. 2d 73, 431 P.2d 973 (Wash. 1967).

83. 535 F. Supp. 1261 (E.D. Pa. 1982).

84. 271 N.W.2d 8 (S.D. 1978), *overruled by Shamburger v. Behrens*, 380 N.W.2d 659 (S.D. 1986).

85. N.J. Stat. Ann. 2A:53A-8 ($25,000 limitation on recovery against a hospital).

86. See Me. Rev. Stat. Ann. 158; Md. Code Ann. H.G. 19-354.

87. See *Hospital Authority of City of Manetta v. Misfeldt*, 99 Ga. App. 702, 109 S.E.2d 816 (Ga. App. 1959).

88. *Harnish v. Children's Hospital Medical Center*, 387 Mass. 152, 439 N.E.2d 240 (Mass. 1982); *Grubb v. Albert Einstein Medical Center*, 255 Pa. Super. 381, 387 A.2d 480 (Pa. Super, 1978).

89. *McConnell v. Williams*, 361 Pa. 355, 65 A.2d 243 (Pa. 1949); *Regula v. Bettigole*, 12 Mass. App. 939, 425 N.E.2d 768 (Mass. App Ct. 1981). The following cases discuss the concept of vicarious liability.

Colo.: *Young By and Through Young v. Carpenter*, 694 P.2d 861 (Colo. App. 1984), *appeal after remand*, 757 P.2d 148 (Colo. App. 1988), *judg. rev'd*, 773 P.2d 561 (Colo. 1989)

Del.: *Durney v. St. Francis Hospital*, 7 Terry 350, 46 Del. 350, 83 A.2d 753 (Del. Super. 1951)

Fla.: *Reed v. Good Samaritan Hospital Association, Inc.*, 453 So. 2d 229 (Fla. App. Dist. 4, 1984); *Irving v. Doctors Hospital of Lake Worth, Inc.*, 415 So. 2d 55 (Fla. App. Dist. 4, 1982), *review denied*, 422 So.2d 842 (Fla. 1982); *Cedars of Lebanon Hospital Corporation v. Silva*, 476 So.2d 696, 10 Fla. L. Week, 2102, (Fla. App. 3d 1985)

Ill.: *Johnson v. St. Bernard Hospital*, 79 Ill. App. 3d 709, 35 Ill. Dec. 364, 399 N.E.2d 198 (Ill. App. Dist. 1, 1979)

Ky.: *Paintsville Hospital Co. v. Rose*, No. 84-SC-14-DG, slip op. (Sup. Ct. of Ky.) (1985)

La.: *Sibley v. Board of Supervisors of Louisiana State University*, 477 So. 2d 1094 (La. 1985)

La.: *Wells v. Woman's Hospital Foundation*, 286 So. 2d 439 (La. App. 1 Cir 1973), *cert. denied*, 288 So. 2d 646 (La. 1974)

Me.: *Hamor v. Maine Coast Memorial Hospital*, 483 A.2d 718 (Me. 1984)

Md.: *Mehlman v. Powell*, 281 Md. 269, 378 A.2d 1121 (Md. 1977)

Miss.: *Hardy v. Brantley*, 471 So. 2d 358 (Miss. 1985)

N.M.: *Armijo v. Albuquerque Anesthesia Services Ltd.*, 101 N.M. 129, 679 P.2d 271 (N.M. App. 1984); *Dessauer v. Memorial General Hospital*, 96 N.M. 92, 628 P.2d 337 (N.M. App. 1981)

N.Y.: *Hill v. St. Clare's Hospital*, 67 N.Y. 2d72, 499 N.Y.S.2d 904, 490 N.E. 2d 823 (1986); *Kladek v. St. Vincent's Hospital & Medical Center of New York*, 128 Misc. 2d 985, 491 N.Y.S.2d 948 (N.Y. Sup. 1985); *Bleiler v. Bodnar*, 65 N.Y.2d 65, 489 N.Y.S.2d 885, 479 N.E.2d 230 (N.Y. 1985)

N.D.: *Benedict v. St. Luke's Hospitals*, 365 N.W.2d 499 (N.D. 1985)

Ohio: *Baird v. Sickler*, 69 Ohio St. 2d 652, 433 N.E.2d 593, 23 O.O.3d 532 (Ohio 1982)

Okla.: *Weldon By and Through Weldon v. Seminole Municipal Hospital*, 709 P.2d 1058 (Okla. 1985)

Or.: *Allen v. Kaiser Foundation Hospital, Inc.*, 76 Or. App. 5, 707 P.2d 1289 (Or. App. 1985); *Themins v. Emanuel Lutheran Charity Board*, 54 Or. App. 901, 637 P.2d 155 (Or. App. 1981), *petition denied*, 292 Or. 568, 644 P.2d 1129 (Or. 1982)

Tenn.: *Edmonds v. Chamberlain Memorial Hospital*, 629 S.W.2d 28 (Tenn. App. 1981)

Tex.: *Gladewater Municipal Hosp. v. Daniel*, 694 S.W.2d 619 (Tex. App. 6 Dist. 1985)

Wash.: *Adamski v. Tacoma General Hospital*, 20 Wash. App. 98, 579 P.2d 970 (Wash. App. 1978).

90. See e.g. *Capan v. Divine Providence Hospital*, 287 Pa. Super. 364, 430 A.2d 647 (Pa. Super. 1980).

91. For examples of fact patterns that have prompted courts to embrace the ostensible agency concept, see *Seneris v. Haas*, 45 Cal. 2d 811, 291 P.2d 915 (Cal. 1955); *Mehlman v. Powell*, 281 Md. 269, 378 A.2d 1121 (Md. 1977); *Grewe v. Mt. Clemens Hospital*, 404 Mich. 240, 273 N.W.2d 429 (Mich. 1978); *Howard v. Park*, 37 Mich. App. 496, 195 N.W.2d 39 (Mich. App. 1972); *Mduba v. Benedictine Hospital*, 52 A.D. 2d 450, 384 N.Y.S.2d 527 (N.Y.A. 1, 1976); *Lundberg v. Bay View Hospital*, 175 Ohio St. 133, 191 N.E.2d 821 (1963); *Adamski v. Tacoma General Hospital*, 20 Wash. App. 98, 579 P.2d 970 (1978). See also *Darling v. Charleston Community Memorial Hospital*, 33 Ill. 2d 326, 211 N.E.2d 253 (1965).

92. For examples of the approach used in the majority of jurisdictions, see *Kuhn v. Banker*, 133 Ohio St. 304, 13 N.E.2d 242 (1938); *Lenger v. Physician's General Hospital, Inc.*, 455 S.W.2d 703 (Tex. 1970).

93. 481 Pa. 256, 392 A.2d 1280 (Pa. 1978).

94. 481 Pa. at 263, 392 A.2d at 1283.

95. See Restatement (2d), Torts 323(a).

96. *Hamil v. Bashline*, 481 Pa. at 269, 392 A.2d at 1286.

97. 481 Pa. at 272, 392 A.2d at 1288.

98. 481 Pa. at 271–274, 392 A.2d at 1286–1289.

99. *Thompson v. Sun City Community Hospital*, 141 Ariz. 597, 688 P.2d 605 (1984); *Robertson v. Counselman*, 235 Kan. 1006, 686 P.2d 149 (Kan. 1984); *Thomas v. Corso*, 265 Md. 84, 288 A.2d 379 (Md. 1972); *Clark v. Ross*, 328 S.E.2d 91 (S.C. App. 1985); *Sherer v. James*, 286 S.C.304, 334 S.E.2d 283 (S.C. App. 1985); *Kallenberg v. Beth Israel Hospital*, 45 A.D.2d 177, 357 N.Y.S.2d 508 (N.Y.A.D. 1974).

100. *McBride v. United States*, 462 F.2d 72 (9th Cir. 1972); *Hiser v. Randolph*, 126 Ariz. 608, 617 P.2d 774 (Ariz. App. 1 1980); *Gooding v. University Hospital Building, Inc.*, 445 So. 2d 1015 (Fla. 1984); *Cooper v. Sisters of Charity of Cinn., Inc.*, 27 Ohio St. 2d 242, 272 N.E.2d 97, 56 O.O. 2d 146 (Ohio 1971).

101. *O'Brien v. Stover*, 443 F.2d 1013 (8th Cir. Iowa, 1971); *Jeanes v. Milner*, 428 F.2d 598 (8th Cir. Ark. 1970); *James v. United States*, 483 F. Supp. 581 (N.D. Cal. 1980); *Mays v. United States*, 608 F. Supp. 1476 (D. Colo. 1985); *Aasheim v. Humberger*, 215 Mont. 127, 695 P.2d 824 (Mont. 1985); *Herskovits v. Group Health Coop.*, 99 Wash. 2d 609, 664 P.2d 474 (1983).

102. *Aasheim v. Humberger*, 215 Mont. 127, 695 P.2d 824 (Mont. 1985).

103. *Mays v. United States*, 608 F. Supp. 1476 (D. Colo. 1985). One court has even gone to the extreme of allowing recovery for the loss of chance despite the plaintiff's inability to establish a statistically measurable chance of survival. The court, in effect, reasoned that since negligence occurred, harm must have occurred regardless of the fact that the harm was so small it was immeasurable. See *James v. United States*, 483 F. Supp. 581 (N.D. Cal. 1980).

Chapter 4

1. See e.g. *McPhee v. Reicherl*, 461 F.2d 947 (3d Cir. Pa. 1972) (holding ophthalmologist to standard of specialist).

2. *Larson v. Yelle*, 310 Minn. 521, 246 N.W.2d 841 (Minn. 1976).

3. See the discussion of the Flexner Report in Rosemary Stevens, *American Medicine and the Public Interest* (1971) 68–73.

4. Robert H. Fletcher, Suzanne W. Fletcher, and Edward H. Wagner, *Clinical Epidemiology: The Essentials* (1982).

5. Id. at 1.

6. Id. at 2–3.

7. 367 Pa. Super. 600, 533 A.2d 436 (1987).

8. 553 A.2d at 439.

9. 553 A.2d at 440–445.

10. Id.

11. Id.

12. 1990 WL 98335 (D. Kan. 87-2536-V 1990).

13. Id. at 3.

14. 363 N.W.2d 318 (Minn. App. 1985).

15. 363 N.W.2d at 322.

16. Id.

17. 363 N.W.2d at 323.
18. Stevens, supra note 3.
19. Id. at 138–139, 212–217, 285–289, 426–427.
20. Id. at 285–289.
21. Id. at 85–94.
22. Id. at 92–94.
23. Id. at 78, 79.
24. Id. at 79.
25. Id. at 80–85.
26. Id. at 92.
27. Id. at 92–97.
28. Id. at 94–97.
29. Id.
30. Id. at 113.
31. Id. at 240.
32. Id. at 238–241.
33. Id. at 286.
34. See *Annual Report and Reference Handbook*, published by the American Board of Medical Specialties.
35. Id. For a current discussion of the specialties and the implications for graduate education, see Martini, "Graduate Medical Education in the Changing Environment of Medicine," 268 JAMA 1097 (Sept. 2, 1992).
36. See the report of Dr. Carlos Martini in *JAMA*, supra note 35.
37. Burton J. Bledstein, *The Culture of Professionalism* (1976).
38. Joan Cassell, *Expected Miracles: Surgeons at Work* (1991).
39. Id. at 3.
40. Id. at 32.
41. Id. at 39.
42. Id. at 153.
43. Id. at 72.
44. Id. at 78–79.

Chapter 5

1. 5 U.S.C.A. 891 et seq. (1989).
2. 333 Cal. App. 660, 663–664, 271 Cal. Rptr. 876 (Cal. App. 1990).
3. 83 Wash. 2d 514, 519 P.2d 981 (Wash. 1974), *Superseded by statute as stated in Gates v. Jensen*, 20 Wash. App. 81, 579 P.2d 374 (Wash. App. 1978).
4. Paul J. Feldstein, *Health Care Economics*, at 3 (3d ed. 1988).
5. Id.
6. Id. at 135.
7. Id. at 314.
8. Id.

9. 333 Cal. App. 660, 271 Cal. Rptr. 876, (Cal. App. 1990).

10. 333 Cal. App. 660, 667, 271 Cal. Rptr. 876, 882 (1990).

11. 192 Cal. App. 3d 1630, 239 Cal. Rptr. 810 (1986).

12. 579 A.2d 177 (D.C. App. 1990).

13. Feldstein, supra note 4, at 328.

14. 110 R.I. 606, 295 A.2d 676 (R.I. 1972).

15. 83 Wash. 2d 514, 519 P.2d 981 (1974).

Chapter 6

1. For a comprehensive review of the reform battle, see Abrams, "Medical Malpractice: An Overview of Legislative Reform and Judicial Response," 2 *BioLaw* S:9–30 (Aug. 1986). For more recent accounts of legislation see Thomas, "The Medical Malpractice 'Crisis': A Critical Examination of a Public Debate," 65 *Temple Law Review* 459 (1992); Ludlam, "The Real World of Malpractice Tort Reform," 23 *Journal of Health and Hospital Law* 321 (1990); Bovbjerg, "Legislation on Medical Malpractice: Further Developments and a Preliminary Report Card," 22 *University of California at Davis Law Review* 499 (1989).

2. For critical discussions of approaches to financing health care and resolving medical malpractice claims, see *Rationing America's Medical Care: The Oregon Plan and Beyond* (Martin A. Strosberg, Joshua M. Wiener, Robert Baker, with I. Alan Fein, eds., 1992); Frances H. Miller, "Medical Malpractice Litigation: Do the British Have a Better Remedy?" 11 *American Journal of Law & Medicine* 434 (1986); Karin E. Grauers, "Medical Malpractice in Sweden," *Trial* (May 1985) at 52–55.

3. See Paul C. Weiler, *Medical Malpractice on Trial* at 11–14 (1991).

4. Weiler, supra note 3 at 13.

5. Taragin, Willett, Wilczek, Trout, and Carson, "The Influence of Standard of Care and Severity of Injury on the Resolution of Medical Malpractice Claims," 117 *Annals of American Medicine* 780–784 (Nov. 1, 1992).

6. See generally Weiler, supra note 3; Epstein, "Market and Regulatory Approaches to Medical Malpractice: The Virginia Obstetrical No-Fault Statute," 74 *Virginia Law Review* 1451 (1968).

7. Danzon, "The Frequency and Severity of Medical Malpractice Claims, 27 *Journal of Law and Economics* 115 (Apr. 1984).

8. Munch, "Causes of the Medical Malpractice Insurance Crisis (1978)," 1977 Report of the ABA Commission on Medical Professional Liability, 10–12 (1977). See also Danzon, supra note 7, at 1–2; John Guinther, *The Malpractitioners* (1978), at 152–158.

9. Learner, "Restrictive Medical Malpractice Compensation Schemes: A Constitutional Quid Pro Quo Analysis to Safeguard Individual Liberties," 18 *Harvard Journal on Legislation* 143, at 145 (1981).

10. Guinther, supra note 8, at 257–276; Learner, supra note 9, at 145.

11. Learner, supra note 9, at 145; Danzon, supra note 7, at 4–7.

12. Guinther, supra note 8, at 277; Learner, supra note 9, at 145.

13. Blodgett, "Malpractice Crisis, Doctors' Premiums Jump," 71 *American Bar Association Journal* 18 (June 1985); Blodgett, "MD's Get Well," 71 *American Bar Association Journal* 25 (Aug. 1985).

14. Karzon, "Medical Malpractice Statutes: A Retrospective Analysis," 2 *Annual Survey of American Law* 693, 693–695 (1984).

15. See generally Abrams, supra note 1.

16. See generally id.

17. Id. at 695.

18. For a detailed description of how joint underwriting associations are structured and funded, see Health Policy Center, Georgetown University, *A Legislator's Guide to Medical Malpractice Issues*, and see statutes in Hawaii, Idaho, and Minnesota.

19. Hawaii Rev. Stat. Sec. 435C (1989)
Idaho Code Sec. 41-4101-4105 (1990), *repealed*
Minnesota Stat. Sec. 62I.02-.16 (1993)

20. Missouri Ann. Stat. Sec. 383.150-.195 (1991)

21. Indiana Code Sec. 16-9.5-4-1 (1991)
Louisiana Rev. Stat. Ann. Sec. 40-1299.44 (1993)
Puerto Rico Laws Ann. Sec. 4105 (1989)
South Carolina Code Ann. Sec. 38-59-20 (1992)
Wisconsin Stat. Ann. Sec. 655.27 (1992)

22. Hawaii Rev. Stat. Sec. 671-31 (1982), *repealed*
Illinois Rev. Stat. Sec. 1065.300-315 (1989), *repealed*
Indiana Code Sec. 16-9.5-4-1 (1991)
Kentucky Rev. Stat. Sec. 304-40-330 (1984), *repealed*

23. Florida Stat. Ann. Sec. 627.351 (1992)
Indiana Code Sec. 16-9.5-8-3 (1991)
Kansas Stat. Ann. Sec. 65-4921 (1992)

24. U.S. Const., amend. XIV, sec. 1.

25. Id.

26. Smith, "Battling a Receding Tort Frontier: Constitutional Attack on Medical Malpractice Laws," 30 *Oklahoma Law Review* 195, 202 (1985).

27. Gerald Gunther, *Cases and Materials on Constitutional Law* (10th ed. 1980), at 671.

28. *McLaughlin v. Florida*, 379 U.S. 633 (1948).

29. *Oyama v. California*, 332 U.S. 633, 68 S. Ct. 269, 92 L. Ed. 249 (1948).

30. *Bernal v. Fainter*, 467 U.S. 216, 104 S. Ct. 2313, 81 L. Ed. 2d 175 (1984).

31. Gunther, supra note 27, at 670. See also *Minnesota State Board for Community Colleges v. Knight*, 104 S. Ct. 1058 (1984).

32. Laurence Tribe, *American Constitutional Law*, 1439–1450 (2d ed. 1988).

33. Id.

34. Id.

35. *Craig v. Boren*, 429 U.S. 190, 97 S. Ct. 451, 50 L. Ed. 2d 397, *review denied*, 429 U.S. 1124, 97 S. Ct. 1161 (1977).

36. Id.

37. *Plyer v. Doe,* 457 U.S. 202, 102 S. Ct. 2382, 72 L. Ed. 2d 786, *review denied,* 458 U.S. 1131, 1035 S. Ct. 14 (1982).

38. *Trimble v. Garder,* 430 U.S. 762 (1977).

39. Tribe, supra note 32, at 1558–1618.

40. See Witherspoon, "Constitutionality of the Texas Statute Limiting Liability for Medical Malpractice," 10 *Texas Tech Law Review* 419, at 462 (1979). The following cases have treated the right to recover damages for bodily injury as a fundamental right: *Kenyon v. Hammer,* 142 Ariz. 69, 688 P.2d 961 (Ariz. 1984); *White v. State,* 203 Mont. 363, 661 P.2d 1272 (Mont. 1983), *overruled by Meech v. Hillhaven West, Inc.,* 238 Mont. 21, 776 P.2d 488 (1989).

41. *White v. State,* 203 Mont. 363, 661 P.2d 1272 (Mont. 1983) [overruled?].

42. Nevertheless, the Montana legislature subsequently restored the limitation on governmental liability. See *Simmons v. Montana,* 206 Mont. 264, 670 P.2d 1372 (Mont. 1983).

43. See generally Martin Redish, "Legislative Response to the Medical Malpractice Insurance Crisis," 55 *Texas Law Review* 759, 770 (1977).

44. 120 N.H. 925, 424 A.2d 825 (1980).

45. Id. at 932 (citation omitted).

46. *Jones v. State Board of Medicine,* 97 Idaho 859, 555 P.2d 399, 411 (1976), *cert. denied,* 431 U.S. 914, 975 S. Ct. 2173; *Arneson v. Olson,* 270 N.W.2d 125 (N.D. 1978); and *Johnson v. Saint Vincent Hospital, Inc.,* 272 Ind. 374, 404 N.E.2d 585 (1980).

47. See e.g. *Gay v. Rabon,* 280 Ark. 5, 652 S.W.2d 836 (1983); *American Bank and Trust Co. v. Community Hospital of Los Gatos, Inc.,* 36 Cal. 3d 359, 683 P.2d 670, 204 Cal. Rptr. 671 (1984); *Otero v. Zouhatr,* 23 N.M. St. B. Bul. 67 (N.M. Ct. App. 1984); *Perna v. Pirozzi,* 12 N.J. 446, 457 A.2d 431 (1983).

48. *Boucher v. Sayeed,* 459 A.2d 87 (R.I. 1983).

49. 459 A.2d at 93.

50. U.S. Const., amend. V, amend. XIV.

51. See e.g. *Roe v. Wade,* 410 U.S. 113, 93 S. Ct. 705, 35 L. Ed. 2d 147 (1973); *United States v. Carolene Products Co.,* 304 U.S. 144, 152 n. 4, 58 S. Ct. 778, 82 L. Ed. 1234 (1938).

52. *Mattos v. Thompson,* 491 Pa. 385, 421 A.2d 190 (1980) (holding entire act unconstitutional because of extreme delay of panel in processing claims).

53. Id.

54. *Wright v. Du Page Hospital Ass'n,* 63 Ill. 2d 313, 347 N.E.2d 736 (1976).

55. *Bernier v. Burris,* 113 Ill. 2d 585, 497 N.E.2d 763 (1986).

56. See e.g. *Woods v. Holy Cross Hospital,* 591 F.2d 1164 (5th Cir. 1979); *Williams v. Lallie Kemp Charity Hospital,* 428 So. 2d 1000 (La. App. 1 Cir. 1983).

57. The following states have enacted some form of pretrial screening panel: Alaska, Arizona, Connecticut, Hawaii (mandatory), Idaho, Indiana (mandatory), Kansas, Louisiana, Maine (mandatory), Massachusetts, Michigan, Montana, Nebraska, Nevada, New Mexico, Virginia (mandatory), Virgin Islands, Utah (mandatory), and Wisconsin. The following states have recently repealed their legislation

dealing with pretrial screening panels: Arkansas, Delaware (found unconstitutional but not repealed), Rhode Island, Illinois, and Tennessee.

58. Sakayan, "Arbitration and Screening Panels: Recent Experience and Trends," 17 *Forum* 682 (1982).

59. Comment, "Constitutional Challenges to Medical Malpractice Review Boards," 46 *Tennessee Law Review* 607, 612 (1979).

60. See e.g. Md. Code Ann. (Cts. and Jud. Proc.), Sec. 3-2A-03.

61. See discussion of screening panels in Redish, supra note 43, at 790–796.

62. See generally Sakayan, supra note 58.

63. See "Ill. Medical Malpractice Review Panel Provisions: A Constitutional Analysis," 17 *Loyola University of Chicago Law Journal* 27 (1986). See also *Cardinal Glennon Memorial Hospital v. Gaertner*, 583 S.W.2d 107 (Mo. 1979), *holding limited by* 807 S.W.2d 503 (1991).

64. 113 Ill. 2d 219, 497 N.E.2d 763, 100 Ill. Dec. 585 (1986) (court struck down for the second time the Illinois enactment of a pretrial screening panel).

65. *Carson v. Mauer*, 120 N.H. 924, 424 A.2d 825 (1980).

66. *Arneson v. Olson*, 270 N.W.2d 125 (N.D. 1978).

67. 497 N.E.2d at 768.

68. 497 N.E.2d at 770.

69. Redish, supra note 43, at 790.

70. See Abrams, supra note 1, at S:18–19.

71. Id. at 932 (citation omitted).

72. *Carson v. Mauer*, 120 N.H. 924, 424 A.2d 825 (1980) presents the view that ceilings violate the right to equal protection.

73. A good exposition of the view that ceilings pass constitutional muster is presented in *Fein v. Permanente Medical Group*, 211 Cal. Rptr. 368, 38 Cal. 3d 137, 695 P.2d 665 (1985).

74. The appeal of *Fein*, supra, was dismissed at 106 S. Ct. 214.

75. For a case holding that the legislature lacks the power to abrogate the collateral source rule, see *Carson v. Maurer*, 120 N.H. 924, 424 A.2d 825 (1980).

76. For the view that abrogation of the collateral source rule is permissible, see *Baker v. Vanderbilt Univ.*, 616 F. Supp. 330 (M.D. Tenn. 1985); *Rudolph v. Iowa Methodist Medical Ctr.*, 293 N.W.2d 550 (Iowa 1980).

77. Punitive damages were eliminated by statute in Illinois, Ill. Rev. Stat. ch. 110 2-1115.

78. *Bernier v. Burris*, 497 N.E.2d 763, 776 (Ill. 1986).

79. Id.

80. Representative states providing for periodic payment of future damages include California: Cal. (Civ. Proc.) Code 667.7 (West Supp. 1990); Missouri: Mo. Ann. Stat. Sec. 383.110 (1990).

81. For a case upholding periodic payments, see *Bernier v. Burris*, 100 Ill. Dec. 585, 497 N.E.2d 763 (Ill. 1986).

82. *Carson v. Mauer*, 120 N.H. 925, 424 A.2d 825 (1980).

83. Id.

84. Jurisdictions that limit attorney fees in medical malpractice cases include California: Cal. (Bus. & Prof.) Code 6146 (West Supp. 1990); Delaware: Del. Code Ann. tit. 18, Sec. 6852 (Supp. 1989).

85. See discussion in Abrams, supra note 1.

86. *Carson v. Maurer*, 120 N.H. 925, 424 A.2d 825 (N.H. 1980).

87. *Boucher v. Sayeed*, 459 A.2d 87 (R.I. 1983).

88. Weiler, supra note 3.

89. Id. at 12.

90. Id. at 13.

91. Id. at 12 (footnotes omitted).

92. 464 F.2d 772, 150 U.S. App. D.C. 263 (D.C. Cir. 1972), *cert. denied*, 409 U.S. 1064.

93. 33 Ill. 2d 326, 211 N.E.2d 253 (1965), *cert. denied*, 383 U.S. 946.

94. 192 Cal. App. 3d 1630, 239 Cal. Rptr. 810 (Cal. App. Dist. 2 1986).

95. The case of Dr. Nork is reported in *American Mut. Liability Ins. Co. v. Superior Court for Sacramento County*, 38 Cal. App. 3d 579, 113 Cal. Rptr. 561 (Cal. App. 3 Dist. 1974); and *Nork v. Superior Court In and For Sacramento County*, 33 Cal. App. 3d 997, 109 Cal. Rptr. 428 (Cal. App. 3 Dist. 1973).

96. For a thoughtful discussion of the role played by the tort system in protecting the public, see Jerry Phillips, "In Defense of the Tort System," 27 *Arizona Law Review* 603 (1985).

97. See Abrams, supra note 1.

98. 243 U.S. 188, 37 S. Ct. 247, 61 L. Ed. 667 (1917).

99. 201 N.Y. 271, 94 N.E. 431 (N.Y. 1911).

100. 42 U.S.C. Sec. 11101 et seq. (1986).

Chapter 7

1. Studies have revealed that juries return defense verdicts in a majority of the medical malpractice cases that go to trial. See e.g. *Report of the Secretary's Commission on Medical Malpractice*, Appendix, at 154 (1973) (defense verdicts in 56% of cases studied during time frame of January 1, 1970, through September 1972). One explanation for these results is that insurers and health care providers are inclined to settle the cases with the most merit and fight the battle in the cases that may go either way—unless the potential damage award is too intimidating to confront in the contested case.

2. 15 *National Law Journal* 1 (Sept. 14, 1992).

3. Id. at 38.

4. *Healy v. White*, 173 Conn. 438, 378 A.2d 540 (1977).

5. Dan Dobbs, *Remedies* at 540–543 (1973).

6. Id.

7. 176 W. Va., 492, 345 S.E.2d 791 (W. Va. 1986).

8. 176 W. Va. 492, 345 S.E.2d at 796 (footnote omitted).

9. 621 F. Supp. 1202 (D.C. Me. 1985).

10. Admission of film found proper: *Lee v. Volkswagen of America, Inc.*, GMBH, 688 P.2d 1283 (Okla. 1984); *Grimes v. Employer's Mut. Liab. Ins. Co.*, 73 F.R.D. 607 (D. Alaska 1977); *Ward v. Hester*, 32 Ohio App. 2d 121, 61 O.O. 2d 124, 288 N.W.2d 840 (Ohio App. 1972). Admission improper: *Transit Homes, Inc. v. Bellamy*, 282 Ark. 453, 671 S.W.2d 153 (Ark. 1984) (film accentuated presentation of preexisting injuries); *Thomas v. C. G. Tate Constr. Co., Inc.*, 465 F. Supp. 566 (D.S.C. 1979) (depiction of burn victim's physical therapy would destroy jury's objectivity).

11. *Hayhurst v. LaFlamme*, 441 A.2d 544 (R.I. 1982).

12. *Franco v. Fujimoto*, 47 Haw. 408, 390 P.2d 740 (Haw. 1964).

13. *Herman by Warshafsky v. Milwaukee Children's Hosp.*, 121 Wis. 2d 531, 361 N.W.2d 297 (Wis. App. 1984); *Watson v. City of Chicago*, 124 Ill. App.3d 348, 80 Ill. Dec. 117, 464 N.E.2d 1100 (Ill. App. 1984).

14. *Tucker v. Union Oil Co. of California*, 100 Idaho 590, 603 P.2d 156 (Idaho 1979); *DeMaris v. Whittier*, 280 Or. 25, 569 P.2d 605 (Or. 1977).

15. 216 N.J. Super. 513, 524 A.2d 455 (N.J. Super. A.D. 1987).

16. 52.4 A.2d at 458–59.

17. 524 A.2d at 459, quoting *Cox v. Valley Fair Corp.*, 83 N.J. 381 at 385, 416 A.2d 809 (1980).

18. For an excellent review and analysis of the case law and reasoning, see *Beagle v. Vasold*, 53 Cal. Rptr. 129, 65 Cal. 2d 166, 417 P.2d 673 (Cal. 1966).

19. Rule:7-1(b), discussed in *Friedman v. C&S Car Service*, 108 N.J. 72, 527 A.2d 871 (N.J. 1987).

20. 53 Cal. Rptr. 129, 65 Cal. 2d 166, 417 P.2d 673 (Cal. 1966).

21. 417 P.2d at 681.

22. 417 P.2d at 682.

23. *McDougald v. Garber*, 135 App. Div. 80, 524 N.Y.S.2d 192 (1988); *Nemmers v. U.S.*, 681 F. Supp. 567 (C. D. Ill. 1988). For a collection of cases, see Annotation, "Loss of Enjoyment of Life as a Distinct Element or Factor in Awarding Damages for Bodily Injury," 34 A.L.R. 4th 293 (1983 and Supp. 1988). For a recent article on the subject, see Hilton and Goldstein, "Damages for the Loss of Enjoyment of Life in Personal Injury Cases," 30 *Defense* 2 (Nov. 1988).

24. *Yosuf v. U.S.*, 642 F. Supp. 432 (M.D. Pa. 1986).

25. 233 Md. 446, 197 A.2d 140 (Md. 1964).

26. 359 F.2d 344 (3d Cir. Pa. 1966).

27. Dobbs, supra note 5, at 549.

28. See e.g. *Morrison v. Stallworthe*, 73 N.C. App. 196, 326 S.E.2d 387 (N.C. App. 1985) (holding that trial court improperly excluded evidence of shortened life expectancy in a case involving a failure to detect cancer).

29. 478 A.2d 976 (R.I. 1984).

30. 478 A.2d at 980.

31. *Ondis v. Pion*, 497 A.2d 13, at 18 (R.I. 1985).

32. California led the country in the struggle to recognize and limit claims for negligent infliction of emotional distress in *Dillon v. Fegg*, 68 Cal.2d 728, 69 Cal. Rptr. 72, 441 P.2d 912 (Cal. 1968) (recognizing the claim and setting forth guidelines).

33. See *Portee v. Jaffee*, 84 N.J. 88, 417 A.2d 521 (N.J. 1980).

34. See *Thing v. La Chusa*, 48 Cal. 3d 644, 257 Cal. Rptr. 865, 771 P.2d 814 (Cal. 1989) (reviewing and critically analyzing the unsuccessful attempts of the California courts to develop workable guidelines).

35. 197 N.J. Super. 385, 484 A.2d 1316 (1984).

36. 197 N.J. Super. at 388–89, 484 A.2d at 1318.

37. *Frame v. Kothari* 212 N.J. Super. 498, 515 A.2d 810 (N.J. Super. L. 1985).

38. 212 N.J. Super. 498, 503, 515 A.2d 810 (1985).

39. 209 N.J. Super. 110, 506 A.2d 1285 (1986).

40. 27 Cal. 3d 916, 167 Cal. Rptr. 831, 616 P.2d 813 (1980).

41. For a good discussion of the historical approach to wrongful death claims, see *Moragne v. States Marine Lines*, 398 U.S. 375, 90 S. Ct. 172, 26 L. Ed. 2d 339 (1970).

42. Dobbs, supra note 5, at 551–569.

43. Id.

44. For an overview of death actions, see generally Stuart Speiser, *Recovery for Wrongful Death and Injury* (3d ed. 1988).

45. *Roberts v. Stevens Clinic Hospital*, 176 W. Va. 492, 345 S.E.2d 791 (W. Va. 1986).

46. 345 S.E.2d at 799.

47. 345 S.E.2d at 804.

48. Lord Campbell's Act, 9 & 10 Vict., c. 93 (1846), allowed families to recover for tort "although the Death shall have been caused under such Circumstances as amount in Law to Felony."

49. The West Virginia Wrongful Death Statute discussed in *Roberts v. Stevens Clinic Hospital*, 345 S.E.2d 791 (W. Va. 1986) is an example of this type of statute.

50. Id.

51. See generally Stuart Speiser, *Recovery for Wrongful Death and Injury* (3d ed. 1988).

52. The Pennsylvania statute takes this approach. See 42 Pa. Cons. Stat. Sec. 8301 et seq. (wrongful death); 20 P.S. Sec. 3371 et seq. (survival statute).

53. See *Incollingo v. Ewing*, 444 Pa. 263, 444 Pa. 299, 282 A.2d 206 (Pa. 1971).

54. 345 S.E.2d 791 (W. Va. 1986).

55. W. Va. Code, Sec. 55-7-6 (1982).

56. See e.g. *Slavin v. Gardner*, 274 Pa. Super. 192, 418 A.2d 361 (Pa. Super. 1979) (upholding verdict of $75,000 in survival action for death of two-and-one-half-year-old girl killed in car accident).

57. *Roberts v. Stevens Clinic Hospital*, 345 S.E.2d 791, at 801 (W. Va. 1986).

58. For example, Pennsylvania Rule of Civil Procedure 238 provides that damages for delay shall be added to an award that is 125% of the defendant's highest offer of settlement.

59. See e.g. *Hawthorne v. Dravo Corp., Keystone Div.*, 352 Pa. Super. 359, 508 A.2d 298 (1986), *appeal denied*, 514 Pa. 617, 521 A.2d 932 (1987) (upholding trial court order denying delay damages for the period between entry of nonsuit [dismissal of plaintiff's case] in favor of defendant and order vacating entry of nonsuit).

60. See e.g. Frankel v. Heym, 466 F.2d 1226 (3d Cir. 1972) (affirming award of $650,000 for pain and suffering and loss of ability to enjoy life of a nineteen-year-old woman who sustained brain damage and other severe physical and medical injuries).

61. 382 F. Supp. 1271 (D. Conn. 1974), *aff'd in part & rev'd in part*, 524 F.2d 384 (2d Cir. 1975), *on remand*, 452 F. Supp. 151 (D. Conn. 1976).

62. 382 F. Supp. at 1277–1278.

63. 382 F. Supp. at 1284.

64. 382 F. Supp. at 1286.

65. Id.

66. Id.

67. 382 F. Supp. at 1298.

68. 421 A.2d 1027, 491 Pa. 561 (1980).

69. 382 F. Supp. at 1294–1295.

70. 421 A.2d at 1036–1038.

71. For a helpful discussion of the evidentiary approach, along with the others, see *Jones & Laughlin Steel Corporation v. Pfeifer*, 462 U.S. 523, 103 S. Ct. 2541, 76 L. Ed. 768 (1983).

72. *Domeracki v. Humble Oil & Refining Co.*, 443 F.2d 1245, 1251 (3rd Cir. 1971).

73. *Norfolk & W.R.R. v. Liepelt*, 444 U.S. 490 100 S. Ct. 755, 62 L. Ed. 2d 689 (1980).

74. See e.g. *Pennsylvania Department of Transp. v. Phillips*, 488 A.2d 77 (Pa. 1985).

Chapter 8

1. Edwards v. Our Lady of Lourdes Hospital, 217 N.J. Super. 448, 526 A.2d 242 (N.J. Super A.D. 1987).

2. 217 N.J. Super. 448, 526 A.2d 242 (N.J. Super. A.D. 1987).

3. 217 N.J. Super. 448, 459–460, 526 A.2d 242, 247–248 (1987).

4. 217 N.J. Super. 448, 461–462, 526 A.2d 242, 249 (1987).

5. 569 F.2d 1221, 1229 (3d Cir. Pa. 1977).

6. *Medvecz v. Choi*, 569 F.2d at 1227.

7. 217 N.J. Super. 448, 526 A.2d 242 (N.J. Super. A.D. 1987).

8. 118 Ill. App. 161, 166 (1905), aff'd. 224 Ill. 300, 79 N.E. 562 (1906).

9. 58 N.M. 686, 275 P.2d 175 (1954).

10. 342 Pa. Super. 375, 492 A.2d 1382 (1985).

11. 114 Or. 1259, 229 P. 372 (1924).

12. 142 F.97 (3rd cir. 1905).

13. *Olsen v. McAtee*, 181 Or. 503, 182 P.2d 979 (1947).

14. 36 Colo. App. 109, 537 P.2d 754 (1975).

15. *Los Alamos v. Medical Center Coe*, 58 N.M. 686, 275 P.2d 175 (1954).

16. *Hoffman v. Memorial Osteopathic Hospital*, 342 Pa. Super. 375, 492 A.2d 1382 (1985).

17. *Gunthorpe v. Daniels*, 150 Ga. App. 113, 257 S.E.2d 199 (1979).

18. *Mandeville v. Courtright*, 142 F. 97 (3d Cir. 1905).

19. *Olsen v. McAtee*, 181 Or. 503, 182 P.2d 979 (1947).

20. *Cholia v. Kelty*, 155 Or. 287, 63 P.2d 895 (1937).

21. *Robinson v. Duszynski*, 36 N.C. App. 103, 243 S.E.2d 148 (1978).

22. *Green v. Hale*, 433 F.2d 324 (5th Cir. Tex. 1970).

23. *Gunthorpe v. Daniels*, 150 Ga. App. 113, 257 S.E.2d 199 (1979).

24. For an overview of trial considerations, including the burden of proof, see James Ghiardi and John Kircher, *Punitive Damages Law and Practice* ch. 9 (1985).

25. 217 N.J. Super. 448, 526 A.2d 242 (1987).

26. See e.g. *Public Service Mutual Insurance Co. v. Goldfarb*, 53 N.Y.2d 392, 442 N.Y.S. 2d 422, 425 N.E.2d 810 (1981) (dentist's insurance policy covered claim based on sexual abuse but company could not be held liable for punitive damages); *Northwestern Nat. Casualty Co. v. McNulty*, 307 F.2d 432 (5th Cir. 1962) (thorough discussion of public policy against insurance coverage of punitive damages), *superseded by statute as stated in United Services Auto Association v. Webb*, 235 Va. 655, 369 S.E.2d 196 (1988).

27. See e.g. *Mazza v. Medical Mut. Ins. Co. of N.C.*, 311 N.C. 621, 319 S.W.2d 217 (1984) (public policy did not preclude coverage under medical malpractice policy for punitive damages against psychiatrist for negligence in abandoning patient).

28. For an in-depth discussion of the public policy issues and case law, see Ghiardi and Kircher, supra note 24, ch. 7.

29. 553 So.2d 537.

30. *Pacific Mutual Life Insurance Co. v. Hascip*, 493 U.S. 1014 (1991).

31. The most recent challenge to a punitive damage award on substantive and procedural due process grounds was rejected by a plurality opinion of the U.S. Supreme Court in *TXO Production Corp. v. Alliance Resources Corp.*, 61 U.S.L.W. 4766, 113 S. Ct. 2711 (1993).

Chapter 9

1. See e.g. *Herst v. Bruhn*, 106 A.D.2d 546, 483 N.Y.S.2d 363 (1984) (while mother who brought action in behalf of son for injuries allegedly sustained at birth did not waive physician-patient privilege as to maternal records merely by bringing action, maternal records for period when infant was in utero were discoverable and she was obliged to authorize the release of these records); *State ex rel. Klieger v. Alby*, 125 Wis. 2d 468, 373 N.W.2d 57 (1985) (court upholds a limited authorization that allows defendant to obtain copies of child's neonatal records but precludes informal pretrial discussion with the treating neonatologists).

2. *Stack v. Wapner*, 24 Pa. Super. 278, 368 A.2d 292 (1976).

3. *Bondu v. Gurvich*, 473 So. 2d 1307 (Fla. App. 3 Dist. 1985).

4. For a discussion of the property right issues, see *Gotkin v. Miller*, 514 F.2d 125 (2d Cir. 1975) (holding that former mental patient does not have a constitutional right of unrestricted access to her hospital records); cf. *Pyramid Life Insurance Co. v. Masonic Hospital Association of Payne County* 191 F. Supp. 51 (W.D. Okla. 1961) (patient has a property right in information in records).

5. For a collection and discussion of the statutes, see 1 *Lane Medical Litigation Guide* Sec. 3.52, identifying the following eighteen state statutes that allow patients access to their records:

Alaska Stat. Sec. 47.30.260
Ariz. Rev. Stat. Sec. 36-509
Cal. Evid. Code Secs. 1040, 1158
Colo. Rev. Stat. Sec. 25-1-801
Conn. Gen. Stat. Sec. 4-104
Haw. Rev. Stat. Sec. 622-57
Ill. Rev. Stat. ch. 51, para. 71; ch. 51, para. 73
Ind. Code Ann. Sec. 34-3-15.5-4
Me. Rev. Stat. tit. 22, Sec. 1711
Mass. Gen. Laws Ann. ch. 111, Sec. 70
Minn. Stat. Ann. Secs. 144.335, 144.651
Miss. Code Ann. Sec. 41-9-65
Nev. Rev. Stat. Sec. 629.061
Okla. Stat. Ann. tit. 76, Sec. 19
Or. Rev. Stat. Sec. 192.525
Tenn. Code Ann. Sec. 53-1322
Utah Code Ann. Sec. 78-25-25
Wis. Stat. Ann. Sec. 269.57

6. *Penman v. Lansing*, 357 Pa. Super. 225, 515 A.2d 948 (1986).

7. See e.g. *Hernandez v. Lutheran Medical Center*, 104 A.D.2d 368, 478 N.Y.S.2d 697 (1984) ($1.00 per page is a reasonable charge in light of employee time involved and duplication charge).

8. For a discussion of the therapeutic privilege to withhold information from the patient to protect her interest, see the seminal informed consent case: *Canterbury v. Spence*, 464 F.2d 772 (D.C. Cir. 1972).

9. *Penman v. Lansing*, 357 Pa. Super. 225, 515 A.2d 948 (1986).

10. *Pardo v. Medical Liability Mutual Insurance Company*, 132 A.D.2d 442, 522 N.Y.S.2d 393 (1987).

11. For example, New York law authorizes a court to order discovery before an action is commenced. N.Y. Civ. Prac. L. & R., Sec. 3102(c); see *Matter of Weiss*, 208 Misc. 1010, 147 N.Y.S.2d 455 (Sup. Ct. 1955). Pennsylvania law provides for the initiation of a lawsuit by serving a summons or a complaint. Pa. R. Civ. Proc. 1007. Once the lawsuit is initiated, a subpoena may be served compelling the production of documents. Pa. R. Civ. Proc. 234. In the alternative a plaintiff could seek equitable relief in the form of an injunction. Cf. *Penman v. Lansing*, 357 Pa. Super. 225, 515 A.2d 948 (1986).

12. 799 F.2d 1354 (9th Cir. 1982) (Langager II).

13. 799 F.2d at 1355.

14. Id.

15. Id.

16. Id.

17. 406 N.E.2d 178, 84 Ill. App. 3d 744, 40 Ill. Dec. 477 (Ill. App. Dist. 1980).

18. 406 N.E.2d at 179. In this action plaintiff was appealing the dismissal of her second complaint. The defendant's motion to dismiss was based on the following

grounds: (1) failure to state a cause of action, (2) failure to allege grounds on which tort relief could be granted, (3) failure to meet the two-year statute of limitations, and (4) in the alternative, Counts II and III were improperly joined with Count I. The negligence claim was Count II.

19. Id.

20. See *Emmett v. Eastern Dispensary & Casualty Hospital* (D.C. Cir. 1967) (hospital and doctor had a duty to disclose medical records based on patient-doctor relationship); *Quiñones v. U.S.*, 492 F.2d 1269 (3d Cir. 1974).

21. See Ill. Rev. Stat. 1973, ch. 51, para. 71 (patient's attorney or physician on demand may examine patient's records).

22. See *Darling v. Charleston Community Memorial Hospital*, 33 Ill. 2d 326, 211 N.E.2d 253 (1965), *cert. denied*, 385 U.S. 946, 86 S. Ct. 1204, 16 L. Ed. 2d 209 (1966) (duty determined by the legal standard of reasonable conduct in light of the apparent risk).

23. 406 N.E.2d at 181.

24. Id. at 183.

25. Id.

26. Id.

27. Id.

28. 473 So. 2d 1307 (Fla. App. 3 Dist. 1985).

29. Id.

30. 473 So.2d at 1311.

31. Id.

32. Id.

33. *Langager v. Lake Havasu Comm. Hosp.*, 799 F.2d 1354, 1355 (9th Cir. 1986) (Langager II).

34. 799 F.2d at 1356.

35. 799 F.2d at 1356–1357.

36. 799 F.2d at 1356.

37. Id.

38. Id.

39. Id.

40. Id.

41. Id.

42. 694 S.W.2d 434 (Tex. App. 5 Dist. 1985).

43. 694 S.W.2d at 435.

44. Id.

45. 694 S.W.2d at 436.

46. Id.

47. 694 S.W.2d at 437.

48. 694 S.W.2d at 436.

49. 310 S.E.2d 326 (N.C. 1984).

50. Id.

51. Id.

52. 310 S.E.2d at 329–333.
53. 310 S.E.2d at 334.
54. Id.
55. Id.
56. Id.
57. Id.
58. 507 So. 2d 596 (Fla. 1987).
59. 507 So. 2d at 599.
60. 507 So. 2d at 598.
61. Id.
62. Id.
63. Id.
64. Id.
65. 507 So. 2d at 599–601.
66. 507 So. 2d at 598.
67. Id.
68. 507 So. 2d at 599.
69. Id.
70. Id.
71. 730 S.W.2d 56, 57 (Tex. App. 1987). The temporary restraining order was granted but expired on its own terms without further extension, thereby making all issues associated with the temporary restraining order moot.
72. Id.
73. Id.
74. Id.
75. Id.
76. 166 Ill. App. 3d 70, 116 Ill. Dec. 612, 519 N.E.2d 504 (1988), *appeal denied*, 121 Ill. 2d 571, 526 N.E.2d 832.
77. Id.
78. Id.
79. Id.
80. 424 So.2d 596 (Ala. 1982).
81. Id.
82. Id.
83. Id.
84. 708 F.2d 1023 (5th Cir. 1983).
85. 708 F.2d at 1027–1028.
86. Id.

Chapter 10

1. Charles Tilford McCormick, *McCormick on Evidence* 33 (3d ed. 1984).
2. Generally, to qualify as an expert witness on any subject, a person must profess

knowledge of the subject on which he or she is to testify. See e.g. *Dambacher v. Mallis*, 485 A.2d 409 (Pa. Super. 1984); the court should inquire "whether the witness has sufficient skill, knowledge, or experience in [the] field or calling as to make it appear that his opinion or inference will probably aid the trier in his search for truth," 485 A.2d 408, 415 (Pa. Super. 1984), quoting *McCormick on Evidence* 33, supra note 1.

3. *Glicklich v. Spievack*, 16 Mass. App. 488, 452 N.E.2d 287 (1983), *appeal denied*, 390 Mass. 1103, 454 N.E.2d 1276 (1983); *Maslonka v. Herman*, 173 N.J. Super. 566, 414 A.2d 1350, *rev'd on other grounds*, 85 N.J. 533, 428 A.2d 504.

4. See e.g. *Sims v. Helms*, 345 So.2d 721 (Fla. 1977) (absent expert medical testimony, lay jury could not have determined, except from pure speculation, whether defendant was negligent in separating uterus from bladder during vaginal hysterectomy); *Roark v. Allen*, 633 S.W.2d 804 (Tex. 1982) (diagnosing of skull fracture outside the experience of ordinary layperson).

5. *Gordon v. Neviaser*, 478 A.2d 292 (D.C. App. 1984) (expert testimony necessary to establish that further injury to plaintiff's shoulder was the result of defendant's surgery); *Walstad v. University of Minnesota Hospitals*, 442 F.2d 634 (8th Cir. Minn. 1971) (absent evidence that defendant lacerated plaintiff's artery during heart catheterization, setting in motion chain of events leading to amputation of leg, plaintiff's theory of causation amounted to conjecture).

6. *Woolley v. Henderson*, 418 A.2d 1123 (M. 1980); *Ziegert v. South Chicago Community Hospital*, 99 Ill. App. 3d 83, 54 Ill. Dec. 585, 425 N.E.2d 450 (1981). For an informative discussion of this topic, see generally Meisel and Kabnick, "Informed Consent to Medical Treatment: An Analysis of Recent Legislation," 41 *University of Pittsburgh Law Review* 407 (1980).

7. *Sard v. Hardy*, 281 Md. 432, 379 A.2d 1014 (1977).

8. See e.g. *Bly v. Rhoads*, 216 Va. 645, 222 S.E.2d 783 (1976), *Superseded by statute adopting statewide standard* (Va. Code Ann. 8.01-581.20), discussed in *Henning v. Thomas*, 235 Va. 181, 366 S.E.2d 109 (1988); *Cross v. Trapp*, 294 S.E.2d 446 (W. Va. 1982).

9. *Nicholl v. Reagan*, 208 N.J. Super. 644, 506 A.2d 805 (1986).

10. See e.g. *Cooper v. Roberts*, 220 Pa. Super. 260, 286 A.2d 647 (1971) (requirement failed to produce equitable results and demeaned the concept of physical integrity of the individual); *Miller v. Kennedy*, 11 Wash. App. 272, 522 P.2d 852 (1974), *aff'd*, 85 Wash. 2d 151, 530 P.2d 334 (1975) (duty to inform of risks inherent in treatment existed as a matter of law).

11. 150 App. D.C. 263, 464 F.2d 772, *cert. denied*, 409 U.S. 1064, 34 L. Ed. 2d 518, 93 S. Ct. 560 (1972).

12. 150 App. D.C. 263, 283, 464 F.2d 772, 791, 792, *cert. denied*, 409 U.S. 1064, 34 L. Ed. 2d 518, 93, S. Ct. 560 (1972).

13. *Cobbs v. Grant*, 8 Cal. 3d 229, 104 Cal. Rptr. 505, 502 P.2d 1 (1972) ("to bind the disclosure obligation to medical usage is to arrogate the decision on revelation to the physician alone") (8 Cal. 3d 244, 104 Cal. Rptr. 514, 502 P.2d 10) (1972).

14. *Cooper v. Roberts*, 220 Pa. Super. 260, 286 A.2d 647 (1971) ("the standard of disclosure within the medical community bears no inherent relationship to the amount

of knowledge that any particular patient might require in order to make an informed choice. [A]ny physician testifying on the issue of the duty of disclosure would be testifying to either what he would have done under similar circumstances, or what he thinks another practitioner should do, neither of which supplies an adequate definition of the 'community standard'") (220 Pa. Super. 267, 286 A.2d 650).

15. *Wilkinson v. Vessey*, 110 R.I. 606, 295 A.2d 676 (1972) ("The decision as to what is or is not material is a human judgment, in our opinion, which does not necessarily require the assistance of the medical profession. The doctor-patient relationship is a one-on-one affair. What is a reasonable disclosure in one instance may not be reasonable in another.") (110 R.I. 606, 625, 295 A.2d 676, 688) (1972).

16. *Cooper v. Roberts*, 220 Pa. Super. 260, 286 A.2d 647 (1971) (plaintiff's difficulty in finding a physician to testify against another physician has to be considered) (220 Pa. Super. 267, 286 A.2d 650).

17. Many journals as well as other sources exist to aid the attorney in finding local medical experts and consultants for both plaintiff's and defendant's cases.

18. See e.g. *Getchell v. Mansfield*, 260 Or. 174, 489 P.2d 953 (1971); *Bly v. Rhods*, 216 Va. 645, 222 S.E.2d 783 (1976).

19. *Sard v. Hardy*, 281 Md. 432, 379 A.2d 1014 (1977).

20. *Canterbury v. Spence*, 150 App. D.C. 263, 464 F.2d 772, *cert. denied*, 409 U.S. 1064, 34 L.Ed. 2d 518, 93 S. Ct. 560 (1972) (experts are ordinarily indispensable to identify for factfinder the risks of therapy and the consequences of leaving existing maladies untreated); *Sard v. Hardy*, 281 Md. 432, 379 A.2d 1014 (1977) (expert testimony required, among other things, to establish whether or not disclosure would be detrimental to the patient); *Cross v. Trapp*, 294 S.E.2d 446 (W. Va. 1982) (expert medical testimony ordinarily required to establish alternative methods of treatment and risks relating to such treatment).

21. 549 P.2d 1099 (Colo. App. 1976).

22. 54 Cal. App. 3d 521, 126 Cal. Rptr. 681 (1976).

23. See generally Jay Katz, *The Silent World of Doctor and Patient* (1984).

24. 69 N.C. App. 588, 317 S.E. 2d 726 (1984).

25. 317 S.E. 2d at 732.

26. Compare the following jurisdictions:

Ariz.: *Revels v. Pohle*, 101 Ariz. 208, 418 P.2d 364 (1966)
Cal.: *Cobbs v. Grant*, 8 Cal. 3d 229, 104 Cal. Rptr. 505, 502 P.2d 1 (1972)
Colo.: *Greenwell v. Gill*, 660 P.2d 1305 (Colo. App. 1982)
Del.: *Robinson v. Mroz*, 433 A.2d 1051 (Del. Super. 1981)
D.C.: *Martin v. Washington Hospital Center*, 423 A.2d 913 (D.C. App. 1980)
Fla.: *Stepien v. Bay Memorial Medical Center*, 397 So. 2d 333 (Fla. App. 1981), *petition dismissed*, 402 So. 2d 607 (Fla. 1981)
Haw.: *Medina v. Figuered*, 3 Haw. App. 186, 647 P.2d 292 (1982) (involving dentist)
Ill.: *Stevenson v. Nauton*, 71 Ill. App. 3d 831, 28 Ill. Dec. 71, 390 N.E.2d 53 (1979)
Ind.: *Emig v. Physicians' Physical Therapy Service*, 432 N.E.2d 52 (Ind. App. 1982)
Iowa: *Grosjean v. Spencer*, 258 Iowa 685, 140 N.W.2d 139 (1966)

Kan.: *Collins v. Meeker*, 198 Kan. 390, 424 P.2d 488 (1967)
Md.: *Thomas v. Corso*, 265 Md. 84, 288 A.2d 379 (1972)
Mass.: *McCarthy v. Boston City Hospital*, 358 Mass. 639, 266 N.E.2d 292 (1971)
Mich.: *Clapham v. Yanga*, 102 Mich. App. 47, 300 N.W.2d 727, *appeal granted*, 412 Mich. 889, 313 N.W.2d 286 (1981), *appeal dismissed*, 335 N.W.2d 1 (Mich. 1982)
Minn.: *Schulz v. Feigal*, 273 Minn. 470, 142 N.W.2d 84 (1965)
Mo.: *Robbins v. Jewish Hospital of St. Louis*, 663 S.W.2d 341 (Mo. App. 1983)
N.J.: *Jones v. Stess*, 111 N.J. Super. 283, 268 A.2d 292 (1970)
N.M.: *Toppino v. Herhahn*, 100 N.M. 564, 673 P.2d 1297 (1983)
N.C.: *Chapman v. Pollock*, 69 N.C. App. 588, 317 S.E.2d 726 (1984)
Or.: *Mayor v. Dowsett*, 240 Or. 196, 400 P.2d 234 (1965)
Pa.: *Chandler v. Cook*, 438 Pa. 447, 265 A.2d 794 (1970)
S.C.: *Burke v. Pearson*, 259 S.C. 288, 191 S.E.2d 721 (1972)
Tenn.: *Runnells v. Rogers*, 596 S.W.2d 87 (Tenn. 1980)
Tex.: *Cohen v. United States*, 540 F. Supp. 1175 (D.C. Ariz. 1982) (applying Texas law)
Utah: *Kim v. Anderson*, 610 P.2d 1270 (Utah 1980)
Vt.: *Largess v. Tatem*, Vt. 271, 291 A.2d 398 (1972)
Wash.: *Douglas v. Bussabarger*, 73 Wash. 2d 476, 438 P.2d 829 (1968)
Wis.: *McManus v. Donlin*, 23 Wis. 2d 289, 127 N.W.2d 22 (1964)

27. *Wilkinson v. Vessey*, 11 R.I. 606, 295 A.2d 676 (1972).
28. 624 P.2d 905 (Colo. App. 1980), *aff'd*, 655 P.2d 405 (Colo. 1982).
29. Id.
30. Id.
31. 624 P.2d 905 (Colo. App. 1980), *aff'd*, 655 P.2d 405, 409 (Colo. 1982).
32. 624 P.2d 905 (Colo. App. 1980), *aff'd*, 655 P.2d 405, 409 note 4 (Colo. 1982).
33. See *McDaniel v. Merck, Sharp, & Dohme*, 367 Pa. Super. 600, 533 A.2d 436 (1987).
34. See, e.g., *Croda v. Sarnacki*, 322 N.W.2d 712 (Mich. 1982) (error found in jury instruction that "only those learned in urology or gynecology can say what should have been done"; Jurors may give less weight to testimony of non-specialists if they choose).
35. *Cornfeldt v. Tongen*, 262 N.W.2d 684 (Minn. 1977); see also *Hudgins v. Serrano*, 186 N.J. Super. 465, 453 A.2d 218 (1982) (unlicensed witness with Ph.D. in pathology who served on faculty of medical school and published articles in medical journals competent to testify).
36. *Piacentini v. Bonnefil*, 69 Ill. App. 2d 433, 217 N.E.2d 507 (1966).
37. 106 Mich. App. 35, 307 N.W.2d 695 (1981).
38. See e.g. *Dow v. Kaiser Foundation*, 12 Cal. App. 3d 488, 90 Cal. Rptr. 747 (1970); *Swanson v. Chatterton*, 281 Minn. 129, 160 N.W.2d 662 (1968).
39. *Carbone v. Warburton*, 11 N.J. 418, 94 A.2d 680 (1953) (witness's acquaintance with the subject in question may be established from evidence of witness's observation of practices of fellow physicians or reading and study of treatises and medical journals on the subject); *Ragan v. Steen*, 229 Pa. Super. 515, 331 A.2d 724 (1974) (surgeon qualified to testify against radiologist despite unfamiliarity with particular treatment

involved where surgeon had referred patients for treatment, was knowledgeable of risks involved, and had personally observed results of administration of massive doses of radiation).

40. See e.g. *Gaston v. Hunter*, 121 Ariz. 33, 588 P.2d 326 (1978) (not necessary that expert witness have personally administered a drug before he can testify to the effects of that drug or its lack of effect; learned medical articles can form the basis for a witness's expert opinion).

41. See e.g. *Harold v. Radman*, 31 Md. App. 184, 355 A.2d 477 (1976) *aff'd*, 279 Md. 167, 367 A.2d 472 (1977); *Gaston v. Hunter*, 121 Ariz. 33, 588 P.2d 326 (1978).

42. *Peters v. Gelb*, 314 A.2d 901 (Del. Super. 1973).

43. *Brown v. Colm*, 11 Cal. 3d 639, 114 Cal. Rptr. 128, 522 P.2d 688 (1974).

44. 114 Cal. Rptr. at 130, 522 P.2d at 690.

45. See also *Grindstaff v. Coleman*, 681 F.2d 740 (1982) (fact that witness was not a physician at time of alleged malpractice did not prevent him from testifying since he became a licensed physician prior to trial and knew prevailing standards of practice in medical profession at the time of incident).

46. *Pike v. Honsinger*, 155 N.Y. 201, 49 N.E. 760 (1898); *Loftus v. Hayden*, 391 A.2d 749 (Del. Super. 1978).

47. *Howard v. Piver*, 53 N.C. App. 46, 279 S.E.2d 876 (1981) (rejecting strict locality rule); *Cronic v. Pyburn*, 170 Ga. App. 377, 317 S.E.2d 246 (1984) (stating that standard is that which is ordinarily employed by the medical profession generally, not dependent on local standards; *overruled by McDaniel v. Hendrix*, 260 Ga. 857, 401 S.E.2d 260) (1991).

48. See e.g. *Simons v. Georgiade*, 55 N.C. App. 483, 286 S.E.2d 596 (1982), *petition denied*, 305 N.C. 587, 292 S.E.2d 571 (1982) (finding physician competent to testify where he has relevant surgical training and experience in communities similar to the locality in which the allegedly negligent surgery occurred); *Tallbull v. Whitney*, 172 Mont. 326, 564 P.2d 162 (1977) (rejecting the locality rule and finding that witness, although unfamiliar with standard of care in defendant's community per se, was familiar with standard of care in locality similar to defendant's in geographic location, size, and character and thus competent to testify).

49. See e.g. *Schenck v. Roger Williams General Hospital*, 119 R.I. 510, 382 A.2d 514 (1977) (finding proximity of Providence, Rhode Island, to Boston sufficient to deem Providence a medical locality similar to New York); *Cook v. Lichtblau*, 144 So.2d 312 (Fla. App. 1962) (finding medical community of West Palm Beach sufficiently similar to that of Miami).

50. Compare the following jurisdictions:

Ariz.: *Gaston v. Hunter*, 121 Ariz. 33, 588 P.2d 326 (1978) (when defendant undertakes to perform work of a specialist, he/she will be held to standard of care applicable to that specialty); *Pollard v. Goldsmith*, 117 Ariz. 363, 572 P.2d 1201 (1977) (the standard of care to be established by expert testimony is nationwide one for specialist and local one for practitioner)

Cal.: *Brown v. Colm*, 11 Cal. 3d 639, 114 Cal. Rptr. 128, 522 P.2d 688 (1974) (standard of care grounded on same or similar locality rule); *Quintal v. Laurel Grove Hospital*, 62 Cal. 2d 154, 41 Cal. Rptr. 577, 397 P.2d 161 (1964) (same or similar locality rule)

Conn.: *Fitzmaurice v. Flynn*, 167 Conn. 609, 356 A.2d 887 (1975) (physician is under a duty to exercise that degree of care and skill which physicians in the same general neighborhood and same general line of practice ordinarily exercise in like cases); *Logan v. Greenwich Hospital Assoc.*, 191 Conn. 282, 465 A.2d 294 (1983) (national standard)

Del.: *Baoust v. Kraut*, 377 A.2d 4 (Del. Super. 1977) (need to show that doctor failed to exhibit the same standard of care and competence as ordinarily adhered to by other surgeons in good standing in the same or similar community)

D.C.: *Morrison v. MacNamara*, 407 A.2d 555 (D.C. App. 1979) (national standard of care applicable to clinical laboratory)

Fla.: *Caputo v. Taylor*, 403 So. 2d 551 (Fla. App. 1981), *petition denied*, 412 So. 2d 464 (Fla. 1982) (expert must be a provider similar to defendant or possess, to court's sufficient satisfaction, the training, experience, and knowledge to provide expert testimony)

Ga.: *Wade v. John D. Archbold Memorial Hospital*, 252 Ga. 118, 311 S.E.2d 836 (1984) (recognizing that state courts have abandoned the locality rule with regard to the standard of care applicable to physicians and holding that the standard of care applicable to hospital's physical therapists is that ordinarily employed by the profession generally)

Idaho: *Buck v. Duane St. Clair*, 108 Idaho 743, 702 P.2d 781 (1985) (national standard of care for board-certified specialists), *disavowed by Grimes v. Green*, 113 Idaho 519, 746 P.2d 978 (1987) (local community standard applies if different from national standard)

Ill.: *Spidle v. Steward*, 79 Ill. 2d 1, 37 Ill. Dec. 326, 402 N.E.2d 216 (1980) (doctor must possess and apply the knowledge of and use the skill and care ordinarily used by a reasonably well qualified doctor in locality in which he practices or in similar localities in similar cases and circumstances); *Duvall v. Laidlaw*, 141 Ill. App. 3d 717, 95 Ill. Dec. 912, 490 N.E.2d 1004 (1986) (expert may base opinion on national or international standard); *Hansbrough v. Kosyak*, 141 Ill. App. 3d 538, 95 Ill. Dec. 708, 490 N.E.2d 181 (1986) (distinguishes standard of care for informed consent from that concerning negligence or medical malpractice)

La.: *Ray v. Ameri-Care Hospital*, 400 So. 2d 1127 (La. App. 1 Cir. 1981) (national standard of care); *Cable v. Cazayou*, 351 So. 2d 797 (La. App. 1 Cir. 1977) (plaintiff must establish that physician deviated from the required standard of care employed by other physicians practicing in same locality and under similar circumstances)

Me.: *Taylor v. Hill*, 464 A.2d 938 (Me. 1983) (national standard established for specialists)

Md.: *Shilkret v. Annapolis Emergency Hospital Association*, 276 Md. 187, 349 A.2d 245 (1975) (criticism of locality rule; national standard of care)

Mass.: *McCarthy v. Boston City Hospital*, 358 Mass. 639, 266 N.E.2d 292 (1971) (national standard of care)

Mich.: *Grewe v. Mount Clemens General Hospital*, 404 Mich. 240, 273 N.W.2d 429 (1978) (same or similar locality standard of care); *Haisenleder v. Reeder*, 114 Mich. App. 258, 318 N.W.2d 634 (1982) (same or similar locality rule, in light of present state of medical science)

Minn.: *Lundgren v. Eustermann*, 370 N.W.2d 877 (Minn. 1985) (same or similar locality rule)

Miss.: *Smith v. Lee*, 484 So. 2d 1028 (Miss. 1986) (expanded the rule established in *King v. Murphy* to a national standard of care); *King v. Murphy*, 424 So. 2d 547 (Miss. 1982) (same or similar standard of care)

Mo.: *Gridley v. Johnson*, 476 S.W.2d 475 (Mo. 1972) (court unwilling to apply same village or similar village standard)

Mont.: *Tallbull v. Whitney*, 172 Mont. 326, 564 P.2d 162 (1977) (excellent discussion on "locality rule" and whether expert is competent to testify as to standard of care when not from same community; customary practice in a rural town is but one factor in determining the standard of care)

Neb.: *Wentling v. Jenny*, 206 Neb. 335, 293 N.W.2d 76 (1980) (expert need only have knowledge of defendant's community in order to testify as to standard of care in community, and does not have to have actually practiced in the community); *Greenberg v. Bishop Clarkson Memorial Hospital*, 201 Neb. 215, 266 N.W.2d 902 (1978) (same or similar standard of care)

N.J.: *Levine v. Wiss & Co.*, 97 N.J. 242, 478 A.2d 397 (1984) (physician required to exercise the skill and knowledge normally possessed by members of the profession in good standing in similar communities)

N.M.: *Pharmaseal Laboratories v. Goffe*, 90 N.M. 753, 568 P.2d 589 (1977) (modified "strict locality rule"; now liable in action for negligence if fail to exercise that degree of care and skill which is exercised by the average practitioner in the class to which he/she belongs, acting in same or similar circumstances)

N.C.: *Wall v. Stout*, 310 N.C. 184, 311 S.E.2d 571 (1984) (same or similar standard of care); *Wiggins v. Piver*, 276 N.C. 134, 171 S.E.2d 393 (1970) (abandoning the locality rule)

N.D.: *Benedict v. St. Luke's Hospital*, 365 N.W.2d 499 (N.D. 1985) (national standard of care applicable)

Oh.: *Allen v. State*, 61 Ohio St. 2d 168, 15 Ohio Op. 3d 190, 399 N.E.2d 1251 (1980) (a physician must use reasonable care and conform to minimal standards of care of same or similar circumstances); *Bruni v. Tatsumi*, 46 Ohio St. 2d 127, 75 Ohio Op. 184, 346 N.E.2d 673 (1976) (locality rule no longer justifiable)

Or.: *Creasey v. Hogan*, 292 Or. 154, 637 P.2d 114 (1981) (Rule of law: Practitioner must exercise that degree of care and skill which an ordinary practitioner in the same discipline in that same community or a similar community would exercise)

Pa.: *Smith v. Yohe*, 412 Pa. 94, 194 A.2d 167 (1963) (same or similar locality rule)

R.I.: *Schenck v. Roger Williams General Hospital*, 119 R.I. 510, 382 A.2d 514 (1977) (experts from other localities may testify as to standard of care)

S.C.: *Hupman v. Erskine College*, 281 S.C. 43, 314 S.E.2d 314 (1984) (national standard of care; locality rule discarded)

Tex.: *Peterson v. Shields*, 652 S.W.2d 929 (Tex. 1983) (Supreme Court reversed lower court's decision to strike expert's testimony from record because expert was not familiar with lymph node biopsies performed in Texarkana or similar community)

Utah: *Jenkins v. Parrish,* 627 P.2d 533 (1981) (same or similar standard of care); *Nixdorf v. Hicken,* 612 P.2d 348 (Utah 1980) (before plaintiff can prevail in a medical malpractice action, he must establish both standard of care required of defendant as a practicing physician in community and defendant's failure to employ that standard)

Vt.: *Seneac v. Associates in Obstetrics and Gynecology,* 141 Vt. 310, 449 A.2d 900 (1982) (need evidence of departure from standard of care and skill ordinarily exercised by physician in similar case)

Va.: *Maxwell v. McCaffrey,* 219 Va. 909, 252 S.E.2d 342 (1979) (expert's testimony not allowed because he did not profess to know standard and skill in area)

Wash.: *Harbeson v. Parke-Davis, Inc.,* 98 Wash. 2d 460, 656 P.2d 483 (1983) (same or similar standard of care); *Pederson v. Dumouchel,* 72 Wash. 2d 73, 431 P.2d 973 (1967) (same or similar standard of care; practice or custom in locality is only one of the elements to consider in determining degree of skill and care required)

W. Va.: *Plaintiff v. City of Parkersburg,* 345 S.E.2d 564 (W. Va. 1986) (locality rule abolished in West Virginia); *Thornton v. CAMC, Inc.,* 305 S.E.2d 316 (W. Va. 1983) (explicitly overruled the locality rule)

Wis.: *Nimmer v. Purtell,* 69 Wis. 2d 21, 230 N.W.2d 258 (1975) (same or similar standard of care); *Francois v. Mokrohisky,* 67 Wis. 2d 196, 226 N.W.2d 470 (1975) (plaintiff has burden of establishing appropriate standard of care or a breach of standard of care)

Wyo.: *Vassos v. Roussalis,* 625 P.2d 768 (Wyo. 1981) (a physician or surgeon must exercise the skill, diligence, and knowledge and must apply the means and methods that would reasonably be exercised and applied under similar circumstances by members of his profession in good standing and in same line of practice)

51. See e.g. *May v. Moore,* 424 So. 2d 596 (Ala. 1982); *Peters v. Gelb,* 303 A.2d 685 (Del. Super. 1973), *aff'd,* 314 A.2d 901 (Del. 1978).

52. *Pederson v. Dumouchel,* 72 Wash. 2d 73, 431 P.2d 973 (1967); *superseded by statute* (Ariz. Rev. Stat. Ann. sec. 12-563 (1976)) discussed in *McGuire v. DeFrancesco,* 168 Ariz. 88, 811 P.2d 340 (1990) (statewide standard applies to specialists and generalists; however, evidence of applicable national standard may present a question of fact).

53. See e.g. *Kronke v. Danielson,* 108 Ariz. 400, 499 P.2d 156 (1972); *Hines v. St. Paul Fire & Marine Ins. Co.,* 361 So. 2d 969 (La. App. 3d Cir. 1978).

54. *Harris v. Campbell,* 2 Ariz. App. 351, 409 P.2d 67 (1965); *Lee v. Miles,* 317 F. Supp. 1404 (N.D. Tex. 1970).

55. See e.g. *Morgan v. Hill,* 663 S.W.2d 232 (Ky. App. 1984) (allopathic doctor incompetent to testify as to standard of care applicable to chiropractors).

56. *Hart v. Van Zandt,* 399 S.W.2d 791 (Tex. 1966); *Ison v. McFall,* 55 Tenn. App. 326, 400 S.W.2d 243 (1964).

57. *Bivins v. Detroit Osteopathic Hospital,* 77 Mich. App. 478, 258 N.W.2d 527 (1977), *rev'd on other grounds,* 403 Mich. 820, 282 N.W.2d 926 (1978) (testimony of thoracic surgeon allopath admissible in case against thoracic surgeon osteopath).

A suit charging negligent failure to refer a patient to another health care provider for appropriate diagnosis or treatment is illustrative. See e.g. *Rosenberg v. Cobill*, 99 N.J. 318, 492 A.2d 371 (1985), where the court observed in a malpractice case against a chiropractor that chiropractors, like physicians, are permitted to use X ray for diagnosis; thus, where the appropriate standard of care requires referral of the patient to a medical doctor, a medical doctor was competent to testify on the chiropractic use of X rays.

58. *Bartimus v. Paxton Community Hospital*, 120 Ill. App. 3d 1060, 76 Ill. Dec. 418, 458 N.E.2d 1072 (1983) (allopathic physician qualified to testify as to standard of care required of osteopath where witness acquired knowledge of standard through training, education, experience, "or the like").

59. 286 N.W.2d 710 (Minn. 1979).

60. Although the trial court granted permission to the plaintiff to reopen her case to include the testimony of the internist, the court ordered that testimony stricken on the basis of a pretrial order. The trial judge added that even if he had allowed that testimony to stand, he nevertheless would have granted the defendant's motion for a directed verdict.

61. 286 N.W.2d at 715.

62. 481 Pa. 256, 392 A.2d 1280 (1978).

63. 368 F.2d 626 (4th Cir. 1966).

64. 368 F.2d at 632.

65. 235 Kan. 1006, 686 P.2d 149 (1984).

66. See e.g. *Cooper v. Sisters of Charity of Cinn., Inc.*, 27 Ohio St. 2d 242, 272 N.E.2d 97 (1971).

67. 235 Kan. at 1021, 686 P.2d at 160.

68. 686 P.2d at 159.

Chapter 11

1. An excellent medical reference book on therapeutic drugs is Louis S. Goodman, Alfred Gilman, Theodore W. Rall, and Ferid Murad, *The Pharmacological Basis of Therapeutics* (7th ed. 1985).

2. Thalidomide, marketed in the early 1960s, is probably the drug most associated with limb defects. For a detailed discussion of thalidomide and the tragedy it wrought, see Morton Mintz, *By Prescription Only* (1967).

3. For a discussion and analysis of many of the seminal cases, see McClellan, "Strict Liability for Drug-Induced Injuries: An Excursion through the Maze of Products Liability, Negligence, and Absolute Liability," 25 *Wayne Law Review* 1 (1978).

4. Id.

5. For a discussion of the early history, see Harvey Wiley, *An Autobiography* (1930); Reiger, "The Struggle for Federal Food and Drugs Legislation," 1 *Law and Contemporary Problems* 3 (1933).

6. 34 Stat. 768 (1906). For an account of the first statute, see Cavers, "The Food, Drug and Cosmetic Act of 1938: Its Legislative History and Its Substantive Provisions," 6 *Law and Contemporary Problems* 2 (1939).

7. *United States v. Johnson*, 221 U.S. 488 (1910).

8. Sherly Amendments to the Pure Food & Drug Act of 1906, 34 Stat. 416 (1912).

9. 21 U.S.C. Sec. 331 (1940).

10. Mintz, supra note 2, at 48–49.

11. 21 U.S.C. Sec. 331 (1940).

12. Mintz, supra note 2 at 149–152, 248–264.

13. See the comments of Senators Kefauver et al. on the reported bill in S. Rep. No. 1744, 87th Cong., 2d Sess. *reprinted in* [1962] U.S. Code Cong. & Ad. News 2884, 2905–2906. (hereinafter S. Rep. No. 1744).

14. For an interesting perspective on the regulatory failure and the response to this tragedy, see Curran, "Governmental Regulation of the Use of Human Subjects in Medical Research: The Approach of Two Federal Agencies," *Daedalus* 542 (Spring 1969). For a detailed discussion of the history of drug regulation in this country, see McClellan, Tate, and Eaton, "Strict Liability for Prescription Drug Injuries: The Improper Marketing Theory," 26 *St. Louis University Law Journal* 1 (1981).

15. 21 U.S.C. Sec. 321 et seq.

16. 21 U.S.C. Sec. 321(p).

17. 21 U.S.C. Sec. 355(i).

18. 21 U.S.C. Sec. 355(j).

19. See generally Goodman and Gillman, supra note 1.

20. See e.g. *Ealy v. Richardson-Merrell, Inc.*, 897 F.2d 1159 (D.C. Cir. 1990) (holding that trial court erred in not granting judgment notwithstanding the verdict (j.n.o.v.) to drug manufacturer because scientific evidence does not support a finding that Bendectin causes limb defects in fetuses); *Ealy* follows the holding in *Richardson v. Richardson-Merrell, Inc.*, 857 F.2d 823 (D.C. Cir. 1988), *cert. denied*, 110 S. Ct. 218 (1989); *accord, Brock v. Merrell Dow Pharmaceuticals, Inc.*, 884 F.2d 166 (5th Cir. 1989); *In re Bendectin Litigation*, 857 F.2d 290 (6th Cir. 1988) (affirming trial court ruling upholding jury special verdict finding that Bendectin does not cause birth defects); cf. *Lanzilotti v. Merrell Dow Pharmaceuticals, Inc.* (Civ. A. No. 82-0183) (E.D. Pa. 1986) (overruling defendant's motion for j.n.o.v. because the evidence allowed reasonable minds to differ as to whether Bendectin caused the plaintiff's birth defects); and *Oxedene v. Merrell Dow Pharmaceuticals, Inc.*, 506 A.2d 1100 (D.C. Cir. 1986) (holding that trial court erred in granting new trial to defendant because evidence supported verdict that Bendectin caused the plaintiff's birth defects).

21. *Stedman's Medical Dictionary* (4th Lawyers' ed.) at 1523 states that the original term referred to the live vaccine (vaccinia, cowpox) virus inoculated in the skin as prophylaxis against smallpox and obtained from the skin of calves inoculated with seed virus. Common usage, however, has extended the meaning "to include essentially any preparation intended for active immunological prophylaxis."

22. *Stedman's*, supra note 21, at 88 defines *antibiotic* as follows: "A soluble substance derived from a mold or bacteria that inhibits the growth of other microorganisms; relating to such action."

23. 21 U.S.C. Sec. 503(b); 21 C.F.R. Sec. 201 et seq.

24. 21 C.F.R. Sec. 330.1.

25. 21 U.S.C. Sec. 321(p) (definitions); 21 U.S.C. Sec. 325 (approval procedures).

26. For an analysis of the "new drug" provision, see *Stanton v. Astra Pharmaceutical Products, Inc.*, 718 F.2d 553 (3d Cir. 1983).

27. 21 U.S.C. Sec. 321(p), 355(j).

28. See *Ciba Corp. v. Weinberger*, 412 U.S. 640 (1973); *USV Pharmaceutical Corp. v. Weinberger*, 412 U.S. 655 (1973); *Weinberger v. Bentex Pharmaceuticals, Inc.*, 412 U.S. 645 (1973); and *Weinberger v. Hynson, Westcott & Dunning, Inc.*, 412 U.S. 609 (1973) (hereinafter "efficacy cases").

29. 21 U.S.C. Sec. 321(p).

30. See "efficacy cases," supra note 28.

31. 21 U.S.C. Sec. 355(j).

32. 21 U.S.C. Sec. 355(i); 21 C.F.R. Sec. 321.1 et seq.

33. 21 C.F.R. Sec. 321.21–22.

34. 21 C.F.R. Sec. 321.53(d).

35. 21 C.F.R. Sec. 314.1 et seq.

36. 21 C.F.R. Secs. 314.50, 314.105.

37. 21 C.F.R. Secs. 201.10, 201.56, 201.57.

38. The *PDR* is published each year by Medical Economics, Inc.

39. Many cases have addressed the issue of whether the salespeople overpromoted a drug or minimized its risks. See e.g. *Love v. Wolfe*, 226 Cal. App. 2d 378, 38 Cal. Rptr. 183 (1964); *later app.* 249 Cal. App. 2d 822, 58 Cal. Rptr. 42 (1967); see also supra note 3 and infra notes 41, 56, 57 and accompanying text.

40. FDA regulations require that advertisements with respect to prescription drugs contain a fair balance of promotional and scientific information. See 21 C.F.R. Sec. 202.1.

41. For a discussion of the means by which drug companies communicate risks to the medical profession, see *Sterling Drug, Inc. v. Yarrow*, 408 F.2d 978 (8th Cir. 1969).

42. 21 U.S.C. Sec. 352(e), (n).

43. 21 U.S.C. Sec. 355(j), 21 C.F.R. Sec. 314.80.

44. 21 C.F.R. Sec. 314.80(c)(1).

45. 21 C.F.R. Sec. 314.80(c)(2).

46. 21 U.S.C. Sec. 502(a).

47. 21 U.S.C. Sec. 501(a).

48. 21 U.S.C. Secs. 355(e), 332, 333.

49. 21 U.S.C. Sec. 357.

50. 21 U.S.C. Sec. 356.

51. The seminal case holding that the drug company is relieved from liability based on an inadequate warning claim if it gave an adequate warning to the physician is *Sterling Drug, Inc. v. Cornish*, 370 F.2d 82 (8th Cir. 1966).

52. 21 U.S.C. Sec. 353.

53. Rheingold, "The MER/29 Story—An Instance of Successful Mass Disaster Litigation," 56 *California Law Review* 116, at 145 (1968).

54. Task Force on Prescription Drugs, Report and Recommendations, Subcommittee on Monopoly of the Select Committee on Small Business, United States Senate (Aug. 30, 1968) (hereinafter Task Force Report), at 26.

55. Id.

56. See e.g. *Incollingo v. Ewing*, 444 Pa. 299, 282 A.2d 206 (1971); *McEwen v. Ortho Pharmaceutical Corp.*, 270 Or. 375, 528 P.2d 522 (1974) (discussing drug company's duty to keep abreast of medical literature revealing risk that birth control pill may cause blindness; duty to warn generalists and specialists).

57. *Incollingo v. Ewing*, 444 Pa. 263, 282 A.2d 206 (1971).

58. *Feldman v. Lederle Laboratories*, 97 N.J. 429, 479 A.2d 374 (1984); *McEwen v. Ortho Pharmaceutical Corp.*, 270 Or. 375, 528 P.2d 522 (1974).

59. See e.g. *Incollingo v. Ewing*, 282 A.2d 206, where a mother took an active role in securing renewals of an antibiotic prescription for her daughter; nevertheless, the court held that her conduct did not relieve the physicians and drug company of their responsibilities to warn about the risks.

60. See e.g. *Tracy v. Merrell Dow Pharmaceuticals, Inc.*, 569 N.E.2d 875 (Ohio 1991) (rejecting a product liability claim against a nicotine chewing gum manufacturer and the clinical investigator based in part on the contributory negligence of the plaintiff in failing to inform the doctor of the complete details of his alcoholism, as well as the plaintiff's failure to stop smoking as directed).

61. As noted earlier, Goodman and Gillman, supra note 1, is a helpful reference on this subject.

62. Goodman and Gillman, supra note 1, at 1066–1095.

63. For a collection of cases, see "Failure to Warn in Use of Vaccine," 94 *American Law Reports* 3d 748 (1979).

64. Id.

65. For cases of doctors prescribing drugs without an adequate diagnosis see infra note 67.

66. For cases representative of claims of improper prescribing of antibiotics, see infra note 67.

67. Chloramphenicol, a broad-spectrum antibiotic marketed in the early 1960s under the trade name Chloromycetin, precipitated numerous claims of blood disorders. See e.g. *Incollingo v. Ewing*, 444 Pa. 263, 282 A.2d 206 (1971); *Stevens v. Parke-Davis & Co.*, 10 Cal. 3d 151, 107 Cal. Rptr. 45, 507 P.2d 653 (1973).

68. *Mulder v. Parke-Davis & Co.*, 181 N.W.2d 882 (Minn. 1970) (physician liable for prescribing drug to patient over period of time, despite awareness of danger of blood disorder).

69. *Incollingo v. Ewing*, 444 Pa. 263, 282 A.2d 206 (1971).

70. A seminal case is *Davis v. Wyeth Laboratories*, 399 F.2d 121 (9th Cir. 1968) (39-year-old man paralyzed from the waist down as a result of polio vaccine).

71. *Davis v. Wyeth Laboratories*, 399 F.2d 121; *Reyes v. Wyeth Laboratories*, 498 F.2d 1264 (D.C. Cir. 1974); *Cunningham v. Charles Pfizer & Co., Inc.*, 532 P.2d 1377 (Okla. 1975).

72. For a general discussion of local anesthetics, see Goodman & Gillman, supra note 1, at 302–321.

73. *Stedman's*, supra note 21, defines an allergic reaction as "any allergic response stimulated by an allergen."

74. *Stedman's*, supra note 21, defines an anaphylactic reaction as a response "manifesting extremely great sensitivity to a foreign product or other material."

75. 718 F.2d 553 (3d Cir. 1983).

76. 718 F.2d at 558–563.

77. See generally "Drugs During Pregnancy: Dangerous Business—The Continued Movement to Provide Adequate Warnings for the Consumer," 62 *Nebraska Law Review* 526 (1983).

78. See Mintz, supra note 2.

79. See 2 Marden G. Dixon and Frank C. Woodside, *Drug Product Liability*, Sec. 15.64.

80. For a general discussion of the problem of the therapeutic orphan, see McClellan, "The Use and Misuse of Drugs in Children," *Juris* 7–9 (Winter 1977).

81. See Nelson, *Textbook of Pediatrics* (12th ed. 1983) at 1814.

82. 42 U.S.C.A. Secs 300aa–10 to 34 (West Supp. 1993). For a discussion of this statute see *Grant v. Secretary of the Department of Health and Human Services*, 956 F.2d 1144 (Fed. Cir. 1992). See also Neraas, "The National Childhood Vaccine Injury Act of 1986: A Solution to the Vaccine Crisis?" 63 *Washington Law Review* 149 (1988).

83. Task Force Report, at 5.

Chapter 12

1. 718 F.2d 553 (3d Cir. 1983).

2. See e.g. *Simonsen v. Barlo Plastics Co., Inc.*, 551 F.2d 469 (1st Cir. 1977); *Corter v. Epsco Industries, Inc.*, 511 F. Supp. 99 (M.D. La. 1980); *McLean v. Alexander*, 449 F. Supp. 1251, *rev'd*, 599 F.2d 1190 (D.C. Del. 1978); *Penzell v. State*, 466 N.Y.S.2d 562, 120 Misc. 2d 600 (1983); *Laster v. Gottschalk*, 75 Mich. App. 290, 255 N.W. 210 (1977).

3. The disadvantages of no joinder are stated succinctly in footnote 25 of W. P. Keeton, Dan B. Dobbs, Robert E. Keeton, and Daniel G. Owen, *Prosser & Keeton* on Torts, Sec. 47 at 327 (5th ed. 1984): "The result of the refusal to permit joinder is that: (1) in the separate suits it is open to each defendant to prove that the other was solely responsible, or responsible for the greater part of the damage, and so defeat or minimize recovery; (2) it is equally open to the plaintiff to prove that each defendant was solely responsible, or responsible for the greater part of the damage, and so recover excessive compensation; (3) the two verdicts will seldom have any relation to one another; (4) different witnesses may be called in the two suits, or the same witness may tell different stories, so that the full truth is told in neither; (5) neither defendant may cross-examine the other, or the other's witnesses, and plaintiff may not cross-examine both in one action; (6) time and expense are doubled."

4. Professor Prosser once stated, "Joint torts is one of those unhappy phrases of indeterminate meaning whose repetition has done so much to befog the law." Prosser, "Joint Torts and Several Liability," 25 *California Law Review* 413 (1937). The term *joint tortfeasor* varies throughout the jurisdictions. Historically, it pertained only to tortfeasors acting intentionally in concert. Modern law, however, has expanded the

definition of *joint tortfeasor* to include those acting together to create a single, insepa-rable wrong. Some jurisdictions have a more strict definition than others. For a helpful discussion of joint tortfeasors, see *Losprogato v. Qualls*, 263 Pa. Super. 174, 397 A.2d 803 (1979).

5. See Fed. R. Civ. P. 18–25. There is usually no reason to refuse joinder if it is merely a matter of procedural convenience. See *Scearce v. Mayor of Gainsville*, 33 Ga. App. 411, 126 E. 883 (1925).

6. See *Prosser & Keeton on Torts*, supra note 3, Sec. 547 at 324–327.

7. See id., Sec. 547 at 327.

8. See id., Sec. 546 at 323.

9. For example, in Pennsylvania, which has adopted a strict definition of joint tortfeasors, there is only contribution among joint tortfeasors. See *Losprogato v. Qualls*, 263 Pa. Super. 174, 397 A.2d 803 (1979). The court in *Losprogato* explains: "The right of *contribution* exists only between joint tortfeasors. Contribution distributes the loss equally or each joint tortfeasor pays his or her pro rata share. Whenever two actions are brought for separately identifiable acts of negligence on the part of the original wrongdoer and the treating physician, the *apportionment* of damages between the two causes should take place." See also *Rocco v. John-Manville Corp.*, 754 F.2d 110 (3d Cir. 1985); *TVSM, Inc. v. Alexander & Alexander, Inc.*, 583 F. Supp. 1089 (E.D. Pa. 1984); *Levy v. First Pennsylvania Bank NH*, 338 Pa. Super. 73, 487 A.2d 857 (1985).

10. See *Prosser & Keeton on Torts*, supra note 3, Sec. 547 at 327–328.

11. A *concurrent tort* is one where there is no consent or agreement, but where the act of the two tortfeasors produces a single, indivisible injury. Thus, if *A* and *B* are hunting and fire simultaneously, both mistakenly shooting *C*, *A* and *B* are concurrent tortfeasors.

12. See Dan Dobbs, *Tort and Compensation*, ch. 1053 at 620–621 (1985); Prosser, supra note 4, at 433–434; Jackson, "Joint Torts and Several Liability," 17 *Texas Law Review* 399, 415–419 (1939).

13. See *Prosser & Keeton on Torts*, supra note 3, Sec. 51 at 341, 344; *Bielski v. Schulze*, 16 Wis. 2d 1, 114 N.W.2d 105 (1962); *Mitchell v. Branch*, 45 Haw. 128, 363 P.2d 969 (1961).

14. At common law the principle established was that there was no right to any contribution among intentional tortfeasors. *Merryweather v. Nixon*, 101 Eng. Rep. 1337 (1799). That general rule has been narrowed and confined significantly by numerous exceptions and limitations, and many jurisdictions have begun to relax the harshness and permit contribution.

15. The following statutes are from those states that have adopted the Uniform Contribution Act:

Alaska Stat. 1962, Sec. 09.16.010
Ark. Stat. 1947, Sec. 34-1001
Ariz. Rev. Stat. Ann. Sec. 12-1501
Colo. Rev. Stat. 13-50.5-101
Cal. Code Civ. Proc. 875
Del. Code Ann. 1974, tit. 0610, Sec. 6301
Fla. Stat. 1983, 768.31

Haw. Rev. Stat. 1976, Sec. 663-11
Ga. Official Code Cenn. 51-12-32
Ky. Rev. Stat. Ann. 1971, 412.030
Ill. Rev. Stat. 1981, ch. 70, para. 301
Mass. Gen. Laws 1984, Sec. 231 Bil
Md. Code Ann. 1957, art. 50, Sec. 16
Miss. Code Ann. 1972, Sec. 85-5-5
Mich. Comp. Laws 1948, 691. 561
Mo. Rev. Stat. 1978, 537.060
N.C. Gen. Stat. 1943 Sec. 1 B-1
N.D. Cent. Code 32-38-01
Nev. Rev. Stat. Reprint 1979, 17.225
N.J. Stat. Ann. 2A:53A-1
N.Y. Civ. Prac. Laws and Rules, Sec. 1401
N.M. Stat. Ann. 1978, 41-3-1
Pa. Cons. Stat. tit. 42, Sec. 8321
R.I. Gen. Laws 1956, Sec. 10-6-1
S.D. Codified Laws Ann. 1967, 15-8-11
Tenn. Code Ann. 29-11-101
Tex. Rev. Civ. Stat. Ann. 2212
W. Va. Code 1966, Sec. 55-7-13
Wyo. Stat. 1977, 1-1-110

16. For a full text of the Uniform Act of 1939 as well as the Commissioner's Notes, see 9 U.L.A. 230–252.

17. See *Bielski v. Schulze*, 16 Wis. 2d 1, 114 N.W.2d 105 (1962); *Mitchell v. Branch*, 45 Haw. 128, 363 P.2d 969 (1961).

18. See supra note 12.

19. In determining the *pro rata* share of tortfeasors in the entire liability, (a) their relative degrees of fault shall not be considered; (b) if equity requires, the collective liability of some as a group shall constitute a single share; and (c) principles of equity applicable to contribution generally apply. See *Early Settlers Ins. Co. v. Schweid*, 221 A.2d 920 (D.C. App. 1966).

20. *Prosser & Keeton on Torts*, supra note 3, Sec. 52 at 348–349.

21. Id., Sec. 52 at 346.

22. Id., Sec. 51 at 341–345 and Sec. 52 at 346. One of the generally recognized distinctions between *contribution* and *indemnity* has been that whereas *contribution* ordinarily operates to distribute a loss equally among joint tortfeasors, *indemnity* seeks to transfer the entire loss imposed on one tortfeasor to another who because of justice and equity must bear the loss.

23. A successive tortfeasor is a tortfeasor whose negligence creates risk of further harm by a second tortfeasor. For example, if *A* hits *P* with his car and leaves him lying in the street, and *B* subsequently hits *P*, causing further injury, *A* and *B* would be considered successive tortfeasors. *A* would be liable for the injury that both he and *B* caused. *B* would be liable only for the injury that she herself caused.

24. See *Prosser & Keeton on Torts*, supra note 3, Sec. 52 at 352–353; Jackson, supra note 12, at 419–420; Prosser, supra note 4, at 434–435.

25. Therefore, when the plaintiff is injured in an automobile accident and brought to a hospital, the physician who operates negligently will not be held liable for the original injury. See *Thompson v. Fox*, 326 Pa. 209, 192 A.2d 107 (1937); *Aubuschun v. Cutt*, 412 S.W.2d 136 (Mo. 1967).

26. For example, suppose *A* hits the plaintiff, fractures his skull, and leaves him dying in the road. *B* comes along and runs over the plaintiff's leg. *A* is liable for both the fractured skull and the broken leg because it was reasonably anticipated that a second car might run the plaintiff over. See *Adams v. Parish*, 189 Ky. 628, 225 S.W. 467 (1920).

27. *Prosser & Keeton on Torts*, supra note 3, Sec. 49 at 332. See Cocke v. Jenner, 80 Eng. Rep. 214 (1614).

28. In Pennsylvania, for example, the courts have held that the Uniform Act precludes recognition of a release as a bar against joint defendants. See 12 U.L.A., 1982 Pocket Part, 34.

29. See generally *Penzell v. State*, 466 N.Y.S.2d 562, 120 Misc. 2d 600 (1983), *Corter v. Epsco Industries, Inc.*, 511 Supp. 99 (M.D. La. 1980); *McLean v. Alexander*, 449 F. Supp. 1251, rev'd, 599 F.2d 1190 (D.C. Del. 1978); *Simonsen v. Barlo Plastics Co., Inc.*, 551 F.2d 469 (1st Cir. 1977); *Laster v. Gottschalk*, 75 Mich. App. 290, 255 N.W.2d 210 (1977).

30. See *Morris v. Kospelich*, 253 La. 413, 218 So. 2d 316 (1969); *Haiger v. Caputo*, 420 Pa. 528, 218 A.2d 108 (1966).

31. See e.g. *Farmers Mutual Auto Ins. Co. v. Milwaukee Automobile Ins. Co.*, 8 Wis. 2d 512, 99 N.W.2d 749 (1959).

32. 579 A.2d 177 (D.C. App. 1990).

33. *Stanton v. Astra Pharmaceutical Products, Inc.*, 718 F.2d 553 (3d Cir. 1983).

34. See *Physician's Desk Reference* (Supp. 1971).

35. See notes 9 and 10.

36. The specific allegation of negligence made against the pediatrician was that she failed to take effective steps to lower the child's temperature after the child was resuscitated. Plaintiffs were, however, aware that most of the damage had been done by the time the pediatrician assumed responsibility for the child's care. Thus, even if they could prove that the pediatrician was negligent, she would be liable only for aggravating the injuries.

37. As discussed earlier, since the plaintiffs gave a joint tortfeasor's release to each defendant who settled, the drug company would receive credit for any money paid to the plaintiffs by any party who was found to be liable to the plaintiffs.

38. *Stanton v. Astra Pharmaceutical Products, Inc.*, 718 F.2d 553, 572 (3d Cir. 1983).

39. Id.

40. 718 F.2d at 555.

41. Id.

42. 579 A.2d 177 (D.C. App. 1990).

43. When the oxygen in a person's blood becomes sufficiently depleted, the person becomes cyanotic, a condition characterized by a dark or dusky color of the skin. This characteristic is caused by the dark, unoxygenated blood in the capillaries beneath the skin. In persons with dark skin, the cyanosis may be virtually undetectable except on mucous membranes and nailbeds. Membranes become pale because when

a person's supply of oxygen is compromised, the body attempts to compensate by shunting blood from nonessential parts, such as the skin and mucous membranes, to vital organs such as the heart, liver, and kidneys.

44. *Pleasant v. Washington Sand and Gravel Co.*, 104 U.S. App. D.C. 374, 262 F.2d 471 (1958).

45. See e.g. 4 Fowler Harper, Fleming James, Jr., and Oscar Gray, *Law of Torts*, Sec. 25.14 at 605–609 (2d ed. 1986) (discussing loss of parental companionship as a compensable element of damages in wrongful death actions); *Dearborn Fabricating & Engineering Corp. v. Wickham*, 532 N.E.2d 16 (Ind. Ct. App. 1988) ("[T]he parent should not have to die for the child to gain relief."); *Hibpshman v. Prudhoe Bay Supply, Inc.*, 734 P.2d 991 (Alaska 1987); *Hay v. Medical Center Hospital*, 496 A.2d 939 (Vt. 1985); *Veland v. Reynolds Metals Co.*, 691 P.2d 190 (Wash. 1984); *Theama v. City of Kenosha*, 344 N.W.2d 573 (Wis. 1984); *Audobon-Extra Ready Mix, Inc. v. Illinois Central Gulf R.R.*, 335 N.W.2d 148 (Iowa 1983); *Berger v. Weber*, 303 N.W.2d 424 (Mich. 1981); *Ferriter v. Daniel O'Connell's Sons, Inc.*, 413 N.E.2d 690 (Mass. 1980).

46. See e.g. Note, "The Parental Claim for Loss of Society and Companionship," 1980 *Arizona State Law Journal* 909; *First Trust Co. v. Scheels Hardware*, 429 N.W.2d 5 (N.D. 1988); *Reben v. Ely*, 705 P.2d 1360 (Ariz. 1985); *Shockley v. Prier*, 225 N.W.2d 495 (Wis. 1975); *Reben v. Ely*, 146 Ariz. 309, 705 P.2d 1360 (1985).

47. In their filings before the trial court counsel for the plaintiff acknowledged the lack of authoritative case law.

48. A pulse oximeter is a machine that provides a continuous digital display of a patient's oxygen saturation. An end-tidal CO_2 monitor is a device that is attached to a patient's endotracheal tube and measures carbon dioxide.

49. *Martello v. Hawley*, 112 U.S. App. D.C. 129, 300 F.2d 721 (1962).

50. *Snowden v. D.C. Transit System*, 147 U.S. App. D.C. 204, 454 F.2d 104 (1971).

51. 207 U.S. App. D.C. 350, 647 F.2d 175 (1980).

52. 508 A.2d 912 (D.C. App. 1986).

53. But see *Rose v. Associated Anesthesiologists*, 501 F.2d 806 (D.C. Cir. 1974) (where granting of *pro tanto* credit resulted in an unjust enrichment to nonsettling defendant found to be negligent, only a *pro rata* credit was awarded).

Suggested Readings in Case Law

This book is designed for use in a two- or three-credit course on medical malpractice in which students concentrate primarily on the discussion of cases and problems in the text and then enhance their study by reading carefully selected cases. This approach to studying law represents the reverse of the one most commonly used in law schools today, where students spend most of their time reading cases, supplemented by text and problems. The suggested cases for student reading follow.

Medical Malpractice Litigation: Threshold Considerations
    a. PROOF OF NEGLIGENCE
        Clark v. Gibbons, 66 Cal. 2d 399, 58 Cal. Rptr. 125, 426 P.2d 535 (1967)
    b. THE ROLE OF A DOCTOR IN THE LITIGATION PROCESS
        Meyer v. McDonnell, 301 Md. 426, 483 A.2d 76 (1984)

The Lawyer's Ethical and Legal Duty of Care
        Rogers v. Robson et al., 30 Ill. Dec. 320, 74 Ill. App. 3d 467, 392 N.E.2d 1365 (1979)
        Rorer v. Cooke, 313 N.C. 338, 329 S.E.2d 355 (1985)

The Common Law of Malpractice
    a. NEGLIGENCE—STANDARD OF CARE
        Incollingo v. Ewing, 444 Pa. 263, 282 A.2d 206 (1971)
    b. INFORMED CONSENT
        Canterbury v. Spence, 464 F.2d 772 (D.C. Cir. 1972)
        Largey v. Rothman, 110 N.J. 204, 540 A.2d 504 (1988)
    c. RES IPSA LOQUITUR
        Clark v. Gibbons, supra
        Ybarra v. Spangard, 25 Cal. 2d 486, 154 P.2d 687 (1944)
    d. NEGLIGENCE AS A MATTER OF LAW
        Helling v. Carey, 83 Wash. 2d 514, 519 P.2d 981 (1974)
    e. BREACH OF CONTRACT
        Sullivan v. O'Connor, 363 Mass. 57, 296 N.E.2d 183 (1973)
    f. WRONGFUL BIRTH
        Berman v. Allen, 80 N.J. 421, 404 A.2d 8 (1979)

General Index

Index of Cases

309